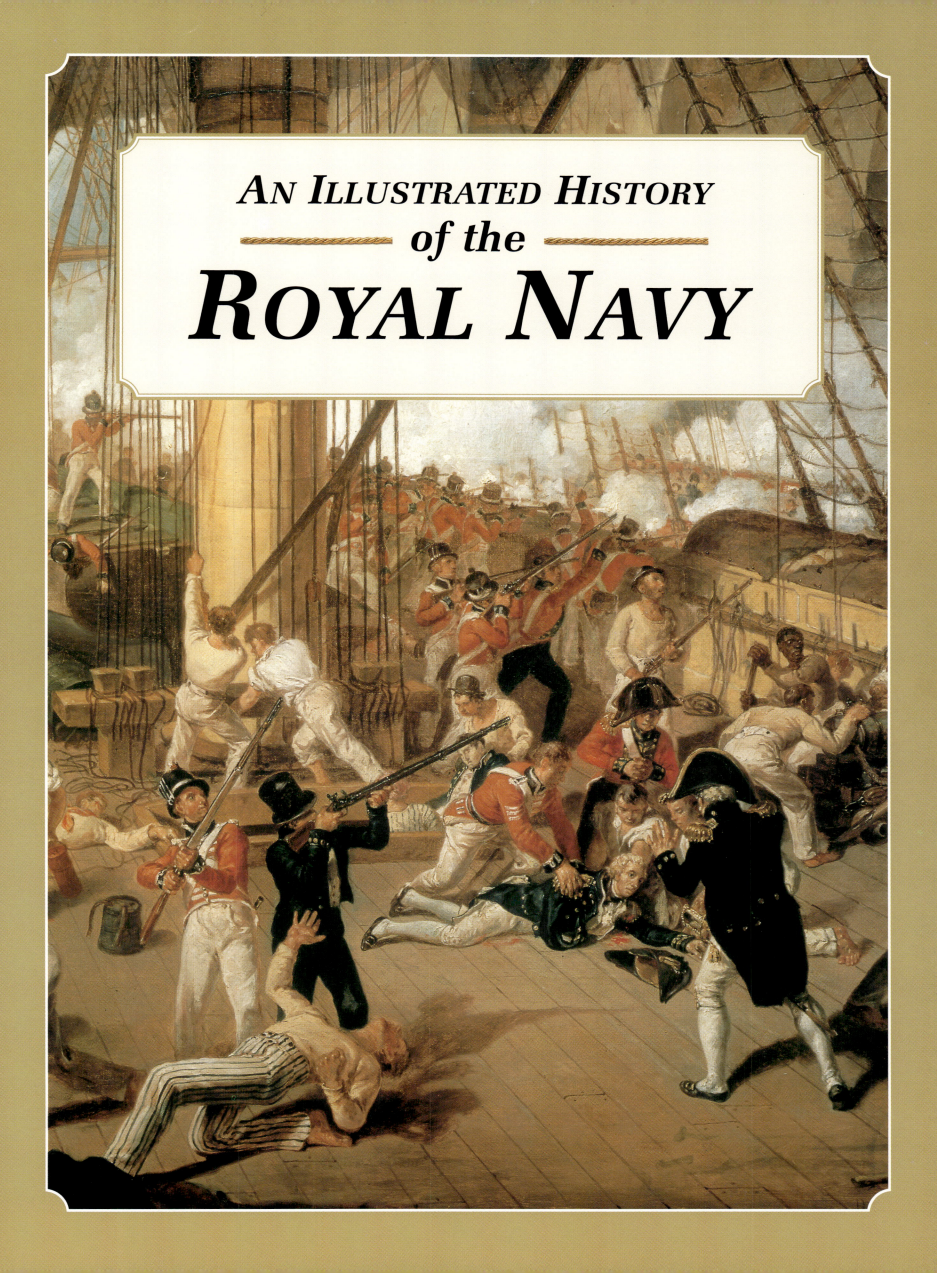

AN ILLUSTRATED HISTORY
of the
ROYAL NAVY

PUBLISHED IN ASSOCIATION WITH THE ROYAL NAVAL MUSEUM

AN *ILLUSTRATED HISTORY* of the ROYAL NAVY

John Winton

Foreword by Campbell McMurray

Consultant Editor: Dr. Chris Howard Bailey

A Salamander Book

5072 An Illustrated History of
the Royal Navy

Published in 2000 by
Salamander Books,
8, Blenheim Court,
Brewery Road,
London N7 9NT

A member of the Chrysalis Group plc

© Quadrillion Publishing Ltd.
and Salamander Books Ltd.,
in association with the Royal
Naval Museum.

ISBN 1-84065-218-7

Credits

Editor:
Philip de Ste. Croix

Designer:
Roger Hyde

Caption and feature writer:
Richard O'Neill

Picture researchers:
Stephen Courtney, Deborah
Potter, Nigel Tallis

Maps:
Michael O'Callaghan, CDA
Design

Cutaway drawings:
Tony Townsend

Commissioned photography:
Rod Tidman

Index:
Michael Forder

Publishing Director:
Will Steeds

Production:
Neil Randles

Colour reproduction:
Pica Colour Separations
Overseas (Pte) Ltd, Singapore

Printed and bound in
Singapore by Star Standard
Industries (Pte) Ltd

The Author

John Winton joined the Royal Navy as a cadet at Dartmouth, served in the Korean War and at Suez, and was for seven years in the Submarine Service. Since his retirement as a Lieutenant-Commander he has written 40 books, fourteen of them novels including the first, *We Joined the Navy*. His several works of naval history include *The Death of the Scharnhorst*, *ULTRA at Sea*, *ULTRA in the Pacific*, *Signals from the Falklands*, *Cunningham: The Greatest Admiral since Nelson* and *The Submariners: Life in British Submarines 1900–1999*. He also writes for a range of publications including the *Naval Review*, the *Daily Telegraph*, and the *Dictionary of National Biography*.

The Consultant Editor

Chris Howard Bailey, Cert.Ed. (Dist.), B.Ed. (Hons), MA, PhD is Keeper of Collections and Director of Publications at the Royal Naval Museum, Portsmouth. She has worked extensively in both the United States and Great Britain in the fields of oral history and education and has had published numerous articles and won many awards for her work. She is on the Executive Committee of the Oral History Society and is a member of the Oral History Association (USA), the Society for Nautical Research, the Society of Authors, and the Museums Association. She is the author of *Down The Burma Road: Work and Leisure for the Below-Deck Crew of the Queen Mary, 1947–1967*; *The Battle of the Atlantic – The Corvettes and their Crews: An Oral History*; *The Life and Times of Admiral Sir Frank Twiss: Social Change in the Royal Navy, 1924–1970* and *St. Richard's Hospital and the NHS: An Oral History*.

Acknowledgements

The production of this book has been quite complex and has involved the work of many people. Particular thanks go to Campbell McMurray, Director of the Royal Naval Museum, and many of the Trustees and staff of the Museum itself, including Rear Admiral Richard Hill, Colin White, Chris Arkell, Denise Smith, Matthew Sheldon, Val Billing, Richard Noyce, Pat Nagle and Lesley Thomas. Thanks are also due to Roger Hyde, Michael O'Callaghan, Richard O'Neill, Rod Tidman, and the picture researchers: Stephen Courtney, Deborah Potter and Nigel Tallis. Special thanks go to Philip de Ste. Croix, Alastair Wilson and Michael Forder for their patient and painstaking attention to detail.

Chris Howard Bailey

Contents

Foreword by Campbell McMurray 6

Foreword

'Cherish merchandise, keep the Admiraltie, That we be masters of the Narrow Sea', wrote Adam de Moleyns, Bishop of Chichester, in 1436. The burden of his pamphlet, *The Libel of English Policie*, could be condensed into a plea for the stimulation of commerce by the state and for the maintenance of a sufficient naval force to control the flow of trade past our shores, and particularly through the Straits of Dover.

Ships, the sea and seafaring have been a profound influence on the people of this country from our earliest beginnings, and the sea has never intermitted its effect on our fortunes from earliest times to the present. Wherever water has flowed, British seafarers have carried their cargoes – while behind them the ships of the Royal Navy have patrolled the world and guarded the peace. Indeed, it is not too much to say that, throughout the three hundred years or so of our history as a world power, the nation's safety, freedom, wealth and prosperity have to a great extent rested on our seafaring prowess and upon the Royal Navy, as it is set out in the preamble to the Articles of War, 'under the good providence of God'.

In this splendid book, lavishly illustrated with visual matter drawn mainly from the collections of the Royal Naval Museum, John Winton has done more than simply bring vividly to life this magnificent tradition and its key role in the defence of an island realm. What he shows us also is that, whichever the way the matter is defined, the Royal Navy and its history, and that of the seafaring community, have been and remain one of our great cultural lynch pins, still among the most powerful forces shaping the national character and helping to sustain our sense of who we are as a people. It is a superb achievement and I commend it to you wholeheartedly.

Campbell McMurray
Director, Royal Naval Museum

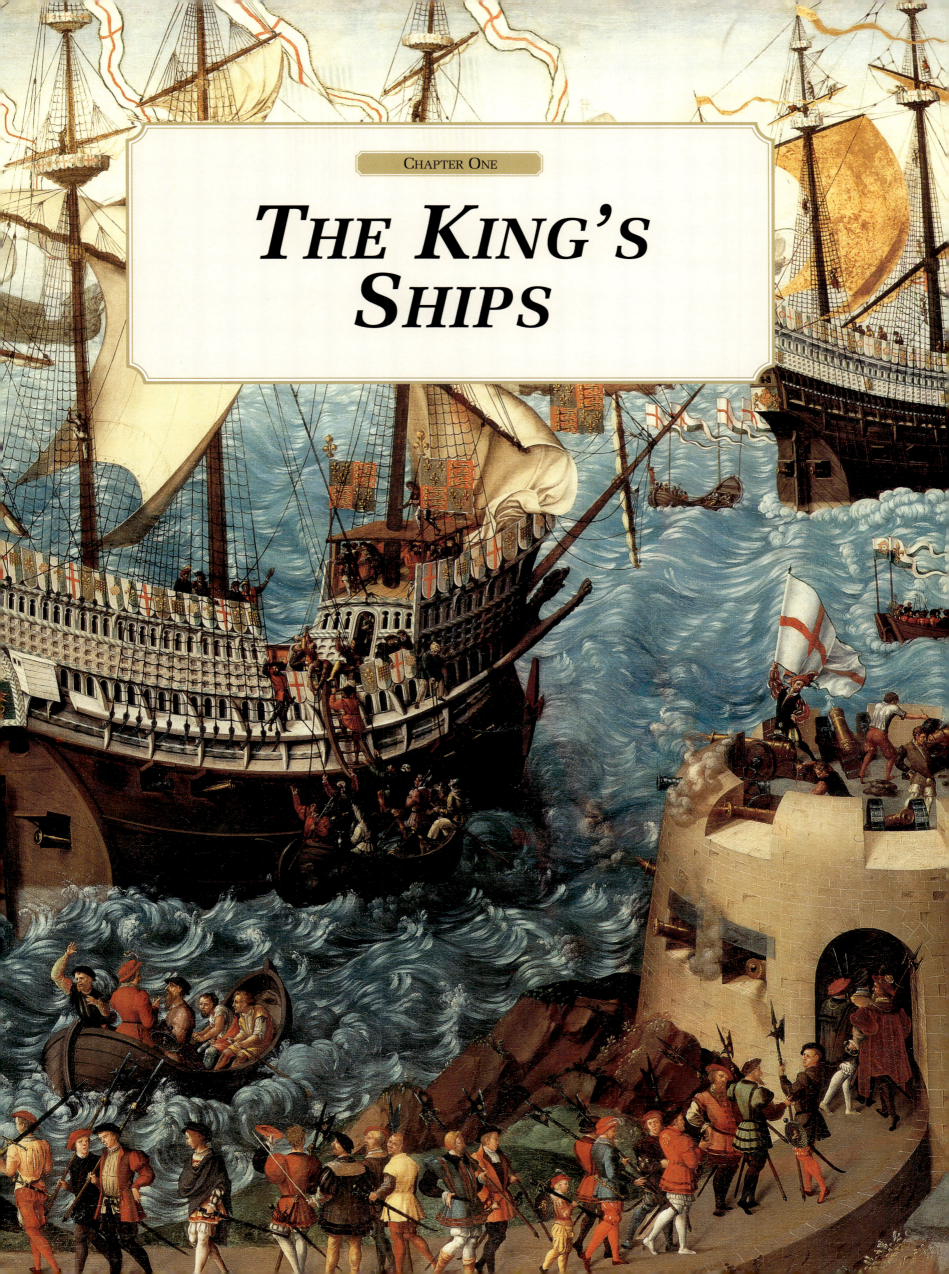

CHAPTER ONE

THE KING'S SHIPS

TIMELINE

▶ **896** King Alfred builds his own ships. Alfred's naval and beach battle against the Danes.

937 King Athelstan's victory over the Danes at Brunanburh (site unknown).

1066 Norman Conquest of England.

Right: A *gold medallion from Beaurains, Arras. The reverse shows the relief of London by the Roman emperor Constantius I and celebrates the overthrow in 296 AD of the empire set up by the rebel Belgic commander of the Roman fleet, Carausius, in 296 AD.*

Previous pages: *Henry VIII's Fleet, 1520 – the embarkation at Dover for the meeting with Francis I at the Field of the Cloth of Gold. The painting is by an unknown artist. The two monarchs, each with a huge retinue, met at a site near Calais in June 1520.*

John was the first English King to lay claim to the lordship of the sea. He ordered that vessels should strike or lower their sails whenever they encountered the 'lieutenant of the King or the admiral of the King or his lieutenant on any voyage ordained by Common Council of the realm'. Merchantmen still dip their ensigns to a passing Queen's ship to this day.

In the 13th century, there were, for the first time, ample written records of events. In March 1205, King John awarded the first prize money, granting to his galleys' crews half of anything they captured from the enemy. In 1208, he ordered the Bailiffs of Portsmouth, Shoreham, Southampton and other places to select their best and strongest men, such of them as were armed, to man the King's galleys. This was the earliest form of impressment of men for the Navy.

King John won one major sea battle in April or May 1213 (the exact date is not known) when he sent a fleet of 500 sail and a force of 700 knights under the Earl of Salisbury to the coast of Flanders. They found a French invasion fleet at a place called Damme, now a small inland town some miles north-east of Bruges, but in the 13th century a seaport with a large harbour.

Many of the French crews were ashore, Salisbury attacked at once. The English seized 300 French ships and burned a hundred more, but then Salisbury rashly landed and was himself defeated by the French King, Philip Augustus. Two thousand English were killed or drowned.

Philip Augustus had won a tactical victory, but had suffered a strategic defeat. He had attempted an invasion by sea without first defeating a powerful opposing 'fleet in being'. Damme gave the English command of the sea, and prevented Philip from either evacuating his army from Flanders or supplying them by sea.

Anxious to follow up his advantage, King John ordered William de Wrotham, Archdeacon of Taunton, and Keeper of the King's Ships, Galleys and Seaports, a sort of medieval First Lord of the Admiralty, to prepare all the King's galleys for sea in November 1213. They were sent to Portsmouth early in 1214 and, on or about 9 February, King John sailed from the Isle of Wight, with his Queen Isabella, his bastard son Richard, and a large army.

This final expedition, made possible by command of the sea, was disastrously defeated in France. It was followed by further defeats for King John, on land at Runnymede in June 1215, when his barons forced him to sign the Magna Carta, and at sea, in 1216, when another French invasion fleet of 680 ships, commanded by the renegade Eustace the Monk, who had until only recently served King John, sailed to put Prince Louis of France on the throne of England. Eustace the

---

THE KING'S SHIPS

Viking raids on England began in 789 AD and continued through the next century. In 851, they overwintered for the first time, camping on the Isle of Thanet. They plundered London and Canterbury, but their fleet was defeated by King Athelstan of Kent at Sandwich in the first real sea-fight in English history, where Athelstan took nine ships and put the rest to flight.

Alfred King of Wessex fought several sea-battles against the Danes and in 896 he ordered the building of improved and larger warships, the first 'King's Ships'. The *Anglo-Saxon Chronicle* records for 896 that the King 'ordered warships to be built to meet the Danish ships; they were almost twice as long as the others (the Danes], some had sixty oars, some more; they were both swifter, steadier, and with more freeboard than the others; they were built neither after the Frisian design nor after the Danish, but as it seemed to himself that they could be most serviceable'.

In that same year, nine King's ships defeated six Danish ships in 'King Alfred's Naval and Beach Battle', the earliest English naval engagement to be properly recorded, fought in an unnamed river estuary on the south coast. Alfred may or may not deserve the title of 'Father of the Royal Navy', but he certainly grasped the strategic truth that maritime foes like the Danes had to be fought and defeated at sea. Hitherto, the English had always regarded the sea as anything but a safeguard; on the contrary, it was seen as a constant source of danger, an open pathway for sea-borne invaders.

Alfred's brisk way with Danes/pirates, i.e. hanging them, laid the foundations of a peace which continued under his grandson, Athelstan, and his great

Left: *Alfred constructing the first English fleet – the frontispiece to* The Imperial Dictionary of Universal Biography.

Below: *A scene from the 11th century Bayeux Tapestry shows King's Harold's ships during Harold's fateful visit to Normandy. Harold's fleet tried to prevent the Norman invasion by patrolling off the Isle of Wight, but in the event William landed in England unopposed in 1066.*

Monk's fleet was dispersed by bad weather, but Louis himself landed at Sandwich.

King John died on 19 October 1216 and was succeeded by his elder son, Henry III, who was then nine years old. John has the reputation of being a bad King, but he had a continuing interest in naval affairs. He published the first primitive form of Navy List, awarded the first prize moneys, introduced a new method of impressing seamen, ordered the first enclosed dockyard (at Portsmouth), laid down regulations for the assembly, organisation and dispatch of large fleets (which always sailed in convoy), and was the first to claim the lordship of the sea. Many aspects of the history of the Navy began to take shape during King John's reign.

grandson Edgar. Athelstan used his fleet to support his army and in 934 an expedition to Scotland went as far as Caithness. The fleet also became an instrument of diplomacy, and Athelstan's help was enlisted by the Saxon king Henry the Fowler, Louis IV of the Franks and Duke Richard of Brittany.

Edgar ordered the 'ship-soke', which required every landowner to provide a ship and the county hundreds the men to man it. This became the 'ship-fyrd' which mustered every year. Under Edward the Confessor the ship muster system was developed, and the fleet campaigned against the Scots and assisted the Danes against the King of Norway.

Sandwich, the main naval base of the Saxon kings, was where King Harold mustered the ship-fyrd in 1066. They sailed to Spithead, where they cruised around the Isle of Wight through the summer and autumn, awaiting the invasion by William of Normandy. Some accounts say that false intelligence led Harold to believe that William's expedition had been abandoned, and so he sent his crews home. The *Chronicle* gives another, wholly believable, version of the first recorded mutiny at Spithead.

In September, the sailors' provisions ran out and 'no one could keep them there any longer' and 'they were therefore given permission to return home'. Thus William the Conqueror was able to land his troops from his ships unopposed. Harold returned from the north to be defeated and killed at Senlac on 14 October. Had his ships still been on station three weeks earlier, the history of England might have been very different.

AN INVASION REPELLED

Henry III's reign began with a great English victory. Louis of France had been defeated at Lincoln in May 1217, but in August Eustace the Monk sailed again with an invasion fleet of 80 ships, with galleys and small craft.

The English commander was Sir Hubert de Burgh, Governor of Dover Castle, who had 16 large and well-equipped ships from the Cinque Ports, and about 20 smaller vessels. When the English ships put to sea from Dover on 24 August 1217, Eustace's fleet was already in mid-Channel, some miles out of Calais and heading almost north on a brisk south-south-easterly wind, steering to round the North Foreland and enter the Thames.

Sir Hubert did not head directly for the enemy but steered across the Channel. Eustace thought he meant to attack Calais, but was unworried, knowing it was well defended. Sir Hubert had no intention of attacking Calais. He steered so as to get to windward of his enemy, thus gaining the weather gauge – one of the earliest examples of this primary fighting tactic in the days of sail.

Once he had his enemy in his lee, Sir Hubert altered to the north and his ships bore down on the French rearguard. The English began by flinging unslaked lime downwind into the eyes of the French a tactic actually pioneered by King John (he also smeared his ships' gunwhales with soft soap to make boarding more difficult). The English followed up with grapnels to prevent their enemies escaping. While the English archers fired a stream of flaming arrows into the French ships, the English men-at-arms swarmed on board and cut down the French rigging and halyards with axes, before engaging the blinded and bewildered defenders in desperate hand-to-hand combats, which were mostly short and brutish and ended in immense slaughter amongst the French.

Some English ships were fitted with iron beaks, which also did tremendous execution. Most of the French ships were sunk or captured. Only 15 escaped. Twenty-five French knights and more than one thousand soldiers were taken prisoner.

Of the three Plantagenet Edwards, who between them reigned for 105 years, Edward III was the most successful at sea. He personally commanded the English fleet at the great victory over the French invasion fleet at Sluys on the Flemish coast on 24 June 1340, and again in the defeat of the Spanish fleet in the action known as 'Les Espagnols sur Mer' on 29 August 1350.

Sluys, fought in the estuary of the river Scheldt, was a particularly bloody defeat for the French and their Genoese allies, who lost 25,000 men and 180 ships. Afterwards, French corpses were washed up all along the neighbouring coast. Edward III himself wrote the report of the victory on board his flagship *Cog Thomas* on 28 June.

Left: In 1939 a magnificent Anglo-Saxon ship burial was uncovered at Sutton Hoo in Suffolk. It may have been the grave of Raedwald, a 7th century king of East Anglia. The photograph shows the Sutton Hoo ship, its form preserved in sand, undergoing excavation. The ship is about 80 feet (24.4m) long and would have been propelled by some 40 oarsmen.

Inset left: This magnificent iron helmet and face-mask from the Sutton Hoo burial, decorated with repoussé plaques and crested with a protective boar symbol, exhibits very close parallels with Swedish examples and is an indication of possible links between the local dynasties and Scandinavia.

'Les Espagnols sur Mer' was fought in mid-Channel off Winchelsea on 29 August 1350, between Edward's ships and a Castilian fleet, allies of the French, who were returning home from a trading expedition to Flanders. It was the first battle which was not a land battle fought on board ship, but a genuine naval engagement, the first in which cannon were used at sea, when ship-handling and ship construction contributed as much as the bravery of the fighting men.

The two fleets met at some speed, so that Edward's ship struck the leading Spanish ship with such force that her seams were sprung by the impact and she foundered just as Edward's knights scrambled aboard the Spaniard and captured her. At the end of the day, the English had taken 14 Spanish ships. The rest escaped.

Despite his victories at sea, Edward III still regarded his fleet primarily as a means of transporting his army to where the really decisive battles on land would be fought. Thus, the medieval Navy was formed specifically for convoy duties. From 1204, when King John lost the Duchy of Normandy to Philip Augustus, the only direct communication between England and the English empire in southern and western France was by ship, around the politically and navigationally hostile coasts of Normandy and Britanny.

CONVOY IN THE MIDDLE AGES

England's main export was wool, through the French town of Calais in the north, and the main import was wine, from Bordeaux in the south-west. Wool convoys sailed regularly, under the command of an official with the ancient title of Wafter of the Wool Fleet. The wine convoys, generally of 200 to 300 ships, sailed to Bordeaux in December, loaded the season's wines, and returned in January or February.

The English kings used convoy as a matter of course. Some medieval convoys had huge numbers of ships by modern standards, King John had sent 500 ships to Flanders. In 1346, Edward III had between 1,000 and 1,100 large ships and 500 small craft assembled in the Solent. After reviewing his fleet, the King embarked from the Isle of Wight on 10 July and sailed the next day, accompanied by the Prince of Wales, many noblemen, 10,000 archers, 4,000 men-at-arms and a number of Welsh and Irish footmen. The King landed at La Hogue on 12 July and the ensuing campaign led to the victory at Crécy on 26 August.

Seventy-five years after Crécy, another fleet assembled in the Solent under another King before another great victory. Henry V took a great interest in his Navy. He ordered large ships to be laid down, such as the *Holy Ghost*, the *Grace Dieu*, and the *Trinity Royal*.

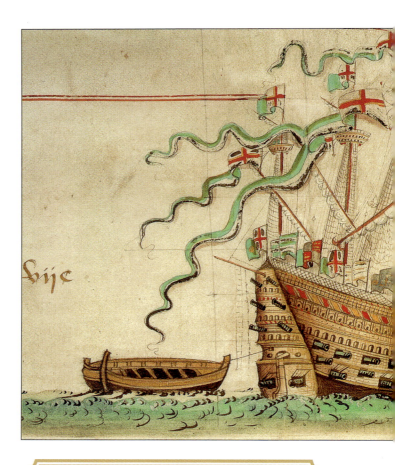

In 1415, Henry V began the campaign with which he intended to enforce his claim to the throne of France. He embarked at Portchester in the *Trinity Royal* on Saturday, 10 August 1415, and ordered her yard to be hoisted to the middle of her mast, as a signal that he was ready for sea, and that all ships in the neighbouring ports were to join his fleet.

Before sailing from Southampton, on 11 August, the King reviewed his fleet of 1,400 vessels carrying his army of several thousand men-at-arms and archers. This was very probably the first Royal Naval Review in any modern sense of the term.

Fair stood the wind for France and the fleet crossed without opposition, entering the Seine on the afternoon of Tuesday 13 August. The army besieged and took Harfleur before going on to the historic victory at Agincourt on St Crispin's Day, 25 October 1415.

Edward III's and Henry V's fleets had sailed, like John's before them, in huge convoys. Without considering why, the English kings knew that the larger the convoy, the better. Contrary to the consensus of opinion in the Victorian Royal Navy, when convoy fell out of favour, there was nothing

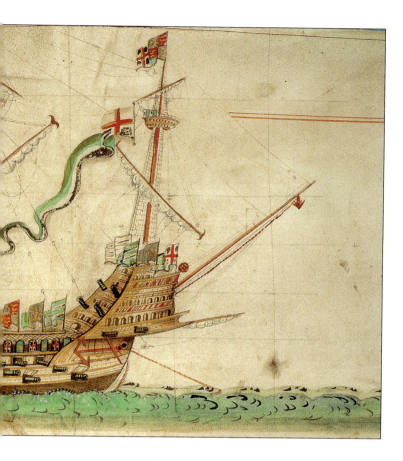

new, or revolutionary, or risky, about convoy, nor did it impose impossible administrative demands. Naval officers of the 13th, 14th and 15th centuries solved several complex problems of convoy organisation. They arranged assembly ports, at both ends of the voyage. They manned, victualled and armed hundreds of ships. They laid down rules for station-keeping, and for-mulated convoy escort tactics. They frequently joined up two halves of a convoy successfully before departure. Similarly, the medieval state was quite capable of carrying out measures such as introducing acts to make convoy compulsory, and imposing penalties on shipmasters who broke away from a convoy.

Throughout the Navy's history, periods of success and naval expenditure have been followed by times of neglect. After an expedition was over, or an emergency had passed, ships reverted to trade or were sold off. When Henry V died in 1422, there were over 30 vessels of 400 to 600 tons, but the Council of Regency for his only son, the nine-month-old infant Henry VI, sold off almost all the ships. By 1430, the Navy had only the *Trinity Royal, Grace Dieu* and *Jesus*, all dismantled, unrigged and laid up, at Bursledon.

THE TUDOR DYNASTY

Henry VII, the first Tudor King, ascended the throne after the defeat and death of Richard III at Bosworth Field in 1485, bringing the Wars of the Roses to an end. Henry VII never had a large fleet, but he knew that the strength of a country was

reflected by the strength of its fleet, and he acted upon that principle in a way that was new in England.

First, he recognised Portsmouth's geographical advantages as a naval base, and began by improving the fortifications, so that it might be a secure base for a permanent Navy. In 1495, he gave instructions for a dry graving dock – the first dry dock ever known in this country – to be built at Portsmouth, thus deciding, once and for all, the town's destiny as a naval port.

The first ship known to have gone into the new dock, on 25 May 1496, was the 600 ton *Sovereign*, which had been built partly from some of the remains of the broken-up *Grace Dieu*. She was in dock for more than eight months, until 31 January 1497, almost certainly because there was no pressing need for her services, and it was thought that a ship lasted longer in dock than afloat.

The next ship in dock was the *Regent*, of about the same size. For her, there was a much greater need for urgency. She was only in dock from 4 March to 23 April 1497. She was at Portsmouth on 1 May and on the 14th she became the Earl of Surrey's flagship in the fleet operating against James IV of Scotland.

Henry VII was a King with the heart and soul of a merchant. He believed in making every penny count and, whenever possible, making other people, and especially his nobles, pay the bills. He has been credited with being the founder of the Royal Navy. In fact, though he did lay down the foundations for building and repairing ships at Portsmouth, he built few ships himself, preferring to hire Spanish ships instead, because their rates were lower.

Apart from the *Sovereign* and the *Regent*, Henry VII seems to have built only two other small warships, the *Sweepstake* and the *Mary Fortune*, both described in the King's Inventories as the 'Kynges New Barke'. They were three-masted, with a main topmast, a mizzen mast, a sprit sail on the bowsprit, and 80 and 60 oars respectively. Both served in 1497 in the fleet under Robert, Lord Willoughby de Broke, against the Scots.

Left: The Mary Rose *from the* Anthony Roll, *a manuscript preserved in the Pepys Library in Cambridge. This key document, a list of all Henry VIII's vessels completed in 1546, includes only slightly stylized portraits of his ships with details of the stores, ordnance and armaments carried on each vessel. The* Mary Rose *was a four-masted warship built in 1509–1511 at the Royal Dockyard, Portsmouth. After a long career, she foundered on 19 July 1545 during a battle against the French fleet off Southsea Castle. More than four centuries later, in 1982, the hull was raised, and she is now preserved and on show at Portsmouth Historic Dockyard.*

Below: Henri Grace à Dieu, the largest ship in Henry VIII's navy as pictured in the Anthony Roll. Though looking superficially similar to the depiction of the Mary Rose above, close inspection reveals that the details of the armament on the various gun decks is quite different.

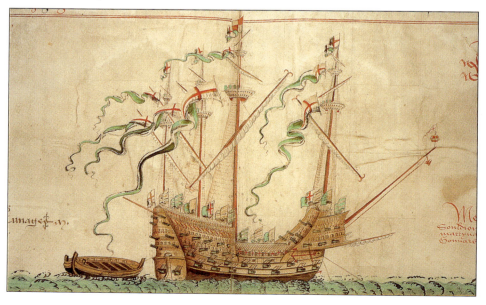

1415 Henry V builds great ships, *Holy Ghost*, *Grace Dieu*, *Trinity Royal*, and sails with 1,400 vessels for France, leading to battle of Agincourt.

1495 Henry VII orders first dry dock in England, at Portsmouth.

1509–11 Building of the *Mary Rose*.

HENRY VIII'S SHIPS

Sweepstake survived into Henry VIII's navy, and was rebuilt in 1511, being renamed *Katherine Pomegranate* in honour of Katherine of Aragon (the pomegranate was part of the coat of arms of the city of Granada, whose capture from the Moors was a resounding victory for Christendom; the pomegranate was often used as a badge after Katherine of Aragon's arrival in England).

After *Sweepstake* and *Mary Fortune*, the next two men-of-war to be built at Portsmouth, in 1509, were the *Peter Pomegranate* and the *Mary Rose*. The smaller *Peter Pomegranate*, at about 400 tons, was armed with 60 obsolete serpentynes (small calibre swivel guns, weighing about 250lb), but the 600 ton *Mary Rose* was, with the recently rebuilt and re-armed *Sovereign*, one of the most formidable warships of her time.

The King himself rode down to Portsmouth in August 1512 to review the 25 ships which had been assembled to reinforce Lord Edward Howard, who was already cruising off the coast of Brittany.

Howard, with his reinforced fleet, met the French fleet of 39 sail off Brest on 10 August. During the battle, the *Regent* grappled with the 'great carrack of Brest' the *Marie La Cordelière*, which either caught fire after a gunpowder explosion or, as one account says, 'a varlet gunner, being desperate' set fire to the powder. The flames spread rapidly to the *Regent* to leeward and both ships were destroyed. Only 120 of the 800 crew of the *Regent* were saved, and only 20 Frenchmen of the reputed 1,500 on board *Marie La Cordelière*.

In the following year of 1513, the French had a fleet of 11 warships, under a more enterprising admiral than the year before, and six galleys, under the veteran commander Prégent de Bidoux, assembled in Brest, with another 16 ships at various ports in Normandy. But they also had the same cautious strategy, of waiting for the English to attack. Howard thus had the tactical advantage, but could not exploit it because he was unable to deal with Pregent's galleys in the enclosed harbour of Brest. Eventually, he personally led an attack in which he was killed, and the leaderless English ships retreated in confusion.

Henry VIII's response to the *Regent* disaster was typical: 'on hearing of the loss of the *Regent*, (he) caused a great ship to be made, such another as was never seen before in England, and called *Henry Grace à Dieu*'.

The *Henry Grace à Dieu* was laid down at Woolwich in the autumn of 1512, and completed and commissioned in 1514. She was of 1,500 tons, with a complement of 349 soldiers, 301 sailors and 50 gunners, and armed with over 180 guns. She also was a good sailer; Admiral Sir William Fitzwilliam reported to the King in 1522 that she

MARY ROSE'S ARMAMENT

Named after Mary Tudor, Henry VIII's sister, *Mary Rose* was 122 feet 4 inches (37.3m) long at the waterline, 37 feet 5 inches (11.4m) in the beam, and drew 14 feet 9 inches (4.5m). She was strongly built, with wooden diagonal braces in her hull, and almost entirely of oak but with her 105-foot (32m) long keel made of two pieces of elm scarfed together. She had four masts: fore, main, mizzen and bonaventure mizzen; and five decks: hold, orlop, main, upper and gun decks with guns on the top three decks, firing through ports on the main and upper decks.

She had two main types of gun, as well as hand guns: larger wrought iron breech-loading guns, mounted on wooden beds or stocks which could be moved about the ship on a pair of wheels fitted on a single axle; and newer bronze muzzle-loading guns, firing iron shot, fitted on elm carriages, which could be run back for cleaning and reloading.

Mary Rose had 79 guns, besides another six in her tops: 33 small calibre pieces called serpentynes, 26 stone guns (i.e. firing stone shot), ten small calibre anti-personnel iron or brass hand guns known as murderers, five brass culverin-type falcons firing three pound shot, and five brass curtalls – heavy guns of some 3,000lb (1,360kg), until then used only as siege weapons on land, so their use at sea in *Mary Rose* was a considerable advance in naval gunnery. *Mary Rose* also carried numerous longbows and arrows.

She had a crew of 30 gunners, 180 soldiers and 200 mariners, although one eye-witness account says that she had 700 men on board when she sank. She was an excellent sailer and could steer up closer to the wind than any other ship in Henry VIII's fleet. Lord Edward Howard, whose flagship she was in the war against France of 1512–13, wrote to the King of her as 'your good ship, the flower I trow of all ships that ever sailed'.

Above: *One of* Mary Rose*'s bronze muzzle-loading guns fitted on its wheeled elm carriage.*

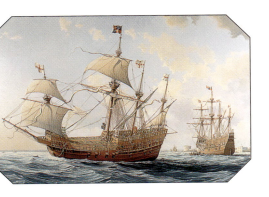

Left: *The hull as it is preserved in No. 3 Dry Dock at Portsmouth and (far left) W.H. Bishop's impression of the ship underway.*

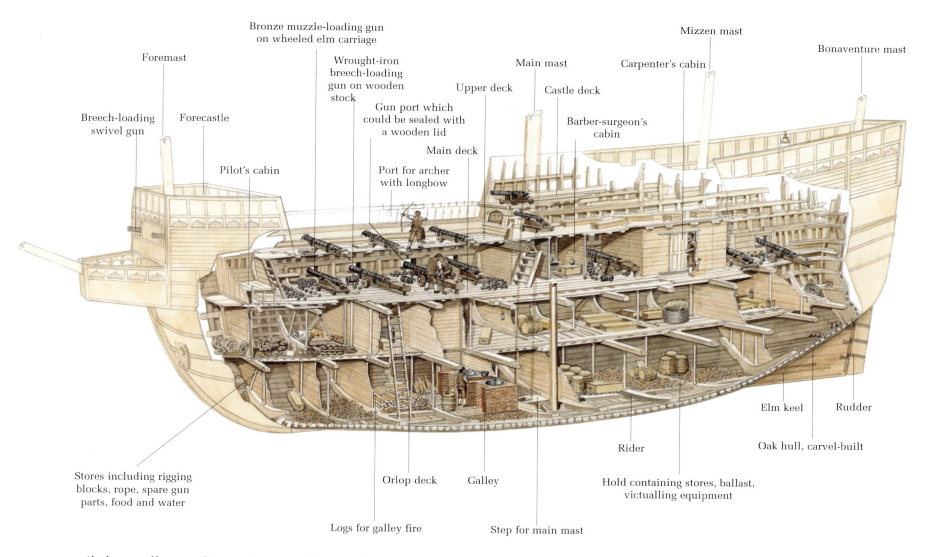

Foremast

Breech-loading swivel gun

Forecastle

Pilot's cabin

Bronze muzzle-loading gun on wheeled elm carriage

Wrought-iron breech-loading gun on wooden stock

Gun port which could be sealed with a wooden lid

Port for archer with longbow

Main deck

Upper deck

Main mast

Castle deck

Mizzen mast

Carpenter's cabin

Bonaventure mast

Barber-surgeon's cabin

Stores including rigging blocks, rope, spare gun parts, food and water

Logs for galley fire

Orlop deck

Galley

Step for main mast

Rider

Hold containing stores, ballast, victualling equipment

Elm keel

Rudder

Oak hull, carvel-built

sailed as well as, or better, than any ship in the fleet, 'weathering all save the *Mary Rose*'.

Henry Grace à Dieu was a splendid ship, forever associated with Henry VIII's name and reign. But she was only one of 85 warships which Henry either built (46), bought (26), or acquired as prizes (13). He also built 13 20-ton 'rowbarges', making a total of 98 warships of various types and sizes added to the Navy in Henry's reign. Of 7,780 men in the fleet in 1547, 1,885 were soldiers, 5,136 mariners and 759 gunners.

Henry took a close interest in guns and gunnery, and during his reign more and ever smaller warships were armed with an ever greater variety of guns. He had a 'pond made and cast' at Deptford large enough to take the *Mary Rose*, which was the beginning of that yard, and he founded Woolwich yard, which more or less grew up around the *Henry Grace à Dieu*.

REFORM AND REGULATION

Henry introduced and enforced new regulations for the control and manoeuvring of fleets at sea and the discipline of their crews. He reformed the administration of the Navy, changing it from the medieval pattern under one official to a committee, known as the Principal Officers of the

Navy, and later the Navy Board, a system of Admiralty which, albeit in a greatly changed form, exists today.

Under Henry VIII, the Navy took the first steps towards becoming a powerful offensive instrument of policy in its own right, rather than an ancillary and a mere means of transport for the army. Thus, in his own way, Henry VIII is more entitled to be called the Founder of the Royal Navy than his father.

Yet it was Henry, for all his flamboyance and authoritarian pride, who had the humiliation of watching one of his ships sink before his eyes, in one of the most dramatic mishaps in all naval history.

Mary Rose was rebuilt in 1536, uprated to 700 tons, and armed with new cast bronze muzzle-loading guns. She was in Henry VIII's fleet in 1544 when, in alliance with the Emperor Charles V of Spain, he was again at war with France and Scotland. Henry himself landed at Calais on 14 July with an army of 30,000 men, and besieged Boulogne, which surrendered on 14 September. In October, Sir Thomas Seymour was appointed vice admiral in command of a fleet to take winter stores to the garrison of Boulogne, who were themselves now besieged by the French. He was then to cruise off the coast, capturing or burning any French vessels he met.

However, Seymour's ships were blown away by storms and he had to return to Portsmouth with

Above: *A cutaway drawing of the* Mary Rose *showing the ship's structure. The heaviest guns were stationed along the main deck, while the upper deck and castle decks were fighting areas where gunners, soldiers and archers were stationed. The orlop deck housed stores and equipment such as rope, rigging blocks, and spare parts for the guns, while the hold contained ballast, stores, victuals and the ship's galley.*

Above: *The encampment of the English forces near Portsmouth, an engraving after an original picture (now lost) in Cowdray House. The* Mary Rose *can be seen sinking in the centre of the picture, just above the town of Southsea Castle, while the 'Great Harry' engages a number of French galleys in the action of 19 July 1545.*

Right: *A detail from the painting of Henry VIII's fleet embarking from Dover in 1520 that is reproduced on pages 8-9. The figure of the King can be seen standing on the upper deck of the ship in the centre background. The King's vessel was the* Kathryn Pleasaunce, *especially built to accommodate the royal party. Twenty-five years later he was personally to witness the loss of the* Mary Rose.

the loss of all his boats and two storeships. Henry was furious, but accepted Seymour's explanation.

Meanwhile, the French King Francis I decided to retaliate by seizing the Isle of Wight, to attack Portsmouth and Southampton, and eventually to march on London. He began to assemble every available warship on the Normandy coast and by the spring of 1545 he had a fleet of 150 large merchant vessels (*gros vaisseaux ronds*) and 60 oared coasters (*flouins*), under the Admiral of France, Claude d'Annebault. The King also summoned from the Mediterranean 25 galleys under Polain, Baron de la Garde, and Leone Strozzi, Admiral of the Galleys of Rhodes, and the best galley commander of his time.

Henry VIII decided that attack was the best form of defence, and dispatched his fleet, commanded by the Lord High Admiral, John Dudley, Lord Lisle (later Earl of Warwick, Duke of Northumberland and Lady Jane Grey's father-in-law), on a raid along the French coast. Lisle entered the Seine estuary and exchanged shots with the French, but it came on to blow and both sides drew off.

The French fleet sailed from Le Havre, Honfleur, Harfleur and other ports on 6 July, carrying an invasion force of more than 30,000 men. Henry had already had news of it. The King's ships were ordered to Portsmouth with all speed.

The King himself left Greenwich on 12 July and arrived with his retinue in Portsmouth on the 17th. The English had about 60 ships and some small craft, and 16,000 men, many of them assembled on Southsea Common. The watchword in the fleet that night was 'God Save The King'. The reply was 'Long to reign over us'.

The French arrived off the Isle of Wight on 18 July. During the day, d'Annebault brought his entire fleet round St Helens Point. His ships stretched in a long line from Brading Harbour along St Helens Roads to Ryde.

When the French were sighted, the English ships weighed and slowly approached. Some desultory long-range fire was exchanged. The English tried to lure the French into the shallows on the Spit Sand, within range of the town's guns, but d'Annebault refused to be drawn, and both sides broke off as night fell.

LIFE IN A TUDOR WARSHIP

A Tudor warship, unless she was very small, was commanded by a captain who had disciplinary control over the whole company, with full powers of summary jurisdiction up to and including the death penalty.

Under the captain, the chief officer was the master, who sailed the ship and managed the seamen. Warships usually had a master gunner, who recruited the gunners and commanded them in action. There was also a lieutenant, to command the soldiers. As the 16th century progressed and naval gunnery developed, the number of soldiers decreased and the gunners increased.

The junior officers included the boatswain, purser, carpenter, surgeon, steward, coxswain, cook and quartermasters, all on different rates of pay. Mariners

On 19 July 1545, the sun rose on a perfect English summer's day. It was slack water, and flat calm. The sea lay like a sheet of shining glass. There was not a breath of wind. Sails hung flat and motionless on the English yards. Such conditions were ideal for the French galleys, and for an hour, during which they were brilliantly handled, they had some excellent shooting practice against the stationary English hulls.

THE LOSS OF THE *MARY ROSE*

At last, a brisk wind sprang up off the land and the English ships began to weigh anchor. The *Mary Rose* had just weighed when she was seen to heel slightly. She was manned and stored for war, with a full complement of men and a full outfit of guns and shot, and would be drawing her maximum draught. Her lower guns might already have been run out for action. Whether or not the order was ever given to shut the gun-ports, it was certainly never carried out. Water flooded in through the openings and the ship rapidly filled and sank. Sir Walter Raleigh, writing in the early years of the next century but very probably using the testimony of eye-witnesses, said that *Mary Rose*: 'by a little sway of the ship in casting about, her ports being within sixteen inches of the water, was overset and lost'.

There seems also to have been some insubordination. Sir Gawain Carew, passing the *Mary Rose* in his own ship at that moment, called out to Sir George Carew 'asking him how he did? who answered, that he had a sort of knaves whom he could not rule'. It also seems possible that *Mary Rose* had what would now be called 'too many Chiefs and not enough Indians'. Nobody thought it their duty to see to such mundane matters as shutting gun-ports when going to sea.

There were only about 40 survivors. Sir George Carew and most of the 400 men on board were drowned, many of them trapped between decks.

Meanwhile, a somewhat anticlimactic battle was in progress. As the English ships advanced on the wind, so the French galleys retreated. They had been ordered to lure the English on, and they had, in any case, the galleys' dread of being rammed and having their oars broken by the great beaks of the sailing ships.

Adroitly handled, the galleys all rowed clear. Then, to their amazement and consternation, they were pursued by a flotilla of small 'roo-barges' (row-barges) which shot out from behind the larger ships. Galleys had no guns aft, so the roo-barges followed close astern, firing into their unprotected poops. Only the great Strozzi himself turned his galley and chased his tiny tormentor, but in a moment the roo-barges had gone about and withdrawn out of danger.

D'Annebault landed troops on the Isle of Wight, hoping Lisle would respond. But Lisle refused to

1512 The *Regent* lost in action with the French off Brest.

1513 *Henry Grace à Dieu* is built.

1536 *Mary Rose* rebuilt and uprated.

1545 Loss of the *Mary Rose* (19 July).

---

were well paid compared with farm workers and artisans ashore. An ordinary seaman's pay was five shillings a month in 1513, with coat and conduct money and free victuals. But it was an inflationary century and there were frequent desertions, requiring pay to be raised to 6s 8d a month in 1545 and to ten shillings a month in 1588.

On board, the seamen lived in very cramped quarters, normally infested with vermin, although hammocks began to be introduced in the 1590s. But the food was good and plentiful compared with on shore. Most voyages were short, so there was fresh meat and fish, and fruit in season. The weekly scale of victualling for a seaman in 1565 was seven pounds of biscuits, seven gallons of beer, eight pounds of salt beef, ¾ pound of stock fish, ¾ pound of butter and ¾ pound of cheese.

Most of the food was cooked in large cauldrons supported on iron bars over a fire-box placed on the deck of a massive brick-built galley situated down in the hold. There were pewter plates,

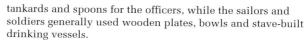

Left: *Tableware recovered from wreck of the* Mary Rose. *The treasure trove of archaeological material such as this recovered from the warship has revealed a vast amount about life in the Tudor Navy.*

tankards and spoons for the officers, while the sailors and soldiers generally used wooden plates, bowls and stave-built drinking vessels.

Many sailors were literate, and books were not uncommon on board, but arrangements were made for those who could not read: hatches and hatch covers had incised marks to show which cover fitted which hatch. Similarly, the chambers of breech-loading guns were clearly marked with the same mark as the gun they fitted.

Gaming was very popular in the Tudor navy. Off watch the sailors played with dice, the officers with backgammon boards. The general impression of the officers and ship's company of a ship such as the *Mary Rose* was of a body of young, generally healthy men, although some showed signs of dietary deficiency in childhood, who were adequately clothed and fed by the standards of the time.

Left: *This fine backgammon set made of oak with spruce and yew inlays was also recovered from the* Mary Rose.

Below: *Other artefacts from the* Mary Rose *throw a fascinating light on life on board a Tudor warship. They include the carpenter's tools (below left) and personal items such as a comb, a wooden seal, a pouch and tokens, a sundial, a die, a ring, a clasp, a whistle and a rosary.*

be drawn. D'Annebault then considered whether he could attack Lisle, but decided it was not feasible and anchored off Bricklesome Bay for the night. Lisle, too, considered whether he could make use of the westerly wind to drive the French down on to the Owers sands, but the wind dropped and so, also, was the plan.

D'Annibault re-embarked his troops after they had looted and burned a few villages. He decided, wisely, not to land in force and carry on with the invasion while the English fleet was still in being. He retired to France. Lisle did not follow.

By August 1545, the French fleet once more under d'Annebault was again at sea, cruising up and down the Channel. They were met off Shoreham on 15 August by Henry's fleet, commanded once more by Lisle. In an attempt to deal with the French galleys, Henry had taken what seems to be the reactionary decision to have his own galleys or 'oared pieces'. Thus the English fleet had a windward squadron under Captain William Tyrrell, 40 sail of 'galleasses, shallops and boats of war', including the new galleasses, powered by sail and oars, *Grand Mistress* (Admiral) and *Anne Gallant* (Vice Admiral), the *Galley Subtille* and the *Greyhound*, with nine Royal pinnaces, 20 pinnaces from the Western Ports and seven boats from Rye. In the van, were 24 heavy ships unders Sir Thomas Clere, Vice Admiral of England. Lisle, the Lord Admiral, had 40 sail in the 'battle': 104 sail in all.

The French attacked with galleys but, as Lisle reported to the King, 'your Highness's shallops and rowing pieces did their parts well, but especially the *Mistress* and the *Anne Gallant* did so handle the galleys, as well with their sides as with their prows, that your great-ships in a manner had little to do'.

D'Annebault did not get up to support his galleys until the evening, but after a shift of wind both sides anchored. Lisle wanted the wind to strengthen so that it would favour his ships and disadvantage the French galleys, but in the morning the French had vanished. Lisle gave chase, but could not catch them. Francis I did not attempt another invasion.

It was an inconclusive action, but it had long-term effects. It seems to have been the first battle in which English ships fired broadsides in action. Thus, these forgotten sea battles off Portsmouth laid the foundations for the great age of Elizabethan naval tactics under Drake and Howard.

Having watched from Southsea Castle the awful spectacle of one of his best ships sinking, Henry VIII at once gave orders that *Mary Rose* should be salvaged. She lay in 40 feet (12m) of water which was not an insuperable depth for recovery. But after four years of failures, the salvage was abandoned. *Mary Rose* then lay undisturbed until 1836, when two pioneer divers, John and Charles Deane, rediscovered the wreck off Spit Sand, and recovered several guns. The hull was eventually raised in 1982 and towed into Portsmouth harbour. The preserved ship is now on display at Portsmouth Historic Dockyard.

A TIME OF EXPLORATION

The 16th century saw the beginnings of voyages of exploration from this country. In 1527, an Englishman, Robert Thorne, suggested the possibility of sailing north of Europe and Asia so as to reach Cathay (China), avoiding the Spaniards and

Right: The basic tools of navigation in a 16th century ship were steering compasses, a protractor and a pair of dividers to enable the pilot to steer a course using charts. The examples shown here were recovered from the Mary Rose. A log reel and sand timer glasses were also used to calculate the speed of the ship by measuring the distance she had travelled in a specific period of time.

Below: A drawing from a manuscript by Matthew Baker entitled Fragments Of Ancient English Shipwrighting *that was part of Samuel Pepys's own library. It dates from around 1586 and shows the profile of an Elizabethan galleon.*

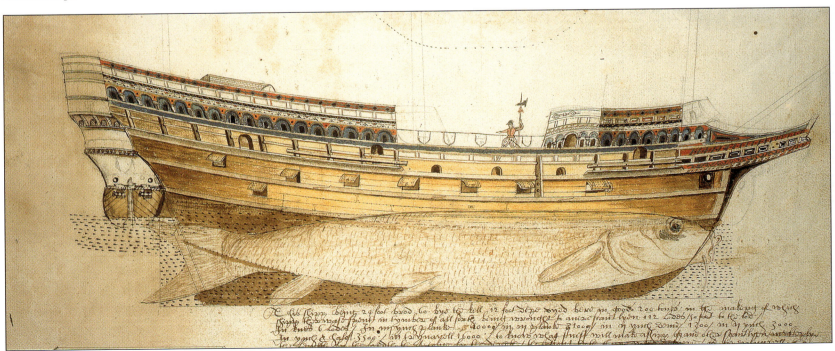

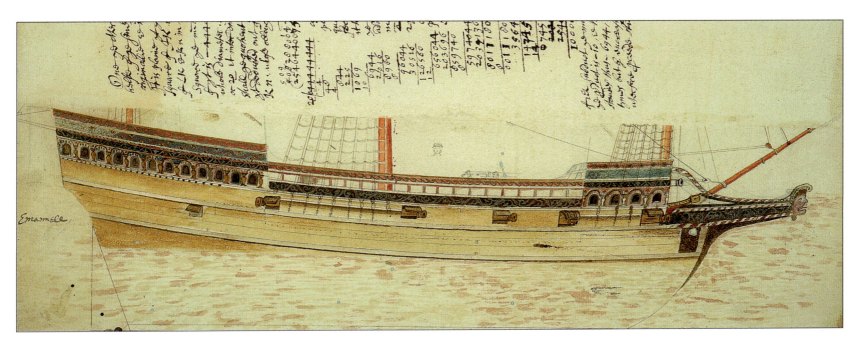

the Portuguese. So the concept of a North-east passage was born.

In 1553, Sir Hugh Willoughby, a soldier and adventurer with no previous experience as a sailor, was appointed captain-general of an expedition to search for the North-east passage. His squadron consisted of the *Bona Esperanza* (120 tons), *Edward Bonaventure* (160 tons), which had the chief pilot, Richard Chancellor, embarked and *Bona Confidentia* (90 tons).

Willoughby's ships sailed in July, and reached the Lofoten Islands, off the north Norwegian coast, in August. After a stay of three days, they sailed northward again, but when they reached latitude 70° and were about to round the North Cape, a gale separated *Bonaventure* from the other two ships.

They sighted land again in August but contrary winds kept the two ships at sea until September when they able to anchor in the harbour of Arzinia in Lapland. Willoughby decided to winter there. However, his expedition lacked all the necessities for surviving an Arctic winter, and everyone on board the ships perished.

After waiting seven days at the rendezvous, Chancellor went on alone and reached the White Sea, where he landed and visited Ivan the Terrible in Moscow. This led in 1555 to the founding of the Muscovy Company, designed to encourage trade between England and Russia.

Chancellor made a second voyage in 1555, during which he called at Arzinia and collected Willoughby's body, goods, and papers, including his Journal, which showed that most of the ship's company had survived until January 1554. Returning from a third voyage in 1556, with a Russian ambassador embarked, Chancellor's ship was wrecked off Petsligo, Aberdeen, and he and most of his crew were drowned.

In the reign of Queen Elizabeth, 'exploration' became almost synonymous with piracy. One of its first and chief exponents was John Hawkins, son of a mayor of Plymouth, whose family had traded with West Africa for some years before Hawkins made his first voyage to Hispaniola (Haiti) in 1562, and extended his family's trade to the transport of slaves to the Spanish West Indies. By so doing, Hawkins offended both the Portuguese, who themselves transported slaves, and the Spanish, who naturally resented this intrusion on their monopoly in the Caribbean.

Hawkins' second voyage in 1564-65 was backed by a syndicate of merchants and by the Queen herself, who lent him the royal ship, the *Jesus of Lubeck*. The voyage was successful and Hawkins and his backers, including the Queen, made a huge profit from the sale of slaves. However, Hawkins' third voyage, of 1567–68, was a disaster. Hawkins was bearing the Queen's commission and was actually flying her standard when the *Jesus of Lubeck* was captured at San Juan de Ulloa in Mexico, and only the Queen's other ships, the *Minion* and the *Judith*, under Francis Drake, his cousin, escaped. This was the start of the long period of hostility between England and Spain which was eventually to lead to open warfare.

DRAKE'S 1577 VOYAGE

It also ignited Drake's hatred of Spaniards, and his desire for revenge on them for what he always regarded as their treachery at San Juan de Ulloa. His chance came in 1577 when a syndicate headed by the Queen engaged him to make the first circumnavigation of the world by an Englishman. Ostensibly, the objects of the expedition were to discover the legendary southern continent of Terra Australia Incognita, and to return through the North-west passage, the sea route from the Atlantic to the Pacific to the north

▶ **1553–54** Sir Hugh
Willoughby and
Richard Chancellor
sail to look for the
North-east passage.
Willoughby and his
crew perish during the
voyage.

1562 John Hawkins
makes first voyage to
Hispaniola.

1577–80 Francis
Drake's circum-
navigation of the
world.

1583 Sir Humphrey
Gilbert sets up the first
English colony in
North America, in
Newfoundland.

of Canada. Actually, the expedition's object was plunder.

The whole enterprise was planned in great secrecy between Elizabeth and her syndicate and Drake so as to keep it from being known to Spain. Drake's crew consisted mostly of experienced seamen, with a few ship's boys, some soldiers, and ten gentlemen adventurers, including John Doughty and his brother Thomas, to whom Drake revealed, in confidence, the true purpose of the voyage. Thomas in turn revealed the secret to Lord Burghley, Lord Treasurer of England, who was horrified by the probable impact of such a voyage on English relations with Spain, already strained by Drake's previous voyages. Burghley did everything in his power to obstruct the expedition, and apparently persuaded Doughty to disrupt it if it got under way.

Drake sailed from Plymouth on 5 November 1577 in command of the *Pelican*, of 100 tons, (renamed *Golden Hind* in the Pacific), with four smaller ships and about 160 men. Drake picked up various Portuguese prizes as he fell in with them. From one he took a Portuguese, Nunez da Silva, a pilot who had considerable experience of Brazilian coastal waters. This was exactly what Drake needed and da Silva stayed for the next 15 months.

Thomas Doughty had begun to cause trouble, inciting the crews to mutiny, when Drake's ships were hardly clear of the Channel. By June 1578, Drake had reached Port St Julian, 200 miles (320km) north of the entrance to the Magellan

Straits. Here, Drake decided to quell the discord which was endangering his ships. He had Doughty arrested, empanelled a jury of 40 men, with John Wynter the Vice Admiral as foreman, and charged Doughty with incitement to mutiny, witchcraft, defamation of Drake and seeking to 'overthrow' the voyage, insubordination and using words treasonable to the Queen and council. Doughty was found guilty of all charges and was beheaded two days later.

Drake sailed through the Straits of Magellan and was driven further south by a storm to about latitude 57°S. The smaller ships had already left him and he was separated by the storm from his only remaining ship, the *Elizabeth*, commanded by Wynter, who decided to return home.

> '*H*ere is such controversy between the sailors and the gentlemen and such stomaching between the gentleman and the sailors, that it doth even make me mad to hear it. But my masters, I must have it left. For I must have the gentlemen to haul and draw with the mariner and the mariner with the gentleman. What! let us show ourselves all to be of a company and let us not give occasion to the enemy to rejoice at our decay and overthrow. I would know him, that would refuse to set his hand to a rope, but I know there is not any such here.'
>
> FRANCIS DRAKE ADDRESSING THE MEMBERS OF HIS
> EXPEDITION AT PORT ST JULIAN DURING HIS
> CIRCUMNAVIGATION OF THE GLOBE, 11 AUGUST 1578

SIR FRANCIS DRAKE

Francis Drake was the supreme fighting seaman of his age. The Spaniards believed he had a magic mirror, which he could look into and see where all their ships were.

He was born at Crowndale, near Tavistock, probably in 1541, the son of a preacher (and a cousin of John Hawkins). He was short and stocky in stature, and had red hair. After serving an apprenticeship in the Thames coastal trade, he made a voyage to the west coast of Africa in 1566.

His feats became the stuff of legend: his raids on the Spanish Main, the attack on Nombre de Dios in 1572, his interception of the mule trains carrying silver across the Isthmus of Panama and his first sight of the Pacific, when he prayed that he might be the first 'to sail an English ship in those seas'.

Then there was the circumnavigation of the world from 1587–1580, the 'descent of the Indies' in 1585 when he sacked San Domingo and Cartagena, the 'singeing of the King of Spain's beard' at Cadiz in 1587, and his celebrated game of bowls on Plymouth Hoe before commanding *Revenge* in action against the Spanish Armada.

When, in August 1578, during the voyage round the world, there was continuing discord between the professional seamen and the gentlemen adventurers of the court, Drake mustered the entire expedition and

made his famous and often quoted speech, in which he laid down the splendid tradition that was to govern the English sea-service. After reminding them all of the desperate and dangerous nature of the service to which they were committed, he told them that their mutinies and discords must cease, and enjoined them to work together, 'the mariner with the gentleman', in a wonderful piece of oratory that is quoted in the panel above.

In 1595, he and Hawkins made another descent on the Indies, which failed. Hawkins died of dysentry off Puerto Rico. Nombre de Dios was sacked, but no treasure was found. Drake contracted yellow fever and died off Porto Bello on 28 January 1596. He was buried at sea.

'Drake's Drum', now at Buckland Abbey, Devon, his old home, was said to have been carried on board his ships, to beat crews to quarters. It is popularly supposed to give a drumbeat whenever England is threatened by invasion from the sea.

'Drake's Prayer', supposed to have been composed by him off Cadiz, was in fact compiled in 1941 from his letters to the government.

Left: Sir Francis Drake, a portrait in the style of Marcus Gheeraerts the Younger. Drake was the foremost sailor of his age and the first Englishman to sail his ship around the globe.

Below: A 16th century astronomical compendium used for calculating position at sea. The latitudes of various towns are inscribed on the open face on the right hand side.

Thus the *Golden Hind*, as she was now called, entered the South Seas alone, but as the Spanish settlements were undefended, Drake was able to make several successful raids along the coast of South America, sacking towns and plundering shipping, his richest prize being the treasure ship *Nuestra Señora de la Concepción*, taken off Lima.

Drake sailed as far north as latitude 48°N, where he turned south again to land at New Albion, near San Francisco. He then sailed across the Pacific to the Moluccas, where he loaded six tons of cloves. For some reason Francis Fletcher, Drake's preacher, who was to write the best account of the voyage, incurred Drake's severe displeasure, and was excommunicated by him.

Drake returned to Plymouth on 26 September 1580, anxiously enquiring whether the Queen were still alive to protect him against Spanish charges of piracy. His treasure, estimated at half a million pounds in Elizabethan currency, was taken by land to the Tower of London, while Drake sailed the *Golden Hind* to Deptford, where he was knighted by the Queen, though she handed the sword to the French ambassador for the actual accolade. The voyage had been a most succcessful enterprise, which paid £47 for every £1 invested in it, and it also put England on the map as a rising sea power.

THE NORTH-WEST PASSAGE

The possibility of a North-west passage to Cathay, over the 'roof' of Canada, continued to preoccupy the Elizabethan imagination. Martin Frobisher made three voyages between 1576 and 1578, which were of great navigational value but commercially profitless. The 'gold' he brought back proved to be valueless.

But the Elizabethan whose name is most closely associated with the search for the North-west passage to Cathay is Sir Walter Raleigh's half-brother, Sir Humphrey Gilbert. He had soldiered in France, Ireland and the Netherlands, but his ambition was always to find the North-west passage, and he published a famous *Discourse* on the subject in 1576.

In 1578, he was granted a charter by Queen Elizabeth to make such a voyage and to found a colony in Newfoundland, of which he was to be the Governor. His first expedition, in 1578, reached only Cape Verde, where it met disaster at the hands of the Spaniards. Gilbert had to return to soldiering, but in 1583, with Raleigh's help and, as he himself said, by 'selling the clothes off my wife's back', he raised enough money for another expedition.

Gilbert sailed from Plymouth in June 1583 in the *Delight*, with the *Ark Raleigh* (the biggest ship in the flotilla, provided by Raleigh), the *Golden Hind, Swallow* and the 10-ton *Squirrel*. The *Ark*

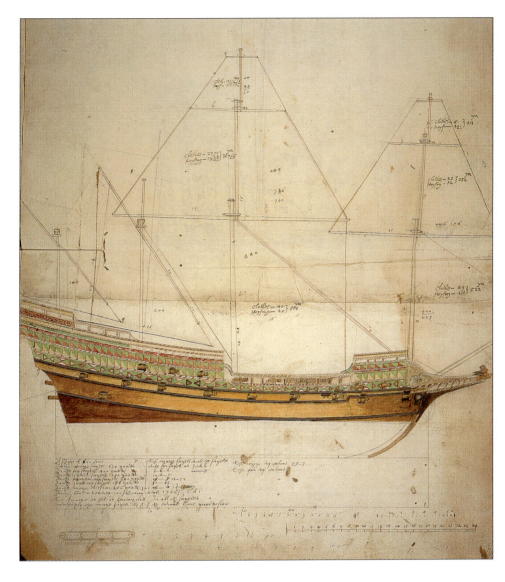

Raleigh soon left and returned home, on the pretext of sickness on board. The rest reached St John's, Newfoundland, where Gilbert took possession of the territory in the Queen's name and, on 5 August 1583, set up the first English colony in North America.

Gilbert soon found the task of imposing discipline and law on the colonists beyond him. He sent the *Swallow* back to England with the sick and disaffected, while he embarked in the *Squirrel* and led the remaining ships south to explore the coast.

The *Delight* ran aground on 29 August and was lost. Two days later, the *Golden Hind* and the *Squirrel* shaped course for England, meeting fierce storms off the Azores. After one storm, Gilbert could be seen from the *Golden Hind*, sitting composedly in the *Squirrel*'s stern, book in hand. When the two ships came within earshot, he called out cheerfully, 'We are as near to heaven by sea as by land'. The *Squirrel* was lost with all hands that night.

Queen Elizabeth's ambivalent attitude towards adventurers like Hawkins and Drake, who repeatedly, deliberately and infuriatingly trespassed upon the commercial monopolies of Spain and Portugal in the New World and Africa, was bound to lead to war with Spain, although Philip II did not act decisively for some time.

Above: *This drawing from Matthew Baker's* Fragments Of Ancient English Shipwrighting *shows the masts and sails, as well as the hull, of a galleon of the Armada period. The low profile of such ships is in marked contrast to the high-sided vessels of Henry VIII's navy. Speed and manoeuvrability were important to men such as Drake and Hawkins who chose to prey on commercial prizes on the high seas.*

▶ **1585** England agrees to support the Dutch in Treaty of Nonsuch. War with Spain becomes inevitable. Lord Howard of Effingham appointed Lord High Admiral. Drake raids Cartagena.

Right: Charles, Lord Howard of Effingham and First Earl of Nottingham, a portrait by Daniel Mytens. He was created Lord High Admiral in 1585 and commanded the English fleet against the Spanish Armada in 1588.

Below: The Chatham Chest, a charitable fund inaugurated in Elizabeth I's reign to aid distressed sailors and their families. It was secured by five locks which opened to five different keys held by five different officers, an expedient intended to prevent misappropriation of the funds.

SIR JOHN HAWKINS

Ironically, it is Hawkins who has the best claim to be the main architect of the Elizabethan Navy which fought against Spain. He succeeded his father-in-law, Benjamin Gonson, as Treasurer of the Navy in 1577, and although his financial probity was occasionally questioned, he put up convincing defences, and generally maintained a comparatively high standard, for his times, of administrative integrity. He improved the pay and conditions of seamen, and in 1590, with Lord Howard of Effingham and Francis Drake, founded the Chatham Chest, a contributory benevolent fund to which seamen paid sixpence a month from their pay for the benefit of the wounded and the widows of those fellow sailors killed in action. Hawkins is still remembered for his ship's order: 'Serve God daily, love one another, preserve your victuals, beware of fire, and keep good company'.

In 1579, Hawkins contracted to maintain 25 ships to a certain standard, although not to repair them or provide shipkeepers, in return for £1,200 a year. He became virtually responsible for designing and building new ships to replace those inherited by Elizabeth from Henry VIII, although he seems to have been much influenced by experiments in ship design carried out in Henry's reign. Hawkins was a privateer by temperament, not concerned with defence, only with attack. Although some larger ships such as the *White Bear* and the *Triumph* were built, the *Revenge*, which was

longer, narrower and had much less superstructure, was typical of the new 'low-charged', 'race-built' galleons, faster, more manoeuvrable, more weatherly, and carrying more guns. Such ships could hold larger but clumsier opponents at bay by 'stand off' tactics, using longer-ranged guns to good advantage.

The decade of the 1580s began with successes for Spanish arms. In the Low Countries, the Duke of Parma won a succession of victories against the rebellious Protestant provinces, who were forced to look for allies. Under the Treaty of Nonsuch, in 1585, England agreed to support the Dutch with a small army. This made war with Spain inevitable.

There was a severe shortage of grain in Spain in the Spring of 1585, and Philip had guaranteed safe conduct to the English and Baltic ships importing grain. But in May 1585 he ordered all these ships to be seized, their guns confiscated, and their crews imprisoned.

The English retaliated by swiftly launching a 'descent of the Indies', the first act of open war: a fleet of 22 sail, under Drake, which sailed from Plymouth in September 1585. While the Spanish commanders were at cross purposes and their defences ill organised, Drake proved himself a master of combined operations, sacking San Domingo, Cartagena, St Augustine in Florida, and then taking off the first Virginian colonists.

A humiliated Philip now decided that he would have to defeat England before he could win in the Netherlands. There had been earlier plans, suggested by the Marquis of Santa Cruz, Philip's naval commander, to invade England directly from Spain, with 55,000 men, and over 500 ships, but Philip knew that such an undertaking was beyond Spain's means. But in April 1586 Parma suggested that he himself would invade England with 30,000 of his men already in the Low Countries, if a Spanish fleet could defeat the English and hold the Narrow Seas long enough for Parma's army to cross.

A SPANISH ARMADA

This would require 150 ships – still a major logistical undertaking. But an angry and mortified Philip, who looked on himself as God's agent, destined by a Catholic God to crush these Protestant rebels, ordered the Armada to be assembled. Santa Cruz, who would command, still wanted to lead a force from Spain, so it was decided that some 19,000 men would sail with the Armada. This meant that troop transports, as well as warships, would be required. The Armada was to sail against England in August 1587.

Such a vast enterprise could not be concealed. By the end of 1586, it was common knowledge in England that the Spaniards were preparing a huge Armada. The largest ship-building programme since the war against France in the 1540s was put in hand, and, in March 1587 Drake was commissioned to lead a fleet of 23 sail, including six of the Queen's large warships and others provided mainly by the city of London, on an expedition to 'impeach' Spain's preparations for war in any way he could.

Drake sailed on 2 April, supposedly to an unknown destination, but knowing very well that his objective was an armed raid on Cadiz. His ships arrived off Cadiz on 19 April and took the place by surprise; 24 Spanish ships were destroyed or captured, with a large amount of arms and equipment. Fourteen royal galleys which tried to defend the harbour were sunk, but no attempt was made to capture or plunder the city.

Having achieved his object, of 'singeing the King of Spain's beard', Drake withdrew. But he had to stay at sea to satisfy the captains of the London ships who had expected to make a profit out of the voyage by privateering. One carrack from the Indies was captured, the *San Felipe*, with a cargo worth about £115,000. Drake returned to Plymouth in July, having narrowly avoided the Marquis of Santa Cruz, who had sailed with a powerful fleet to look for him. By the time Santa Cruz returned to Spain, it was too late for the Armada to sail in 1587.

On 5 July 1588, Gilbert Lee, captain of the *Rat of Wight*, arrived in Portsmouth to report that on 25 May (by the Spanish calendar) one hundred and three score sail of small and great ships had departed from Lisbon. The Spanish Armada had sailed at last.

That it sailed at all was remarkable. The organisation of the Armada had encountered every sort of difficulty. There were not enough heavy guns, and no means of manufacturing them in Spain, not enough ships for the men who had assembled, and were eating food faster than it could be provided for them. When the Marquis of Santa Cruz died in February 1588, it seemed the Armada would never sail. But Santa Cruz was replaced by Alonso Pérez de Guzmán, Duke of Medina Sidonia, an inexperienced admiral but a very good organiser, who got the Armada to sea before it bankrupted the national treasury, as seemed likely at one time.

However, the splendid fleet that Medina Sidonia led down the Tagus late in May 1588 had grave deficiencies. The Armada had made such prodigious demands on manpower that many of the so-called sailors were actually landsmen who had never been to sea before, and many of the

soldiers were the rawest of recruits. Only about thirty of the 130 ships were properly fitted out as warships. The guns were of every size and calibre and many of them were old or unsuitable for shipboard use. With no base once it had sailed, the Armada had to take with it all the food, water, powder and shot needed for a voyage of incalculable length.

A FATAL FLAW

The Armada's plan of action had one serious defect which, in the event, was to prove fatal. Spain had no large deep water port in the Netherlands. Therefore Parma would have to be ready in all respects to embark immediately the Armada arrived. Furthermore, before Parma's troop barges could reach the protection of the Armada's guns, they would first have to make their way out through shallow coastal waters, where a flotilla of heavily armed shallow draught Dutch warships commanded by Justin of Nassau was lying in wait. Thus, the Armada's whole scheme depended upon timing. It would, in fact, probably require divine intervention.

The English fleet, of about 150 ships, 40 of them Queen's ships, assembled in the Downs and at

Above: Drake's capture of the Nuestra Señora del Rosario, *21 July 1588. Having captured the Spanish flagship, Drake realised that her formidable artillery was not set up for repeated firing in a mobile fight. This intelligence helped to formulate the English fleet's tactics during the running battle up the Channel. The engraving was published as one of a series of ten charts made by John Pine in 1739 that were based on tapestries by Cornelis Vroom and Francis Spiring..*

1587 Drake raids Cadiz 'singeing the King of Spain's beard'.

1588 Spanish Armada sails from Lisbon. The Armada is defeated by the English fleet and scattered by storms as it flees north (July).

1589 Drake's expedition to Lisbon is a failure.

1590 Hawkins founds the Chatham Chest, a benevolent fund for seamen.

Plymouth. The Lord Admiral, Howard of Effingham, was comparatively inexperienced as an admiral, but he had under him captains such as Drake, in the *Revenge*, Hawkins, in the *Victory*, and Frobisher, in the great galleon *Triumph*. The English ships were generally better sailers than the Spaniards, and could keep up a higher rate of fire at a greater range. The English also had the advantage of sailing in familiar waters, near their home ports, where they could replenish with ammunition and stores.

The Armada was sighted off the Lizard on 19 July (29 July by the Calendar introduced by Pope Gregory XIII in 1582, used by the Spaniards but not by the English; thus English dates are ten days in arrears, although the days of the week remain the same).

FIRST ENCOUNTERS

The first engagements, on Saturday and Sunday, 20 and 21 July, were led by Drake who captured the galleon *Nuestra Señora del Rosario* and sent it into Dartmouth. There was a further action off Portland on 23rd and then, on 24th, an encounter between Drake's *Revenge* and the straggling Rostock hulk, *El Gran Grifon*, flagship of the supply squadron, off the Isle of Wight. Medina Sidonia had to send galleasses back to rescue her.

Four days of fighting had left the English ships very short of ammunition, and Howard sent 'divers barks and pinnaces unto the shore' for supplies. He obtained some but not enough. The English ships were also very short of direction. So far, battles had developed more or less as individual ship's captains had decided, and there was little sense of their ships being components of a corporate fleet or squadron. By contrast, the corporate discipline in the Armada, fostered by the belief that they were engaged on a divine mission, was excellent.

On Wednesday evening, 24 July, the Armada and Howard's ships lay becalmed, and quite close to each other, off the Needles. That night, Howard held a council of war on board his flagship *Ark Royal*. As a result of this conference, he organised his fleet in four squadrons. He himself, as the Admiral, was in the centre, Drake, as Vice Admiral, was on the right or seaward end of the line, with Hawkins, Rear Admiral, inshore and to port of him. On the port, landward, wing was Frobisher, the junior flag officer.

The English now reasoned that Medina Sidonia was sure to make a move into the Solent and seize the Isle of Wight. This would provide him with a large deep water harbour of refuge while he established communications with the Duke of Parma. He could safely wait there until he received word that Parma was ready. Once past the Isle of Wight, there was nowhere else he could take shelter.

Philip's orders to Medina Sidonia had been quite specific and inflexible: he was to proceed directly and join the Duke of Parma. However, it seems that Medina Sidonia's advisers strongly urged him to capture the Isle of Wight, and it does seem that he did make some move in that direction, although his own account is silent on the point.

Dawn broke on Thursday 25 July with the Armada off Dunnose Head, and both fleets still almost becalmed. Soon, the wind picked up from the south-west and the Armada was under way, keeping as close to the shore as possible. The English followed, intending somehow during the day to slip as many ships as possible through to landward of the Armada, and thus block the entrance to the Solent.

At dawn that day, the ships of Frobisher's landward squadron were off Dunnose Head, to the north and east of the Armada, and ahead of its van. As the light strengthened, two ships, the *Santa Ana* and the Portuguese galleon *San Luis*, could be seen straggling astern of the Armada. They were engaged by Hawkins and then by Howard. Medina Sidonia sent ships, including his own flagship, the *San Martin*, back to help the stragglers.

San Martin was hotly engaged by Frobisher and it was while he was thus occupied that the breeze sprang up from the south-west, leaving the *Triumph* in the Armada's lee, and effectively cut off. It was a perilous situation for Frobisher, and very similar to one he had experienced off Portland a few days earlier.

The great galleon *Triumph* was, of course, a tremendous prize for the Spanish ships. Gleefully they crowded on sail to bear down and capture her. Still becalmed, *Triumph* got out her longboats to try and pull herself clear of danger. Lord Sheffield's *White Bear* and the *Elizabeth Jonas* came round the Armada's flank to assist *Triumph*. Even so, she might still have been taken but, luckily for her, a wind suddenly got up, veered

Below: *A woodcut of* Ark Royal *which was Lord Howard of Effingham's flagship during the Armada campaign. On 26 July he conferred six knighthoods on fellow officers on her deck. She was the first of a long line of notable warships to bear this famous name.*

and freshened. Shaking out her sails, and casting off her boats, *Triumph* managed to get under way and slipped clear.

CHANGES OF COURSE

There is no admission in Spanish accounts that Medina Sidonia diverted from the course ordered by Philip and entered St Helens Road, but it seems likely that he did. The wind freshened and stayed in the south-west, ideal for his purpose, and then as he steered for Spithead the wind changed, again very suitably, to north-east. As he went, he was followed and harried by Howard, who must have thought his worst fears of a Spanish invasion were about to be realised. Then, seemingly inexplicably, Medina Sidonia turned back to the south-west and appeared to abandon any attempt to reach Spithead.

Hawkins and Drake, commanding the two most southerly and seaward English squadrons, also drop out of the English narratives for a time, but it was certainly those two who attacked the Armada's right wing later in the forenoon. The wind had backed to south-west again, and Drake

and Hawkins, by steering out to sea, gained the weather gauge of the Armada.

The brunt of the attack was borne by the Portuguese galleon *San Mateo*, supported by the 52-gun *Florencia*, the most heavily-armed Spanish ship. However, as the battle developed and more ships were involved, *San Mateo* and the other ships were forced backwards, slowly giving ground as they retreated into the middle of the supply squadron which they were escorting, and throwing them into confusion.

Wind, tide, and the harassing English ships, gradually edged the Armada's seaward wing northwards and eastwards, across the eastern entrance to the Solent, thus making sure they could never now enter the Solent, and driving them ever nearer the dangerous shoals and rocks of the Owers Bank, stretching out from Selsey Bill.

The leading Armada ships were within 40 minutes of striking and disaster, with discoloured shoal water ahead, and seas actually breaking over uncovered black rocks clearly to be seen, when Medina Sidonia noticed, or more likely had his attention drawn to, the imminent danger. He fired a gun from his flagship, and bore away to the south-east. The ships in his landward wing, some of whose captains had been reluctant to follow him to the north because they knew and feared the Owers Bank, turned away from Spithead and followed the seaward wing to the south-east.

By ten o'clock that forenoon, the whole Armada was streaming away to the eastward. With the westerly wind behind them, all hope of entering the Solent had gone forever. The English ships had forced Medina Sidonia to take the course ordered by his master. The Duke had no choice now but to go on and meet Parma at Calais.

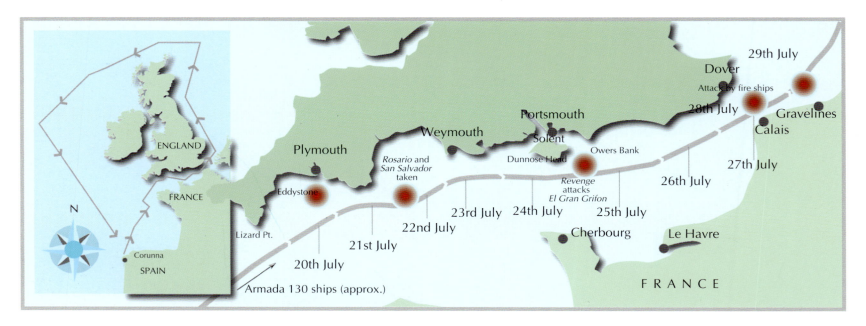

Above: *A map that shows the course of the Armada from the time it set sail from Corunna on 10 July to the return of the vanquished fleet which was forced to flee northwards and sail around the British Isles to regain home waters. The detail (right) shows the actions fought in the English Channel.*

Above right: *Augustine's Ryther's chart showing the Spanish fleet anchored in tight formation in the Calais roads being engaged by English ships. It was the use of fire-ships at this juncture that broke the Spanish resolve.*

1591 Sir Richard Grenville's action off the Azores.

1596 Earl of Essex leads successful expedition to Cadiz.

1599 Threat of another Spanish invasion.

1604 Peace with Spain confirmed by the Treaty of London.

Although the English ships had done well, and had surprised the Spaniards with their line-ahead formation and their raking gunfire, their 'morris dance on the waters', as Drake put it, they had done very little real damage. The Armada was short of ammunition, with stores and water much reduced, when it reached Calais, but it was still essentially a large convoy, still in a tight fighting formation, still intact and formidable, having lost only three galleons.

But when Medina Sidonia reached Calais roads, on 27 July, he found that Parma would not be ready for another week. The Armada was forced to anchor in the roads, exposed to the weather and vulnerable to English attacks.

THE 'HELL-BURNERS'

Next day, Sunday 28 July, Howard's ships were anchored only a culverin's shot (about 2,000 yards, 1,830 metres) up-wind and up-tide of where the Armada lay in its tightly packed anchorage. Anybody who saw the Armada, counted its ships and its guns, could not doubt that victory would surely go to Spain. The only niggling uncertainty, more than a little worrying, was the sight of some eight or nine strange,

unidentified ships joining Howard's fleet that Sunday evening.

Actually, the newcomers were harmless supply ships, but every man in the Armada had heard of the floating bombs, the 'hell-burners', the *maquinas de minas* (mine-machines), designed by Federigo Gianibelli, and used at the siege of Antwerp in 1585. Gianibelli was known to be in England (he was building an inoffensive and eventually futile boom across the Thames at Gravesend). Thus, by that Sunday, every officer and man in the Armada was unusually sensitive to any rumours about fireships or 'hell-burners', or indeed any ship or event which appeared strange or untoward.

In fact, the English had already discussed the question of fire-ships. When the English commanders conferred on that Sunday morning, they decided they could not wait for fire-ships from England. Eight ships were selected from the fleet, one belonging to Drake himself, another to Hawkins. Their guns were left loaded. There was no time to remove them, and in any case the detonations might add to the fire-ships' effect and cause greater alarm amongst the enemy. This decision, perhaps accidental, perhaps intentional, in fact did more to destroy Spanish morale than anything else.

The tide was flowing at nearly three knots towards the Armada, with an extra three-quarters of a knot of North Sea current backing it up. The fire-ships had to cover a distance of about a mile and a half (2,400m). So, from the moment the first flames were sighted, the Armada had about 30 minutes to act.

Medina Sidonia sent pinnaces out to windward to intercept the fire-ships and tow them clear. In spite of the wind, tide, and current, bearing the flames down on the Armada at a furious rate, the pinnaces did tow two fire-ships clear. But then the flames reached the guns in one of the other ships, and there was a series of shattering detonations.

Here, at last, were the terrible sounds the Spaniards had half-expected, half-dreaded, to hear. Those ships which had arrived the previous evening must have been Gianibelli's handiwork after all. These, then, were the diabolical hell-burners of Antwerp, the *maquinas de minas* designed and fashioned as though by the Devil himself.

Something close to panic broke out in the Spanish ships. Medina Sidonia said later that he gave the order for his flagship to weigh, and also for the rest to do the same, intending to return and recover the same position when the fire-ships had passed. That may or may not have been his intention but it was impossible to carry it out in practice. Most of the ships simply cut their cables and fled, slipping rapidly away down to leeward. They were to regret the loss of those anchors and cables in the weeks to come.

But worst of all, the fire-ships had broken the Armada's tight formation, in a way all the mid-Channel manoeuvres of Howard and Drake had failed to do. Once broken, it was never properly reformed. Medina Sidonia did anchor and fired a gun to signal to the others to do the same. Few heard it, and only three or four ships obeyed, or were able to obey. The great galleass *San Lorenzo* ran aground under the guns of the fortress of Calais, where she was plundered by Howard's men the next day.

Off Gravelines on Monday 29 July the English ships closed to within killing range of their long guns and inflicted the final and irreversible defeat on the Spanish Armada. Medina Sidonia's surviving ships fled to the north, intent only on getting home to Spain. Many of them were wrecked on the coasts of Scotland and Ireland on the way.

A NATION REJOICES

The countrywide relief and euphoria at the defeat of the Spanish Armada greatly stimulated that sense of national pride and identity which was already such a feature of Elizabethan England, and encouraged a spate of triumphalist literature.

England may have been swept by a wave of relief and euphoria, but there was an outbreak of plague in the fleet even before Howard had called off the pursuit of the Armada. Within days, hundreds of men were dying in the streets of the seaport towns.

In 1589, an expedition was despatched under Sir Francis Drake, in command of the ships, and Sir Henry Norris, commanding the troops, to Lisbon with the object of destroying the survivors of the Armada. Troops were landed at Corunna and Lisbon but they achieved nothing and disease decimated their numbers.

> '*...which fire in the dead of night put the Spaniards into such a perplexity and horrour (for they feared least they were like unto those terrible ships,which Frederic Jenebelli three yeeres before at the siege of Antwerpe had furnished with gunpowder, stones and dreadfull engines...) that cutting their cables wheron their ankers were fastened, and hoisting up their sailes, they betooke themselves very confusedly unto the maine sea.*'
>
> RICHARD HAKLUYT'S ACCOUNT OF THE REACTION OF THE SPANISH FLEET TO THE ATTACK BY FIRE-SHIPS ON THE NIGHT OF 28 JULY 1588

The Queen was so furious at the failure that she did not employ Drake again for another five years. Meanwhile, Sir John Hawkins advocated the strategic policy of blockading Spanish trade from the Azores, but the idea was much in advance of its time because Elizabethan ships could not keep at sea long enough. However, efforts continued to intercept the incoming Spanish treasure *flota*. The gallant failure of Sir Richard Grenville off the Azores in the *Revenge* in 1591 showed that an attack on a convoy, which the *flota* essentially was, was one of the most dangerous undertakings any naval commander could attempt. By contrast, an expedition to Cadiz in 1596, under the Earl of Essex and Lord Admiral Howard, was a rousing success. The city was caught by surprise and seized, being later ransomed for £180,000. The English destroyed 24 large ships and a great many smaller ones, captured 1,200 guns, and caused damage estimated at 20 million ducats.

Nevertheless, Spain had by then recovered from the defeats of 1588. Another Armada, unknown to the English, was launched in 1597. It was competently planned and carried out, and it might well have succeeded where its predecessor failed had its ships not been scattered by gales.

The Elizabethan era ended with the death of the Queen in 1603, and the war against Spain with the Treaty of London a year later. Unlike Spain, where there was a spirit of national disillusion, England was optimistic, even triumphalist. Success at sea had affected the way Englishmen thought of themselves and their country. The Navy had suddenly become fashionable. Stories of seafaring adventure and discovery, such as Hakluyt's *Principal Voyages and Navigations*, were bestsellers. Navigation had become a subject for the educated gentleman, and had itself been refined into a science. Where the illiterate shipmaster of the Middle Ages had been guided largely by guess and by God, the Elizabethan navigator needed to know how to read his instruments and his charts, his tide tables and tables of declination.

Above: *Sir Richard Hawkins, the son of Sir John Hawkins, commanded a ship in the Armada campaign. Later in his career he was captured by Spaniards off South America and held hostage until a ransom was paid in 1602.*

Left: *Queen Elizabeth I, a portrait by John Bettes. Her penchant for fine clothes and elaborate jewellery is evident in this likeness. Her reign was marked by naval triumph at home and remarkable voyages of exploration and discovery abroad.*

From Piracy
To
Permanency

Previous pages: The Battle of North Foreland, 1666, an oil painting by W.L. Wyllie.

Below: A detail from a painting by Hendrik Vroom showing the arrival of the English fleet at Flushing in 1613.

Below right: 'Great Ships' of the Jacobean Navy entering the Solent pictured in The Return of Prince Charles and the Duke of Buckingham by Hendrik Vroom, 1623.

King James I inherited 45 King's ships and could call upon some 200 merchantmen of over 100 tons. But he was not much interested in the Navy and under a regime of benevolent neglect by the Lord High Admiral, Charles Howard, Earl of Nottingham, the Navy was allowed to decay. No new ship was laid down until Phineas Pett's *Prince Royal*, 1,200 tons, and the first three-decked ship built for the Navy, in 1609. Under Sir Robert Mansell, appointed Treasurer in 1604, and Sir John Trevor, Surveyor since 1598, corruption in the Admiralty became rampant. 'The whole body is so corrupted,' wrote Sir John Coke, Commissioner of the Navy, 'as there is no sound part almost from the head to the foot'.

The Jacobean Navy was riddled with scandal, and disfigured by fraud, embezzlement and mal-administration on a scale so massive it led to two commissions of enquiry. The first of these, in 1608, reported damning evidence of scandalous misuse of public funds. Bribery and corruption were rife. Places were bought and sold. Charges for travel, pilotage and stores were grotesquely inflated. Worn-out ships were commissioned to use up stores and to provide places for the dependants of officials who were themselves corrupt, where they were not incompetent. But James disregarded the findings, and the recommendations for remedial action. A second inquiry, ten years

Above: George Villiers, Duke of Buckingham – a full-length portrait by the Dutch artist Daniel Mytens. A court favourite, Buckingham was appointed Lord High Admiral of the Navy in 1619.

later, again reported scandalous mismanagement. This time, James suspended the Navy Board and appointed a 12-man commission, including Sir John Coke, who began to put much needed reforms in place.

The reforms were assisted by the appointment in 1619 of a new, young and energetic Lord High Admiral, King James's favourite, George Villiers, Earl, Marquis and finally Duke of Buckingham. He proved to be a surprisingly good Lord High Admiral, who did improve the Navy's effectiveness, albeit from an unusually low level. New ships were built. Officers and men had a pay rise. By 1625, when Charles I acceded to the throne, and the country was once again at war with Spain, the fleet had 25 seaworthy capital ships. Sir John Coke said in 1626 that this strength was 'better than ever it was in my memory and exceeded the navies of former times'.

Yet, ironically, it was a time of consistent failure at sea. Pirates from Algiers and privateers from Dunkirk and the Channel ports had been infesting British coastal waters for years, in fact, it was one of the charges laid against Buckingham at his impeachment that he had failed to protect the country's shipping and harbours from these predators. A punitive expedition to Algiers, of 6,000 tons of shipping and 2,000 men, left England in October 1620 and returned the following summer, having achieved nothing.

However, this expedition, for which Buckingham as Lord High Admiral must bear chief responsibility (although Viscount Wimbledon, the soldier who led the venture was incompetent), was not quite the nadir of the 17th century Navy. The expedition to Cadiz in 1625, an attempt to repeat a former glory, is generally reckoned to be the lowest water mark of seamanship in the whole history of the Royal Navy.

Planning was non-existent. The organisation, if it can be so called, was chaotic. The men were mostly unpaid and barely trained. Many were sick when they sailed, or sickened soon after, and many died. The ships were ill-found and ill-equipped. Incapable officers were chosen and there were fresh suspicions of corruption. Many ships could not maintain proper station and kept on colliding with each other. Some captains did not even know where the expedition was supposed to be going, or where they should rendezvous if they became separated from the main body. Viscount Wimbledon was once again in command. The expedition achieved nothing. Another expedition in 1626 was turned back by bad weather in the Bay of Biscay.

No further expeditions were mounted against Spain, although the war went on until 1630. Instead, fresh hostilities began against France, but with a similar lack of success. Expeditions to the port of La Rochelle to relieve the beleaguered Huguenots failed.

After Buckingham's assassination on 23 August 1628, King Charles chose to replace the office of Lord High Admiral with an Admiralty Commission which lasted until May 1638. Although peace with France was concluded in 1629, there was still a need for ships to patrol the Channel where piracy was rife. In 1634, Charles introduced Ship Money, a special financial rate first raised in the maritime counties of England and Wales and extended in 1635 to include

inland shires. It was used to pay for the maintenance of the fleet at sea rather than new ships, but 12 ships and pinnaces were built between 1632 and 1637, including, in the latter year, the 1,500 ton *Sovereign of the Seas*, the largest English warship built until that time.

Although Charles I enlarged the Navy and, through Ship Money, devised a contentious means of financing it in peace time, the early

Above: *Peter Pett, the designer of the 100-gun* Sovereign of the Seas. *The portrait is attributed to Sir Peter Lely.*

Below: *The* Sovereign of the Seas, *a three-decked warship, was launched in 1637.*

Top: Antelope, 1648, drawn by Willem Van der Velde. She was a ship of the Royalist Squadron in exile.

Above: Van der Velde was renowned for his detailed and accurate portraits of ships. This drawing shows the 60-gun Constant Reformation of 1618.

Right: Admiral Robert Blake led the English fleet in its struggle with the Dutch for supremacy of the seas. This engraving is by the 19th-century artist J. Mollison.

▶ **1628** Assassination of Buckingham.

1634 Charles I introduces Ship Money.

1642 Outbreak of Civil War, Navy declares for Parliament.

1649 Execution of Charles I. Commonwealth institutes a major shipbuilding programme.

Stuarts had not the same regard for the Navy as the Tudors had had, nor did the Navy have the same regard for them. Almost the whole Navy, some 35 ships, was solidly for Parliament at the outbreak of the Civil War in 1642.

Ironically, it was King Charles's death which was of the greatest benefit to the Navy. After the execution of the king, the new Commonwealth was soon forced to spend vast sums on ship build-ing to defend itself against the threats, real or imagined, of invasion by enemies such as the Dutch, who were bitter commercial rivals, and the great Catholic powers of France and Spain, whose leaders were outraged by the manner of Charles's death and who were natu-rally sympathetic to the exiled house of Stuart.

The first Anglo-Dutch war, which began in 1652, had two main causes: commercial rivalry and, to a certain extent, wounded pride. Cromwell's Navigation Act, passed in October 1651, restricted Dutch trade because under its terms only English vessels or vessels of the country of origin could import goods into Britain or her colonies, and colonial exports could only be exported in English ships. In the East Indies, English trade was becoming a serious rival to the

Dutch, who had ousted the Portuguese. Further, England laid claim to the 'British seas', an undefined area around Britain in which foreign ships had to strike their flags to English warships. The Dutch naturally resented having to observe this humiliation in waters which were as much theirs as England's. In May 1652, a Captain Young, commanding an English frigate, fired on and then captured a Dutch warship for refusing to strike his ensign to the British flag. Four days later, a Dutch fleet under Admiral Maarten Tromp, at sea to protect Dutch merchant shipping against just such English demands, met Robert Blake's force off Dover. Blake had 15 sail against Tromp's 42 but attacked at once and eventually captured two Dutch ships. There were more engagements in the next three months, when English ships attacked Dutch convoys. England straddled the only sea routes which incoming and outgoing Dutch trade could take, and the Dutch ships thus had constantly to run the gauntlet of attack along the south coast of England.

WAR WITH THE NETHERLANDS

Robert Blake was a soldier, who had distingushed himself in the defence of Bristol in the Civil War and who had been appointed with Richard Deane as 'general at sea' in 1649. He had never commanded a ship, let alone a fleet, until he was 50 years old, but he was to prove one of the ablest sea captains in British history.

On 28 September, off the Kentish Knock, a sand bank in the southern North Sea, 68 English ships under Blake met and defeated a Dutch fleet of 59 ships under Witte De With, capturing four ships. However, in November, Blake foolhardily engaged Tromp's fleet of over 100 sail with his own fleet of barely 40 ships off Dungeness in Kent. Blake was forced to withdraw to the Thames, leaving Tromp to hoist a broom triumphantly to his masthead, to signify he had swept the Channel clear of English.

This drastic defeat led at once to drastic reforms. The sailors' pay was increased. The fleet was organised into three squadrons, the van, the middle and rear, each with three flag officers, (which were to become 'the white', 'the red' and 'the blue'). Articles of War were drafted and published, and were codified in statute law in 1661. They defined a wide range of offences, including murder, mutiny, theft, desertion, sodomy, striking an officer, and sleeping on

Above: *The Battle of Scheveningen, 1653, by Jan van Beerestraten.*

Left: *Van der Velde's annotated sketch of Scheveningen is an invaluable eye-witness record of war at sea from an age before photography.*

Above: *Instructions to the Commissioners of the Admiralty for the hastening of ships for Barbadoes (sic) signed by Oliver Cromwell, 22 January 1654.*

watch, the penalty being death in many cases.

In February 1653, these reforms contributed to the defeat inflicted on Tromp in a three-day running fight off Portland, when the Dutch lost 12 warships, 43 merchantmen, and 1,500 men, out of a fleet of 70 warships and 150 merchantmen. In June, the Dutch suffered another heavy defeat off the Gabbard shoal, losing 20 ships while Blake and his fellow 'generals at sea', Richard Deane and George Monck, lost none at all. The final decisive victory of the war was off Scheveningen in July 1653, when Tromp himself was killed.

Oliver Cromwell, who had become Lord Protector in December 1653, concluded the Treaty of Westminster in April 1654, bringing the first Dutch war to an end but, some thought, treating the Dutch too leniently.

Under the Commonwealth, the Navy could for the first time be termed a disciplined force, instead of an assembly of men and ships who were still basically privateers. Blake's orders for the running battle off Portland, for instance, laid down that there was to be no 'straggling for loot'. No merchantmen were to be sought until the enemy fleet had been defeated.

The English not only had better discipline than the Dutch, but better and bigger guns, mounted in bigger ships, and made the first use of a new tactic, the line of battle, in which ships ranged alongside their opponents' vessels and exchanged broadsides.

Having made peace with Holland in 1654, Cromwell then made war against Spain in the same year. The 'Western Design', an almost Elizabethan scheme whose first objective was to capture Hispaniola, was launched under William Penn, to establish a base for trade with the

Right: George Monck, a portrait by Sir Peter Lely. Monck was created Duke of Albemarle by Charles II in recognition of the important role that he played in the restoration of the monarchy.

▶ **1652** First Dutch War. Victories of Robert Blake, general-at-sea, at Dungeness (May) and Kentish Knock (28 September).

1653 Blake's victory at Portland (The Three Days' Battle) (February). George Monck and Richard Deane victorious at the Gabbard (North Foreland) (June) and Monck victorious at Scheveningen (First Texel) (July). Cromwell becomes Lord Protector.

Below: Portraits from 'Flagmen of Lowestoft' by Sir Peter Lely, a series depicting the commanders at the Battle of Lowestoft. These portray Sir Fresheville Holles and Sir Robert Holmes (below) and Sir John Lawson (below right). They offer a valuable insight into the diversity of naval officers' dress at this period. Note Lawson's fighting dress of breastplate and thick buff coat.

Right: George Monck, a portrait by Sir Peter Lely. Monck was created Duke of Albemarle by Charles II in recognition of the important role that he played in the restoration of the monarchy.

Americas and for further attacks on Spanish territory. It was a failure, except for the capture of Jamaica, a most valuable prize, although it was considered a very poor reward at the time.

Blake was sent to the Mediterranean in the winter of 1654, for operations against pirates along the African coast, but also to prepare for hostilities against Spain. He made a successful attack on the fortified pirate harbour of Tunis. He established a blockade of Cadiz and the Spanish coast, and lay in wait for the treasure fleet bringing silver from the Americas. A squadron of seven frigates under Richard Stayner captured two treasure ships in September 1656, but the greatest victory was achieved by Blake himself off Santa Cruz on Tenerife in April 1657.

In a brilliant four-hour action against ships and forts, Blake destroyed all the ships anchored in the harbour. He was as lucky as Drake had been.

Fortunate shifts of winds took him into harbour and out again. Little treasure was captured but, significantly, this was considered of minor importance. Clearly, under the Commonwealth, the freebooting and looting of the Tudor days were becoming things of the past.

This was Blake's last exploit. Sickening of scurvy and dropsy, and not fully recovered from his wounds, he died on board his flagship *St George* on 7 August 1657, the day she entered Plymouth Sound.

OLD RIVALRIES, NEW TENSIONS

From the restoration of the monarchy in 1660, another war against the Dutch was probable. The old commercial rivalry between the two East India Companies remained, with new tensions over trade along the Guinea coast of Africa. A new Navigation Act in 1660 further irritated the Dutch. Charles II and his court wanted to prove themselves as successful at sea as the Commonwealth had been. There was also a feeling amongst some of the leading figures, especially the King's brother, James, Duke of York, and Monck, now Duke of Albemarle, that the Dutch had been let off too lightly after the first war, and there was unfinished business to be attended to.

In August 1664, a squadron of the King's frigates, lent to the African Company, crossed the Atlantic and captured New Amsterdam, which was renamed New York, after the Duke of York, patron of the African Company. There were attacks on Dutch convoys in the winter of 1664/5, although war was not officially declared until March 1665.

The first battle, fought about 40 miles (65km) south-east of Lowestoft on 3 June 1665, between

Above: *The* Naseby *by Willem Van der Velde. Having returned Charles II from exile, she was renamed the Royal Charles.*

Left: *The Duke of York and Albany's Maritime Regiment of Foot, 1664, painted by Richard Simkin.*

Below: St Andrew *at sea by Willem Van der Velde the Younger.*

To all his Ma^{ts} Officers ... whom these may Concern.

'*P*ermitt the Bearers hereof Jasper Margrave, John Hoad, William Hutcherson (late prisoners released out of Zealand) to passe to his Ma^{ts} Shipp the Royall Charles, where they are to be entered. And the purser of his Ma^{ts} said shipp is to furnish them with Cloaths and necessaries fitting for them, Given at the cockpit the 23rd day of February 1655.'

A LAISSER-PASSER SIGNED BY THE DUKE OF ALBEMARLE

an English fleet of 109 ships and 103 Dutch ships, was one of the great classic battles of sail. Hearing that the Dutch fleet, commanded by Admiral Jacob van Wassenaer-Opdam, had captured a English convoy of 20 ships off the Dogger Bank, James Duke of York, Lord High Admiral and admiral of the red, sailed from the Gunfleet in his flagship the *Royal Charles*, 80 guns, (formerly the *Naseby*), with Edward Montagu, Earl of Sandwich, and Prince Rupert in command of two of his squadrons.

Battle was joined at 4 a.m., when the two fleets passed each other on opposite tacks in line ahead, each ship firing as an enemy came within range. But this formal tactic soon became a general mêlée in the centre of which the two flagships *Royal Charles* and *Eendracht* (76 guns) engaged each other. After the Dutch had failed to board the *Royal Charles*, a chain shot killed many officers and men beside James, who was spattered with their blood. One account (possibly by William Penn) said: 'At 12 came A shot from Opdam yt killed ye Earl of Falmouth [Charles Berkeley] Lord Musgrave [Muskerry] and Mr Boyle [younger son of the Earl of Burlington]'.

Eendracht was hit in her powder room and blew up with tremendous loss of life, and the Dutch began to give way. Vice Admiral Jan Evertsen took over command after Opdam's death and conducted a retreat towards the Texel estuary, being much aided in this regard by the failure of the English to follow up their victory. The Dutch lost 32 ships, with casualties of about 4,000 killed and 2,000 taken prisoner. The English lost only the *Charity*, taken early in the battle, 283 men killed and 440 wounded.

In August, an attempt by the Earl of Sandwich, who had taken over command from James, to intercept the Dutch East Indies Fleet as it sheltered in the neutral harbour of Bergen in Norway failed completely, and only brought

Above: *A portrait of the Dutch Admiral Michiel De Ruyter by Ferdinand Bol, who was a pupil of Rembrandt.*

1654 Treaty of Westminster ends First Dutch War. Cromwell begins war with Spain.

1657 Blake defeats Spanish fleet at Santa Cruz (April).

Below: *Ludolf Bakhuyzen's painting showing the loss of the Royal Charles in 1667, when she was towed away as a result of De Ruyter's daring foray into the Medway.*

Denmark into the war on the Dutch side in 1666.

The next fleet engagement began in the southern North Sea on 1 June 1666 between 56 English ships under Albemarle and 85 Dutch ships commanded by Admiral De Ruyter. Despite his numerical disadvantage, Albemarle chose to attack and a particularly bloody four-day battle took place, in which Admiral Sir George Ayscue's flagship, the *Royal Prince* (90), ran aground on the Galloper Sand, was captured and burned, and both Prince Rupert's flagship *Royal James* (82) and Albemarle's *Royal Charles* were badly damaged. Prince Rupert, commanding the White squadron, who had been detached down Channel to intercept a supposed French squadron which never appeared, rejoined on the third day. By the end of the fourth and final day both sides were exhausted. In all, the English lost 17 ships and 8,000 men, the Dutch six ships and about 2,000 men.

By contrast, the next battle, fought about 40 miles (65km) south-east of Orfordness in Suffolk on St James's Day, 25 July, was a brilliant success for the English fleet, of 89 ships and 17 fireships, jointly commanded by Prince Rupert and the Duke of Albemarle, against a Dutch fleet of 85 ships, 20 fireships and ten smaller vessels under Admiral De Ruyter.

The decisive phase began when Admiral Cornelis Tromp's rear squadron broke through the English line and attacked the English rear Blue squadron, under Admiral Sir Jeremy Smythe in the *Resolution* (74). But Smythe's ships resisted strongly and gained the upper hand. This engagement with Smythe in the rear turned into a westward pursuit of De Ruyter, while the main battle between van and centre headed eastward.

The Dutch van and centre both gave way, three flag officers including Jan Evertsen being killed, and the Dutch were then in full retreat. Although the withdrawal was handled most skilfully by De Ruyter, the Dutch lost 20 ships and 4,000 men killed or drowned. *Resolution* was the only English loss.

A fortnight later, on 9 August, Sir Robert Holmes with a few 'lesser' frigates, fireships and a number of ketches attacked a huge assembly of Dutch ships laden with imports from the east in the river Vlie and at Terschelling. Boats manned by raiding parties set two Dutch warships and the astonishing number of 165 merchantmen on fire, in what was called Holmes's Bonfire.

Peace negotiations began in March 1667. Because the government felt that peace was assured, and was very short of money, the main fleet was laid up in ordinary, i.e. in reserve with all their stores taken ashore, in the Medway. But in June, De Ruyter sailed up the Thames and into the Medway, broke a chain boom at Gillingham, landed armed parties at Upnor, captured or burned 16 ships and, most humiliatingly of all, towed away the *Royal Charles* with her royal standard still flying at the main.

The Treaty of Breda in July 1667 ended the second Dutch war, with the Dutch in command of the Narrow Seas. De Ruyter blockaded the Thames and London for a month. Samuel Pepys recorded in his diary that he sent his wife and father out of London with as much gold as they could carry to bury in his father's garden in Huntingdonshire.

THE THIRD DUTCH WAR

It was Charles II himself who caused the third and last Dutch war. Despite a triple alliance concluded in 1668 between England, Holland and Sweden, made to counterbalance the success of the French King Louis XIV's campaign in the Spanish Netherlands, Charles began to negotiate with Louis for an Anglo-French alliance against the Dutch. In the Treaty of Dover in 1670, Charles undertook to declare war against the Dutch and, furthermore, to declare himself a Catholic in return for money to fit out the fleet.

In May 1672, a vast Anglo-French invasion fleet, consisting of over 70 ships of the line and over 80 fireships, transports and smaller vessels, assembled in Solebay on the Suffolk coast of East Anglia. James, Duke of York, flying his flag in the *Royal Prince* (120), was in command, with the Earl of Sandwich, in his flagship the *Royal James* (100), commanding the rear, and the French Admiral D'Estrées, in the *St Philippe* (78), commanding the van.

However, De Ruyter, flying his flag in the *Zeven Provincien* (82), discovered the invasion fleet and

launched a pre-emptive strike on 28 May, running before a stiff north-east wind to bear down on the anchorage with his fleet and fireships. Due to a failure in communication, the French turned away to the south-east and took no part in the main action, where the Dutch admiral Van Ghent and Sandwich fought a fierce duel in which Van Ghent was killed, the *Royal James* was burned to the waterline and Sandwich was drowned when a boat crowded with survivors capsized.

James himself came under fire and was forced to shift his flag twice during the day. That evening the English disengaged and allowed the Dutch to

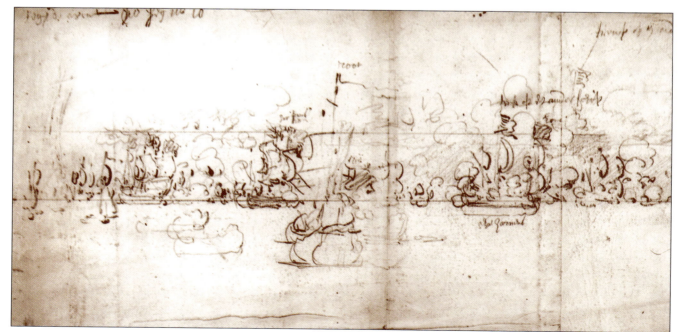

Top and above: *The burning of the* Royal James *during the Battle of Solebay painted by Willem Van der Velde the Younger. Note how the finished oil differs from the preliminary sketch as the artist seeks to heighten the drama of the scene.*

Left: *This eyewitness sketch of the 1st Battle of Schooneveld, 1673, also by the younger Van der Velde, includes annotations of ships' names and other details appended in the artist's own hand.*

Above: *Tromp's flagship occupies the foreground in the younger Van der Velde's painting of the Battle of Texel, 1673. Tromp is believed to have commissioned the painting.*

▶ **1660** Restoration of the monarchy. James, Duke of York, is Lord High Admiral.

1664 Squadron of King's frigates captures New Amsterdam. Second Dutch War declared.

1665 James' victory at Lowestoft (3 June). Earl of Sandwich's raid on Bergen.

Below: *HMS* Royal Prince *in 1679 painted by Jan Karel van Beecq. Pepys recorded in his diary entry for 10 April 1661 how he visited her in dock: 'endeed, it hath one and no more rich cabbins for carved work, but no gold in her'.*

withdraw. The English fleet suffered severe losses and 2,500 men died. The Dutch lost two ships but De Ruyter's masterly handling of his fleet that day disabled the English fleet for a month, gave the Dutch command of the Channel once more and, most importantly, thwarted the Anglo-French invasion of the Netherlands.

Prince Rupert took over command of the combined fleet in 1673 after James, a Catholic, had resigned the office of Lord High Admiral as a result of the Test Act. Rupert made two attempts to destroy the Dutch fleet off the Schooneveld in May and June 1673, but De Ruyter's brilliant handling of his ships foiled both attempts and, furthermore, opened up Dutch ports once again to incoming convoys.

The final battle of the war took place off the Texel on 11 August 1673. The Dutch managed to separate the French van from the main body so that it took no part in the battle in the rear between Sir Edward Spragge and Cornelis Tromp, in which Spragge was killed. The battle was broken off with honours even, but De Ruyter had once more foiled the invasion and Charles II was forced to end a war which had always been unpopular in the country and in Parliament with the Treaty of Westminster in February 1674.

The pressures and, ironically, the failures, of the Dutch Wars, and the results of the Restoration, which the Navy had made possible, transformed the Navy from a loose and unsettled collection of warships and a ragged regiment of officers and men unsure of their duty and their purpose, other than personal profit through privateering, into the reliable naval shield of a first-class naval power.

The royal patronage of Charles II, and the active service of James, Duke of York, raised the Navy's status in the country. The four principal Navy offices, of Treasurer, Controller, Surveyor and Clerk, which had all been revived, with three naval commissioners, and James, Duke of York, as Lord High Admiral, constituted a body which could for the first time be properly called the Admiralty.

A framework was created for the entry, training, promotion and retirement of a class of regular officer. The Navy rid itself of most of the rough-and-tumble shellback captains of old and replaced them with men of birth and education, making the naval officer a distinctly polite person. Captains could nominate boys to enter the Navy under the 'King's Letter Boys' scheme. A professional examination for the rank of Lieutenant was introduced.

SAMUEL PEPYS

Samuel Pepys was born in London in 1633 and educated at St Paul's School, and Trinity Hall and Magdalene, Cambridge. A Latin classicist and a mathematician, he was also a talented musician (he played the flute, the viol and the flageolet) and learned shorthand.

He was the protégé and employee of his first cousin once removed, Edward Montagu, one of the Commonwealth's generals-at-sea, who obtained for him a post as a clerk in the Exchequer. After Cromwell's death, Montagu turned towards the Royalist cause and at the Restoration he was again a general-at-sea, taking Pepys to sea with him as his secretary. When Charles II returned with the fleet from

There was less change on the lower deck. The Navy was still manned by a nucleus of men who simply preferred naval service, but with further recruitment from the 'maritime community', such as merchantmen, fishermen, and river bargees. The press gang was necessary in time of war. However, a distinction was introduced between 'able' and 'ordinary' seamen. Wages were raised. Gratuities were paid to seamen or their families in the event of death or mutilation. The Articles of War were formally codified in law.

The main driving forces behind these reforms were two civil servants, Sir William Coventry and Samuel Pepys. Sir William Coventry was appointed the Lord High Admiral's secretary in 1660 and became an 'extra Commissioner' on the Navy Board in 1662. An able and industrious man, he might well have become famous as 'the Saviour of the Navy' had he not been completely overshadowed by Pepys.

The Navy had made possible the restoration of Charles II. It also brought about the dethronement of his brother James II – by doing nothing. James had converted to Catholicism in 1669, and soon after he succeeded to the throne in February 1680 he began to promote Catholicism with all the extra zeal of the convert. Such was his zeal that he eventually alarmed even the Catholics, who feared a Protestant backlash.

Alarm and unrest in the country at James's behaviour came to a head with the birth on 10 June 1688 of a son to James by his second wife Mary of Modena. As long as James had no son, Protestant England could look forward to the eventual accession of the Princess Mary, James's eldest daughter by his first wife Anne Hyde. But this baby Prince James (later, the Old Pretender) would be brought up as a Catholic, and England could be a Catholic kingdom once more.

On 30 June seven dignitaries sent an invitation to William, Prince of Orange, Mary's husband and thus James's son-in-law, to come to England at once with an armed force. Their messenger was Admiral Arthur Herbert, later Earl of Torrington, who crossed over to Holland disguised as an ordinary seaman.

William, who had spent much of his political life trying to counter-balance the overweening

▶ **1666** Four Days' Battle (1-4 June). Prince Rupert and the Duke of Albemarle's victory off Orfordness – St James's Day or North Foreland Battle (25 July).

1667 Dutch sail up the Medway and tow away the *Royal Charles*. Treaty of Breda.

1672 Third Dutch War. James, Duke of York's reverse at Solebay (28 May).

Holland, Montagu was created Earl of Sandwich. One of his first steps was to obtain for Pepys the post of Clerk of the Acts to the Navy Board.

Despite his fondness for heavy drinking, the theatre and fast women, Pepys worked very hard and very long hours, and soon became the most influential member of the Board. He was a master of paperwork, of which his famous diary, begun on 1 January 1660, was only a part. During the Second Dutch War, only Pepys's energy and his campaign to drive out corruption prevented a complete breakdown of supplies to the fleet.

In 1673 Pepys became the first Secretary to the Admiralty, one of the most important civil servants in the country. After the Third Dutch War, it was Pepys who launched a vigorous programme of recovery and reform. By 1678 he had made the Navy a powerful, well-disciplined force, and the office of Lord High Admiral an efficient government department.

He was MP for Castle Rising, 1673–78, and for Harwich in 1679, and became the accepted spokesman in Parliament for the Navy he had created and its administration. However, his fortunes followed those of James, Duke of York. James was accused of betraying the country to France and Pepys himself of selling naval secrets to France.

After six weeks in the Tower of London, Pepys was out of office for five years, and the Navy suffered grievously from inept administration in his absence.

In 1684, the year Pepys became President of the Royal Society, Charles II made him Secretary for Admiralty Affairs, a post he kept when James became King in 1685. In 1686 he set up a special commission to assist the Navy Board, which once again restored competent administration to the Navy. But after James's dethronement, Pepys was again falsely accused of treason, forced to resign, and retired into private life.

When Pepys died in May 1703, after a long illness, his friend John Evelyn said of him 'a very worthy, industrious & curious person, none in England exceeding him in the knowledge of the Navy'.

Below: *A sample of Pepys's handwriting from the catalogue collection of his papers in the National Maritime Museum, London.*

Left: *Pepys's diary offers a wonderful insight into his public and private life, such as when he climbed into the stern lantern of the* Royal Sovereign *(inset) in company with 'my Lady Sandwich' and party!*

Left: *A Barbary ship. Piracy was a major threat – Pepys sat on the Tangier Committee which concerned itself with safeguarding maritime trade routes.*

Above: A splendid pair of drawings that lay bare the anatomy of late 17-century naval warships. The upper plan details the external structure of a 'ship of war of the third rate', while the lower drawing shows the internal layout of a first rate warship. The component parts are numbered and identified in the accompanying keys. The engraving is after a Phillips print of 1690.

power of the Catholic French King Louis XIV, and thus prevent most of Europe falling under the domination of a despotic Catholic monarchy, accepted the invitation at once and, while keeping a wary eye on Louis XIV, set about assembling an expeditionary force.

Meanwhile, James was behaving with his usual insensitivity, especially towards his own service, the Navy, which was strongly opposed to Roman Catholicism. At a time when he must have known that anti-Catholic feeling was running high, ashore and afloat, James appointed a Catholic, Sir Roger Strickland of Sizergh, Rear Admiral of England, in command of the fleet.

James's fleet assembled as early as June 1688, but instead of going across at once to observe the Dutch ports, it stayed in the Straits of Dover. By September, James had realised that Strickland was not the man to command, and replaced him

with the Earl of Dartmouth who, as the danger of invasion increased, moved the fleet to the Gun-fleet, off the Essex coast.

The fleet looked imposing: 40 men-of-war, 18 fireships and three yachts. But it is very doubtful if more than a third would have given battle. Only half the officers could be relied on, and there were 'cabals' (secret meetings) in every ship.

Louis XIV, who stood to gain from a Catholic England, sent an envoy to London to offer assistance. The French had a very good navy, largely due to the efforts of Louis' able minister Colbert. But James refused, saying he would not be patronised. Also, even James must have realised that sailors who would fight to the death to defend England would not lift a finger in support of France and popery. Rebuffed, Louis turned his attention to Germany, and his army attacked the Rhineland in September 1688.

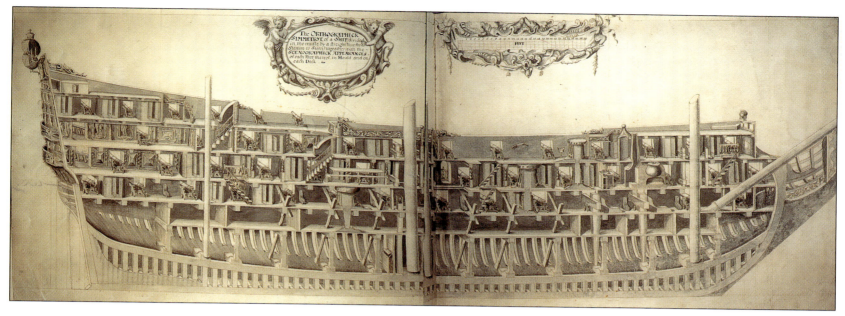

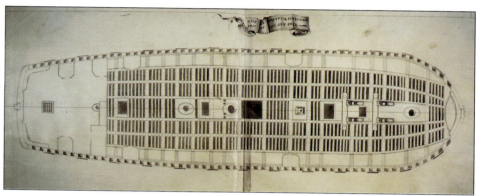

Until then, William had had to keep his army in Holland, to guard against a French invasion. Now, he could look across the North Sea to England. He collected his fleet at the mouth of the Maas, of 50 ships of the line, 25 frigates, 25 fireships, and about 400 transports carrying 4,000 horses, 11,000 foot soldiers, and huge amounts of stores and ammunition.

After one false start in October which was turned back by bad weather, William sailed again on 1 November 1688, with Admiral Herbert in supreme command flying his flag in the *Leijden* (62), and William himself on board the *Briel* (30).

William was embarking upon an appallingly dangerous and difficult course of action – an amphibious operation, a landing upon a potentially hostile shore, always a perilous undertaking, without command of the sea. Furthermore, it was November. The usual season for naval operations in the Channel was May to August. The days were short, and getting shorter. Bad weather was almost inevitable. One gale could wreck his whole enterprise, as it had wrecked the Spanish Armada, exactly a century before.

But William of Orange, always the realist, counted upon a quick passage. Dutch fishing boats had reported on the English fleet's disposition and morale for months. William reckoned that the English navy was not likely to interfere with his enterprise. The rest he left in the hands of the Lord.

William's fleet set out in a 'Protestant' north-easterly, heading for the Humber, probably the first objective. But the wind strengthened and veered to the east. The fleet turned south and ran close to the English at the Gunfleet.

Dartmouth had weighed anchor on 30 October, expecting the Dutch to use the easterly wind. But when the Dutch appeared, the wind direction and the state of the tide prevented Dartmouth from following until 3 November.

Wind and weather continued to favour William. The east wind providentially changed to south-west, allowing William to land at Brixham on 5

November. The same wind increased to storm force and drove Dartmouth back to shelter in the Downs on 7 November. James ordered a fresh sortie a week later, but Dartmouth's ships were once again scattered by a storm. He made a token appearance off Torbay on 19 November, but he was by then outnumbered, and he knew that any action he took now would be only a gesture. Dartmouth and his fleet made a full submission to William on 12 December.

James fled to exile in France. William and Mary were proclaimed King and Queen on 13 February 1689. England was to be Protestant, with government by a Parliamentary democracy, instead of a Catholic monarchy. It was called a 'Glorious Revolution', which had been allowed to happen by the Navy's inaction.

WAR WITH FRANCE

The accession of William and Mary led to the War of the English Succession, or the Nine Years' War, the first of several wars against France, spread over more than a century. Louis XIV declared war against the Dutch ten days after William landed at Brixham. The Dutch replied with their own declaration of war in March 1689, but England delayed until after an inconclusive engagement in May between Admiral Herbert and the Comte de

Top: *This longitudinal section through a ship, published in 1680 in Dummer's Draught, was created to show 'the Scenographick Appearances of each part thereof'.*

Above: *One of a set of plans showing the cabins of a First Rate from an anonymous manuscript of 1680. This is a plan of one of the gun decks.*

▶ **1673** Inconclusive actions between Anglo-French fleet under Prince Rupert and Dutch fleet under de Ruyter at Schooneveld (May and June), and De Ruyter's brilliance at the Texel (11 August). As a result of the Test Act, Duke of York resigns as Lord High Admiral. Pepys becomes Secretary to the Admiralty.

1674 Treaty of Westminster ends Third Dutch War.

1679 Pepys resigns. New Admiralty Commission formed.

1684 Admiralty Commission dismissed. Pepys returns as Secretary of the Admiralty.

1688 'Glorious Revolution'. James II flees to exile in France.

1689 William crowned King William III. Declaration of war with France (War of the English Succession).

Below: *The Battle of Barfleur by Ludolf Bakhuyzen. On 19 May 1692 an Anglo-Dutch fleet under Admiral Sir Edward Russell defeated the French fleet of Comte de Tourville in a fierce engagement off Cap Barfleur on France's Cotentin peninsula.*

Châteaurenault in Bantry Bay, where the French were landing troops and stores in support of James II. The French outnumbered Herbert and had the weather gauge, and Herbert was fortunate to escape without serious damage. Both sides claimed victory. William declared war on France five days later, and also created Herbert Earl of Torrington.

Another result of William's accession was a much closer co-operation between the English and Dutch navies, which was to be the basis of Anglo-Dutch naval operations for the next 25 years. The first real test of this co-operation came in 1690, when on 21 June a powerful French force of 68 ships of the line, formed by combining the Brest and Toulon fleets and commanded by the Comte de Tourville, was sighted off the Lizard. By the 25th de Tourville, whose object was to blockade the Thames, was off the Isle of Wight. Torrington, flying his flag in *Royal Sovereign* (100), was also at sea in the Channel, with 34 ships of the line, and 22 Dutch ships of the line under Admiral Cornelis Evertsen, 'the Younger'.

Torrington was only a few miles to the east of the French but declined action and stood up Channel, keeping his fleet 'in being'. Four days later, he was ordered to engage the enemy. In the action which took place off Beachy Head on 30 June, the Anglo-Dutch attack was badly organised, with the Dutch van and the English rear engaging more or less independently and half-heartedly, and both being badly mauled. Torrington himself, in the centre, stood off at long range to windward.

In the evening, the French were beginning to overpower the Dutch, when luckily the wind dropped. Torrington placed his ships between the Dutch and the French, where they anchored with all sail set, while the strong ebb tide carried the French ships out of range. In the end, the Anglo-Dutch fleet lost five badly damaged ships which were scuttled. De Tourville lost none.

The French now had command of the Channel, and the way was open to London, where there was panic. Astonishingly, de Tourville now hesitated in his moment of victory, and abandoned the pursuit of his enemy, pleading sickness and lack of stores. He sailed back down the Channel, burning Teignmouth as he went.

When Torrington anchored off the Nore, he was relieved of his command and later court-martialled, when he argued that he had kept his 'fleet in being', thus ensuring that no invasion could be safely attempted. He was acquitted, but never served at sea again.

In 1691, Torrington was succeeded, after some political intriguing, by Admiral Edward Russell (later the Earl of Orford), one of the first 'gentle-

Left: *A portrait of Sir Cloudesley Shovell by Michael Dahl. Shovell fought and was wounded at Barfleur. He later served under Sir George Rooke in the Mediterranean and was made Commander-in-Chief of the fleet in 1705.*

Right: *The parts of a ship for a lay person, an illustration from a French tactical manual, L'Art des Armées navales (1697) by Paul Hoste. It was engraved by Bernard after Goussier.*

men' officers of the Navy, bred to the sea as a permanent career. He had been appointed Treasurer of the Navy in 1689 and had served in 1690 as an Admiral of the Blue under Torrington.

During the winter of 1691/2, the French began to assemble ships, troops and stores in northern French ports for an invasion of England to restore James II to the throne. De Tourville expected reinforcements from the Toulon fleet but when

these failed to arrive he put to sea from Brest, flying his flag in the *Soleil Royal* (104), with 44 ships of the line and entered the Channel on 17 May 1692.

Russell had had intelligence of the invasion plans and had assembled at Portsmouth a huge Anglo-Dutch fleet, of 36 Dutch ships of the line in the White Squadron, and 63 English ships in the Red and Blue Squadrons. Russell himself flew his flag in the *Britannia* (100).

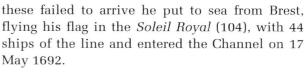

THE BATTLE OF BARFLEUR

The two fleets met off Cap Barfleur on the Cotentin peninsula on 19 May 1692 and both battle lines engaged each other in fierce fighting. There was dense fog in the battle area in the afternoon, when de Tourville disengaged and withdrew to the west. Both fleets anchored for the night, neither having lost a ship. De Tourville continued sailing westward towards the Channel Islands for two days, pursued by Russell. The *Soleil Royal* was chased by Vice Admiral Sir Ralph Delavall with the Red Squadron and ran aground near Cherbourg on 22 May. *Soleil Royal*, *Triomphant* (76) and *Admirable* (90) were all destroyed by fire, de Tourville having shifted his flag to the *Ambitieux* (96).

On 23 May, Sir Cloudesley Shovell, Rear Admiral commanding the Red Squadron (who had first gone to sea as a 13-year old cabin boy in 1664), was ordered to enter the bay of La Hogue and destroy the remaining 12 French ships of the line that were anchored there among the invasion transports. Shovell had suffered a severe thigh wound and his place was taken by Vice Admiral Sir George Rooke, commanding the Blue Squadron.

On that day and the next, Allied fireships, boats and even ships of the line penetrated the bay and,

Above: *The two plates reproduced here are also from the superbly produced L'Art des Armées navales by Paul Hoste. They explain fleet evolutions and rules of engagement in some detail, and are indicative of the growing analysis of the theory of war at sea that was a feature of the 17th century.*

1690 Defeat of Herbert by the French admiral Comte de Tourville, Beachy Head (30 June).

1691 Admiral Russell's *Sailing and Fighting Instructions* issued.

1692 Russell's defeat of de Tourville at Barfleur (19 May) and La Hogue (23-24 May).

1693 Smyrna convoy overwhelmed by the French off Cadiz.

Right: *A colour lithograph of Greenwich Hospital by T. Boys. The hospital for disabled seamen was established by Queen Mary in 1694, and the buildings were designed by Christopher Wren, John Vanburgh and Nicholas Hawksmoor.*

in a battle fought close inshore and watched by crowds who, it was said, included James II, destroyed every one of the 12 ships of the line, and many of the transports. In places the water was so shallow that the French sent cavalry into the attack, and there was the unusual sight, for a sea battle, of French troopers being pulled off their horses and drowned by sailors with boathooks.

The victory at Barfleur and La Hogue was complete and decisive. It removed the threat of a French invasion, and restored both English pride after Beachy Head and English command of the Channel.

After Barfleur, the French did not seek another fleet action. In fact, they changed their main naval strategy from the *guerre d'escadre*, of fleet actions, to the *guerre de course*, attacking trade. In June 1693, a huge convoy of 400 English, German, Dutch, Danish and Swedish merchantmen sailed down the Channel, bound for Smyrna on the coast of Turkey. The main English and Dutch fleets escorted the convoy as far as Ushant and then turned back, believing the convoy was now safe from attack.

From Ushant, the convoy was taken on by Sir George Rooke and Rear Admiral van der Goes. At about noon on 17 June, south of Cape St Vincent, Rooke was suddenly confronted by a French fleet of some 80 ships. Unknown to Rooke, the French had learned of the Smyrna convoy, and de Tourville from Brest and Admiral D'Estrées from Toulon had rendezvoused at Lagos Bay, east of Cape St Vincent, to lie in wait for it. Rooke did his best, but he was taken by surprise and outnumbered. The French sank or captured 92 vessels, with an estimated worth of between one and six million pounds. Rooke collected 54 of the survivors into another convoy, and other ships scattered to Gibraltar, Cadiz, Malaga or Madeira. But, otherwise, the Smyrna convoy was an unmitigated disaster.

In 1694, William and Mary granted a charter to found Greenwich Royal Hospital, for seamen who had been injured or grown old in the service of the Crown, and work began on buildings designed by Wren, Vanbrugh and Hawksmoor on a site alongside Charles II's new palace at Greenwich. In

DOCKYARDS

The 17th and 18th centuries saw a huge expansion in the size and capabilities of the naval dockyards. Portsmouth had the first enclosed dock, begun by King John in 1212, the first dry graving dock, under Henry VII in 1495, and it was greatly enlarged by Henry VIII in 1527. Under the Commonwealth, Portsmouth had a new dry dock completed in 1658 and two ropewalks, built alongside each other, three storeys high and over 1,000 feet (305m) long.

By the reign of George III, Portsmouth Dockyard had grown into a considerable business enterprise. A guide book of 1775 said 'it resembles a town in the number of its dwelling houses, offices, storehouses, lofts and other edifices for carrying out the various purposes of the Yard'.

Chatham was begun in 1547 and was the premier yard a century later. Visiting in 1724 Daniel Defoe described Chatham as 'the chief

Above: *The west prospect of Portsmouth, an engraving by S. and N. Buck dating from 1749, showing the dockyards and boathouses. Below is a 1755 plan of Chatham Dockyard by T. Milton.*

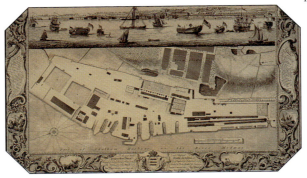

arsenal of the Royal Navy of Great Britain. The buildings here are indeed like the ships themselves, surprisingly large, and in their several kinds beautiful'.

A new dockyard, established in Plymouth in the 1690s, expanded rapidly in the early 18th century, with a site for a Gun Wharf purchased in 1718, and further enlargement including a rope-yard in the 1740s. During the war of 1739–48 Plymouth had two dry docks and three building slips. Further enlargement was planned in 1761 and another dock was completed in 1763. A powder magazine was built at Keyham Point in 1784, and another dry dock, the Union, was completed in 1789.

Deptford was a naval dockyard in the reign of Henry VII and its first naval dock was constructed in 1542, when the yard was considerably improved and enlarged in the last years of Henry VIII's reign. By the later Stuart period of the 1660s and 1680s, Deptford was a large and most important naval dockyard, which was always closely linked with the names of the Pett family, master shipwrights, who designed many well known warships of the period.

There were also dockyards at Woolwich and Sheerness. A dockyard was begun in Jamaica in 1733. The first Commissioner of the Dockyard at Gibraltar was appointed in 1756, and served until the end of the Seven Years War in 1763. Bermuda was first surveyed by Captain Hurd in 1794, and land was bought and wharves and storehouses built in the next ten years.

Left: *Admiral George Rooke by Michael Dahl. Rooke became Commander-in-Chief of the fleet in 1697.*

Far left: *Sir Godfrey Kneller's 1701 portrait of Admiral John Benbow. He died of wounds at Port Royal in 1702 after losing a leg to chain-shot while bringing Ducasse to action.*

1694 Royal Hospital at Greenwich founded on land donated by Queen Mary.

1695 Dockyard established in Plymouth.

1697 Capture by Rooke of neutral Swedish merchant-men on their way to France in the Channel. Peace of Rijswick.

1702 War of the Spanish Succession. Rooke's attack on Spanish treasure fleet in Vigo Bay (12 October).

1704 Capture of Gibraltar (July). Drawn battle between Anglo-Dutch fleet under Rooke and Franco-Spanish fleet under the Comte de Toulouse, Malaga (13 August).

Below: *A view of Gibraltar, an aquatint by T. Sutherland after Whitecombe, published in 1816. Gibraltar was captured by an English and Dutch force under Sir George Rooke in July 1704, and was ceded to England by the Treaty of Utrecht in 1713.*

practice, naval seamen contributed sixpence a month from their pay towards the upkeep of the hospital. Merchant seamen also had to contribute sixpence of their pay, because at that time there was still no real distinction between the two navies. A registry of all seamen would have helped to resolve the situation, but an attempt to create one in 1696 failed.

An uneasy peace was signed at Rijswick in September 1697, but the political tensions which had caused the war remained and were compounded by the death of the childless King Carlos II of Spain in 1700, when the Spanish empire passed to Phillippe of Anjou, younger son of the heir to the French throne. After French aggressive incursions into Italy and the Spanish Netherlands, the English, the Dutch and the Austrians formed a Grand Alliance to oppose France in 1701.

William III died in March 1702, after a fall from his horse which stumbled while the King was out riding. He was succeeded by Anne, second daughter of James II (when Duke of York) and Anne Hyde, who had been brought up as a Protestant. Queen Anne declared war against France in May 1702.

AN ALLIANCE AGAINST FRANCE

The new war, the War of the Spanish Succession, began for the Navy with an incident which became famous. John Benbow ran away to sea as a young man and served in the Navy as a master's mate until he was courtmartialled for making disparaging remarks about his captain. He then left the Navy and went to sea as a private trader.

He rejoined the Navy in 1689, becoming captain of the *Britannia* through the good offices of Lord Herbert, then First Lord of the Admiralty. He served at Beachy Head and La Hogue, and was promoted to Vice Admiral and made Commander-in-Chief in the West Indies in 1702.

On 19 August 1702, Benbow was in command of a squadron of seven ships of the line, flying his flag in the *Breda* (70), when he encountered four French ships of the line and a frigate, commanded by Captain Jean Ducasse in the *Heureux*, off Santa Marta, on the north coast of Colombia. A five-day battle began, during which the *Breda* was supported only by the two 48s *Ruby* and *Falmouth*, while the rest of Benbow's captains deliberately ignored his signals and took no part. Benbow was eventually forced to break off the action on 24 August after he was badly wounded by a chain shot which smashed his right leg. The squadron returned to Jamaica, where Benbow died of his wounds a few days later.

The captains of the four ships were court-martialled. Kirby and Wade, of the *Defiance* and *Greenwich*, were condemned to death by shooting, and the other two dismissed the Service.

The outstanding admiral of the war, indeed of

his generation, was Sir George Rooke. He was the second son of an influential and wealthy Canterbury family and entered the Navy as a volunteer. He served in the Second Dutch War, was captain of the *Deptford* at Bantry Bay in 1689, and became commander-in-chief of the fleet in 1697. After a miserable failure to seize Cadiz in September 1702, Rooke attacked the Spanish treasure fleet with its escort of 13 French ships of the line in Vigo Bay on 12 October.

The treasure ships and their escort lay behind a harbour boom, guarded by protective batteries. Rooke's force of 25 Anglo-Dutch ships, led by Vice Admiral Hopsonn in *Torbay* (80) and Admiral Van der Goes in *Zeven Provincien* (90), landed troops to seize the batteries, while *Torbay* broke through the boom. After fierce fighting, ten French ships of the line were destroyed and 11 treasure ships captured.

After another ignominious failure, to take Barcelona in 1704, Rooke made a sudden decision to capture Gibraltar, which he believed was weakly defended. Flying his flag in the *Royal Katherine*, and accompanied by Prince George of Hesse-Darmstadt, Rooke landed 1,900 English and 400 Dutch marines on 21 July 1704, who cut off the Rock from the mainland and, despite suffering many casualties from the resolute defenders, called upon the Spanish Governor, Don Diego de Salinas, to surrender the fortress. After a bombardment on 23 July, storming parties of marines established footholds in the defences. The Governor surrendered on 26 July and Gibraltar was taken in the name of Archduke Charles of Austria. However, Rooke soon lowered the Austrian standard and took possession of the Rock in the name of Queen Anne.

Rooke, with 53 Anglo-Dutch ships of the line, beat off a Franco-Spanish fleet of 50 of the line under the Comte de Toulouse off Malaga on 13 August, giving the Allies command of the western Mediterranean for the rest of the war. But when Rooke withdrew his ships to refit, the marines on the Rock had to withstand a siege which lasted

Above: Admiral Sir George Byng. Byng served with Rooke at the capture of Gibraltar in 1704, and later defeated a Spanish fleet under Don Antonio de Gastaneta off Sicily on 31 July 1718. He was created Viscount Torrington in 1721.

Below: Eating utensils and tableware recovered from the wreck of HMS Invincible, a 74-gun warship that was captured from the French in 1747 and lost in 1758. Seen here are a spoon, plate, bowl, stoneware jug and glass bottle.

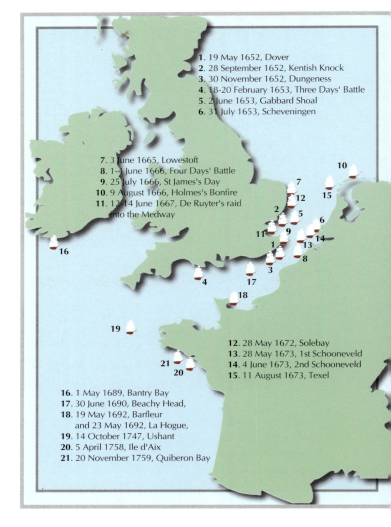

1. 19 May 1652, Dover
2. 28 September 1652, Kentish Knock
3. 30 November 1652, Dungeness
4. 18-20 February 1653, Three Days' Battle
5. 2 June 1653, Gabbard Shoal
6. 31 July 1653, Scheveningen
7. 3 June 1665, Lowestoft
8. 1-4 June 1666, Four Days' Battle
9. 25 July 1666, St James's Day
10. 9 August 1666, Holmes's Bonfire
11. 12-14 June 1667, De Ruyter's raid into the Medway
12. 28 May 1672, Solebay
13. 28 May 1673, 1st Schooneveld
14. 4 June 1673, 2nd Schooneveld
15. 11 August 1673, Texel
16. 1 May 1689, Bantry Bay
17. 30 June 1690, Beachy Head,
18. 19 May 1692, Barfleur and 23 May 1692, La Hogue,
19. 14 October 1747, Ushant
20. 5 April 1758, Ile d'Aix
21. 20 November 1759, Quiberon Bay

until February 1705, when the Spanish besiegers finally marched away. In an action off Marbella on 10 March 1705, Admiral Sir John Leake defeated an attempt by a French squadron under Admiral de Pointis to land troops on Gibraltar, leaving the Rock in British hands, where it has remained to this day. (The Royal Marines observe 24 July as a Memorable Date, and they wear 'Gibraltar' as a battle honour on their cap badge, a unique privilege.)

By the time Rooke died in 1709, the war was drawing to a close. Rear Admiral Charles Wager had attacked the Spanish plate fleet off Cartagena in the West Indies in 1708, and the Navy had enforced a partial grain blockade on France in the North Sea and the Mediterranean, to hasten peace negotiations which concluded at Utrecht in 1713.

Although the Navy continued to be busily employed implementing the agreements reached at Utrecht, removing Austrian troops from Spain, and placing the Duke of Savoy's army in Sicily, for some 20 years Europe enjoyed a period of stability unusual for the 18th century. France and Britain (England became Britain after the Act of Union in 1707) formed a Triple Alliance in 1717 to safeguard European security. In 1718, a squadron under Admiral Sir George Byng prevented an attempt by Spain to break the Utrecht Treaty and seize territory she had lost in Italy by defeating a Spanish fleet off Cape Passaro, Sicily.

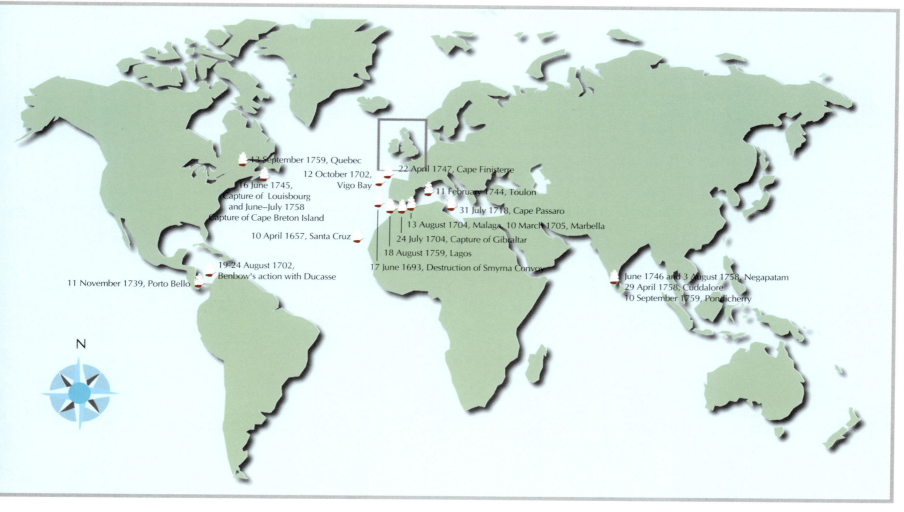

13 September 1759, Quebec

12 October 1702, Vigo Bay

22 April 1747, Cape Finisterre

16 June 1745, Capture of Louisbourg and June–July 1758 Capture of Cape Breton Island

11 February 1744, Toulon

31 July 1718, Cape Passaro

13 August 1704, Malaga   10 March 1705, Marbella

24 July 1704, Capture of Gibraltar

10 April 1657, Santa Cruz

18 August 1759, Lagos

17 June 1693, Destruction of Smyrna Convoy

19-24 August 1702, Benbow's action with Ducasse

11 November 1739, Porto Bello

June 1746 and 3 August 1758, Negapatam
29 April 1758, Cuddalore
10 September 1759, Pondicherry

N

IMPROVEMENTS ASHORE

Ashore, it was a period of improvement and consolidation for the Navy. The office of Lord High Admiral became a permanent bureaucracy, under commissioners who formed the Board of Admiralty, with the First Lord, who could be either an admiral or a civilian, a member of Cabinet. The first Admiralty building, built in 1699, had faulty foundations and was demolished, the present Admiralty building being built on the same site in 1725. The victualling service, to supply ships all over the world, improved from 1700 onwards. A permanent Sick and Wounded Board, who were also responsible for prisoners of war, was established in the 1740s, and the Royal Naval Hospital, Haslar, Gosport, was founded in 1746.

Despite the peace, the clouds of another war were gathering. Friction between Britain and Spain over trading rights in central America were to lead to conflict in Europe. In 1726, Vice Admiral Francis Hosier was appointed in command of a squadron of 16 ships and was sent to the West Indies in April, with orders to prevent the sailing of Spanish treasure ships, but without engaging in hostilities – an impossible order to carry out.

Hosier began by blockading Porto Bello, on the north side of the Isthmus of Darien, but then

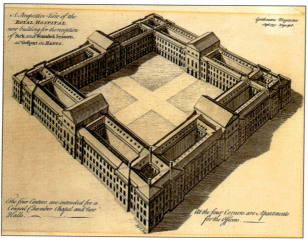

cruised off Cartagena, where his continued inaction became a joke among the Spaniards. His seamen suffered severely from yellow fever, which eventually caused over 4,000 deaths, including those of two admirals, eight captains and 50 lieutenants. Hosier himself became a victim. His body was placed in the bilges of his ship and brought home for permanent burial.

Vice Admiral Edward Vernon, born in 1684, joined the Navy as a volunteer in 1700. He served at the capture of Gibraltar and at the battle off Malaga, became a post captain in 1706, and served in various commands until the end of the war in 1713. He was known as 'Old Grog', because of the grogram boatcloak or, in some accounts, breeches he always wore on board. In 1740, Vernon ordered that the daily ration of rum issued to the seamen

Above: A map illustrating the location of the major naval battles described in this chapter. The inset map shows the waters around Britain in greater detail.

Left: 'A perspective view of the Royal Hospital now building for the reception of sick and wounded seaman, at Gosport in Hants.' This etching of the Royal Naval Hospital at Haslar first appeared in the September 1751 edition of Gentleman's Magazine.

1705 Leake's action off Marbella (10 March).

1708 Wager's action off Cartagena.

1713 Peace of Utrecht.

1715 First Jacobite rising.

1718 War for Sicily. Byng's victory over a Spanish squadron, Cape Passaro.

of the fleet should be diluted in the proportion of three parts of water to one of rum – hence the name 'grog' for watered-down rum.

Vernon was elected to Parliament in 1722 and took a leading part in all naval debates. He was particularly incensed by the incident of Jenkins' Ear, a result of the growing tensions between Britain and Spain in the Caribbean, when Spanish coastguard officers arrested a British trader called Captain Robert Jenkins and sliced off his ear.

The incident actually happened in 1731, but Parliament did not hear of it until 1738, when it aroused tremendous indignation in the country and forced a reluctant government to declare war on Spain. After a boastful speech in Parliament, Vernon was given command of a squadron of only six ships and ordered 'to destroy the Spanish settlements in the West Indies and distress their shipping by every method whatever'.

To the surprise of everybody who had expected him to fail and thus make himself look ridiculous, Vernon took the fort of Porto Bello in November 1739, seized the town and held it to ransom while he destroyed all warlike stores. This *coup* was so well received at home that the government had no other course but to send Vernon reinforcements of ships and men for further operations against Spain, and the War of Jenkins' Ear merged into the War of the Austrian Succession, in which Britain supported Austria against Spain.

In October 1743 the war entered a new phase when France made a 'second Family Compact' with Spain and took an active part in the war, leading to a major fleet engagement off Toulon on 11 February 1744 (before war had been formally declared) between the British Mediterranean Fleet of 28 ships of the line commanded by the C-in-C, Admiral Thomas Mathews, and a combined Franco-Spanish fleet of 15 French ships of the line, commanded by Admiral La Bruyère, and 12 Spanish ships under Admiral Don Jose de Navarro.

Mathews led the centre, flying his flag in the *Namur* (90), with Rear Admiral Sir William Rowley in the van, and Vice Admiral Richard Lestock commanding the rear. Lestock had been C-in-C in the Mediterranean until relieved by Mathews in 1742, and there was no love lost between the two.

After a pursuit of three days, the battle finally began, but Mathews' approach was so inept that only he and Rowley were engaged. Lestock was miles astern, and took no part. The general action, which lasted all day, ended inconclusively and the enemy escaped. Mathews did not pursue, thinking the enemy were trying to lure him away from his duty of protecting the Italian coast. The only captain to distinguish himself that day was Edward Hawke, in the *Berwick*, who captured the Spanish *Poder* (60).

The failure off Toulon enraged the country. Mathews resigned and Lestock came home under arrest. Courts martial followed. Mathews was found guilty of closing to attack before forming the line, even though it was shown that there had not been enough time to form the line. He was cashiered, along with several of his captains.

Lestock, who had been most at fault, argued that he had ignored Mathews' signal to engage because the signal for line of battle was still flying and while it was flying he could not follow his chief's action, as the line had not been properly formed. On this technicality in the *Fighting Instructions* he was acquitted.

The Navy had now become a world-wide force. While a strong fleet was still maintained in the Mediterranean, at home a squadron under Vernon prevented any effective French support of the Young Pretender during the Jacobite rising of 1745. In June of that year, the West Indies squadron under Commodore Sir Peter Warren, together with naval forces north of Carolina, the Newfoundland squadron, and colonial privateers who were serving under him, captured the fort

1725 Admiralty building constructed.

1726 Hosier ordered to prevent sailing of Spanish treasure ships from West Indies.

1733 Opening of Royal Naval Academy in Portsmouth.

Above: *Admiral Sir Edward Hawke. Hawke was knighted in recognition of his attack on the French convoy off Finisterre on 14 October 1747 during which six of the French escort ships were captured. The mezzotint is by James McArdell after G. Knapton.*

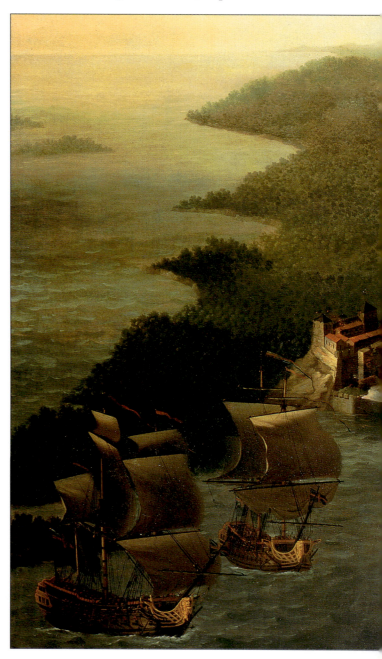

and harbour of Louisbourg, from where the French controlled the mouth of the St Lawrence river, supplied their Newfoundland fishing fleets, and threatened New England and Nova Scotia.

In June 1746, Commodore Edward Peyton fought an inconclusive action with a French force off Negapatam on the Coromandel coast of southern India. But this failure was followed the next year by a smashing success off Cape Finisterre, when on 3 May a squadron of 13 ships of the line, under Vice Admiral George Anson, flying his flag in the *Prince George* (90), intercepted two French convoys, one bound for India and the other for Canada. The French escort was inadequate and although the French admiral de la Jonquière did his brave best, Anson captured four ships of the line, two frigates and seven of the merchantmen in a hopelessly one-sided battle.

On 14 October, after eight weeks patrolling between Ushant and Finisterre, another squadron of 14 ships of the line under Rear Admiral Edward Hawke (of Toulon fame), flying his flag in the *Devonshire* (66), encountered a French convoy on its way to the West Indies. The French escort was outnumbered by about two to one, but the French admiral L'Etenduère handled his ships with great skill and bravery so that the whole convoy escaped, after a nine-hour running battle. But only his flagship, the *Tonnant* (80) and the *Intrépide* (74) escaped, both badly damaged. The other six French ships of the line were all captured. These two reverses contributed greatly to France's agreement to peace which was concluded by the Treaty of Aix-La-Chapelle in 1748.

ANSON'S EXPEDITION

George Anson, who was raised to the peerage for his exploit off Finisterre, was already famous in the country for his circumnavigation of the world from 1740–44. Born in 1697 in Staffordshire, he joined the Navy as a volunteer in 1712, and served as a midshipman in the Baltic under Sir John Norris and as a lieutenant under Byng at Cape Passaro. Promoted to post captain in 1724, he

Above: *Admiral George Anson was renowned for his voyage of circumnavigation around the globe. This engraving by James McArdell is based on Sir Joshua Reynold's famous portrait.*

Left: *The capture of Porto Bello on 11 November 1739 by Admiral Vernon during the War of Jenkins' Ear. The painting is by Samuel Scott.*

Below right: *The log of the* Gloucester *records the deaths of many of Anson's crew from scurvy during his voyage around the world. The entry for 19 August 1742 shown here refers to 'their Ships Company being so much weaken'd by Sickness, Death & Fatigue'*

served for some years off the coast of Carolina where a county was named after him. In 1740, he was given command of a small squadron of six ships, with the rank of commodore, and ordered to the Pacific where he was to harry Spanish possessions and, if possible, to capture one of the treasure ships which sailed yearly from Acapulco in Mexico to Manila.

There was difficulty in manning and equipping the expedition, and the numbers had to be made up with pensioners from Greenwich Hospital. After some eight months' delay, the squadron sailed in September 1740: Anson in the *Centurion* (60), with the *Gloucester* (50), *Severn* (50), *Pearl* (40), *Wager* (28), and the sloop o'war *Tryal* (8). There were also two victualling ships.

The weather was very bad in the south Atlantic, and the ships were scattered. The *Wager* ran aground and was lost. The *Severn* and the *Pearl* turned back and never reached Cape Horn. Mortality from scurvy was high. When the *Centurion* arrived at Juan Fernandez in June 1741, she had only 30 men fit for duty. The *Gloucester* arrived some time later, in even worse plight, followed by *Tryal*.

Of the 961 men who left England in these three ships, 626 had died, but Anson pressed on with the men he had left, and attacked and looted Spanish settlements. He discovered that he had

missed that year's treasure ship. *Tryal* and *Gloucester* were by then unseaworthy and were condemned, *Gloucester* being set on fire, while Anson set sail for China in the *Centurion* alone.

The *Centurion*'s crew suffered severely from scurvy during the crossing of the Pacific and Anson had less than 200 men left when he reached Macao. However, he was able to pick up some Spanish negroes, Indians, Dutchmen and Lascars at Macao, bringing his numbers up to 227. With this reduced and motley crew, *Centurion* encountered the Spanish treasure ship *Nuestra Señora de Covadonga* off Manila on 20 June 1743. The Spaniard was no match for *Centurion* and struck her flag after a 90-minute engagement.

Anson's luck held to the end. On the last leg of his journey home, thick fog allowed the *Centurion* to pass safely through a French fleet cruising in the Channel, and Anson anchored at Spithead on 15 June 1744.

The Spanish treasure, valued at £500,000, the largest amount brought back to England in a single ship, made the survivors of the voyage wealthy men, and Anson himself very rich. It was landed at Portsmouth, sent up to London, and paraded in triumph through the streets in a procession of 32 wagons, the ship's company marching with colours flying and band playing.

In 1748 Richard Walter, *Centurion*'s chaplain,

SCURVY

Of the six ship's companies who set out with Anson in 1740, only four men died from enemy action, but over 1,300 from disease, mainly scurvy. Scurvy, caused by a deficiency of Vitamin C in the diet, usually became apparent after about six weeks on salt provisions, lacking fresh fruit and vegetables. Because it made men weak long before it killed them, scurvy was responsible for many shipwrecks.

Scurvy manifested itself in many ways, but the first scorbutic (i.e. scurvy-related) symptoms were usually swellings on the gums, teeth falling out, and extensive blotches and a loss of resilience in the skin, so that even a slight pressure left a depression for some time. There followed a dull lethargy which deepened until the sufferer could be roused from it only at the danger of his life, and which resulted eventually in death.

One naval surgeon, James Lind, the father of nautical medicine, was shocked by the enormous losses from scurvy incurred during Anson's voyage. In 1747, he carried out the first controlled dietary experiment in history, and discovered that the juice of oranges and lemons was a sure safeguard against the disease. He published his findings in his *Treatise of the Scurvy* in 1753, but because of administrative indolence and indifference Lind's discovery was not widely promulgated. It was not until 1795, and only then at the insistence of Sir Gilbert Blane, one of Lind's followers, that an issue of lemon juice was officially adopted in the Royal Navy, and scurvy was virtually eliminated at sea. But in those intervening 40 years, tens of thousands of sailors died unnecessarily of the disease.

James Lind went on to write *An Essay on the Most Effectual Means of Preserving the Health of Seamen*, published in 1757, and in 1768 *An Essay on Diseases Incidental to Europeans in Hot Climates*, the first ever handbook on tropical medicine. In 1758 he was appointed physician in charge of the new naval hospital at Haslar, Gosport, where he remained until 1783, when he was succeeded by his son John.

Although scurvy had been eradicated, it reappeared on the polar expeditions of the 19th century, when the Admiralty, for reasons of economy, replaced lemons with limes which had only half the antiscorbutic value of lemons.

The real cause of scurvy was only found when vitamins were discovered in 1912.

Below: *The medical resources aboard an 18th-century warship were not extensive. They might include leech jars and simple, non-specialist reference books for the layman, such as this example from HMS Bounty.*

published *A Voyage Round The World*, an account of Anson's circumnavigation which has become one of the classic books on the sea. In the same year, Lord Sandwich became First Lord of the Admiralty in 1747, and left the executive administration of the Navy almost entirely to Lord Anson, who thus virtually acted as First Lord, and who in 1751 actually did become First Lord.

Anson was a determined reformer, who could justifiably be called the Father of the Navy. He drew up new Articles of War; significantly improved the administration of the dockyards, which for years had been sinks of waste, inefficiency, and corruption; put the establishment of guns and all stores on a more satisfactory footing; devised a system of 'rating' warships, whereby ships were rated in six divisions according to the number of guns they carried; introduced a regulation uniform for officers (although it was to be some years before the majority of officers conformed to it); set up a major naval base at Halifax, the new capital of Nova Scotia; and disbanded the old marine regiments, replacing them with a new permanent corps, under Admiralty administration, organised in three divisions based upon the main naval bases of Chatham, Portsmouth and Plymouth.

The only mistake Anson made was to appoint Admiral John Byng as Commander-in-Chief in the Mediterranean at the start of the Seven Years War in 1756 and, having appointed him, fail to give him an adequate fleet. The war was caused by the alarm aroused among the continental powers by the aggressive intentions of Frederick the Great of Prussia, who was Britain's ally, in which Britain and Prussia were opposed by Russia, France, Poland, Austria, Sweden and Spain, and it was fought, not just in Europe, but in Africa, India, where Clive won his great victory at Plassey, Canada, with the capture of Quebec, and America, with the capture of Pittsburgh.

John Byng, the fourth son of Admiral Sir George Byng, had had a successful but unremarkable naval career before he was sent out to the Mediterranean to relieve Minorca, which was

Left: A portrait engraving of Admiral John Byng by Richard Houston after Thomas Hudson. The son of Admiral Sir George Byng, Viscount Torrington, John Byng was executed on the deck of HMS Monarch *on 14 March 1757, after a court martial had found him guilty of neglect of duty following his failure in an action off Minorca.*

Above: An 18th-century compass made by G. Adams of Fleet Street, London, 'Instrument Makers to His Majesty'.

29th Decem.r 1756.
'M.r Shales. We have order'd the following Provisions to be sent for Supply of his Majestys Stores at Portsmouth, Viz.t Bread 2000 Bags, Pease 2000 Bushells Butter 10000 lbs Cheese 40000 lbs Vinegar 2000 Gallons Hops 30 Bags. And We have order'd our Agent at Dover to send one thousand Bags of Bread to Portsmouth from thence, We are Your Affectionate Friends, signed Ja. Wallace, Robt Pett.'

LETTER FROM THE VICTUALLING BOARD TO HENRY SHALES, ITS AGENT IN PORTSMOUTH

Left: Navigational instruments recovered from HMS Invincible *include this octant used for taking measurements of the Sun, an hourglass and a lead for sounding depth.*

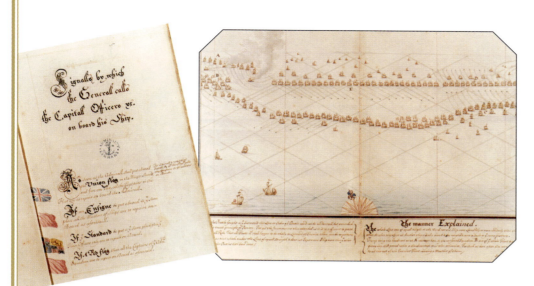

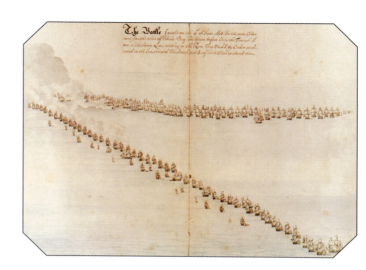

FIGHTING INSTRUCTIONS

Fighting Instructions, a code of 21 tactical signals, first issued by Blake, Deane and Monck in 1653, established the line of battle as a standard formation and imposed a form of tactical discipline on the fleet

In 1673, James, Duke of York published his *Sailing and Fighting Instructions*, the first comprehensive book of tactics for the Navy, giving 26 sailing and fighting instructions, in particular emphasising the importance of maintaining the line in battle.

In the Summer of 1691, Admiral Edward Russell, (later created Earl of Orford), issued his *Sailing and Fighting Instructions*, which incorporated Dutch as well as English experience and were to be the basis of British naval tactics until 1783. The *Instructions* promulgated ideas such as massing fire power and maintaining control of the fleet, and again emphasised that the main tactic was the line of battle, with the British ships gaining the weather gauge, to close the enemy down wind in line ahead and engage the enemy's full battle line, the British van with the enemy's van.

The courts martial of Mathews and Lestock after the action off Toulon in February 1744 showed every serving admiral and captain the dire consequences if,

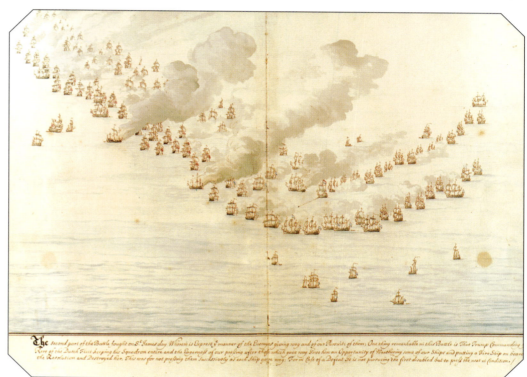

beset by the French. The Admiralty seemed unaware of the importance of the island, for Byng was given a small, weak and poorly equipped fleet of only 13 ships of the line, although there were over 50 in commission.

Byng met a French squadron some 30 miles (50km) east of Port Mahon, the island's capital, on 20 May 1756. His tactics were inhibited by the current *Fighting Instructions* which laid down that fleets should only fight in line ahead, van to van, rear to rear, unless the enemy was clearly retiring, when the signal 'General Chase' could be hoisted, and room for manoeuvre was then possible.

With such little scope for initiative, and having very much in mind the fate of Mathews 12 years earlier, Byng did hoist the 'General Chase', but it was an inconclusive action, with some damage and casualties on both sides. However, the French

retreated, leaving Byng at least technically the victor. But he made no attempt to engage them again or take any offensive action, Instead, he sailed away to Gibraltar – a gross error, unworthy of any C-in-C. Port Mahon held out for another month before surrendering, and Minorca was lost.

At home, there was a public outcry. Byng was court-martialled, found guilty of negligence, condemned to death, and executed by shooting at Portsmouth on the morning of 14 March 1757, an event famously mocked by Voltaire in *Candide*: 'that in this country [England] it is a good thing to kill an admiral from time to time *pour encourager les autres*'.

The world-wide nature of the Seven Years' War was well demonstrated by events in the years 1758 and 1759. In April 1758, Admiral Sir Edward Hawke, who had succeeded Byng in the Mediterranean, fought a confused action off the

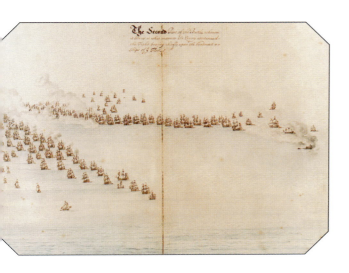

Above and left: *Watercolour illustrations from a copy of* Fighting Instructions *dated c.1680. The surprising*

depth of the tactical analysis in the commentary is revealing of the real professionalism of the navy at this time.

in their eagerness to engage the enemy, they went beyond the strict rules of the *Fighting Instructions*. The effect was to stifle almost all initiative in battle for the next 20 years.

The *Fighting Instructions* denied any flexibility of action to a commander in the presence of the enemy and made no allowance for local conditions of wind and weather. Rigid adherence to such tactical doctrine contributed to Byng's debacle off Minorca in 1756, which lost the British the useful base of Fort Mahon, and to Graves's action off Chesapeake Bay in 1781, which led to the loss of the American colonies.

However, at the battle of the Saintes in 1782, Rodney seized the chance to sail through one of the gaps in the ragged French line. This had the lasting result of introducing into the *Fighting Instructions* the tactic of breaking the line of battle, and throwing the enemy line into confusion, by sailing through the gaps between their ships, and engaging them from the opposite side. This was precisely the tactic used at Trafalgar.

Ile d'Aix which prevented a large French convoy leaving Rochefort for America. Off India, Vice Admiral George Pocock fought three actions with varying success against the French Admiral Comte D'Ache, at Cuddalore in April and Negapatam in August 1758, and at Pondicherry in September 1759. In a short campaign from June to July 1758, Admiral the Hon. Edward Boscawen captured Louisburg and the whole of Cape Breton Island.

On the afternoon of 18 August 1759, Boscawen met a French squadron under Commodore De La Clue off the southern coast of Portugal. In a sharp action, the French *Centaure* (74) was taken and Boscawen's flagship, the *Namur* (90), was disabled aloft. Boscawen shifted his flag to the *Newark* (80). When the boat taking him across was hit by a round shot, Boscawen plugged the hole with his wig. Boscawen continued the chase all night and when the French took refuge in Lagos Bay the next day, he pursued them under the principle of 'hot chase', and captured or burned three more French ships. The French flagship, the *Océan* (80), ran hard aground, and was set on fire, while De La Clue was mortally wounded.

Meanwhile, in Canada, French settlers were fortifying their settlements against the advance of English settlers. Quebec 'was the key to the

1746 Failure of Peyton at Fort St David, Negapatam, southern India. Foundation of the Royal Naval Hospital at Haslar, Gosport.

1747 Anson's victory off Finisterre (22 April). Hawke's victory off Ushant (14 October). James Lind conducts dietary experiment in attempt to discover a cure for scurvy.

1748 Peace of Aix-La-Chapelle.

Above left: *Powder barrels and a worm for clearing debris from gun barrels recovered from HMS Invincible.*

Left: *French fireships attacking the English fleet off Quebec on 28 June 1759 painted by Dominic Serres the Elder. In the event, this attack was foiled and Saunders landed Wolfe's forces below Quebec. In a combined operation, they overwhelmed the French and captured the city on 13 September 1759.*

conquest of upper Canada', and in the autumn of 1759 an expedition was launched to capture the city. The naval commander was Vice Admiral Sir Charles Saunders in the *Neptune* while Major General James Wolfe commanded the troops. Brilliantly navigated by Master (later Captain) James Cook, the fleet took a large force up the St Lawrence river and landed them below the plains of Abraham on 13 September. Seamen landed guns and hauled them up the Heights of Abraham. While Wolfe attacked and took the city, the fleet lay off and above Quebec, to support and supply the troops, as well as denying supplies and reinforcements to the French defenders.

After the failure of an amphibious assault on Rochefort, Hawke hauled down his flag in a fit of pique and came ashore. But in 1759 he was appointed in command of the Western Squadron, blockading Brest, where the French fleet was assembling, preparing to join and escort yet another invasion force of troopships waiting in the Morbihan. But with Hawke waiting outside, the French admiral Conflans could not get to sea. Despite the lack of regular supplies of fresh food and water, Hawke stayed on watch unbroken from May until early in November when a westerly gale blew him off station and allowed Conflans to escape.

QUIBERON BAY

Hawke's ships reached Torbay, and after two days for repairs were at sea again to resume their watch. The gale was still blowing hard when Hawke reached the French coast and learned that his enemy had escaped. But they were sighted off Quiberon Bay on 20 November 1759 and Hawke hoisted the signal for 'General Chase'. Every ship crowded on sail to pursue the French into the bay as darkness was falling, using the French ships as their pilots to keep clear of the many rocks and shoals. The master of Hawke's flagship, the *Royal George* (100), ventured to warn the admiral of the dangerous shallows ahead, but Hawke replied: 'You have done your duty in pointing out to me the danger. Now lay me alongside the enemy's flagship.'

Hawke had 23 ships of the line and a squadron of ten small ships commanded by Commodore Duff, while Conflans had 21 ships of the line and three frigates. Thus numbers lay marginally on Hawke's side, but Conflans was convinced that Hawke would never attack in such narrow waters and in such dreadful weather.

Conflans had misjudged his opponent. In a fierce action before darkness finally fell, six French ships of the line were taken, burned or wrecked. Some escaped out of the bay under cover of darkness, but others broke their backs on the shallow bar at the entrance to the Vilaine

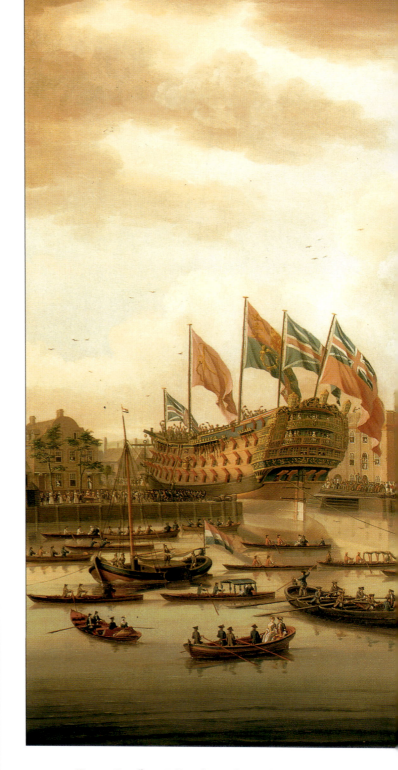

estuary. Even Conflans' flagship, the *Soleil Royal* (80), grounded while putting to sea and was burned by her crew to prevent capture. The French lost seven ships of the line in all, over 2,500 men killed or drowned, and many of the surviving ships were unfit for further sea service. Hawke lost two ships, the *Resolution* (74) and *Essex* (64), both of which ran aground early in the battle and were wrecked by the gale where they lay.

Quiberon Bay was a smashing strategic victory, which once again averted the threat of invasion. The most lasting salute to this justly named 'Year of Victories' was 'Heart of Oak', by David Garrick, still sung today to music by Dr Boyce:

Right: An oil painting by Harold Wyllie of the Battle of Quiberon Bay, 20 November 1759. Admiral Sir Edward Hawke showed considerable daring during his pursuit of the French in darkness into the shallow waters of the bay. He won a decisive strategic victory.

Come cheer up, my lads! tis to glory we steer,
To add something more to this wonderful year:
To honour we call you, not press you like
    slaves;
For who are so free as the sons of the waves?
        Heart of oak are our ships,
        Gallant tars are our men;
        We always are ready:
        Steady, boys, steady!
    We'll fight and we'll conquer again and again.

Above: The Royal
George *at Deptford
showing the launch of
the* Cambridge *in 1757,
painted by John
Cleveley the Elder.
Although an excellent
representation of a
first rate and a launch
ceremony, in fact the
Royal George never
visited Deptford. This
picture illustrates the
hazards of interpreting
art as documentary
evidence of history.*

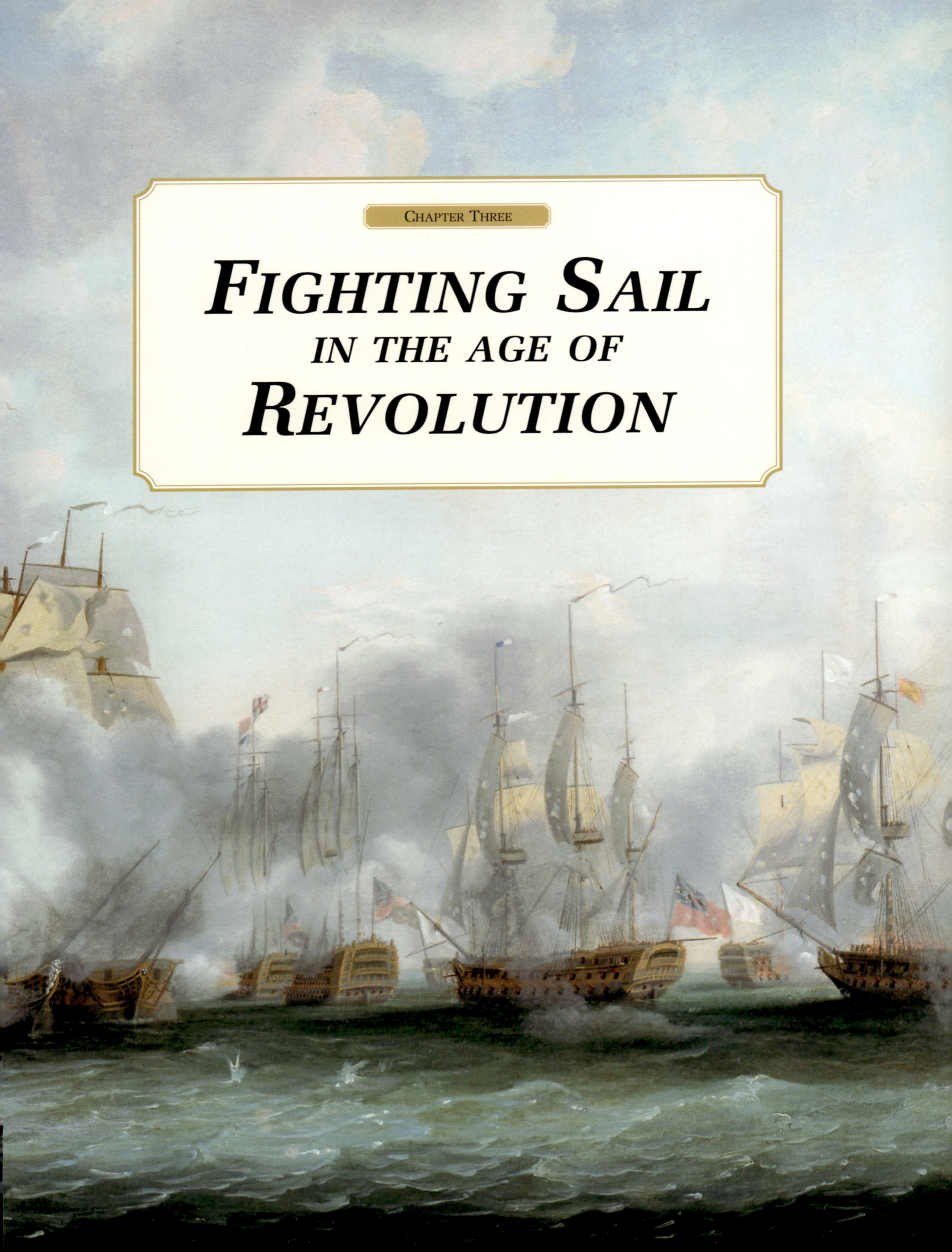

FIGHTING SAIL
IN THE AGE OF
REVOLUTION

Previous pages: *The Battle of the Saintes in 1782, when Rodney defeated a French fleet under de Grasse, secured Britain's dominance in the West Indies. The painting is by Nicholas Pocock.*

Below: *A view of the Royal dockyard at Deptford in 1793. The coloured engraving is by William Woollett after a painting by Richard Paton and John Hamilton Mortimer RA.*

Throughout the 18th century, and into the 19th, the Navy expanded at an almost exponential rate. Although there were periods of decline in years of peace, in wartime the average annual money spent on the Navy, financed by an efficient tax system and sound public credit, rose from £2.4 million from 1702–13 to £15.2 million from 1793 to 1815. In 1714, the Navy had 197 ships, including 63 ships of the line. By 1809, the Navy's peak, it had 193 ships of the line, and a total of 979 ships.

The ships grew much larger. Between 1688 and 1755, the average size was 1,056 tons; between 1756 and 1815, it was 1,714 tons. The number of seamen and marines serving in the active fleet in wartime was 48,000 in 1713, rising to 85,000 in 1762 and reaching 142,000 in 1813. The number of lieutenants increased from 360 in 1715 to 1,350 in 1783, and 3,270 in 1813. The number of captains rose from about 260 in 1715 to 800 in 1813, and there were also 600 commanders in 1813, a rank which did not exist a century earlier.

On shore, there was a huge building programme: docks, wharves, slipways, storehouses, powder magazines and hospitals. Dockyard facilities were greatly improved and enlarged. Permanent overseas bases were established in Gibraltar, Minorca, Port Royal Jamaica, English Harbour Antigua, Halifax, Bombay (where the East India Company had a dry dock) and, at the start of the 19th century, Malta.

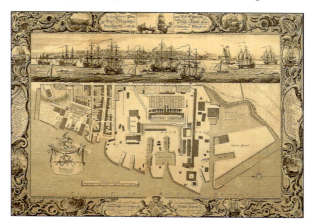

Above: *A plan and west elevation of the dockyard at Plymouth drawn and engraved in 1756 by T. Milton. The 17th and 18th centuries witnessed a huge expansion in the size of the naval dockyards.*

Between 1779 and 1781, the sailing qualities of ships were enormously enhanced by the introduction of copper sheathing on hulls to combat shipworm. By the 1790s, the standard two-deck, 74-gun ship of the line was a most formidably efficient weapon system, combining hull strength, firepower and weight of metal, speed, and good sailing qualities and seaworthiness.

Such ships needed good officers and skilled crews. Most of the officers had first gone to sea when they were boys: Anson at 14, Hawke and Hood at 14, Horatio Nelson at 12. Many of them were the sons and nephews of naval officers, and the rest were boys recommended by friends, relatives and people of political or social importance.

Every boy learned his trade at first-hand, climbing the rigging, handling sails, tying knots, crewing the guns. This almost exclusive concentration upon naval expertise meant that the boys were deprived of a normal education. Schoolmasters in ships, tried in 1702, were a failure. The Admiralty became so concerned that it established a Royal Naval Academy at Portsmouth in 1733. Cadets were to spend three years there (two of which counted as sea service) before joining their ships. But the Academy made a poor start, and almost foundered. It was unpopular with serving officers, who feared it would diminish their influence over entrants, which indeed it did, and with parents who preferred to send their son to a captain they knew, who could be trusted to keep an eye on him.

The popular notion of the Navy, nowadays so deeply ingrained in the public imagination that it is probably indelible, is that the sailors were largely an unwilling and cowed mob, who had been virtually shanghaied to sea, where they were brutally flogged for any misdemeanour and fed the most appalling food.

In fact, Britain had the largest pool of experienced sailors available to any nation, the great majority of whom took pride in their service. The food in warships was of high quality when it was first supplied, although it deteriorated when on board for protracted periods, but in general it was much better than the average sailor could expect if he had stayed at home instead of joining the Navy. Sailors were supposed to be robbed of all their money by rascally pursers. There were some dishonest pursers, but it was normally the purser himself, who sometimes had to wait years for his accounts to be passed, who stood in the most financial risk. Sailors were supposed to be frequently flogged within an inch of their lives. There were brutal captains, but a brutal captain was an inefficient one, and most captains found that flogging was a very time-wasting and inflexible system of punishment.

Nepotism, or 'interest' as it was called in the Navy, whereby everybody helped their friends and relatives as much as they could, was supposed to be a bad system, open to corruption. On the contrary, it was generally an effective system, approved by everybody, not least by the Admiralty, whereby ships were officered and manned more quickly and efficiently than they otherwise could have been, and many an able officer was promoted when he was still young. When a good captain, and there were many of them, commissioned a new ship, he often took the entire ship's company of his old ship with him, who all volunteered to stay with a captain they knew and respected.

An Uncertain Peace

Britain obtained major territorial gains by the Peace of Paris which brought the Seven Years War to an end in 1763. But the peace was uneasy, with Britain isolated, and the Bourbon states of France and Spain clearly waiting for a chance to regain their lost possessions, although France failed to back Spain's attempt to claim the Falkland Islands in 1771.

France's opportunity came with the revolution in America, whose relations with Britain had been deteriorating for some time until, by the spring of 1775, they were in a state of virtual hostility, which turned to actual bloodshed at Lexington and Concord, near Boston, in April.

Above: Captain Lord George Graham in his cabin by William Hogarth. Hogarth called such pictures 'conversation pieces', and the informality of the scene contrasts sharply with the more formal conventions of portraiture of the period. The ship is believed to be the 60-gun Nottingham.

Below: How the hammocks were arranged on the lower deck of the Bedford, c.1780. They were slung from hooks at intervals of 14 inches (36cm) per man.

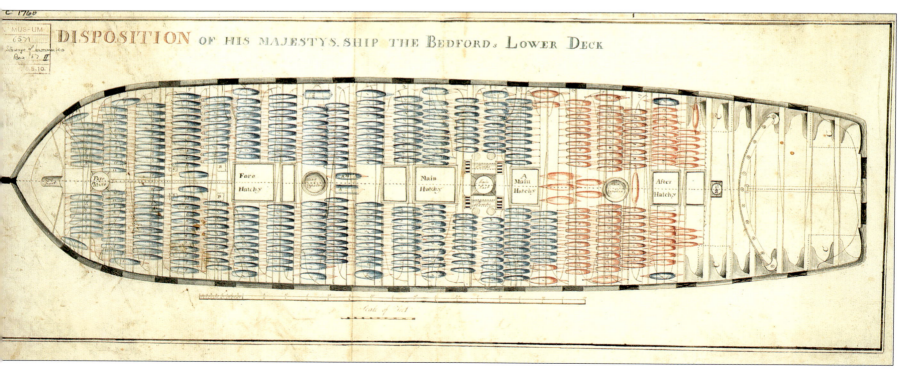

DISPOSITION OF HIS MAJESTYS SHIP THE BEDFORD, LOWER DECK

▶ **1776** Cook sails for third voyage to north-west coast of America. Lord Howe captures New York. British victory on Lake Champlain (13 October).

1777 Burgoyne and the British army surrender at Saratoga. France enters the War of American Independence on the side of the Americans.

1778 Inconclusive action off Ushant (27 July) followed by court martials of Keppel and Palliser.

1779 Cook killed at Kealakekua Bay, Hawaii. Byron's action with the French off Grenada (6 July). French capture Grenada and St Vincent. Duel between *Bonhomme Richard* (John Paul Jones) and *Serapis* off Flamborough Head (23 September).

Although the British initially had complete control of the sea, Lord North's government at home never properly appreciated the true situation across the Atlantic and failed to send forces strong enough to crush the rebellion. Vice Admiral Lord Howe sailed to New York, which he captured in the autumn of 1776. Commodore Sir Peter Parker joined him in New York having been repulsed at Charleston.

Benedict Arnold realised that the British would advance down the axis of Lakes Champlain and George to isolate New England and that, if they succeeded in breaking through, the revolution would be over. He built a Lilliputian fleet on Lake Champlain, of miscellaneous small vessels, including 'gondolas', small flat-bottomed craft of about 53 feet (16m) in length, powered by oars, with a single fore and aft sail, armed with a 12-pound gun at the bows, and a few 9-pounders. By October 1776, he had a fleet of four row galleys, eight gondolas, three schooners, and a sloop, a total of 94 guns and about 700 men.

The British also had a fleet on Lake Champlain, of some 20 gunboats, the schooners *Carleton* and *Maria*, a captured gondola, and the three-masted ship *Inflexible*, mounting 18 12-pounder guns, which had been prefabricated, dismantled, carried across land, and reassembled on the lake. The army, commanded by Sir Guy Carleton, the leader of British forces in Canada, was embarked in some 680 flat-bottomed boats.

The British sailed down the Lake on a brisk northerly wind on 11 October, but overshot Arnold's ships, sheltering behind an island on the western side. The British dared not leave Arnold's ships behind, as this would endanger their supply lines, so they tacked back to engage and trounce the rebel fleet with their superior weight of fire. Arnold's ships slipped away under cover of fog that night, but there could be no final escape, They were hunted down and, in another action on 13 October, all but three were sunk. It was, as one American general said, 'the defeat and almost total ruin of our fleet'.

Carleton's army could now go south and join the army of General Howe (the admiral's brother) in New York. New England would be cut off and the revolution would collapse. But it was not to be so simple. The best campaigning season was now over for the year. The weather was growing much colder, travel was much more difficult, there was ice on tracks and rivers, food and forage were much scarcer.

Carleton's troops were obliged to return to Quebec for the winter. When, under General Burgoyne, they moved south again in 1777, General Howe was no longer in New York. On 17 October 1777, Burgoyne was surrounded at Saratoga by an American army which out-numbered his by more than two to one, and surrendered. So, as it turned out, the delay caused by Arnold's gondolas had actually saved the

THE CARRONADE

The short-barrelled carronade entered the fleet in the 1780s. In the 1770s a Scottish artillery officer, General Robert Melville, had invented a gun for use on ship carriages which was only five feet (1.5m) long and fired a 68-pound ball, with a charge of only 5.5 pounds (2.5kg) of powder. The much reduced charge and barrel length were made possible by reducing the 'windage' on the ball, i.e. by making it a snugger fit in the bore. For instance, a 32-pounder cannon had a bore diameter 0.3 inch (7.6mm) greater than the ball, while the carronade 32-pounder bore was only 0.15 inch (3.8mm) greater than the same ball.

The gun became known first as the 'smasher' but soon acquired its name from its manufacturers, the Carron Iron Works, at Falkirk, Scotland. It was a most effective gun which could fire the same size of ball as the 32-pounder cannon, but only weighed about the same as a 6-pounder, and it relied on the weight of the ball, rather than its impetus, to do the damage.

The carronade was the first gun to be cast with a dispart sight, i.e. a raised spur of metal set on top of the mid-length reinforcing ring which, when sighted from the top of the breech ring, gave the true line of the bore. The angle of the barrel was governed by a screw thread elevating mechanism which was a much better way of fixing the elevation once it had been set than the wooden wedges of the cannon, and unlike them, was not liable to fly out when the gun was fired.

Below: *A 32-pounder carronade on a replica slide mount. The drawings (right) are from a treatise on ordnance by William Congreve (1811).*

Right: *'Subtraction', an etching by H. Heath dated 1830. This satire plays on the widespread public perception of the risks of war, and the appalling effects that could be wrought by concentrated artillery fire, particularly at sea.*

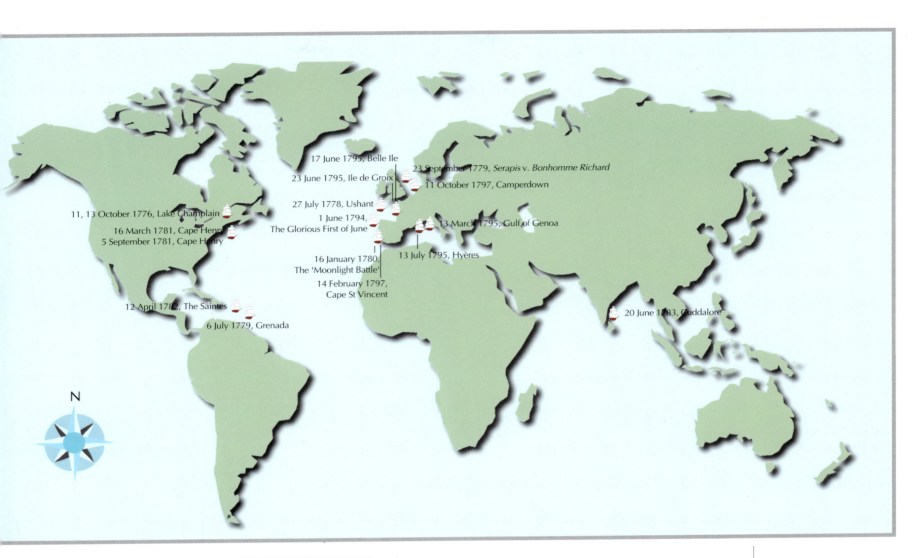

17 June 1795, Belle Ile

23 June 1795, Ile de Groix

23 September 1779, *Serapis* v. *Bonhomme Richard*

11 October 1797, Camperdown

27 July 1778, Ushant

11, 13 October 1776, Lake Champlain

1 June 1794, The Glorious First of June

13 March 1795, Gulf of Genoa

16 March 1781, Cape Henry

5 September 1781, Cape Henry

16 January 1780, The 'Moonlight Battle'

13 July 1795, Hyères

14 February 1797, Cape St Vincent

12 April 1782, The Saintes

6 July 1779, Grenada

20 June 1783, Cuddalore

N

The carronade carriage was a block of timber with a bolt at its outboard end parallel to the ship's side which fitted through a carronade loop, cast beneath the gun about midway along its length. The carriage ran on a stationary timber 'slide'.

Being comparatively light and requiring fewer men to serve it, the carronade was an ideal gun for mounting on the upper deck, and it suited the British style of close-in fighting. However, it did present a fire risk to the lowest ship's rigging and the hammocks which lined the upper deck, because the mouth of its short barrel only just protruded through the bulwarks.

The first major engagement in which the carronade proved its worth was Rodney's victory over the French at the Saintes in 1782, and it went on to be a most potent weapon in the French Revolutionary and Napoleonic wars.

revolution. That seemingly insignificant little skirmish on Lake Champlain had been, as the historian Mahan described it, 'a strife of pygmies for the prize of a continent'.

THE FRENCH ENTER THE FRAY

The surrender at Saratoga was the signal for France to join the conflict on the American Rebels' side. An American mission to Paris had already secured a secret loan of one million *livres* in May 1776, and a treaty of commerce and friendship between France and the Rebels was signed in February 1778. The war now ceased to be colonial and became global.

The first fleet action took place on the afternoon of 27 July 1778, about 70 miles (113km) west of Ushant, when Admiral Augustus Keppel, flying his flag in the newly-commissioned *Victory* (100), with the Channel Fleet of 30 of the line, met Admiral the Comte D'Orvilliers, flying his flag in *Bretagne* (110), with the Brest squadron of 30 ships of the line.

A conclusive victory for the British would have had incalculable political and military effects on the war just beginning. Instead, it was inconclusive, and is now largely remembered for the behaviour of Vice Admiral Sir Hugh Palliser,

Above: *The final decades of the 18th century saw the Royal Navy called into action across much of the globe, from the Caribbean and North American waters in the west to India in the east.*

Below: *An 18th century naval officer – a portrait by Gardner of Commodore Hotham in the 1780s. Hotham was later promoted to the rank of vice admiral.*

Above: *On 15 December 1778 Rear Admiral Barrington fought an action against French ships off the island of St Lucia in the West Indies. Two weeks later, Barrington captured the island. This painting of the engagement is by Dominic Serres, and is a fine representation of the 18th century line of battle.*

leading the rear squadron in *Formidable* (90), who failed to support Keppel at a critical time. Keppel and Palliser were both later court-martialled. Both were acquitted, but while Keppel had public houses named after him – a sure sign of popularity in England – Palliser's house in Pall Mall was burned by a mob.

A French fleet under Count D'Estaing arrived in American waters in July 1778, with orders to engage Howe's fleet. In August, the French attempted a landing on Rhode Island, where the British occupied Newport. D'Estaing put to sea to meet Howe, but both fleets were scattered by a hurricane.

The war now spread to the West Indies. In September 1778, a French force from Martinique captured the British island of Dominica. In December, Rear Admiral Samuel Barrington captured the French island of St Lucia, and the British occupied Savannah, Georgia. In 1779, D'Estaing took St Vincent and then Grenada. There followed, on 6 July, an action in St George's Bay, Grenada, between D'Estaing and the recently appointed C-in-C Leeward Islands, Vice Admiral John Byron, with 21 ships of the line. The British ships were maladroitly handled by Byron and the

result was a tactical victory for the French which, however, D'Estaing failed to follow up.

Meanwhile, in June, Spain had entered the war against Britain and laid siege once more to Gibraltar. By August 1779, a combined Franco-Spanish fleet of 66 ships, the so-called 'false armada', cruised the Channel unopposed, and there was a fresh threat of an invasion, which in the event never took place.

Individual ship engagements had not so far been a marked feature of naval warfare, but the American War of Independence saw one of the most famous and most bitter ship-to-ship actions of all time.

John Paul Jones was a Scotsman who served in the British merchant marine before being commissioned in 1775 in the Continental Navy, the name by which the Navy of the United States was known between the Declaration of Independence in 1776 and the Congress resolution founding the US Navy in 1794. In 1779 he was given command of an old East Indiaman of 900 tons, renamed *Bonhomme Richard* after Benjamin Franklin, Jones' patron and the United States representative in Paris who used the pen-name 'Poor Richard' in some of his writings.

Below: *A sea service flintlock musket dating from c.1795. Flintlocks remained in service until the early 19th century when they were superseded by more reliable percussion muskets.*

Jones sailed from Lorient on 14 August 1779, to go, as he said, 'in harm's way', with the new frigate *Alliance*, commanded by a half-mad Frenchman, Pierre Landais, the frigate *Pallas* and two smaller vessels. On 23 September, off Flamborough Head, he met a Baltic convoy of 44 sail, escorted by the new frigate *Serapis* (50), commanded by Captain Richard Pearson, and the sloop *Countess of Scarborough* (22).

Serapis covered the convoy while it escaped intact to the north. *Pallas* took the British sloop, while *Alliance* played no part except to fire indiscriminately at friend and foe. *Serapis* and *Bonhomme Richard* engaged each other just after sunset, sailing parallel, exchanging broadsides, each attempting to sail ahead or astern of the other to rake the enemy's decks with unopposed fire. In a furious battle which lasted more than two hours, *Bonhomme Richard*, heavily out-gunned from the outset, lost all but two of her 18-pounder guns. When *Serapis* ranged alongside, so close that the two ships' rigging was entangled, and tried to board, Pearson shouted across 'Has your ship struck?' John Paul Jones reply was 'I have not yet begun to fight!'.

Nevertheless, he was on the brink of defeat when *Serapis* caught fire. He managed to get a boarding party across, and Pearson struck, having lost 128 men killed or wounded, while Jones' casualties were 150 men. When *Bonhomme Richard* sank two days later, Jones transferred to the *Serapis*, and sailed to the Texel where he was received as a hero. Pearson and the survivors of his crew were released later. Pearson also had a hero's welcome. He was court-martialled, acquitted and knighted, as the saviour of the Baltic convoy.

ADMIRAL SIR GEORGE RODNEY

After Spain's entry into the war, Britain was threatened at Gibraltar, Minorca, and in the West Indies, where the French took back Grenada and St Vincent. The situation was retrieved by Admiral Sir George Rodney who, in 1779, was appointed C-in-C on the Leeward Islands station for the second time.

George Brydges Rodney, one of the ablest admirals of the 18th century, joined the Navy in 1732 aged 13 and, through his influential connections and natural ability, was rapidly promoted: lieutenant at 19, post captain at 23. He commanded *Eagle* in Hawke's action off Finisterre in 1747 and conducted a successful blockade of Brest in the Seven Years War. As C-in-C in the Leewards, he reduced Martinique and seized St Lucia, Grenada and St Vincent from the French.

Rodney sailed from Plymouth on 29 December 1779, flying his flag in the *Royal George* (100), with a fleet of 21 of the line and nine frigates, escorting a convoy bound for Gibraltar and the West Indies. On 8 January 1780, he intercepted the Spanish Caracca fleet, consisting of the *Guipuscoana* (64) and six frigates, escorting a convoy of 16 ships taking wheat and naval supplies to Cadiz, and captured convoy and escort intact. For Rodney, whose finances were chronically in a parlous state (he had spent some years in Paris to escape his many creditors), the prize money, estimated in Gibraltar to be worth £400,000, was very welcome.

Eight days later, some 12 miles (20km) south of Cape St Vincent, Rodney met a Spanish fleet of 11 of the line and two frigates, commanded by Admiral Don Juan de Langara, in what became known as the 'Moonlight Battle'. The Spaniards at once turned to flee for Cadiz, but Rodney, though confined to his cabin with gout, was a resolute admiral with an equally resolute flag captain in Charles Douglas. He ordered the Spaniards to be pursued and his copper-bottomed ships, running before a strong westerly wind, were faster than the

Top of page: 'Mr B seeking the bubble reputation' – a colour aquatint by George Cruikshank after a painting by Captain Marryat, dated 1835. The ferocity of the hand-to-hand fighting aboard a warship is plain to see.

Above: A short general-purpose sword, known as a hanger, dating from c.1800. This type of sword was used by naval officers before the introduction of regulation swords in the Navy in 1805. The brass hilt is decorated with a crown and foul anchor.

Above: *The Spanish ship San Domingo blows up in the course of the Moonlight Battle which was fought on 16 January 1780. In this battle, the first fleet action to be fought at night, Rodney defeated a Spanish force off Cape St Vincent. The painting is by Richard Paton.*

1780 Russia, Sweden and Denmark form the League of Armed Neutrality against Britain. Rodney's 'Moonlight Battle' victory over a Spanish fleet off Cape St Vincent (16 January).

1781 Rodney takes Dutch island of St Eustatius. Arbuthnot's failure to secure conclusive victory over the French off Chesapeake Bay (Cape Henry) on 16 March, and de Grasse's action in Chesapeake Bay on 5 September lead to surrender of the British army at Yorktown.

1782 Rodney's victory over a French fleet under de Grasse at The Saintes off Dominica (12 April).

enemy and caught them up at about 4 p.m. Rodney ordered his ships to leave their windward position and, ignoring the danger of a rocky coast, cut between the enemy and their port. At about 5 p.m., the Spanish *San Domingo* (70) blew up, with only one survivor from a ship's company of 600.

Darkness fell, but Rodney continued the pursuit and the action went on under a bright moon. By 2 a.m., six of the enemy ships of the line, including Langara's flagship *Fenix* (80), were captured. In worsening weather, one prize was wrecked and another stranded, and several of Rodney's own ships were only extricated by good seamanship from the dangers of a lee shore. However, the stores brought in Rodney's convoy temporarily relieved Gibraltar.

Despite Rodney's successes, the political situation deteriorated even further for Britain when Russia, Sweden and Denmark formed the League of Armed Neutrality against Britain late in 1780, so as to safeguard the League's shipping from British attack while trading with belligerents. To forestall the Dutch joining the League, Britain declared war against Holland in December 1780. This gave Rodney the chance of further prize money by taking the Dutch island of St Eustatius on 3 February 1781. The treasure was immense, but matters were complicated for Rodney because British mercantile interests were involved. The resulting lawsuits dragged on for years.

DECISIVE BATTLES

The battles of 1781, which decided the outcome of the American revolution, took place off Cape Henry in Chesapeake Bay, when British ships attempted to prevent French aid reaching the rebels. The first was an indecisive action on 16 March, some 40 miles (65km) north-east of Cape

Henry, between a French squadron, of eight ships of the line and two frigates, under Commodore des Touches, flying his flag in the *Duc de Bourgogne* (80), and a British squadron of eight of the line and four frigates, commanded by Rear Admiral Marriott Arbuthnot, flying his flag in the *Royal Oak* (74).

After an hour's exchange of fire, both sides lost sight of each other in haze, and the French ships stood out to sea, leaving Arbuthnot nominally in command of the Bay. But the French squadron was still intact. This was to have serious consequences for the British army ashore.

By September 1781, the army under Lord Cornwallis had advanced from South Carolina as far as Virginia, and while awaiting reinforcement by sea, it encamped near Yorktown, where it was soon surrounded by rebel forces, including French troops. Meanwhile, in August, the French admiral Comte de Grasse had brought his fleet of 24 of the line up from the Caribbean to Chesapeake Bay. To counter this threat, Rodney sent his second-in-command Rear Admiral Samuel Hood, with 14 of the line, to reinforce Rear Admiral Thomas Graves who stood off the Bay. This brought Graves' fleet up to 19 of the line,

CAPTAIN COOK

James Cook was born in 1728, the son of a Yorkshire labourer, and was largely self-educated. He went to sea as an apprentice in the east coast coal trade in 1746. In 1755 he joined the Navy as an able seaman, but with his natural aptitude for mathematics by July 1757 he had been promoted to master (the officer responsible for a ship's navigation) in the *Solebay*. In 1759 he was master of the *Pembroke* in the assault on Quebec, when he distinguished himself by his survey of the St Lawrence River, which enabled the big ships of the fleet to ascend it – the first to do so.

After the end of the Seven Years War in 1763, Cook spent five years surveying the Newfoundland coast in his own schooner, the *Grenville*. His observations of an eclipse of the Sun in 1766 impressed the Royal Society who appointed him an official observer for an expedition to Tahiti to record observations of the transit of the planet Venus across the face of the sun. The expedition was then to go on and search for the continent Terra Australis Incognita, believed to exist in the south.

Cook, now promoted to lieutenant, sailed from Plymouth on 25 August 1768 in the Whitby collier 'cat' *Endeavour*. He had no chronometer, although John Harrison had by then produced the first reliable

with Graves flying his flag in the *London* (98), Hood commanding the rear and Rear Admiral Drake the van.

On 5 September, de Grasse's fleet lay at anchor inside the Bay, apparently unaware of Graves' ships closing from sea. In the action which took place some 12 miles (20km) north-east of Cape Henry, Graves had the weather gauge and the advantage of surprise. But he fumbled his approach, and his ships lacked firm direction, so that, even after two and a half hours of indecisive action, Hood's rear squadron had still not become engaged. Graves still had the chance of a resounding victory, which would redeem the British cause on land, but he continued to dither, while spasmodic and desultory fighting went on until 5 September.

De Grasse himself seemed reluctant to engage his enemy as closely as he could have done, but his main object was, after all, to reinforce the rebel army, and he was doing that, actually reentering Chesapeake Bay on 11 September. Two days later, Graves held a council of war, a sure sign of weakness, at which it was decided, in view of the action damage to the British ships and the shortages of bread and water, to return to New

York to refit. Thus Graves sailed north, leaving de Grasse in command of Chesapeake Bay. Deprived of the expected support from sea, Cornwallis was defeated and forced to surrender his army at Yorktown on 19 October 1781. The American colonies were lost. The war had cost the Americans just under £50,000,000, but they had gained their independence, a prize without price.

Meanwhile, the war at sea went on. In the Indian Ocean, Vice Admiral Sir Edward Hughes fought five actions against the brilliant and aggressive French admiral Pierre André de Suffren, the last off Cuddalore on the east coast of India on 20 June 1783, after which de Suffren was able to raise the blockade of Cuddalore.

By then, the naval dominance of the West Indies had been settled, when Rodney foiled a French plan to take Jamaica. Rodney had gone home on sick leave, but he returned to the West Indies in February 1782, bringing with him another 17 ships of the line to reinforce his fleet. The final sea battle for the West Indies took place between Rodney, with 36 of the line, and de Grasse, with 32 of the line escorting a large convoy of merchant

Above: *In 1714 the Admiralty offered an award of £20,000 for the first chronometer that could be used accurately to determine longitude. Cook tested a number of timepieces such as this on his voyages.*

timepiece, but calculated his longitude accurately by measuring the angular distance between the Moon and a fixed star.

Endeavour reached Tahiti in April 1769 without a single case of scurvy, the result of Cook's attention to his ship's cleanliness below decks, and to his sailors' diet, which included pickled cabbage, and orange juice. The Tahitians greeted Cook and his ships with great hospitality, although he was irritated by their constant thieving.

The transit of Venus was duly recorded on Saturday 3 June 1769, and Cook went on across the Pacific, charted the coast of New Zealand, showing it to be two separate islands, and the eastern coast of Australia, and returned to England in July 1771.

Promoted Commander, Cook was given command of two more Whitby 'cats', the *Resolution* and the *Adventure*, and sailed on 13 July 1772 for a second voyage in which he finally proved that a habitable continent in the South Pacific did not exist. In January 1773, he became the first navigator to cross the Antarctic circle.

When the *Resolution* arrived at Portsmouth on 29 July 1775, Cook was promoted post captain, and elected a Fellow of the Royal Society. In June 1776, he sailed again, with the *Resolution* and another Whitby 'cat', the *Discovery*, on a voyage to the north-west coast of America. In January

Right: *A chart of Placentia in Newfoundland drawn by James Cook during his period of service there aboard HMS Northumberland in 1762.*

1778 Cook discovered the Polynesian-inhabited Hawaiian group of islands which he named the Sandwich Islands, in honour of the First Lord of the Admiralty, the Earl of Sandwich.

Cook sailed north through the Bering Strait as far as the ice would let him and then returned to the Sandwich Islands in January 1779 to refit. He was treated by the natives as a Polynesian god. But entertaining a god greatly strained local resources and Cook's departure in February 1779 was greeted with relief.

Unfortunately, *Resolution* sprung her foremast two days later. Cook had to return for repairs, his god-like reputation shattered, to be met by intense hostility. After the theft of a ship's boat, Cook went ashore to take one of the local chiefs hostage against the boat's return. But a large mob had gathered, who stabbed him to death before his marine bodyguard could drive them off. It was a miserable end for a man who had raised what would become the science of hydrography to a high plane of meticulous accuracy. From now on, the Admiralty would accept nothing less than James Cook's standard of chart-making.

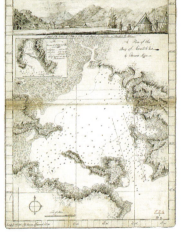

Left: *On his third voyage Cook sailed north through the Bering Straits. This plan and sketch of the Harbour of St Peter and St Paul was made on that occasion by Edward Riou.*

Below: *Riou's survey of Kealakekua Bay on the island of Hawaii. It was here that Cook was killed by rioting islanders on 14 February 1779.*

Above: *One of the first actions of the War of the First Coalition was Lord Hood's destruction of part of the French fleet at Toulon on 18 December 1793. Three French ships of the line were towed away as prizes and nine were destroyed to prevent recapture by the French. This engraving by T. Sutherland after a painting by T. Whitcombe was published in 1816 in a collection entitled Naval Achievements.*

ships, off The Saintes, a small group of islands in the channel between Guadaloupe and Dominica.

THE BATTLE OF THE SAINTES

The action began at 7 a.m. on 12 April 1782, when the opposing lines of battle slowly sailed past each other on opposite tacks, exchanging broadsides as they passed. But at about 9.15 the wind suddenly veered four points (45°). The French station-keeping grew ragged in the lee of Dominica. Gaps appeared in their line. Rodney, flying his flag in the *Formidable* (90), seized the chance to sail through one of these gaps. He was followed by the *Duke* (90), the *Bedford* (74) and three more ships. Rear Admiral Sir Samuel Hood followed suit, with all 12 of his rear division. The British thus gained the weather gauge, while the French tried desperately to reform their line on their leeward ships. But they never recovered their fleet formation and, in a day-long battle, lost the 74s *Glorieux*, *César*, *Hector* and *Hercule*, all of which struck.

Late in the afternoon, the ex-British *Ardent* also struck, and was followed at 6.29 that evening by de Grasse's flagship, *Ville de Paris* (104), Hood in his flagship *Barfleur* (90) accepting de Grasse's surrender. Four hundred of *Ville de Paris*'s crew had been killed, and her upper deck was so thickly covered in blood that when Hood's officers went on board it flowed over the tops of their shoes.

To Hood's great indignation, Rodney did not pursue the enemy. Sixteen minutes after *Ville de*

'The Spanish left one brig on fire before they left her, but our boats crew whent aboard of her and made some plunder out of her ... she was lading with guns for the iseland. Then the boats rowed about 3 leegs up the river and then they fell in with a planters shugar store house with about 200 boxes of shugar. Our boats toke 6 boxes of the same and some of the other boats some and the rest they set on fire with the house and burnt it down and then they returned back and brought into the fleet 3 brigs and one ship, and one they burnt. 3 of them lading with flower and provisions for the iseland and the other lading with seder and mahoggamy from the Spanish Maine. Three of them American bilt ships and two Spanish ships. The shugar that our ships boats toke every man received one and a half pounds each.'

PRESSED MAN ABLE SEAMAN JOHN GOLDSMITH WRITING
ABOARD HMS *PROTHEE* IN 1782

Paris struck, Rodney signalled his fleet to bring to (i.e. bring their ships to a stop, with all sails set) on the port tack, and his ships remained stopped all night. In Hood's opinion, many more enemy ships could have been taken if they had been vigorously pursued immediately after the battle. As it was, the disorganised French fleet was allowed to escape, to join the convoy and a Spanish squadron of nine ships of the line. Hood was eventually sent after the enemy but, as he pointedly wrote in his report to Rodney, he missed the main body of the French fleet by only one day.

The French losses at The Saintes were six ships, over 2,000 men killed and wounded, and many more taken prisoner. The British lost no ships, but

had over 1,000 casualties. It was a great victory. Nevertheless, many of Rodney's own officers thought he had 'botched his battle'.

Peace negotiations had been taking place while the fighting had been going on, and resulted in the Treaty of Versailles in 1783. Britain had lost the American colonies, but retained Canada, and Gibraltar, whose siege had finally been lifted in that year.

When the French Revolution broke out in 1789, William Pitt's government deliberately stayed aloof and took no part in the first coalition against France. Pitt actually reduced the Navy in 1792, confidently looking forward to 15 years of peace. But after Louis XVI's execution on 21 January 1793, the government at once ordered the French minister to leave England. France declared war on Britain and the Dutch Republic on 1 February. There was to be war for the next 22 years, with only a brief respite in 1801–1803, after the Treaty of Amiens.

THE FIRST COALITION

Britain then joined the First Coalition, of Austria, Prussia, and Holland, and the Navy immediately resumed the tactic of blockade, arresting all French merchant ships and preventing neutral ships from taking grain to France. The first battle of the war came after several weeks of patrolling in the Western Approaches by the Channel Fleet of 26 ships of the line under Admiral Howe. On 28 May 1794, Howe's flagship, the *Queen Charlotte* (100), sighted a French fleet of 26 of the line,

under Admiral Villaret-Joyeuse, escorting a large convoy bringing grain from America to France where there was a grave famine.

Joyeuse had the weather gauge and for three days fended off Howe's attempts to reach the grain convoy. Some skirmishing took place until at last, on 1 June, Howe's ships bore down on the French line, intending to break through at several points. *Queen Charlotte, Marlborough, Defence, Royal George* and *Queen* succeeded, but the rest misunderstood the orders, or merely failed to carry them out, and for a time there was a chaotic mêlée, in which six French ships of the line struck, *Le Vengeur du Peuple* (74) foundered after a furious duel with the *Brunswick*, and Joyeuse's flagship, *Montagne* (120), was badly damaged and suffered 300 killed.

It was a victory, dubbed 'The Glorious First of June', but the grain convoy, which many thought Howe should also have captured, escaped.

Above: *On 5 January 1795 the British warship* Blanche *fought a five-hour long engagement with the French ship* La Pique *in West Indian waters. This engraving from Naval Achievements shows the moment when* Blanche *prevailed and* La Pique *was captured.*

Right: *A view from the southwest of Forts Bourbon and Louis on the island of Martinque published by Rev. C. Williams in 1796. Fort Louis was captured by a naval landing party on 20 March 1794, and two days later Fort Bourbon and the rest of the island also fell to the forces of Admiral Jervis and General Grey.*

Richard Howe was the very pattern of an 18th century naval officer. Nelson once called him 'our great master in naval tactics and bravery'. He was a post captain at 20, and served with distinction in the War of the Austrian Succession and in the Seven Years War, when he led the line at Quiberon Bay. Hawke said of him: 'I have tried my Lord Howe on most important occasions. He never asked me how he was to execute any service entrusted to his charge, but always went straight forward and performed it'. He commanded the British fleet, supporting his brother, General Sir William Howe, in the early stages of the American War of Independence, and it was Howe who finally relieved Gibraltar in 1782. But, by the 'Glorious First of June', he was 68 years old and weary after weeks at sea. A younger fleet commander might well have pursued and captured the grain convoy.

As in earlier years, the war rapidly spread worldwide. In the Mediterranean in 1793, Admiral Viscount Hood occupied Toulon and Corsica, but had to disengage from both. In the West Indies, Vice Admiral Sir John Jervis, with Lieutenant General Charles Grey, captured Martinique in March 1794. In March of the following year, Vice Admiral William Hotham had an inconclusive engagement against the French in the Gulf of Genoa, and a second action off Hyères in July, when one French 74 caught fire and blew up but a wind change deprived him of the chance of a more decisive victory.

In June 1795, Vice Admiral William Cornwallis skilfully extricated his squadron from a vastly superior French force off Belleisle, and Admiral Viscount Bridport's Channel Fleet fought a spirited action off the Ile de Groix, Quiberon Bay, in which three French 74s were taken as prizes. In September, Vice Admiral Sir George Elphinstone (later Lord Keith), with a naval brigade commanded by General Alfred Clark, took the Dutch colony at the Cape of Good Hope.

The Royal Navy retired from the Mediterranean in 1796, but there were more gains that year in the

West Indies, when Rear Admiral Sir Hugh Christian took St Lucia, St Vincent and Grenada. In February 1797, Rear Admiral Henry Harvey and Lieutenant General Ralph Abercromby captured Trinidad from the Spanish.

Britain's retreat from the Mediterranean was taken as a sign of weakness in the Coalition, and was the signal for Austria to leave the Coalition in 1797, as Holland and Prussia had done in 1795, leaving Britain to stand alone against France. However, it was in this year of 1797, when Britain's fortunes were at a low ebb, that the Navy won one of the greatest battles in its history.

JERVIS AND CAPE ST VINCENT

John Jervis has the reputation of being one of the sternest and grimmest officers of the 18th century Navy, but he was very popular with the lower deck, largely because of the circumstances of his early life. He joined the Navy aged thirteen, with no money over his pay. His father had not honoured a draft of £20 he had drawn on him, but Jervis paid back the sum, shilling by shilling, in three years. This left him so poor he could not afford to pay his mess expenses, so he withdrew from the gunroom and did not eat with the other midshipmen, or associate with them except during instruction or on duty. Instead, he made friends amongst the warrant officers, and this close companionship with the lower ranks of the Navy gave him a deeper knowledge of the British sailor than any other naval officer of his time.

Jervis was made a post captain at the age of 25, and served under Saunders at Quebec in 1759. In 1782, in command of the *Foudroyant* in the War of

American Independence, he pulled off a spectacular *coup* by capturing the French ship of the line *Pégase*, and was made a baronet. In 1795, he was appointed commander-in-chief in the Mediterranean, where he began upon an ultimately triumphant campaign.

In January 1797, Jervis was using the Tagus river in Portugal as an advanced base for his fleet. There he heard of the sailing of a huge Spanish fleet which intended to join the French and Dutch fleets at Brest and clear the Channel for yet another proposed invasion of Britain. Jervis's 15 of the line and four frigates weighed anchor on 18 January and sailed, with Jervis flying his flag in the *Victory*, to cruise off Cape St Vincent.

The Spanish fleet of 27 ships of the line, commanded by Admiral Don José de Cordova, flying his flag in the gigantic *Santissima Trinidad* (136), sailed from Cartagena, intending to put in at Cadiz on their way north. A strong easterly blew them through the Strait of Gibraltar and far to the westward, so that they had to beat back to Cadiz. They were off Cape St Vincent when Jervis met them on the foggy morning of 14 February 1797.

Jervis was not only outnumbered but outgunned, with a total of 1,232 guns against the Spaniards' 2,308, but he had some star-studded names in his fleet; Commodore Horatio Nelson, flying his broad pendant in the *Captain* (74), who had joined Jervis from Gibraltar on 13 February, Captain Thomas Troubridge in the *Culloden* (74), Rear Admiral William Parker, flying his flag in the *Prince George* (98), Captain James Saumarez in the *Orion* (74), and Captain Cuthbert Collingwood in the *Excellent* (74)

But, impressive though the Spanish ships might have appeared, they were undermanned, with a large proportion of untrained men. Furthermore, they were by then in a state of considerable disorder, having lost all cohesion as a fleet, and

Above: *Admiral William Hotham fought an inconclusive action with the French on 14 March 1795 in the Gulf of Genoa. Two French ships,* Ça-Ira *and* Censeur, *were captured.*

Above: *Sir John Jervis, a portrait by Sir William Beechey. Admiral Jervis won a famous victory against a much larger Spanish fleet on 14 February 1797 off Cape St Vincent. He was created Earl St Vincent by George III in recognition of this triumph.*

were sailing in two straggling divisions some distance apart, with several ships trying to make Cadiz independently.

Jervis led his ships in line ahead between the two enemy groups, first engaging the lee division. Meanwhile, the larger weather division was sailing down on a parallel opposite course to the British line. Jervis signalled his ships to tack in succession to engage the enemy, but the leading Spanish ships were by then so far ahead that they looked as though they would escape.

It was at this point that Nelson ordered the *Captain*, fourth from the British rear, to wear ship (bringing the ship on the other tack by bringing the wind round the stern, as opposed to tacking, when the wind is brought round the bow). *Captain* hauled out of line and, followed by Collingwood in the *Excellent*, sailed across the intervening water to cross the bows and engage the *Santissima Trinidad* and two other ships of the line.

This was a very bold manoeuvre, totally contrary to the *Fighting Instructions* and thus a court martial offence, because no signal had yet been made allowing ships to act independently. *Captain*'s log shows that Nelson gave the order to wear ship at 12.50 p.m. It is a measure of the almost telepathic *rapport* which Jervis and Nelson had already established between them that *Victory*'s log shows that at 12.51 p.m., only a minute after Nelson's order to haul out of line and head

directly for the enemy, Jervis actually signalled to his fleet 'Take up Suitable Stations and Engage Enemy as arriving up in succession', thus giving Nelson permission to do exactly what he was already doing.

Captain came under such intense fire that her foremast and her wheel were shot away, but she still succeeded in getting alongside the *San Nicolas* (80) which was at that time entangled with the *San Josef* (112), both Spanish ships being under a heavy fire from the *St George*. *Captain* had embarked some soldiers of the Welch Regiment who were acting as Marines, and when Nelson called for a boarding party, the soldiers, with as Nelson said 'an alacrity that will ever do them credit', swarmed up the sides of the *San Nicolas* to overpower her crew and then go on to take the *San Josef*. Nelson later described this as his 'patent bridge for boarding enemies'.

The Spanish lee division was by now coming to assist the weather division. Jervis decided that it would be prudent to withdraw his ships, some of them badly battered, rather than begin another encounter with fresh enemies. He signalled his fleet to bring to, to cover his own disabled ships and the four Spanish ships of the line which had been taken as prizes.

Meanwhile, the remaining Spanish ships, now thoroughly demoralized and keeping no sort of fleet order, made their escape as best they could. It was a great victory, but it could have been even better had Jervis pursued his enemy through the night. However, he was created Earl St Vincent, the title being suggested by George III himself, and Nelson was knighted. 'St Vincent' became one of the Welch Regiment's proudest battle honours.

THE SPITHEAD MUTINY

The news of Jervis' victory was well received in the country, but it was followed on 16 April by the stunning news that the Channel Fleet under Admiral Bridport had mutinied at Spithead. Nor was it just one ship, or even a few disaffected ships. The whole fleet was involved. Bridport's own flagship, the *Royal George,* 15 other ships of the line, and every frigate at Spithead, all refused to obey Lord Bridport's order to weigh anchor.

The mutinies at Spithead and later at the Nore are often popularly supposed to have been

Above: *A colour etching by Thomas Rowlandson of a midshipman, 1799.*

Right: *This portrait by Thomas Hudson shows Admiral Pocock wearing the first official naval uniform, introduced in 1748.*

Above: *A cabin-boy, again by Rowlandson.*

Above: *Watercolour illustrations of some of the signal flags that were used by the Navy for communication between ships.*

Right: *The manoeuvre during the Battle of Cape St Vincent when Nelson in* Captain *hauled his ship out of line and set course for the Spanish windward division to engage the Santissima Trinidad.*

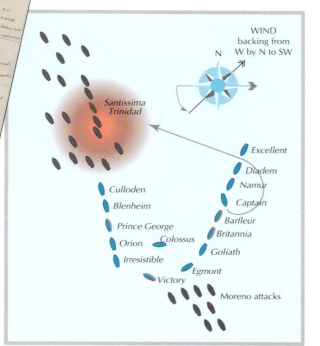

caused by resentment at brutal punishments in the fleet, and the ruthless behaviour of the press gangs ashore. Punishment rested entirely in the hands of individual ship's captains, who had the power to decide the scale and even the nature of the punishment.

Ill-treatment, which had previously been the subject of several ineffectual seamens' petitions to the Admiralty, was certainly one cause of the mutinies at Spithead and the Nore. But the main grievance was pay. In 1795, under the pressure of war, the pay of a private soldier was raised to one shilling a day. It was only justice that the pay of an ordinary seaman should be similarly increased. The Admiralty did not do so. Lord Spencer, the First Lord, received several warnings that trouble was brewing in the fleet over the question of pay, but he evidently believed that, as in the past, the matter could be ignored.

However, there had recently been a small but significant change in recruiting for the Navy. Under the desperate need to man the Navy, Pitt's Government passed the Quota Acts of 1795 and 1796. Under these, towns and counties were required to provide men for the Navy according to their size. Thus, Yorkshire's quota was 1,081, and Rutland's 23; London had to provide 5,704, Newcastle 1,240, and Bristol 666.

Many of the Quota men were the uttermost sweepings of local gaols: small-time criminals, pickpockets, poachers, beggars, ne'er-do-wells and local 'hard cases'. But some men enlisted voluntarily, attracted by the bounties offered which could amount to as much as £70. Amongst them were men of some education and professional background: discredited or bankrupted businessmen, disgraced lawyers, failed school teachers, and men of some previous standing in their communities whose families wished them to disappear to mitigate some scandal.

THE PRESS GANGS

Impressment for naval or military service goes back to Anglo-Saxon times, and was first made legal by an Act of Mary Tudor in 1556. It applied equally to service ashore and afloat. Cromwell's 'New Model' army, for instance, was largely recruited by impressment. But naval service was always so unpopular and the need for seamen always so great, that impressment was used by the Royal Navy (and by the navies of other countries) through much of its history in time of war.

It was an inefficient, expensive and inhumane way of obtaining men. To try and improve it, in 1768 the Admiralty established the Impress Service, which at its peak employed a full admiral, and 130 other officers, and set up an office in many seaports and other towns, where the officer in charge would hold pre-signed but undated warrants for pressing men, ready for use when the need arose.

The heyday of the press gangs, in the popular imagination and in fact, was in the wars from 1793 to 1815. The general public were, in theory, safeguarded from the press gangs' activities. Each gang had to be commanded by a commissioned officer, bearing a warrant recently signed by a magistrate. The gangs could only seize able-bodied seaman or watermen, who had to be British subjects between the ages of 18 and 55 years, and not carrying a certificate of exemption. There were other exemptions, for apprentices, masters and mates of merchantmen, crews of merchantmen outward bound and Trinity House vessels. Landsmen, being theoretically volunteers because they did not use the sea as a profession, were immune from impressment.

All other seamen and mariners were liable to impressment but in practice nobody in authority ever questioned too closely whether a pressed man was actually a seaman or a mariner. Many men were pressed through the Vagrancy Acts, by which local magistrates cleared their gaols and rid themselves of their worst characters by drafting them into the Navy.

Often, some or even all of an inward merchantman's crew were pressed. A man who had spent months or even years at sea, and was looking forward to seeing his wife and family, would be pressed aboard a man-of-war and forced to spend more years at sea. Many foreigners were illegally pressed (there were 71 foreigners, of 12 different nationalities, serving on board *Victory* at Trafalgar, and the number was even higher on some ships).

Captains of men-of-war were always on the lookout for men, hoping to exchange their worst for a merchantman's best, while the merchant skippers became adept at concealing their best men on board. A warship convoying merchantmen to a foreign port would press their men on arrival. A cartel ship (a cartel being an agreement between warring nations for the exchange of prisoners-of-war while the war was still on) was a much sought-after target, for it would yield hundreds of able-bodied British seamen, recently released from French, Spanish or Dutch prisons, who could be pressed at once.

Impressment ceased, for all practical purposes, at the end of the Napoleonic War in 1815, but the right to operate press gangs was still retained until the need for them was finally ended by the introduction of continuous service in the Royal Navy in 1853.

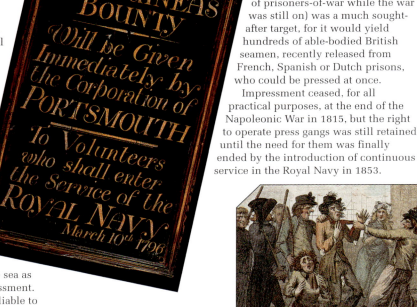

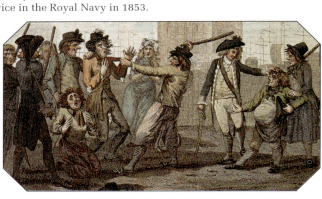

Above: *Cruikshank's satire 'The Battle of the Nile' – even Nelson's crews contained illegally pressed foreigners.*

Left: *A bounty board dating from 1796 offering two guineas to volunteers prepared to serve in the Navy.*

Below: *'Manning The Navy', a cartoon from 1790. The ruthless behaviour of press gangs did little for the Navy's image ashore.*

Right: A fine portrait of Admiral Lord Howe, 'Black Dick', by John Singleton Copley. Howe was a strict disciplinarian, but was still popular with ordinary seamen. In 1797 he received the initial petitions from the leaders of the Spithead Mutiny.

1783 Hughes' action against de Suffren off Cuddalore (20 June). Peace of Versailles.

1793 Louis XVI executed in France. The First Coalition (Austria, Britain, Holland and Prussia) at war with Revolutionary France.

1794 French West Indian colonies are captured. Howe's victory on the Glorious First of June.

It is impossible to determine precisely the part Quota men played in the 'Breeze' at Spithead, but certainly they must have introduced new awareness, literacy and some smattering of knowledge of the law to the messdecks. For the first time there were now men in the Navy able to point out the wrongs done to the sailor, and ways of putting those wrongs right.

Whoever they were, the leaders of the mutiny preserved their own anonymity while they succeeded in involving almost every man on the lower deck, from 'old salts' to newly-pressed men, from raw ordinary seamen to senior petty officers; honest men and crooks, native Englishmen and foreigners, young and old, all took part, and not one gave the game away. They made their plans and kept them secret for weeks, on messdecks where privacy was impossible, where 'narks' abounded, only too ready to relay news of disaffection to the quarterdeck, and where the least whisper of mutiny could mean the cat or the noose.

By March 1797, the leaders had prepared a 'humble petition', soberly and respectfully phrased, addressing itself only to the particular grievance of pay. Written out separately, but all clearly copies of the same original, the petitions were smuggled ashore and sent to Admiral Lord Howe, retired but still the titular C-in-C of the Channel Fleet (Bridport was his second-in-command).

'Black Dick' was very popular with the lower deck, who thought of him as the sailors' friend and their best hope at this time. But he was now seventy-two, and a martyr to gout. He was at Bath, taking the waters for his affliction. However, he took the petitions up to London but, once again, Lord Spencer did nothing.

After a month's silence, the sailors decided 'Black Dick' had let them down. They prepared another petition, directly to Parliament, and decided to refuse to put to sea until the demands were met. On 13 April, Captain Patton visited the *Queen Charlotte* and was astonished and dismayed to see sailors gathering in groups and arguing together on the upper deck. Some had even trespassed onto the sacred quarterdeck, with the officers doing nothing to stop them.

When Patton got ashore, he had a message sent by the newly-installed 'Semaphore' on Southsea

PUNISHMENT

Punishments were many and various. Floggings were frequent, though not as frequent as popularly imagined, because many captains found flogging an inflexible and time-consuming punishment. The penalty for mutiny was death – rarely carried out – or flogging through the fleet: 300 to 500 lashes, administered 20 to 30 lashes at a time, the convicted man being rowed from one ship to another to undergo his punishment. If a doctor pronounced the man unfit for further lashes, the remainder would be held over and administered on another occasion, when his back had healed.

One eyewitness of this terrible procedure, which was called 'going through the fleet', said: 'I believe no man has ever been known to hold up his head after going through the Fleet. The heavy launch is fitted with a triangle, to which the wretch is tied, as if to a cross. It takes some hours to row (sometimes against wind and tide) through the Fleet. The torture is, therefore, protracted till, to

Right: 'The Point of Honor', a satire by George Cruikshank that pictures the grim scene as a miscreant is about to be flogged on the upper deck of his ship with the whole crew assembled to witness the ordeal.

Below: Mutiny on the Bounty – an event that was popularly, but wrongly, supposed to have been caused by Captain Bligh's brutal punishment of his crew.

Right: A 19th century cat 'o nine tails. Popular lore held that it had nine lashes because flogging by 'a trinity of trinities' was both more effective and more efficient. It was not unknown for offenders to die after such a punishment.

beach, which was relayed to the Admiralty roof (in three and a half minutes) via Portsdown Hill, Telegraph Hill near Petersfield, Blackdown, Hanscomb, Cabbage Hill, Putney, and Chelsea Hospital: 'Mutiny brewing at Spithead'.

On 16 April the Admiralty sent Bridport orders to prepare to put to sea. He replied that he was convinced his crews would not sail. Nor would they. When the signal was hoisted to weigh anchor, nothing happened. Instead, the sailors of the *Queen Charlotte* manned the fore shrouds and gave three ringing cheers, the signal for the mutiny to begin, answered at once from every other ship.

Left: *An engraving by B. Cole of the Old Admiralty building near Whitehall in London. In 1797 news of the incipient mutiny was relayed to the Admiralty from Southsea beach by semaphore in less than four minutes.*

24th June 1797

My Lord...

'*The Queen Charlottes Ships Company in general, whilst I served with them, and they were under their late Captain [-] Douglas (before he was much affected by the complaint of which he died) were taken together one of the most patient, orderly and well disposed crew I would ever wish to command. But how they became so much changed as to be deemed principals on occasion of the late disturbances in the Channel Fleet is more than I can account for ...*'

LETTER FROM EARL HOWE TO LORD KEITH, HIS SUCCESSOR AS C-IN-C OF THE CHANNEL FLEET

---

use a sailor's phrase, "their very soul is cut out". After this dreadful sentence they almost always die.'

Men could be gagged, with a piece of iron or wood inserted in their mouths, for swearing or insolent language. Running the gauntlet, a penalty for theft, meant a man having to go between two lines of his messmates who each beat him with a rope's end as he passed. In keel-hauling (not actually done in the Navy after about 1770), a man was dragged underwater from one side of the ship to the other, a process in which many drowned.

The punishment for desertion was, in theory, death, but again it was rarely carried out, for men were too scarce. In the late 18th and early 19th centuries, desertion ran like an epidemic through the Navy. On average during the Napoleonic wars, men deserted at the rate of some 600 a month. Nelson calculated that in the war up to 1803, 42,000 men deserted from the fleet, and a third of those who 'ran' in the naval word, were permanently lost to the Navy. Most of the deserters were good men, for more able seamen deserted than ordinary seamen, and more ordinary seamen than landsmen ('landsmen' was the rate given to men without any naval training who served on board warships). Even the exertions of the press gangs could not make up the deficiencies caused by desertion.

DELEGATES AND ADMIRALS

The mutiny, though it remained a very polite affair, now began to gain momentum. Every ship sent two Delegates, who met daily in the *Queen Charlotte's* Admiral's cabin and virtually ran the fleet, enforcing discipline and maintaining the usual ship's routine. Captains were paid all the proper marks of respect when entering or leaving their ships. But the Delegates themselves were paid the same marks of respect.

Lord Spencer and the rest of the Board were slow to realise the extent of the mutiny. They sent Bridport orders to sail which were so far removed from reality that even Bridport thought them ridiculous. Lord Spencer himself came down to Portsmouth. Concessions were made, *very* reluctantly, on pay, but not on food, leave or the redress of grievances. An Admiralty pardon was offered, which the Delegates rejected. The only pardon worth having was the King's. Their petition must be met in full and put into effect by Act of Parliament. There was a furious argument in the Great Cabin between three admirals and the Delegates, when the admirals were lucky not to be assaulted.

After bureaucratic delay in drafting the Act, and an easterly wind which kept the ships from sailing, the mutiny broke out again in a much

Above: *An aquatint of the Board Room of the Admiralty in 1808 by Thomas Rowlandson and Pugin, part of a series produced for the London publisher Ackermann. Lord Spencer, the First Lord, and the members of the Board initially underestimated the gravity of the situation when the Spithead mutiny was brewing.*

Right: *A Georgian naval officer's hat and hatbox.*

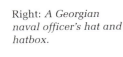

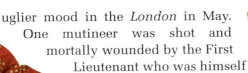

Above: *The neckerchief worn by Lt Haswell of HMS* Pallas *when he led a boarding party against the French corvette* La Tapageuse *in 1806. The bullet hole was made by a musket ball that grazed his head. The patriotic sword and scabbard (top right) were awarded to him by Lloyds of London in recognition of his gallantry.*

Right: *Richard Parker who was executed on board the* Sandwich *on 30 June 1797 for having led the mutiny at the Nore.*

1795 Hotham's action in the Gulf of Genoa (14 March). Cornwallis' retreat from Belleisle (17 June). Bridport's action off Ile de Groix (23 June). Office of Hydrographer of the Navy is established.

1796 Christian takes St Lucia, St Vincent and Grenada.

1797 Jervis' victory off Cape St Vincent (14 February). Mutinies at Spithead and the Nore. Seamen's Bill is passed and able seamen's pay is raised. Duncan's victory over the Dutch at Camperdown (11 October).

uglier mood in the *London* in May. One mutineer was shot and mortally wounded by the First Lieutenant who was himself then nearly hanged. The tense situation was calmed by one of the *London*'s Delegates, AB John Fleming, who might have been a Quota man, and made an excellent advocate.

A hundred officers were put ashore, including two admirals, the Captain of the *London*, the Captain and many of the officers of the *Duke*, and all the officers of the *Glory*. Portsmouth, Gosport and Southsea were suddenly filled with un-employed and homeless naval officers, their chests and swords.

The Seamen's Bill was passed on 8 May 1797. A new Royal Pardon was issued, Lord Howe visited the fleet with Lady Howe, had himself rowed to every ship, and later took wine with the Delegates. All the Delegates' demands were granted, if not at once, then at least in principle. It was a famous victory for ordinary men who combined irresistibly to get their rights. Apart from the trouble in the *London*, there was no bloodshed. No Spithead mutineer was court-martialled, imprisoned, flogged, sentenced to death or hanged.

FURTHER UNREST

The same could not be said of the mutiny in the North Sea Fleet which began in the old depot ship, the *Sandwich* at the Nore in May. It lasted until well into June before it collapsed, when 412 mutineers were court-martialled, 29 imprisoned, nine flogged, 59 sentenced to death and 29 were hanged, including Richard Parker, the mutiny's leader.

There were also mutinies at the Cape, in the East Indies, and off Cadiz when, later in the year, 'Spithead-tainted' ships joined the Mediterranean Fleet. John Jervis was not Bridport or Lord Spencer. He was the grimmest disciplinarian in the Navy and, furthermore, he was in a difficult situation, commanding a fleet some way from home, off an enemy coast.

Thus, when 'Old Jarvey' dealt with a mutiny, there were no Royal Pardons, no Delegates, no debate, no delay at all. He hanged mutineers first, and notified the Admiralty later.

Later, the unrest at the Nore spread to Admiral Duncan's fleet, then lying in Yarmouth Roads. Duncan had been blockading the Dutch fleet in the Texel since the Dutch became the allies of France in 1794. A mutiny in his ships laid the country open to a Dutch invasion, and Duncan took typically robust steps to deal with it. He quickly identified and isolated the ring-leaders in his flagship, the *Venerable* (74), and by the force of his personality won the rest of the ship's company over to his side. In the *Adamant* (50), he seized one mutineer by the collar and holding him with one hand suspended him over the side, saying: 'My lads, look at this fellow – he dares to deprive me of the command of the fleet'. The rest of the crew cheered and the situation was thus defused.

Adam Duncan had served as a midshipman in the *Centurion* with Keppel, and as a post captain commanded the *Valiant*, Keppel's flagship in the expedition to Belleisle in 1761. He commanded the *Monarch* in the 'Moonlight Battle' in 1780 and served under Howe at the relief of Gibraltar.

Having dealt with the mutiny, Duncan sailed again for the Texel but his ships deserted him one by one and returned to England until only the *Venerable* and the *Adamant* were left. However, Duncan stayed off the Texel, and fooled the Dutch by making signals, as though to a fleet just over the horizon.

Duncan's ships did return to him, one by one, but he had to take them back to Yarmouth Roads in October 1797 to refit and revictual, leaving frigates to stand guard over the Texel. When one of them appeared, flying a signal that the enemy ships were out, Duncan sailed at once with 16 ships of the line (including Captain Bligh in the *Director* (64)) and sighted the Dutch fleet of 16 of the line and seven frigates under Vice Admiral Jan de Winter, flying his flag in the *Vrijheid* (74), about three miles (5km) northwest of Camperdown (Kamperduijn), on the Dutch coast.

Duncan attacked just after noon without waiting to form a line of battle, engaging the Dutch van with nine ships while Vice Admiral Richard Onslow in the *Monarch* (74) took on the rear with seven ships. A ferocious battle began, lasting over three hours, in which the British had the advantage of heavier guns and the weather gauge. In the rear, five Dutch ships struck to Onslow, including Rear Admiral Reynties' flagship *Jupiter* (74). Ably assisted by Bligh in the *Director* in the van, Duncan fought a personal battle with de Winter's ship *Vrijheid* which finally struck at 3.15 p.m., when de Winter himself was the only man left unwounded on his flagship's deck. Four more Dutch ships in the van also struck, making Duncan's victory complete.

Duncan was remarkably magnanimous in victory. When de Winter came on board *Venerable* to surrender, Duncan refused to accept his offered sword and shook his hand instead. Thus the year of 1797, which had seen so much turmoil in the fleet, ended on a graceful note of victory.

Above: *The Battle of Camperdown, 11 October 1797, painted by Philippe Jacques de Lotherbourg. Earlier in the year, Admiral Duncan had acted decisively to quell a mutiny among his men and this victory over a Dutch fleet did much to restore morale.*

Left: *A moment of magnanimity – Admiral Duncan refuses the sword proferred by the defeated Dutch Admiral de Winter after the Battle of Camperdown and offers to shake his hand instead. The painting is by Samuel Drummond.*

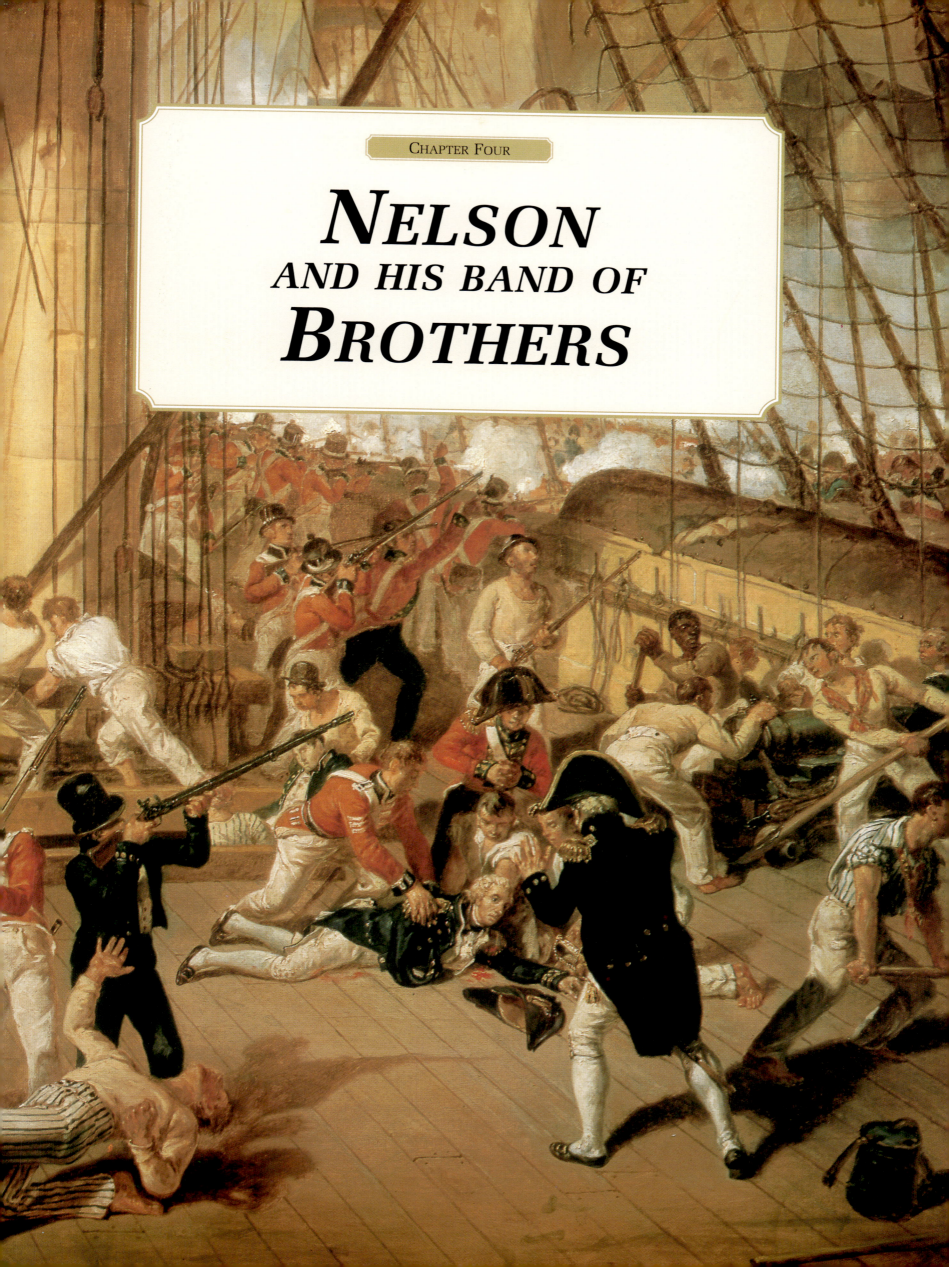

NELSON
AND HIS BAND OF
BROTHERS

Previous pages: *Nelson falls mortally wounded at the Battle of Trafalgar. He was shot by a marksman firing from the fighting top of the French warship* Redoutable. *The painting is the work of Denis Dighton.*

Below: *Youthful Intrepidity: Young Nelson's Attack and Chase After a Bear, a plate that first appeared in Edward Orme's biography of 1806. Nelson's personal courage in the face of danger was well documented.*

'What has poor Horace *done*,' wrote Captain Maurice Suckling to the Rev Edmund Nelson, 'who is so weak, that he above all the rest should be sent to rough it out at sea? But let him come; and the first time we go into action, a cannon-ball may knock off his head, and provide for him at once.'

So Horatio Nelson was entered on the books of the *Raisonnable* (64), his uncle's ship, as a midshipman, in November 1770, when he was 12 years and two months old, and joined her in March 1771. His career was in many ways very typical of a naval officer of the late 18th and early 19th centuries, but in some curious manner everything he did or said was raised to a higher degree of intensity than normal. He seemed to live his life at the extreme limits of emotion and ambition. He was, for instance, sublimely brave, with a reckless disregard for personal danger, but he also displayed a hypochondriac's obsessive preoccupation with the state of his health.

Above: *Rear Admiral Lord Nelson, KB, a portrait by the Austrian court painter Heinrich Füger. It was painted in 1800 in Vienna, which Nelson visited on his journey back to England from Italy.*

In his first years in the Navy, Nelson had a great variety of sea experience. In 1773, he sailed with an expedition in search of an Arctic route to the Pacific. He was then appointed midshipman in the frigate *Seahorse* and served in the East Indies until 1775 when he was invalided from his ship with malaria. He passed the examination for lieutenant in April 1777, at the age of 19, and served in the War of American Independence. He was second lieutenant of the frigate *Lowestoft* which sailed for Jamaica in April 1777, then in September 1798 he was first lieutenant in the *Bristol* (50) and finally in December he was given his first command, the brig *Badger*. In June 1779, a few months short of his 21st birthday, he was made post captain and appointed in command of the frigate *Hinchinbroke*.

From February to April 1780, Nelson was senior officer in command of a disastrous expedition to attack the Spanish fort at San Juan in Nicaragua. The fort was eventually taken, largely because of Nelson's leadership, but the expedition suffered many casualties from yellow fever and illness, including Nelson, who became too sick to take up his next appointment in command of the frigate *Janus*. He arrived back in Portsmouth in the *Lion* in December so sick he could only just make the coach journey to London. After convalescence, he took command of the frigate *Albemarle* in August 1781, bound for the North American station, where he served until the end of the war in 1783.

In 1784, Nelson went to the West Indies in command of the frigate *Boreas* for his only

peacetime commission as a captain. There he met and, in 1787, married Frances Nesbit, the widowed niece of the President of Nevis. When he returned home, the peacetime Navy was shrinking, and he had to spend the next five years on half-pay.

PERSONAL INJURY

When the War against Revolutionary France began in 1793, Nelson was re-employed and given command of the *Agamemnon* (64) in January. He served under Lord Hood in the Mediterranean and then, from January to August 1794, took part in a campaign to capture Corsica from the French. On 12 July, during the siege of Calvi, he was struck violently in the chest and face by splinters, stones and sand from a battery hit by an enemy shell. Although he was in great pain, he wrote to Lord Hood that evening: 'I got a little hurt this morning; not much, as you may judge from my writing'. At first the surgeons hoped to save his sight, but he was eventually blind in his right eye.

However, Nelson remained in command of the *Agamemnon* and in 1795 was one of the very few captains to distinguish himself in Hotham's two actions, in the Gulf of Genoa in March, and off Hyères in July. He was promoted commodore, flying his broad pendant in the *Captain*. Having distinguished himself by his unorthodox tactics in John Jervis' victory off Cape St Vincent in February 1797, he was created a Knight of the Order of the Bath. His promotion to Rear Admiral of the Blue followed shortly thereafter. He hoisted his flag in the *Theseus* (74) and returned home.

In July 1797, Nelson led an attempt to capture a Spanish treasure ship at Santa Cruz, Tenerife, in the Canary Islands. Everything went wrong and during an assault on the mole of Santa Cruz Nelson had his right elbow shattered by grapeshot. He was laid in the bottom of a boat which began to row back to *Theseus*. But when the *Fox* cutter was sunk nearby, leaving the water full of struggling figures, he insisted that his boat should pick up as many survivors as possible.

The boat passed within hailing distance of the *Seahorse* (38), commanded by Captain Thomas Fremantle, who was taking part in the action and had left his wife on board, but Nelson refused to approach the ship. When he was warned that in his present state he might die, he said 'Then I will die; for I would rather suffer death than alarm Mrs Fremantle by her seeing me in this state, when I can give her no tidings whatever of her husband.' Then, twisting a rope round his left arm, he climbed *Theseus*' side unaided, crying 'Let me alone! I have got my legs left, and one arm.' His right arm was amputated 'very high, near the shoulder' in *Theseus*' cockpit that evening by Thomas Eshelby, the ship's surgeon, assisted by M. Louis Remonier, a Royalist Frenchman.

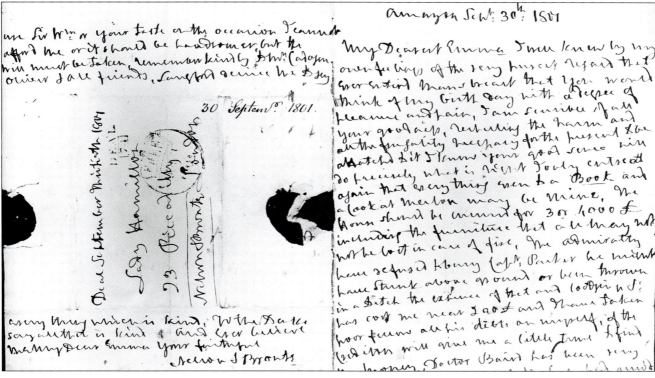

Above and left: *Examples of Nelson's handwriting before and after he lost his right arm during the assault on Santa Cruz in 1797. Nelson wrote the letter (above) to William Suckling in 1795 with his right hand. By contrast, the letter to Emma Hamilton (left) dated HMS* Amazon *30 September 1801, was written with his left hand.*

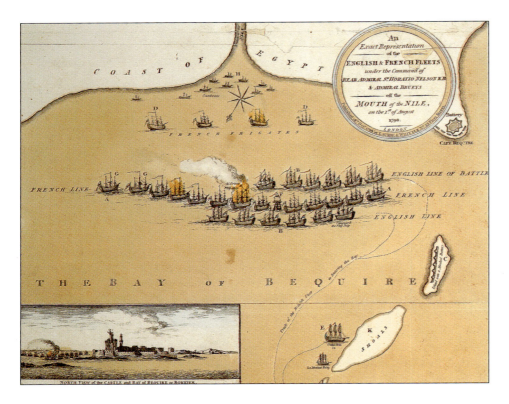

Above: *A plan of the Battle of the Nile that was published in London in October 1798, less than three months after the action had taken place. Admiral Brueys' flagship,* L'Orient, *is shown on fire in the middle of the French line.*

Below: *One of a series of colour mezzotints produced by Robert Dodd to commemorate Nelson's victory at the Battle of the Nile. This shows the beginning of the Battle of the Nile: the attack at sunset. Nelson's flagship, the 74-gun HMS* Vanguard, *is in the foreground.*

Nelson was invalided home, but had recovered by March 1798, when he hoisted his flag in the *Vanguard* (74) and rejoined Jervis, now Earl St Vincent, off Cadiz. St Vincent gave Nelson command of a detached squadron, whose individual captains became known as the 'band of brothers', to search for and destroy a French fleet believed to be assembling and about to sail from the French Mediterranean ports.

Napoleon Bonaparte himself was in command of this expedition, and his first move was to capture and garrison Malta. He then went on to Egypt, where he landed a large army unopposed, and prepared for an extended campaign in the East. He intended nothing less than the conquest of the world.

Nelson had by then arrived in the Mediterranean, and was on his way to Toulon to watch the movements of the French fleet, but the *Vanguard* was dismasted by a severe gale off Sardinia in May and was very nearly wrecked. She was rigged with makeshift 'jury' masts, and was able to get underway again four days later. On

31 May, Nelson wrote to St Vincent, 'My pride was too great for man, but I trust my friends will think I bore my chastisement like a man. It has pleased God to assist me with His favour, and here I am again, off Toulon.'

But the French fleet, with a great convoy of troop transports for the invasion of Egypt, had already sailed, actually on the day before *Vanguard* was dismasted. Nelson made all possible speed to the secret *rendezvous* with his frigates, of which he always complained he never had enough, but they were not there. Their captains had been convinced that the *Vanguard* was so badly damaged she would have to be repaired in dockyard, and so they had returned to Gibraltar.

Deprived of what he called 'the eyes of the fleet', Nelson sailed down the coast of Italy in search of the French. When he heard of the capture of Malta, he decided that the next French objective must be Egypt, particularly as a strong westerly wind had been blowing for days. He therefore took his fleet to the eastern Mediterranean but unluckily just missed the French fleet, having passed them during the night before they reached Egypt. He returned to Sicily to revictual with water and fresh meat, before sailing again for the east.

THE BATTLE OF THE NILE

Nelson's squadron arrived off Alexandria on 1 August 1798, and sighted the French fleet, commanded by Admiral François Paul d'Aiguillers Brueys, flying his flag in the *L'Orient* (120), at anchor in Aboukir Bay, near the Rosetta mouth of the Nile, about 15 miles (24km) east of Alexandria. Brueys, with his 13 ships of the line, 11,000 men and 1,190 guns, seemed to have the advantage of numbers over Nelson's 14 of the line, one of which was small, 8,000 men and 1,012 guns. But Brueys' revolutionary captains were inexperienced in war; even Brueys himself thought them ignorant and boorish. His ships were all undermanned, some of them lacking a quarter or even a third of their proper complement. Discipline was poor, and Brueys was well aware that his fleet was not equal to a British squadron of anything like the same strength.

By contrast, Nelson's squadron was very probably the finest ever assembled in the age of fighting sail. His captains, the 'band of brothers', with names like Hood, Saumarez and Troubridge, were all professional fighting sailors, skilled and experienced in war, who knew Nelson's mind and were determined to carry out his orders to 'use your utmost endeavours to take, burn, sink or destroy'.

Brueys had seen Nelson's ships but, despite his misgivings about his fleet, he was not unduly

Left: *Dodd's depiction of the scene near midnight during the Battle of the Nile when the French flagship* L'Orient *exploded.*

▶ **1800** Capture of Malta.

1801 Hyde Parker's and Nelson's victory over the Danish fleet at Copenhagen (2 April). Saumarez's actions off Gibraltar.

1802 Peace of Amiens concludes war of the Second Coalition against France.

worried. Clearly, being at anchor, he was at a tactical disadvantage, and large numbers of his men were ashore in watering and stores parties. But he believed his ships were anchored in unassailable positions, protected as they were on two sides by shoals and breakers, with frigates on the flanks and shore batteries on Aboukir Island. Also, it was late afternoon and the sun was beginning to go down. A night attack, Brueys thought, was most unlikely.

Brueys had totally misjudged his opponent. Nelson repeatedly said 'I will bring the French Fleet to Action the moment I can lay hand upon them'. He had discussed all the possibilities of a night attack with his captains, so that they all knew what to do. As Berry, *Vanguard*'s captain said, Nelson had studied the dispositions of Brueys' ships 'with the eye of a seaman prepared for attack'. Nelson noted that 'where there was room for a French 74 at single anchor to swing, there was room for a British 74 to anchor'. His ships would pass around the enemy's van and attack from the enemy's shore side.

Although Troubridge's *Culloden* ran aground during the approach, the first five British ships, led by Captain Foley's *Goliath*, anchored at the closest possible quarters inside the French van, which had their weakest and oldest ships, and poured in an overwhelming fire. Five French ships struck within two hours.

Below: *Dodd's view of the Battle of the Nile on the morning of 2 August. The French frigate* Sérieuse *can be seen driven ashore at the left of the picture. The French lost 11 of their 13 ships of the line, and Brueys was killed in the action.*

Above: *A satirical engraving by the caricaturist James Gillray entitled Dido in Despair, which is typically acerbic in its travesty of Lady Hamilton. She laments: 'Ah, where, & ah where, is my gallant Sailor gone? He's gone to Fight the Frenchman, for George upon the Throne.'*

▶ **1801–03** Matthew Flinders aboard the *Investigator* surveys the coasts of Australia.

1803 War with France again declared.

1805 Calder's action off Cape Finisterre (22 July). Battle of Trafalgar, death of Nelson (21 October). Strachan's action in the Bay of Biscay (November).

By 7 o'clock it was quite dark, and the ninth and tenth of Nelson's ships, arriving in a confused and smoke-laden battle scene, had the heaviest casualties. In the centre Brueys' *L'Orient* engaged Captain Darby's *Bellerophon*, dismasting her and killing 200 of her crew. *Majestic* also suffered casualties and her captain Westcott was killed.

Brueys was killed by a shot from *Swiftsure*. *L'Orient* caught fire and when the flames reached her magazine, blew up with a huge explosion which scattered spars, debris and bodies for some distance all around. Her captain Louis de Casabianca, and his ten-year-old son Jacques, the boy of Mrs Felicia Hemans' ballad, 'who stood on the burning deck, Whence all but he had fled' were also killed.

The explosion on board *L'Orient* was a climactic moment in the struggle which seemed to knock the heart out of the French. In all they lost nine ships and two frigates captured, and *L'Orient* and *Timoléon* (74), and two frigates, burned. Only Rear Admiral Villeneuve, with his flagship the *Guillaume Tell* (80) and the *Généreux* (74), and two frigates, escaped. The French suffered casualties of 1,450 men killed and 1,479 wounded, and another 3,105 sent on shore by cartel, against British casualties of 288 killed and 678 wounded. The British lost no ships. When morning came, it revealed a scene for which, as Nelson said, victory was scarcely an adequate word.

The victory at the Nile made Nelson an international celebrity. It also greatly diminished Napoleon's reputation. He and his army were now stranded in Egypt, and it had been convincingly demonstrated that the French were not invincible, after all.

In September, Nelson arrived in Naples with part of his squadron, to be welcomed by Sir William Hamilton, the British Minister, and his wife Emma, with whom Nelson fell in love.

Nelson involved himself deeply with Emma and with Naples affairs, encouraging King Ferdinand to oppose the French. The outcome was disastrous. In December Nelson, by then created Baron Nelson of the Nile, had to rescue the King and the Hamiltons and take them to Palermo in Sicily, where his love affair with Emma deepened.

In June 1799, Lord Keith succeeded St Vincent in the Mediterranean, Nelson transferred his flag to the *Foudroyant*, and himself commanded in the Mediterranean while Lord Keith was absent from August to December, Nelson finally struck his flag in the Mediterranean in July 1800, and spent the next four months travelling home overland with the Hamiltons, visiting European cities such as Trieste, Vienna, Prague, Dresden and Hamburg, where he was fêted as the victor of the Nile.

Despite the scandal of his affair with Emma Hamilton, resulting in the wrecking of his marriage, Nelson was promoted Vice Admiral in January 1801. In February, he hoisted his flag in the *St George* as second-in-command to Admiral Sir Hyde Parker for an expedition to the Baltic, mounted to defeat an armed coalition of northern Powers, headed by Russia, which could become a serious threat to British interests.

The Baltic had been of strategic importance to Britain and a source of essential supplies for the Navy for centuries. A naval presence in the Baltic presented a northern threat to France. Over the years, hundreds of British merchantmen and neutral carriers made the annual journey through the Sound bringing the hemp, timber and tar on which Britain's naval and mercantile strength both depended.

THE BAND OF BROTHERS

In August 1798, immediately after the Nile, Nelson's captains formed 'The Egyptian Club'. Their first action was to present their admiral with a sword and a portrait. The club's members, the 'band of brothers' forged in the Mediterranean campaign, included James Saumarez, Samuel Hood, Thomas Foley, Henry Darby, Thomas Hardy, Alexander Ball and Edward Berry. Later 'brothers' included Thomas Troubridge and Richard Keats.

It is a measure of Nelson's greatness that although he was both vain and quick-tempered, he was able to command the absolute devotion of the best officers of his time. This devotion he returned. Ball said: '...to his officers, his men, to the particular ships themselves, his affections were as steady and ardent as those of a lover.' A later member of the band,

THE BATTLE OF COPENHAGEN

Hyde Parker, with a fleet of 18 of the line and 35 smaller vessels, was persuaded by Nelson that, failing a direct attack on the Russian fleet, the best initial objective would be an attack on the Danish fleet in the strongly defended harbour of Copenhagen. Nelson himself was to lead the attack, with 12 of the line, five frigates, two sloops, five bomb vessels and two fireships.

Nelson negotiated the Outer Channel leading to Copenhagen on 1 April 1801, and stationed his squadron only two miles from the Danish fleet of 18 warships, hulks and floating batteries. Nelson planned to lead ten of his ships and the five frigates up the narrow King's Deep Channel and anchor the *Edgar* (74) opposite the Danish fifth in line. The succeeding ships would then pass her, each in turn, to take up their positions on the disengaged side.

The attack began on the morning of 2 April 1801, and went wrong at once, even before the *Edgar* was in position. The *Bellona* (74) and the *Russell* (74) both went aground on the Middle Ground Shoal, and *Agamemnon* (64) failed to take up her proper station. But when his remaining ships were in position, Nelson began an intense and sustained bombardment of the Danish ships. The Danish Admiral Fischer's flagship *Dannebrog* caught fire and he was forced to shift his flag to the *Holstein*, but the rest of the Danish ships, forts and floating batteries put up such a stout resistance that Hyde Parker, who was some

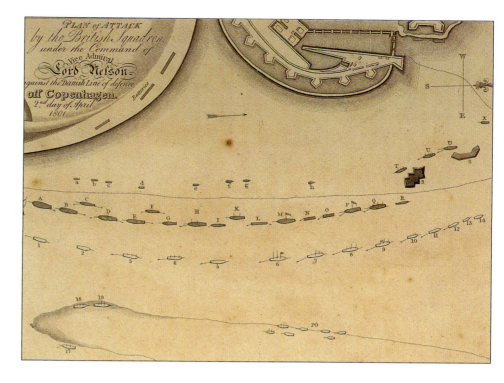

distance away, feared heavy British losses and signalled 'Discontinue the engagement'.

Nelson had previously shifted his flag into the *Elephant*. which drew less than *St George*. She was hotly engaging the *Dannebrog* and two floating batteries ahead of her when the signal lieutenant told Nelson of Hyde Parker's signal. Nelson told him to acknowledge receipt but to keep 'Number 16', the signal for close action, still flying. Then he said to *Elephant*'s captain, Foley, (who had led the squadron in *Goliath* at the Nile) 'You know, Foley, I have only one eye. I have a right to be blind sometimes.' He raised his spy-

Above: A plan of the Battle of Copenhagen which was fought on 2 April 1801. It was the occasion when Nelson famously ignored a signal to disengage by raising his spyglass to his blind eye and observing 'I really do not see the signal'.

George Duff, said: 'He is so good and pleasant a man that we all wish to do what he likes without any kind of orders.'

Coming from a relatively humble background, Nelson showed that aristocratic hauteur was not essential to high command. Not only, as at Copenhagen, would he disregard the orders of superiors if he judged them mistaken; he also would take his captains into his confidence, fostering a spirit of mutual dependence. The qualities of leadership in which he excelled, he encouraged in others: aggression without recklessness; imagination; determination; painstaking logistics. His determination to forge an elite was apparent even in the appearance of his ships, with their 'Nelson chequer' paintwork.

The spirit of teamwork was furthered by the signalling methods of Howe, Kempenfelt and Home Popham, resulting, after 1790, in less rigid *Fighting Instructions* and thus increased flexibilty in command. Flexibility and trust were, indeed, Nelson's watchwords, never better expressed than in his message to Collingwood (who would lead the second division at Trafalgar in the *Royal Sovereign*) on 9 October 1805: 'I send you my plan of attack… . But, my dear friend, it is to place you perfectly at ease respecting my intentions, and to give full scope to your judgement for carrying them into effect. We can, my dear Coll, have no little jealousies.'

Left: Silver and glassware from the services that Nelson took to sea with him.

Right: A pair of French portrait busts in Rouen delftware (c.1810) depicting Nelson (right) and the Emperor Napoleon.

Far right: The rear division at Trafalgar. In battle, Nelson's rapport with his captains was remarkable.

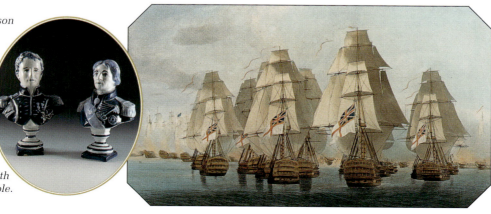

▶ **1806** Nelson buried in St Paul's Cathedral (9 January). Duckworth's victory off San Domingo (6 February). Royal Naval Academy renamed Royal Naval College.

1807 Capture of Curaçao (1 January). Slave trade abolished by Act of Parliament.

glass to his right eye and said 'I really do not see the signal'.

Dannebrog blew up, whereupon some of the Danish spirit seemed to ebb away. There was still sporadic fire up and down the line, but the main battle was over, after some five hours of fighting. It now remained to disentangle Nelson's ships from the confined shoal waters, during which *Defiance* and *Elephant* ran aground. Nelson transferred back to the *St George* for the night, and was heard to say, 'Well I have fought contrary to orders, and perhaps I shall be hanged. Never mind; let them!'.

Nelson himself negotiated an armistice with the Danish Crown Prince. When, in May, Hyde Parker was recalled, Nelson succeeded him as C-in-C. He was also created Viscount Nelson of the Nile and Burnham Thorpe.

The northern coalition had dissolved and Nelson came home, landing at Yarmouth on 1 July. He then took command of the Squadron of a Particular Service for home defence against the threat of invasion. On 15 August 1801, Nelson led the Squadron in an attack against the invasion vessels assembling at Boulogne. It was repulsed with heavy losses, largely because the French used chain anchor cables in their harbour defences instead of the usual hemp ropes.

RESUMPTION OF HOSTILITIES

The war was formally ended by the Treaty of Amiens in March 1802, but the peace proved to be only a brief truce. Britain declared war on France again on 16 May 1803. Nelson, now a Vice Admiral of the Blue, was appointed Commander-in-Chief in the Mediterranean, hoisting his flag in the *Victory* (100) on 18 May.

For the next two years, Nelson kept watch on Toulon to prevent the French ships there from escaping and joining forces with others from French and Spanish ports (Spain having declared war against Britain in December 1804). Villeneuve, now the French fleet commander, sailed from Toulon in January 1805 but was driven back by bad weather. Early in April, Nelson learned that Villeneuve had sailed again. This time, he broke out into the Atlantic, and got clear away.

Napoleon had escaped from Egypt in August 1799 and reached France in October, becoming First Consul in December. Now, as Emperor of the French, he had a grand scheme to conquer Britain. He ordered Villeneuve to the West Indies, to take command of a combined fleet which would join

Above: *Looking aft towards* Victory*'s poop deck. Eight crew manned the wheel in rough weather.*

ABOARD THE VICTORY

HMS *Victory*, commissioned in 1778, is now preserved in dry dock at Portsmouth. A short time aboard will disabuse the visitor of any romantic ideas of life at sea in Nelson's time. Even when touring her with a party of 30 or so, one feels claustrophobic – and wonders how her full complement of around 820 officers and men could endure many months at sea with minimal cooking facilities, sanitation and medical care.

The *Victory* was one of the biggest wooden warships. Some 2,000 oak trees went to the construction of her two-foot thick, double-skinned hull, extending 226 feet (68.9m) from taffrail to figurehead. At Trafalgar, this fighting machine carried 30 32-pounders on her lower gun deck, 28 24-pounders on her middle gun deck, 30 12-pounders on her upper gun deck, 12 12-pounders on her quarter deck, and two 12-pounders and two 68-pound carronades ('smashers') on her fo'c'sle.

A 32-pounder gun crew comprised 14 men, but if the ship was fighting on both sides, the crew was split and seven men operated the opposite gun. Within moments of fire being opened, the gun decks were obscured by thick, choking smoke: the gunners – on the lower deck, two lieutenants, five midshipmen, two mates, 15 gun captains, and 210 guns' crews – laboured in a cramped inferno of noise and darkness, with the ever-present threat of agonizing splinter wounds when enemy shot shivered the *Victory's* timbers.

In battle, Nelson's gunners had two advantages. One was the flintlock firing mechanism that in most British ships had replaced the slow-match. The other was the fact that Nelson and his captains sought battles of attrition, and so looked to engage with the French downwind. The consequent heel of British ships sometimes prevented lower-deck guns from firing, but ensured that most shots struck home in French hulls: French gunners habitually fired high.

During the War of 1812, the frigate HMS *Macedonian* was so badly battered by Stephen Decatur's *United States* that Captain Carden struck his flag. When he remarked on the victor's magnificent gunnery, Decatur showed him guns bearing the words 'Nelson' and 'Victory' – served by men who were veterans of Nelson's fleet.

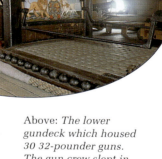

Above: *The lower gundeck which housed 30 32-pounder guns. The gun crew slept in hammocks slung above the guns, and ate at mess tables erected in the cramped space between them (below).*

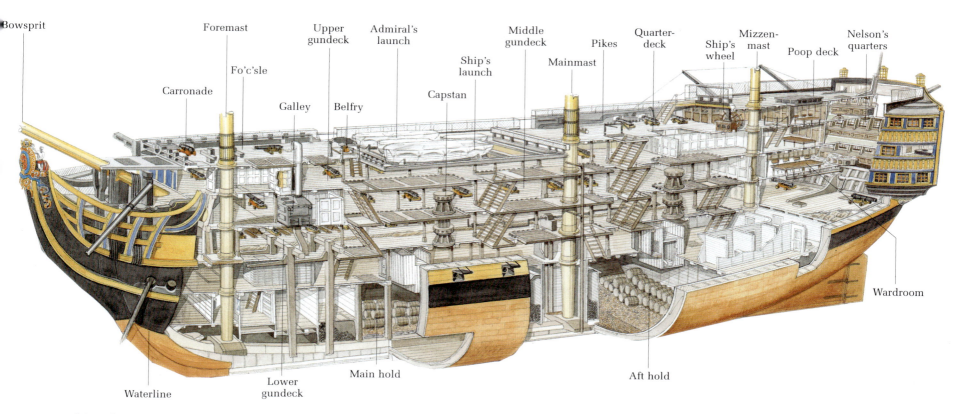

Bowsprit · Foremast · Upper gundeck · Admiral's launch · Middle gundeck · Pikes · Quarter-deck · Mizzen-mast · Poop deck · Nelson's quarters

Fo'c'sle · Ship's launch · Mainmast · Ship's wheel

Carronade · Galley · Belfry · Capstan

Waterline · Lower gundeck · Main hold · Aft hold · Wardroom

him from various Mediterranean and Atlantic ports. Once assembled, his fleet would advance across the Atlantic, defeat the British western squadron off Brittany, and seize temporary command of the English Channel, thus enabling the French Grand Army to cross the water for the invasion of Britain.

Nelson sailed for the West Indies at once, but in a chase which lasted until July, he missed his quarry. As soon as Villeneuve heard of Nelson's arrival in the West Indies, he sailed hastily back to Europe, without waiting for the other squadrons to join him. Napoleon's grand scheme was thus still-born. After an inconclusive action, in which he lost two ships, fought in fog off Ferrol against a squadron under Sir Robert Calder on 22 July, Villeneuve reached the safety of Cadiz on 20 August, where he joined forces with a Spanish squadron.

Nelson followed Villeneuve back across the Atlantic and, having made sure that Villeneuve had not returned to the Mediterranean, where he was still the Commander-in-Chief, Nelson sailed for England in the *Victory*, reaching his home at Merton early on 20 August 1805.

Nelson rejoined his fleet off Cadiz on 28 September. He was welcomed, as he had ordered, in silence, with none of the customary salutes and hoisting of colours. This was because he expected a fleet action at any moment, but it made his arrival all the more dramatic.

His first unpleasant task was to send Sir Robert Calder back to England for court martial. There had been a popular clamour at home after Calder's

inconclusive action of 22 July to which the Government had been forced to respond. Calder, who thought he had done well, was astonished and indignant and broke down in tears. As a result, Nelson did not send Calder home in a frigate, as he had been instructed to do, but allowed Calder to return in his own ship, the *Prince of Wales*, thus weakening the fleet by one 90-gun ship on the eve of Trafalgar.

Meanwhile, Villeneuve would have much preferred to stay in Cadiz and it would have made strategic sense if his 'fleet in being' had done so. But Napoleon ordered him to take his fleet to the Mediterranean and, to ensure that his order was obeyed, he sent another admiral to take command of the fleet. Villeneuve knew this, and the humiliation drove him to take his ships to sea on 19 October and head south-east for the Straits of Gibraltar.

Within minutes, Captain Blackwood in the frigate *Euryalus* had signalled the news of the combined Franco-Spanish fleet's sailing to Nelson. Once at sea, Villeneuve changed his mind and thought of returning to Cadiz. Finally, he decided to stand on and face his opponent. The last great fleet action of the days of fighting sail was about to take place off Cape Trafalgar.

When Nelson rejoined his fleet, he had called his captains, his band of brothers, on board *Victory* to brief them on his plan of action. 'It was new – it was singular – it was simple!' he wrote to Lady Hamilton on 1 October. 'When I came to explain to them the Nelson touch, it was like an electric shock.'

> **25.4.1804:** ' *We are all tir'd of being at sea on salt provisions for we have not been in an English port this 6 months and don't expect of 5 or 6 more to be in one.* '
>
> LETTER FROM SEAMAN JOHN BOOTH TO HIS WIFE WRITTEN ON BOARD HMS *AMAZON* OFF TOULON

Above: *A cutaway drawing of HMS Victory. At the Battle of Trafalgar she was crewed by 821 men, comprising 11 officers, 48 non-commissioned officers, 80 petty officers, 204 able seamen, 195 ordinary seamen, 90 landsmen, 40 boys, four Royal Marine officers and 149 Marines. She displaced around 3,500 tons, and her maximum speed in fair weather was eight knots. At extreme range (c.1 mile/ 1,600m), the shot from the large 32-pounder guns on the lower gundeck could penetrate two feet (61cm) of solid oak.*

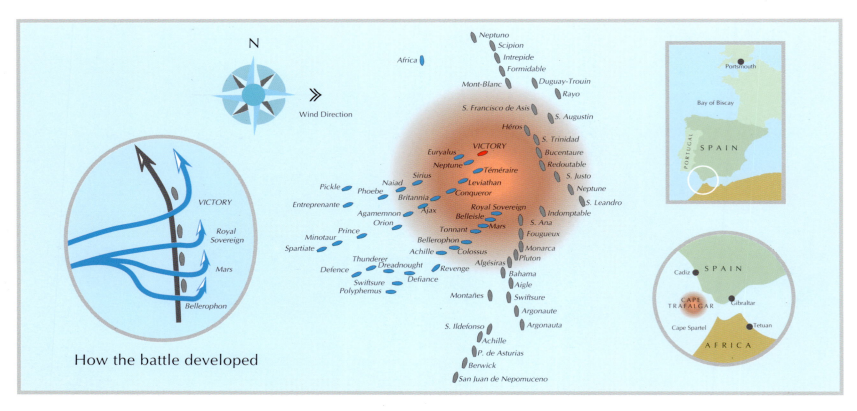

How the battle developed

1808–14 Naval support of British operations in the Peninsular War.

1809 Captures of Cayenne and Martinique. Gambier's fumbling of the action in the Basque and Aix Roads (April). Walcheren expedition to seize control of the Schelde estuary ends in failure.

Right: This engraving of the Battle of Trafalgar was published in December 1805, just weeks after the action. It shows Victory *leading the windward line of ships (left) and* Royal Sovereign *leading the leeward advancing towards the great arc of French and Spanish ships that were sailing north towards Cadiz.*

THE PLAN OF BATTLE

Nelson still intended to lay his ships close alongside the enemy, in the time-honoured way, so that they could pour in fire 'as fast as she could suck it' until, as every English sailor confidently expected (and with good reason), the enemy struck. But he intended a more flexible, original approach. He would have his fleet in three divisions. One, of 16 ships, he would lead himself. Collingwood would lead another. There would also be an advanced squadron of eight of the fastest ships, lying up to windward. Collingwood would aim to cut the enemy's battleline 12 ships from its rear. Nelson himself would go for the centre, where he expected Villeneuve to be. The enemy ships not attacked at first, in the leading section of their fleet, would need time to turn and come back. In the meantime, Nelson and Collingwood would defeat their opponents in detail. It was a startling plan (some of his captains wept when they heard it) but, in the event, Nelson had fewer ships than he expected and thus had no windward squadron. But as Nelson wrote in a

memorandum he circulated to his admirals and captains on 9 October, 'The whole impression of the British fleet must be to overpower from two or three ships ahead of their commander-in-chief (supposed to be in the centre) to the rear of the fleet'. However, as Nelson also said, 'Nothing is certain in a sea fight'.

At dawn on Monday 21 October 1805, Nelson's fleet was off the Straits of Gibraltar, with the towering cliffs of Cape Trafalgar visible to the eastward. These were the same waters where in February 1797 Nelson had, in the close proximity of enemy ships, stopped to rescue Hardy, who had gone away in a jolly boat, exclaiming 'By God, I'll not lose Hardy! Back that mizzen-topsail.'

The weather that morning was fine, with stretches of autumn mist. The sea was smooth, with a ground-swell from the west, the sky was clear, and the wind was light and west-north-westerly, as *Victory*, leading the windward line of 12 ships, and *Royal Sovereign* wearing Colling-wood's flag, leading 15 ships, sailed down towards the enemy, of 33 ships of the line, 18 French and 15 Spanish, by then stretched out in a great arc almost five miles (8km) long, heading north for Cadiz. Villeneuve flew his flag in the *Bucentaure* (80) in the centre. The French van was commanded by Admiral Dumanoir in the *Formidable* (80), the Spanish rear by Admiral Gravina in the *Principe de Asturias* (112).

Towards noon, the bands on board the British ships struck up the National Anthem, followed by 'Rule Britannia' and 'Britons Strike Home'. Nelson wanted to make one more general signal to 'amuse the fleet'. He said to John Pasco, *Victory*'s Signal Lieutenant, 'I wish to say to the fleet, ENGLAND CONFIDES THAT EVERY MAN WILL DO HIS DUTY. You must be quick, for I have one more signal to make, which is for close action'. Pasco suggested

EXPECTS for CONFIDES, because 'expects' was in the Signal Book and would save seven hoists. 'That will do,' Nelson said, 'make it directly.'

As it passed down through his fleet, Nelson's signal was greeted with cheers. Blackwood said it was 'truly sublime'. Collingwood, however, said he wished Nelson would stop signalling, 'We all know what to do.' 'Number 16', the signal for close action, followed and remained at *Victory*'s top-gallant masthead until it was shot away.

Nelson's plan to attack in two lines put the leading ships in both columns at extreme peril during the approach, when they were exposed to the enemy's broadsides for some time (Collingwood for ten minutes) before they themselves could reply. For that reason, Nelson placed three of his strongest ships, *Victory*, *Temeraire* (98) and *Neptune* (98) at the head of his line. They suffered severe damage and heavy casualties as they closed, but once they got alongside their enemies and could bring their own broadsides to bear, they did all that Nelson could possibly have hoped from them. The battle began three minutes before noon and continued for some four hours, by which time no less than 20 enemy ships had been captured or struck their colours.

At about 1.15 pm, Nelson was pacing up and down his quarterdeck with Hardy when he was mortally wounded by a shot from a French sharpshooter in the fighting top of the *Redoutable* which had grappled with the *Victory* and at one stage had even tried to board her. Nelson was carried below and lived only a few hours. *Victory*'s log recorded: 'Partial firing continued until 4.30 when a victory having been reported to the Right Honourable Lord Viscount Nelson K.B. and Commander-in-Chief he then died of his wound'.

The weather worsened during the day and a full gale (which Nelson had foreseen) was blowing by midnight. The ships of both fleets were scattered and in the event only one French and three Spanish prizes were brought into Gibraltar, all the rest being recaptured, sunk or driven ashore.

Collingwood took command of the fleet that evening, flying his flag in the *Euryalus* because *Royal Sovereign* had been so badly damaged. *Victory* was also badly damaged and was taken in tow first by *Polyphemus* and then by *Neptune*, who brought her into Gibraltar on 28 October.

Trafalgar did not prevent the invasion of Britain, because Napoleon had already begun to

Above inset: *The celebrated marine artist Nicholas Pocock painted vivid depictions of Nelson's great actions. This scene shows Trafalgar at the moment when the* Victory *cut through the Franco-Spanish line.*

Above: *Here Pocock has captured the end of the action at Trafalgar. The damage to the ships – particularly to sails, masts and rigging – is very evident. The painting is dated 1807.*

Top of page: *A poignant moment – with flags at half-mast HMS* Victory *is shown arriving at Spithead with Nelson's body on board on 4 December 1805. The painting is by the Victorian artist John W. Carmichael.*

Above: *The undress uniform coat that Nelson was wearing at the Battle of Trafalgar when he was shot. The hole caused by the bullet that struck him can be seen in the left shoulder.*

disperse his Grand Army in the late summer of 1805 for an offensive against his continental enemies. But Trafalgar did comprehensively destroy the main Franco-Spanish fleet, and gave Britain command of the Channel, the Atlantic and the West Indies for the remaining ten years of the Napoleonic War.

A HERO'S FUNERAL

Nelson's body had been placed in a leaguer filled with brandy which was placed in his fore cabin and covered with a silk Royal Standard. Marines mounted guard on it by day and night. After some refitting of her shattered mast and sails, *Victory* sailed on 3 November, arriving at Spithead at 1.30 on the afternoon of 4 December. When *Victory* arrived, all the walls and vantage points of Portsmouth were packed with even more people than had seen Nelson sail in September. The town had shared the national feelings of joy and relief at the news of the great victory, and the shock and grief of Nelson's death at the moment of that victory. In Nelson, Portsmouth felt it had lost one of its own.

Victory sailed again for the Medway on 10 December. Lord Nelson was given a magnificent State funeral, and was buried in St Paul's Cathedral, in a coffin made from wood from the

Royal Sovereign
HONOURED FATHER

'This comes to tell you I am alive and hearty except three fingers; but that's not much. It might have been my head. I told brother Tom I should like to see a greadly battle, and I have seen one, and we have peppered the Combined rarely; and for the matter of that, they fought us pretty tightish for French and Spanish. Three of our mess are killed, and four more of us winged. But to tell you the truth of it, when the game began, I wished myself at Warnborough with my plough again; but when they had given us one good duster, and I found myself snug and tight, I set to in good earnest, and thought no more about being killed than if I were at Murrell Green Fair, and I was presently as busy and as black as a collier. How my fingers got knocked overboard I don't know, but off they are, and I never missed them till I wanted them. You see, by my writing, it was my left hand, so I can write to you and fight for my King yet. We have taken a rare parcel of ships, but the wind is so rough we cannot bring them home, else I should roll in money, so we are busy smashing 'em and blowing 'em up wholesale.'*

AN ACCOUNT OF TRAFALGAR WRITTEN BY AN UNNAMED
SAILOR TO HIS FATHER IN ENGLAND

mainmast of the French flagship *L'Orient*, on 9 January 1806.

The threat of invasion had been lifted, but the war went on, indeed the Navy was escorting convoys as far as China as late as 1815. Fourteen days after Trafalgar, Commodore Sir Richard Strachan in the *Caesar* (80), with three 74s and four frigates, met four French ships of the line, fugitives from Trafalgar, off Cape Ortegal, the north-west shoulder of Spain. After a long chase, Strachan engaged them and the French, the *Formidable* (80), and the 74s *Duguay-Trouin*, *Mont Blanc*, and *Scipion*, all struck. The *Duguay-Trouin*, renamed *Implacable*, served in the Royal Navy as a boys' training ship, and survived until 1949 when, by then in a decrepit state, she was deliberately sunk in the Channel.

After the defeat of their main fleet, the French adopted the policy of the *guerre de course*, attacking British trade at sea. A squadron of five ships of the line and four frigates, under Rear Admiral Leissègues, escaped the Brest blockade and sailed from Cadiz for the West Indies. They were pursued by Admiral Sir John Duckworth, with six of the line and two frigates. Duckworth caught the French ships on 6 February 1806, while they were provisioning and watering, at the eastern end of the island of San Domingo. In a fierce engagement lasting one and a half hours, three French of the line were captured. The remaining two were driven ashore in an attempt to escape, but they were destroyed by boats of the British squadron. Only the frigates escaped.

While the Royal Navy had command of the Channel and the Atlantic, the war in the next three years continued world-wide. In the Caribbean, Captain Brisbane led a squadron of five ships to capture the island of Curaçao on New Year's Day 1807. Later that year, Gambier led an expedition to Copenhagen. In March 1808, Saumarez was appointed in command of a strong squadron in the Baltic which he held for the next five years, returning to England each winter. In the same year, the Navy supported the opening operations of the Peninsular camapign in the Spanish Peninsula.

In January 1809, Captain James Lucas Yeo in the *Confiance* (24) supported the Portuguese troops who took the town of Cayenne in French New Guinea. In February, Rear Admiral Sir Alexander Cochrane, flying his flag in the *Neptune*, commanded the naval forces which supported troops under Lieutenant General George Beckwith who captured Martinique. In the summer of 1809, the Navy escorted and supported an invasion force which attempted to seize control of the estuary of the Schelde at Walcheren, which the French were using as a naval base. The campaign, in which over 100 ships took part and lasted from July to December, finally ended in failure.

In April that year, there was one of those controversies which occurred in the Navy from time to time, when an opportunity was missed, resulting in mutual recriminations, The French Admiral Willaumez sailed with ten of the line from Brest to join a smaller French squadron already anchored in the Basque and Aix Roads (Oléron Roads), preparatory to sailing for the West Indies. Willaumez was followed by the Channel Fleet under Admiral Gambier and blockaded in the Roads.

Captain Lord Thomas Cochrane was selected by the Admiralty to join Gambier off Rochefort and lead a group of fireships against the French in the Roads, where they lay, protected by a stout triangular boom. The red-headed Cochrane was something of a firebrand and already a naval celebrity. In command of the sloop *Speedy* in 1800 he had made a reputation for seizing Spanish prizes. In 1801, the exasperated Spaniards specially commissioned a 32-gun ship, the *Gamo*, and sent it against Cochrane. The two met in May 1801 south-west of Barcelona and the *Gamo* was defeated.

The fireships and explosion vessels, each loaded with several hundred barrels of gunpowder, were launched on the night of 11-12 April. The first fireship broke through the boom, whereupon the French cut their cables in a frantic attempt to escape and all but two of them ran ashore. The chance was now there for a comprehensive British victory, but Gambier, who in any case disliked Cochrane, did not come to assist him until late the following day. The chance was lost. Only three French ships were taken or burned, and a British East Indiaman was recaptured (although it later blew up).

Cochrane, who was MP for Westminster, later opposed a parliamentary vote of thanks to

Gambier because of the excessive caution he had shown, and he pressed for Gambier to be court-martialled. Gambier was court-martialled but the Admiralty, who had appointed him, ensured that he was honourably acquitted. It was Cochrane whose career was ruined. The Admiralty refused to employ him again and, after a scandal over a Stock Exchange fraud in 1814, Cochrane was expelled from the Navy and from Parliament.

In 1811, one of Nelson's protégés, Captain William Hoste, fought an action worthy of Nelson himself. In March, the French Rear Admiral Dubourdieu was dispatched from Ancona with four French frigates, three Venetian frigates, four

▶ **1810** Home Popham's capture of Cape of Good Hope. Cochrane's capture of Guadeloupe.

1811 William Hoste's victory at Lissa (13 March). School of Naval Architecture established in Portsmouth.

Above: *A Sailor's Observation of the Lamented Death of Lord Nelson, an engraving by Thomas Rowlandson after George Woodward that was published in 1805. The public mood of grief after Nelson's death was profound. Huge crowds gathered to observe his Lying in State at Greenwich and the State funeral at St Paul's Cathedral.*

smaller vessels, and 500 troops, with orders to occupy the island of Lissa, off the Dalmatian coast, which Hoste, with a squadron of four frigates, was using as a base.

Hoste's frigates, the *Amphion, Active, Cerberus* and *Volage*, met Dubourdieu's squadron north of Lissa just after dawn on 13 March. Hoisting the signal 'Remember Nelson', Hoste gave battle and after three hours' furious fighting Dubourdieu was killed when his flagship *Favorite* was driven ashore and blew up. Two other Franco-Venetian frigates, *Bellona* and *Corona*, were captured, and the rest fled.

This almost ceaseless naval activity, year after year, demanded equal exertions on the part of the press gangs, who were not particular what kind or what nationality of men they pressed. Thus, *Victory's* ship's company at Trafalgar included Frenchmen, Spaniards, Scandinavians, Hindus, Germans, Italians, Portuguese, Swiss, Dutch, Kanakas and Americans. Even then, in spite of the press gangs' best efforts, *Victory* was under-manned, although Nelson's name had brought nearly 200 volunteers to the ship.

The presence of Americans serving on board British ships had political consequences. The press ganging of American citizens was one of the reasons – the other being British restrictions on trade – for the outbreak of war between Britain and the United States in 1812.

The United States Navy was minute compared to the Royal Navy. Its total strength only equalled the British squadron which patrolled between Halifax and Bermuda, and there were further British squadrons in Newfoundland and the West Indies.

THE WAR OF 1812

However, the US Navy was in no way overawed, and the War of 1812 was notable for the number of its single ship-to-ship engagements, many of which ended in American victories. On 13 August 1812, the frigate *Essex* became the first American warship to capture a Royal Navy warship, the sloop *Alert*, which she did in an battle lasting only eight minutes, after pretending to be a merchant ship. Six days later, about 500 miles (800km) south-east of Halifax, the American *Constitution*, commanded by Captain Isaac Hull, captured and later burned the frigate *Guerrière*.

These losses were merely pin-pricks to the Royal Navy, but they were tremendous boosts to American morale. US Navy successes continued with the capture of the British brig *Frolic* by the American sloop *Wasp* on 15 October 1812. Only ten days later, Stephen Decatur in the frigate

---

NELSON: THE IMMORTAL MEMORY

Few have been mourned like Nelson. 'Our men are such soft toads,' wrote a midshipman after Trafalgar, 'that they do nothing but sit and cry… .' During Nelson's funeral procession, led by the Prince of Wales, the Royal Dukes, 30 admirals and 100 captains, Nelson's chaplain and secretary, John Scott, noted that even London's beggars left their pitches to pay tribute. 'Many did I see, tattered and on crutches, shaking their heads with plain signs of sorrow. This must truly be the unbought affection of the heart.'

With an eye to lasting fame, Nelson had asked to be buried in St Paul's because, he believed, Westminster Abbey's marshy site meant that it would one day sink into the Thames. The Abbey, anxious to take a share of the crowds that flocked to his tomb, exhibited a life-sized wax image so realistic that it moved Lady Hamilton to tears. She may well also have wept at her shabby treatment by the nation: she got nothing, save what Nelson himself left her, while William Nelson, his brother ('a dull, stupid fellow', wrote Collingwood) was granted an earldom and some £100,000. With the title went an annual pension of £5,000.

The immediate flood of 'Nelson souvenirs' included fine paintings by Arthur Devis and Turner, many cheap prints and oleographs, and a plethora of 'fairings' – plaster figures and busts,

jugs, mugs and plates. From the 1830s, his lasting memorial took shape: the planning of Trafalgar Square, London, by Charles Barry, and the erection there on a 170-foot (52m) column of a 16-foot (5m) high statue. The work was completed in 1849; Landseer's massive lions at the column's base appeared some 20 years later.

Rum is still called 'Nelson's Blood' because, it is said, sailors furtively tapped the cask in which his body was shipped home. In fact, his remains, preserved first in brandy and then in spirits of wine, were treated with all reverence. And the three white lines on sailors' collars do not commemorate Nelson's three major victories. 'The Immortal Memory', the toast drunk annually at Trafalgar Day banquets, needs no such spurious props.

Left: Nelson's celebrity spawned a host of commemorative items. Illustrated here are a Staffordshire group of the death of Nelson and a ceramic plant holder bearing his image (below left).

Left: Relics of Nelson were carefully preserved after his death. Here his uniform coat is seen next to a table that he used aboard HMS Victory. *On it stand a mask of his face, a miniature of Lady Hamilton, his watch, a snuff box and two shoe buckles.*

United States defeated the frigate *Macedonian* after a two-hour action, some 600 miles (950km) west-south-west of Madeira, and became the first American captain to bring a captured British warship into an American harbour.

On 29 December 1812, some 30 miles (50km) east of Bahia, *Constitution* had a second success under another captain, William Bainbridge, when she reduced the frigate *Java* to a battered hulk in a close-range action lasting just under two hours. On 24 February 1813, off the coast of British Guiana, another famous US Navy name was in action when *Hornet*, commanded by Commander James Lawrence, met and defeated the sloop *Peacock* which sank with heavy loss of life after an 11-minute battle.

The next single-ship engagement was an exception to the run of American victories and was the most famous action of its kind in all naval history. The American commander was once again James Lawrence, now promoted to Captain. His ship was the 38-gun *Chesapeake*, one of the six original frigates authorized in 1794 as the foundation of the United States Navy. In May 1813 Lawrence was at Boston, with orders to intercept British vessels on their way to Canada.

His opponent was Captain Philip Vere Broke, commanding the 38-gun frigate *Shannon*, who lay off Boston with the *Tenedos* (38), waiting for *Chesapeake* to come out. *Shannon* was short of water and would soon have to retire to Halifax, leaving the coast clear for *Chesapeake*, so Broke sent Lawrence a challenge by letter: 'Sir, As the *Chesapeake* appears now ready for sea, I request that you will do me the favour to meet the *Shannon* with her ship to ship to try the fortune of our respective ships . . .' To even the odds, Broke sent the *Tenedos* away.

Lawrence had no need to respond, indeed it would have been more sensible to have ignored the challenge. But he had formed a poor opinion

of British ships and British officers, whom he considered were overrated. Although his crew were inexperienced and he was short of three officers, Lawrence sailed out on 1 June, to do battle.

Lawrence had badly misjudged his adversary. Philip Broke was one of the best captains in the Royal Navy, a devotee of gunnery who had trained his guns' crews to a high pitch of efficiency. The battle, one of the fiercest of all time, lasted only 11 minutes, in which 146 of *Chesapeake*'s 376 men and 85 of the *Shannon*'s 330 were killed or wounded. More men were killed or wounded per minute in these 11 minutes of action between Cape Ann and Cape Cod than in all Nelson's and Villeneuve's ships at Trafalgar.

Shannon's men boarded *Chesapeake*, who struck four minutes later. Lawrence was mortally wounded, but his repeated dying words, 'Don't give up the ship', became legendary in the US Navy who hailed him as a hero although he should have been courtmartialled had he survived. Broke took *Chesapeake* to Halifax and then to Britain.

The war against America was brought to a somewhat indeterminate end by a peace treaty signed at Ghent in 1814. Napoleon, whose prestige and authority had been catastrophically damaged by his disastrous campaign in Russia, abdicated in April that year. But the peace lasted only until Napoleon escaped from Elba and returned to France in March 1815. The so-called Hundred Days culminated in Napoleon's final defeat at Waterloo in June, bringing more than a century of sea conflict between Britain and France to an end.

In all that time, it was the Royal Navy which had enabled Britain to challenge France with such success, denying opponents command of the sea, winning the great sea battles, safeguarding seaborne trade and supporting the army. The Navy's last contribution to the Napoleonic War was made by the *Northumberland* (74), which took Napoleon to exile on the island of St Helena in October 1815.

Above: *The capture of the* Chesapeake *by HMS* Shannon, *1 June 1813. This famous single-ship engagement took place off the coast of Massachusetts and lasted a mere 11 minutes. The engraving is by Bailey after T. Whitcombe.*

His Majesty's Ship the *Volontaire*, at Port Mahon, 2nd August 1812.

'*I* shall indeed regret leaving the *Volontaire* as I have as good a set of Messmates as ever met in one Ship, and a Captain who may hereafter perhaps be of service in promoting my Interest.'

Pelorus, off the Isle de Bas, Coast of France, 25th June 1815

'*B*y the Bumboat Man I yesterday acquainted my dearest Mary that we were going to cruize in company with *Wanderer* under the orders of Captain Dowers ... The *Pelorus* sails astonishingly – she will I think come up with anything she may chase and will of course be as quick in retreating from a superior force. Our crusing ground is certainly a most excellent one and all hands seem in excellent spirits at the chance of making Prize Money – all French vessels no matter under what flag they may be are lawful Prizes – I hope we shall do something this cruise.'

LETTERS WRITTEN BY THOMAS PECKSTON

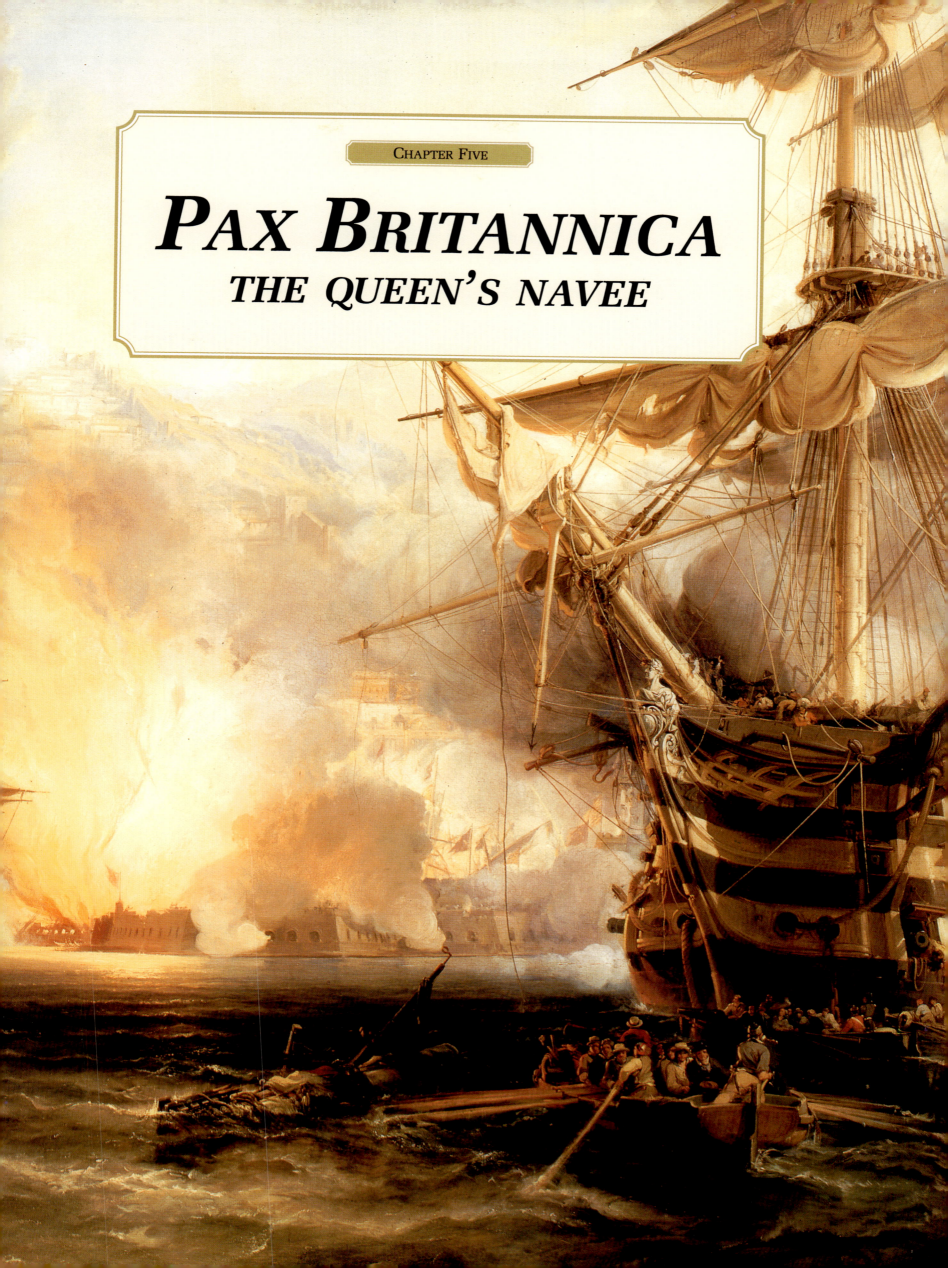

PAX BRITANNICA
THE QUEEN'S NAVEE

Previous pages: *A glow of flame marks the explosion of the mole head battery during the bombardment of Algiers on 27 August 1816. Lord Exmouth's flagship* Queen Charlotte *is shown in the centre of this dramatic painting by George Chambers.*

Below: *Negotiations between the Dey of Algiers and Lord Exmouth's representatives over the contentious issue of piracy proved ineffectual, and in the end an unequivocal show of naval force proved necessary.*

After the great French war, as after every great war, there was a very rapid and drastic reduction of the Navy. In 1815, there were 713 ships in commission: 100 ships of the line, and 613 frigates, sloops, brigs, and smaller vessels. By 1820, these numbers had plummeted to 134 ships in commission, including 14 of the line and 120 smaller vessels, having dropped as low as 121 in 1818.

Manpower was cut just as dramatically, from 140,000 in 1815 to 23,000 in 1820, having been as low as 19,000 in 1817. But while the men were discharged to shore, the officers continued in the naval service, on half pay, liable to be called upon at any time. Their numbers actually increased from 5,017 to 5,664 between 1815 and 1820, some having been promoted to increase their half-pay.

Every officer not employed was on half-pay, for there was no scheme for retiring redundant officers. Advancement was governed largely by seniority, particularly from the rank of Captain upwards. No Captain or Admiral could be promoted while there was a more senior officer above him in the list. Thus, the decommissioning of so many ships in such a short time meant that there was suddenly a glut of officers, most of whom remained in their present ranks, with little or no hope of further employment or promotion.

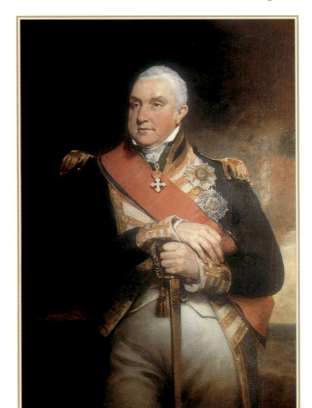

Above: *Admiral Lord Exmouth who commanded the expedition to subdue the pirate port of Algiers in 1816. He was made a viscount for this action. The painting is the work of William Owen.*

There were 50 officers competing for every appointment. Officers without political or family connections, 'interest' as it was called, could wait 30 years between appointments. For most, it was a case of literally waiting to fill dead men's shoes.

The war might be over, but piracy continued. In the Mediterranean, the Turks in Algiers, Tunis and Tripoli made a profitable business from piracy and from ransoming their European captives. In 1816, press and public opinion forced the Admiralty to take action. Lord Exmouth, the Commander-in-Chief, was charged with no less a task than to abolish slavery, and was ordered to 'show the flag' by taking the fleet to all three pirate ports.

Tunis and Tripoli agreed to Exmouth's demands, but the Dey of Algiers refused. Exmouth's squadron arrived off Algiers on the evening of 26 August 1816. It consisted of the *Queen Charlotte* (100), flying Exmouth's flag, with the *Impregnable* (98), wearing the flag of Rear Admiral David Milne, four more ships of the line, two heavy and two light frigates, four gun brigs, five bomb vessels, five small gunboats, a sloop fitted out as an 'explosion vessel', and a squadron of six Dutch frigates under Vice Admiral Baron von Theodorus van Capellan, all supported by the Rocket Troop of the Royal Horse Artillery, Royal Sappers and Miners.

When the Dey refused an ultimatum requiring him to give up his European captives, Exmouth's ships anchored in the positions he had carefully planned for them beforehand, and opened fire at 3 in the afternoon of 27 August. After hours of bombardment which lasted until nearly midnight, all the Algerian ships in the harbour had been set on fire or sunk, all the enemy batteries had been silenced, and much of the town and port reduced to rubble.

The Algerians suffered over 7,000 casualties. The British losses were comparatively light: 128 killed and 690 wounded, most of them in the *Impregnable* whose captain had not anchored in the position Lord Exmouth had ordered. The Dey surrendered, apologised to the British consul, paid tribute money and released over 1,600 European slaves, none of whom were British. But, inevitably, piracy and slavery were not abolished. In a few years' time, pirates were operating along the north African coast, much as before.

June 30th 1814

'*That strict discipline and subordination are essentially necessary; indeed are the main spring, the very life and soul of the Navy and Army is a truth that no one in the least acquainted with either would attempt to deny; but that it should be carried on in the extent it is towards Midshipmen of the Navy is unnecessary, indjudicious and unjust.*

A young man entering the Navy must be prepared for every rebuff – must almost stifle every feeling – must be prepared to put up with everything he meets with, even if it should appear to him oppression and injustice – he must smother every thought of manly pride – for he is scarce looked upon as a gentleman – must bear abusive language without complaint – for complaint against his superiors, even if he procured redress at the time would effectually bar the doors of promotion against him – and no Captain would receive him...'

MIDSHIPMAN JOHN BLUETT WRITING ON BOARD
HMS *TONNANT* IN 1814

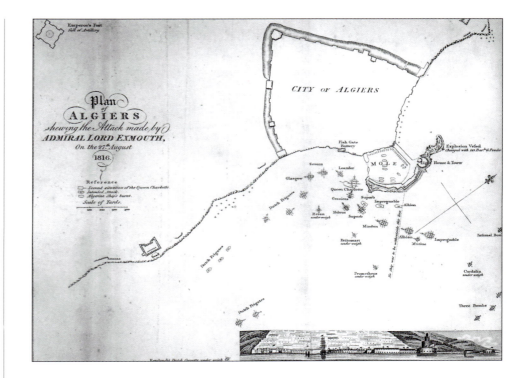

A TIME FOR REFORM

Even this early in the century, there were slow signs of much-needed reform in the Navy. In 1823, an experiment was carried out in the *Thetis* (46): the rum ration was halved, and tea and cocoa were issued every day instead. For months sailors from *Thetis* were beaten up by others ashore who thought they would be responsible for a cut in the rum ration. The experiment was judged a success; in 1824, the daily rum ration was halved to a quarter of a pint per man throughout the Navy. The custom of having 'banyan' or meatless days was also abolished, and meat was issued every day of the week. In 1831, the beer ration was abolished; in 1850, the rum ration was halved again, and the evening grog issue abolished.

The problem which was to trouble the Admiralty for much of the 19th century was: how, without using compulsion, to maintain an effective peacetime navy which could be rapidly augmented in time of emergency? Every reform moved the Navy a little further towards a permanent state of manning. In June 1827, an Admiralty Circular announced that henceforth petty officers of first or second class could not be punished by flogging, except by sentence of a court-martial. Captains could, however, still disrate petty officers by summary punishment on board, as in the past. When a ship paid off, the petty officers were to be discharged to the flagship as supernumeraries and, after leave, they were to be given another sea-going appointment, at the same pay and rate as before. Also, to improve the status of the petty officers, they were permitted to wear the badge of their rate, the second class petty officer a white cloth anchor on his sleeve, the first class an anchor surmounted by a crown.

Above: A plan of Algiers showing the attack made by Lord Exmouth's ships. This was first published in 1819 in A Narrative of the Expedition to Algiers in the Year 1816 *by Abraham Salamé, who was the British government's interpreter during negotiations with the Dey.*

Below: A plate from Jenkins's Naval Achievements *showing the defences of Algiers coming under severe bombardment by the British ships. The engraving, dated 1817, is by T. Sutherland after a painting by T. Whitcombe.*

Right: William Peel and his 'Jacks' at Lucknow during the Indian Mutiny. Peel, who entered the Navy direct from his school, Harrow, enjoyed an extremely distinguished service career until his premature death from smallpox, aged 33.

▶ **1819–20** Parry spends winter in the Arctic with *Hecla* and *Griper*.

1821–29 Greek War of Independence.

1824–26 Burma War.

1825 Rum ration halved throughout Navy. The custom of 'banyan' (meatless) days abolished.

Officers' entry to the Navy was also reformed, to a certain extent. In the previous century, officers had generally entered at an early age through 'interest'. No qualifying examination was required of 'captain's servants', as the youngest entrants were called. Many very young boys, well under ten years of age, were borne on a ship's books, with the captain drawing their pay, until they were old enough, normally at 12 or 13, to go to sea.

Another area in need of reform was the Royal Naval Academy at Portsmouth. Established in 1733, it was never popular and by 1801 Lord St Vincent was urging the abolition of an institution he described as 'a sink of vice and abomination'. Instead, in 1806 the Academy was reconstituted under the name of the Royal Naval College, with the Rev. James Inman (a well-known mathematician) as Headmaster. The first School of Naval Architecture was founded by Inman at Portsmouth in 1811 and amalgamated with the College five years later. It survived, with around 24 students, until its closure in 1834.

Success at the College led to extra seniority in the Navy. When the future Admiral Astley Cooper Key went to sea as a College Volunteer in 1835, he was awarded a year's time in recognition of his achievement of winning the College silver medal in 1833. This enabled him to sit the examination for the rank of lieutenant after only five years' service rather than the normal six.

However, many boys continued to enter straight from school. One such was William Peel, son of

the Prime Minister Sir Robert, who joined up from Harrow as a Volunteer First Class in April 1838. From a humble beginning on the line of battleship *Princess Charlotte*, flagship of the Mediterranean Fleet, he proceeded to captaincy and a KCB, winning the Victoria Cross in the Crimea and leading *Shannon*'s Naval Brigade in the Indian Mutiny in the 1850s.

The recruitment and entering of ship's companies remained the responsibility of the ship's captain as late as 1837, and this could be a major problem. Popular or particularly successful captains had an easier task, for they might well make up almost their full number from men who fol-

FROM SLOPS TO SERVICE DRESS

Although officers began to wear uniform in 1748 and warrant officers in 1787, seamen (except in ships where wealthy and ostentatious captains outfitted their own men, often in colourful gear like the 'pantomime' costumes of the barge crew of the *Harlequin*) remained in 'slops' for close on another century. Slops, ready-made clothes sold aboard, had been introduced in 1628 'to avoid nasty beastliness' – in other words, to lessen the occurrence and spread of diseases among men who might otherwise have only one vermin-ridden outfit.

Along with the establishment of educational facilities for officer cadets, boy seamen and various specialists, the increasing professionalism of the Victorian Navy was reflected in the issue of uniforms to lower ranks. From 1857, the seaman's uniform was established as a blue cloth jacket and blue or white trousers; one blue serge and one white drill frock (blouse) with a square blue collar bearing three rows of white tape, worn tucked into the trousers; a pea jacket; a black silk scarf (descendant of the bandanna worn by gunners to absorb sweat); a black canvas hat encircled by a ribbon bearing the ship's name in gold letters; and a working cap, either with a small peak like that worn by officers or, in summer or in tropical climes, a broad-brimmed straw hat. Special badges to denote non-substantive specialist rank, such as signaller or engineer, were introduced in 1869.

Boatswain, 1820

Midshipman 1823

Lieutenant 1852

Captain 1852

Above and right: A series of plates produced by the artist Richard Simkin in the latter part of the 19th century that illustrate Naval officers' full dress uniforms in the first half of the 19th century. In 1857, ratings were also issued with uniforms.

Admiral 1832

Men who enrolled for continuous service, and boy seamen reaching the age of 18, got their uniform (including a pair of shoes) free, although they could opt for cash in lieu. From 1859, bedding, formerly charged against pay, was also issued free: two hammocks, a mattress and cover, and a blanket. As well as an increase in basic rations, ships were allowed to open canteens, where seamen might purchase such delicacies as bacon, eggs and fruit. In 1892, these privately-run enterprises, accused of profiteering, were taken over by the Royal Naval Canteen Board – the joint ancestor, with similar boards for other services, of the modern NAAFI.

lowed them from their previous commands. Matters were also easier if few other ships had commissioned recently, or if the ship was bound for a favoured destination. However, to complete the roll captains sometimes had to resort to bribery, persuasion and advertising. Recruiting rendezvous were often set up in the commissioning port and in London, and sometimes also in Liverpool and Bristol. Nonetheless, negative factors such as an unpopular captain, an unpopular destination (usually one unattractive to potential deserters, such as West Africa) or competition from other recruiting captains could mean that it took months to complete a crew.

PAX BRITANNICA

At the end of the Napoleonic wars Great Britain was the most powerful state in Europe – arguably, in the world. The Royal Navy gave Britain overwhelming force at sea, to defend Britain herself, the Empire, and oceanic trade, and to conduct offensive operations, and interdict enemy trade, in time of war. The so-called Pax Britannica of the 19th century was upheld by force. France, though defeated, remained a potential enemy. The threat, real or imagined, of a cross-Channel invasion, with periodic 'scares', was a consistent *leitmotiv* in 19th century history.

Despite the intensity of its world-wide naval operations, the Navy continued to mount voyages of exploration and discovery, even at the height of the French wars. George Vancouver served as a midshipman in James Cook's second and third voyages, and was also present at Rodney's victory at The Saintes.

Although he was a somewhat unlikeable man, with little of Cook's humanity, Vancouver was a

worthy successor, and a most able navigator in his own right. He sailed in the new ship *Discovery*, 530 tons, in April 1791 on a voyage during which he surveyed the coasts of south-west Australia and New Zealand, and visited Tahiti and Hawaii. In 1792, he reached the Californian coast and sailed north, where he named Puget Sound, after Lt Peter Puget of *Discovery*, and the island which bears his own name. In 1794, the Polynesian King Kamehameha formally ceded the island of Hawaii to the King of England. Vancouver accepted this, but it appears never to have been ratified. Vancouver went on to survey Prince William Sound in Alaska before returning home in October 1795.

Francis Beaufort, one of the major figures in 19th century hydrography and meteorology, and a future Hydrographer of the Navy, first made his name with a survey of the south coast of Asia Minor, in command of the frigate *Fredericksteen*. He began in 1810, and produced a series of charts, views and descriptions of the ancient cities along the coast. He was shot and badly wounded by a Turkish fanatic in 1812. He later published his own account, in *Karamania*.

Beaufort was Hydrographer of the Navy from 1829 to 1855, a longer period than any other holder of the office, before or since. He joined the Navy in 1787, aged 13, served at the Glorious First of June and in the expedition to Buenos Aires in 1806–07 (when, incidentally, he made surveys of the River Plate). Besides his famous Scale to indicate the force of winds, Beaufort introduced an astonishingly wide-ranging series of innovations: in 1831, the establishment of a scientific branch to include the Hydrographic Department, the Royal and Cape observatories, the Nautical

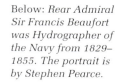

Below: Rear Admiral Sir Francis Beaufort was Hydrographer of the Navy from 1829–1855. The portrait is by Stephen Pearce.

Left: A riotous scene entitled 'The Midshipman's Birth' (sic) shows the lighter side of life aboard in the 1840s. Drink, cards, music, and practical jokes are very much in evidence as, in the words of the original caption to the drawing, 'frolics are the order of the day'.

Right: The search for the North-west passage preoccupied 19th century maritime explorers, but Sir John Franklin's expedition in 1845–47 ended in disaster when he and all his men died. Several expeditions were sent out to search for him – this scene shows HMS Assistance *under the command of Captain Sir Edward Belcher who searched for Franklin between 1852–54.*

1827 Victory of Codrington's British French and Russian Fleet over a Turco-Egyptian Fleet, Navarino (20 October). Admiralty circular announces abolition of flogging of petty officers except by sentence of court-martial.

1828 Names of steam vessels first published in Navy List.

1829 Anti-slavery patrols off Africa (and continuing for many years).

1830 Gunnery school established at Portsmouth – HMS *Excellent* commissioned.

Right: In 1825 William Parry organised an expedition to search for the North-west passage using the strongly built bomb vessels Hecla *and* Fury *which were able to withstand the pressure of pack ice. This engraving shows the two vessels trapped in ice in Prince Regent Inlet west of Baffin Island. On this occasion the party survived, but only* Hecla *returned safely to England.*

Almanac and the Chronometer offices; in 1834, the first publication of *Notices to Mariners*; in 1842, the establishment of a compass branch and the first publication of the annual *Admiralty Tide Tables*; in 1849, the publication of the Admiralty *Manual of Scientific Enquiry*; and, throughout Beaufort's tenure, the production of thousands of charts and hundreds of world-wide surveys, including a 'Grand Survey of the British Isles'.

ARCTIC EXPLORATION

The 19th century was an era of Arctic exploration. In 1818, an expedition commanded by Commander John Ross, with two ships, the *Isabella*, and the brig *Alexander* – commanded by a future Hydrographer of the Navy, Lieutenant William Edward Parry – sailed to search westward of Baffin Bay for the North-west passage. A second expedition sailed the same year, under Captain David Buchan, in the *Dorothea*, to attempt to reach the North Pole. With him, in command of the brig *Trent*, was another future explorer, John Franklin, who had been signal officer in the *Bellerophon* at Trafalgar. Neither Ross nor Buchan achieved their main objects, although Buchan's expedition survived severe hardships to survey thousands of miles of the north American coastline and explore the Mackenzie River.

The experience of 1818 showed that for proper exploration ships must winter in the ice. Two robust bomb vessels, *Hecla* and *Griper*, sailed under Parry in May 1819, and passed through 110°W in September, thus winning the £5,000

prize offered by the Government to anyone who could penetrate so far west inside the Arctic circle. Parry wintered on Melville Island, floating free of the ice in May 1820, and finally breaking out in August, having lost only one man.

A second expedition of 1819 under Franklin reached Hudson's Bay in August, travelled overland to the mouth of the Coppermine River and, having wintered there, went on by canoe to the Arctic Sea in June 1821. They explored the coast to the east, in very bad weather and being very short of provisions because of the rivalry between the two trading companies in the territory. Cold, hunger and fatigue eventually broke down even the strongest. Some died, some were murdered. The survivors reached Hudson's Bay again in June 1822. 'Thus terminated,' Franklin wrote, 'our long, fatiguing, and disastrous travels in North America, having journeyed by water and land (including our navigation of the Polar Sea) 5,550 miles.'

THE BATTLE OF NAVARINO

On 20 October 1827, the very last sea engagement fought purely between wooden walls took place in the Bay of Navarino, on the south-west coast of Greece. Greece had been part of the Ottoman Empire and under Turkish domination for centuries, and the Treaty of Vienna after the end of the Napoleonic wars maintained Greece's subject status. However, the Greeks rebelled for national independence (supported by a number of well-known Englishmen, notably Admiral Cochrane and Lord Byron), beginning with a minor revolt in the southern province of Morea in 1821.

In 1826, when Ibrahim Pasha, son of Mehemet Ali, ruler of Egypt, had almost defeated the Greeks and put down the rebellion, Russia decided it did not want Greece wholly under Turkish rule again. The British and French governments had been neutral, disapproving of the Greek revolt but

Above: *Vice Admiral Sir Edward Codrington who commanded the British, French and Russian fleet at the Battle of Navarino.*

Left: *The Battle of Navarino, 20 October 1827, painted by Thomas Luny. Codrington's flagship* Asia *is seen in the centre of the action.*

Below: *A climactic moment during the Battle of Navarino – a Turkish ship of the line explodes. Codrington won a decisive victory, but questions were asked about the efficacy of the Navy's gunnery.*

taking no steps to suppress it. Now, they also decided that hostilities must end. In the Treaty of London of 1827, Russia, France and Great Britain decreed an armistice between Turkey and Greece, which the Turks rejected. The navies of the three great powers were called upon to enforce it.

The combined British, French and Russian fleet, of four British, four French and four Russian ships of the line, three British, one French and four Russian frigates, and six smaller vessels, was commanded by Vice Admiral Sir Edward Codrington who, not for the first or the last time in British naval history, was placed in a very difficult position. Lacking a clear and un-equivocal lead from his government, he was apparently supposed to threaten force without actually using it. Thus, he was open to criticism whether he brought the Turkish and Egyptian fleets to action or not.

The Turco-Egyptian fleet, of seven of the line, 15 frigates, 26 corvettes, and 17 smaller vessels, lay at anchor in a great horse-shoe formation in Navarino Bay. As Codrington, flying his flag in the *Asia* (84), took his ships up to the Bay, he did not know whether or not he would have to fight. But he certainly acted as though he was sure he would, for he anchored his ships well inside the Bay, almost within the enemy horse-shoe. There was provocation on both sides. Shots were exchanged between boats. More shots followed, and a general ship-to-ship gun action broke out, which lasted for some four hours.

It was a somewhat one-sided battle. Ibrahim Pasha lost one ship of the line, 12 frigates, 22 of his corvettes, and several smaller vessels, with casualties of about 4,000 men. The combined fleet lost no ships but many were badly damaged. Codrington was recalled to London and was fortunate to be cleared of a charge of disobeying orders.

At Navarino, the British sailors had confidently expected the Turks to give up almost at once. 'We expected them to strike speedily,' wrote one sailor, 'and many were the enquiries whether they had "doused the moon and stars yet".' But no Turkish ship struck all day.

PROBLEMS OF GUNNERY

The hard truth was that the Royal Navy's gunnery, which had been good enough to beat the French and Spanish in the Napoleonic war, was no longer good enough for the demands of the 19th century. In the War of 1812, the larger, better armed and better fought American frigates had proved too much for their British opponents, with the famous exception of the *Shannon* and the less well-known *Phoebe*.

The poor performance of the Navy's guns aroused concern, but no immediate action was taken to remedy the situation. A number of pamphlets at the time placed the blame squarely on 'defective ship's guns', but the problem was more deep-rooted than that.

The fact was that the Navy had as yet no official policy regarding gunnery: no official system for testing new techniques or weapons, none for disseminating information about developments in gunnery science, and no mechanism for maintaining, let alone improving, standards of gunnery.

The responsibility for training gun crews was left to individual captains, including how often and in what manner practice was carried out. As a result gunners on certain ships received intensive training, with regular drills and firing practice, under the eye of conscientious captains like those under Exmouth in the Mediterranean or Broke of the *Shannon*; but on many other ships, handling of the guns was left to the gun captains, who were untrained in the science of gunnery.

It was not until 1829 that positive steps were taken to improve the situation. The first move was made by a Commander George Smith, who produced and submitted to the Admiralty a 'Prospectus of a plan for the improvement of naval gunnery, without any additional expense', in which he proposed the creation of an establishment for the training of gun crews and the testing of new gunnery equipment.

His proposal was well received, and in June 1830 the Board authorised the creation of just such a gunnery school under Smith's captaincy. The school was housed in HMS *Excellent*, established as a sixth rate in Portsmouth with a complement of 200, including Royal Marine Officers. The mooring in Portsmouth harbour offered a clear range for firing across the mudflats without any risk to life or property. In 1832, after two years' experience of the new school, Smith was promoted to Captain, but was immediately relieved, to his annoyance, by Captain Sir Thomas Hastings.

Right: *The launch of the 84-gun HMS* Thunderer *at Woolwich on 22 September 1831 in the presence of King William IV and Queen Adelaide.* Thunderer *took part in the capture of Acre in November 1840.*

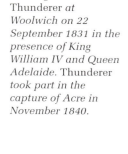

Above: *19th century shot and rammers. Concerted efforts were made to improve standards of gunnery in the early Victorian Navy.*

Right: *A scene showing the gundeck of a man-of-war in c.1850. The establishment of the gunnery school in HMS* Excellent *improved both the standards of gunnery training and the scientific evaluation of new ordnance*

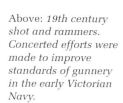

In February 1840, the C-in-C Portsmouth received a new prospectus from the Admiralty which, though nobody realised it at the time, was to revolutionise the bluejacket's world. The first paragraph introduced some startling new ideas:

'Their Lordships having had under their consideration the propriety and expediency of establishing a permanent corps of seamen to act as Captains of Guns, as well as a Depot for the instruction of the officers and seamen of His Majesty's Navy in the theory and practice of Naval Gunnery, at which a uniform system shall be observed and communicated throughout the Navy, have directed, with a view to the formation of such establishment, that a proportion of intelligent, young and active seamen shall be engaged for five or seven years, renewable at their expiration, with an increase of pay attached to each consecutive re-engagement, from which the important situation of Master Gunner, Gunner's Mates, and Yeoman of the Powder Room shall hereafter be selected to instruct the officers and seamen on board such ships as they may be appointed to in the various duties at the guns, in consideration of which they will be allowed 2 shillings per month, in addition to any other rating they may be deemed qualified to fill, and will be advanced according to merit and the degree of attention paid to their duty, which, if zealously performed, will entitle them to the important situations before mentioned, as well as that of Boatswain.'

These were revolutionary concepts indeed. Key words and phrases stood out in the paragraph – *permanent* corps, *uniform system*, engaged for five or seven years, *renewable*, increase of pay at each *re-engagement*, advanced according to *merit*. The introduction of a scheme of fixed-term and renewable employment, with pay increases at each re-engagement, and advancement by merit, would lead to the transformation of an under-valued, under-paid and often under-skilled

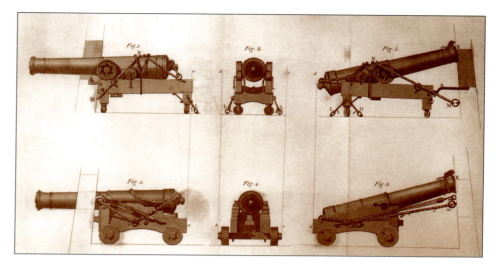

Above: *Drawings from An Elementary Treatise on the Mounting of Naval Ordnance (1811) by William Congreve. One of the pioneers of rocketry, Congreve developed rocket projectiles at Woolwich Arsenal that were subsequently used in the Napoleonic Wars.*

way of life into a professional, permanent career.

Training aboard the *Excellent* under Captain Hastings was to be equally revolutionary – in both style and content. Sailors were not simply ordered to do something, under the threat of punishment, but personally shown the best way to do it. They also had a great deal to learn. Under the old regime, sailors needed to be clever with their hands, and agile in the rigging, but little else. Much more than this was required of the *Excellents*. They had to learn: 'the names of the different parts of a gun and carriage, the dispart in terms of lineal magnitude and in degrees how taken, what constitutes point blank and what line of metal range, windage – the errors and the loss of force attending to it, the importance of preserving shot from rust, the theory of the most material effects of different charges of powder applied to practice with a single shot, also with a plurality of balls, showing how these affect accuracy, penetration and splinters, to judge the condition of gunpowder by inspection, to ascertain its quality by the ordinary tests and trials, as well as by actual proof.'

Though sailors were not formally required to be literate, they were encouraged to acquire skills of

Left: *HMS* Excellent *seen in her early days as a gunnery training ship. She was moored in Portsmouth Harbour where she could safely fire across the mudflats.*

Right: *The Beagle in the Beagle Channel off Tierra del Fuego in 1833, as sketched by Conrad Martens. Accompanying Captain Robert Fitzroy on the voyage was Charles Darwin.*

Below: *A watercolour by Owen Stanley of* Beagle *in Sydney harbour in Australia. The voyage of survey lasted nearly six years.*

reading, writing and cyphering in order to get the most benefit from this training. Under Hastings' sympathetic training methods they were eager to learn, and those who were already literate often taught their mates.

The original *Excellent* had been Collingwood's ship at St Vincent. She was broken up in 1834, and replaced by the *Boyne*, who was herself replaced by the *Queen Charlotte* in 1859. But they were all renamed *Excellent*, as was the shore establishment on Whale Island which eventually replaced them and which was enlarged and extended by spoil and waste brought by convict labour later in the century. The first building on shore, 'The *Excellent* House That Jack Built', was erected in 1864.

WIDENING HORIZONS

The Royal Navy's tradition of exploration was continued in the 1830s by one of the most famous of all voyages. The 235 ton sloop *Beagle* had been assigned to the surveying service in 1825, and had carried out a survey of the Magellan Strait in 1826 under the command of Captain Philip King. In 1831 she was recommissioned and sailed again in December under Captain Robert Fitzroy, to complete previous surveys of South America and to carry out a chronometer traverse of the world.

Fitzroy wanted to have 'some scientific person on board' and asked Beaufort, the Hydrographer of the Navy, if he could recommend anyone. Thus Charles Darwin joined *Beagle* to share Fitzroy's cabin and enjoy his friendship, and to record the natural history of the seas and territories,

including the Galapagos, Tahiti, New Zealand and Australia, which they visited in a voyage which lasted until 1836. The final results were published in a series of books about the voyage, beginning in 1839, and going through many editions, leading to *The Origin of Species*, and Darwin's celebrated theory of evolution.

Navarino was the last naval battle where the sea and sky were clear of boiler smoke and the air of the sound of steam engines. The first steam vessels saw action in the Navy in 1824, when the 3-gun wooden paddler *Lightning* went with the bombships to Algiers, and the 100-ton paddle tug *Diana*, built at Kidderpore in India in 1823, was purchased to take part in the first Burma War.

The war, from 1824–26, the result of resentment of growing British power and influence in India, coupled with xenophobia and local ignorance of just how powerful Great Britain now was, was a expedition to punish acts of aggression against East India Company territory and property.

Diana was used to tow vessels, including the 20-gun corvette *Larne*, which was commanded by Commander Frederick Marryat the novelist, up river where they provided naval brigades, as happened often in the 19th century, to serve ashore with the soldiers.

THE STEAM AGE

It was the great engineer Marc Isambard Brunel who persuaded a reluctant Admiralty that their conservatism must give way and steam must be introduced into the Navy. The Admiralty conceded that steam vessels might possibly be useful in manoeuvring warships in confined waters and harbours. In 1819, the Admiral ordered the tug *Comet*, a wooden paddle steamer of 238 tons and 90 nominal Horse Power (H.P.), which was completed in 1822, having been preceded in 1821 by the somewhat similar *Monkey*, of 212 tons and 80 nominal H.P.

These ships brought a new breed of men, the stokers, into the naval service. Old-fashioned naval officers did not regard stokers as proper seamen, indeed they could hardly bring themselves even to look upon them as fellow human beings, but the rate of stoker was officially instituted in 1826, with pay of 46s. 0d., rising to 54s. 3d., per month; they were paid 50 per cent more when in the tropics with steam up (this was money well earned).

In these early days, the Navy had no corps of engineer officers. Training for 'Engineer Boys' began as early as 1828, but generally engineers had no formal training or terms of apprenticeship. Engineering staff generally came with the ship, supplied by the engine builder, as was the case on *Comet*, *Monkey*, *Lightning* and *Diana*. Lacking any formal status, ranks, terms of service or uniforms, they were described simply as 'engineers' and were indeed no more than engine-drivers. This remained the case until 1837, when an Order in Council gave them warrant rank

Left: *A giant of the Victorian age: Isambard Kingdom Brunel. He was an enthusiatic supporter of steamships and screw propulsion, and and was engaged as a consultant by the Admiralty. His vessel, the* Great Western, *was the first steamship to provide a regular service across the Atlantic.*

(below the Carpenter) and the uniforms of Gunners, Boatswains and Carpenters. That year, the RN College in Portsmouth began to give instruction in 'steam'. In 1841, to distinguish engineers from other officers, engineers had to wear 'engineers buttons', with a steam-engine and a crown embossed on them. Another Order in Council in 1847 gave engineers commissioned rank, equal to the old navigating masters, and their names first appeared in the Navy List. But they still had to mess by themselves. Nobody wanted oily overalls in the wardroom.

Not until December 1827 were steam vessels allowed to use the prefix 'HMS' and their names

Left: *The steam-powered paddleship* Lightning *towing the* Royal Sovereign *into Portsmouth Harbour on 31 July 1827. Built at Deptford and launched in 1822,* Lightning *was the second steam-propelled vessel (after* Comet) *to enter service with the Royal Navy. She saw service at Algiers in 1824, the first such operational deployment of a British steamship.*

103

Right: A model of the Rhadamanthus, the first paddle steamer warship to cross the Atlantic, although she was not under steam power for the whole journey.

1839–42 The Opium War.

1839 Capture of Aden. *Volage* and *Hyacinth* engage war junks in Canton River.

1840 Syrian campaign; bombardment and capture of Acre.

1841 Possession taken of Hong Kong. Engineers given 'Engineers' Button' to distinguish them from other officers.

1842 Capture of Woosung; surrender of Shanghai.

1844–45 *Rattler* v. *Alecto* trials. Navy orders many screw ships.

were not published in the Navy List until January 1828. In that year, Lord Melville, the First Lord, replying to a request from the Colonial Department that a steamer be employed to carry mails from Malta to Corfu, minuted that My Lords Commissioners '. . . felt it their bounden duty to discourage to the utmost of their ability the employment of steam vessels, as they considered that the introduction of steam was calculated to strike a fatal blow at the Naval Supremacy of the Empire . . .'

Much of the prejudice against steam was simply that, but, while paddle wheels were the means of propulsion, there was also some practical justification for it. Paddles prevented guns from being mounted along a substantial part of the hull, and were themselves vulnerable to enemy fire (although, in fact, on the only two occasions a paddle wheel actually was damaged in action, the ship was able to maintain an only slightly reduced speed using the other wheel).

SCREW PROPELLERS

This situation changed utterly when the British inventor Francis Pettit Smith and the Swedish engineer John Ericsson both patented screw propeller designs in 1836. The question of which was the more efficient, paddle wheels or screw propeller, was decisively settled in the famous trials between two frigates of about equal size and engine power, the *Rattler*, fitted with a propeller, and the paddle steamer *Alecto*. In 1845, in a series of races under steam, under sail, and under steam and sail, over some 70 miles (112km) between the Nore and Yarmouth Roads, the *Rattler* beat the *Alecto* by several miles. In a later trial, in March 1845, with the ships secured together at their sterns and both going full speed ahead on their engines, the *Rattler* towed the *Alecto* stern first at a speed of 2.7 knots. It was a convincing result, but in fact the Admiralty were already convinced. They had ordered screw ships for the Navy in the previous year, and now ordered more. Although paddle steamers remained in naval use as dockyard tugs well into the second half of the 20th century, the future indubitably lay with the screw propeller.

The *Rattler* v *Alecto* trials were the most significant technical event of the 1840s, which was a busy decade for the Navy. There was a war in Syria, another consequence of the decline of the Ottoman Empire. In November 1840, a fleet

STEAM AND SCREW

The period 1815 to 1860 saw the end of the age of wood and sail, and the transition to a battle fleet of iron, propelled by steam. The process was long-drawn out, and some false trails were followed, but by and large the Navy embraced the new technology with enthusiasm. The Admiralty first used steam in 1816, when a steam tug was hired for towing trials. The first naval ship, a tug named *Comet*, was ordered in 1819. The first steam warships arrived in 1828; they were paddle-driven, which was a disadvantage in a fighting ship because the machinery and paddles were vulnerable, and the broadside was limited. A further disadvantage, which applied also to vessels propelled by a screw, was that the vibration of the machinery tended to shake wooden ships apart.

The screw was first successfully demonstrated at the same time as iron was introduced as a shipbuilding material. The Royal Navy's first iron warship was HMS *Albert*, a paddle gunboat ordered in 1840, but after 1845 the Navy ceased its iron shipbuilding programme while trials into the resistance of iron to shellfire were carried out, and means of overcoming the problems of fouling of iron hulls, so much

Right: The paddle warship Salamander was built at Sheerness and launched in 1832. The machinery of such paddle-driven vessels vibrated excessively and was deemed vulnerable to broadsides

Below: Launched in 1840, HMS London was a two-decker wooden ship of the line converted to screw propulsion. She was damaged at the bombardment of Fort Constantine in 1854.

worse than with copper-bottomed ships, were sought, as well as a means of correcting magnetic compasses in iron ships.

In the meantime, purpose-designed wooden steam-propelled battleships were built from 1847 onwards. They were screw-propelled, because it was realised that the screw was better at propelling a ship, and that the disadvantages of vulnerability and limited gunpower did not apply. Masts and yards were retained because the steam machinery, though adequately reliable, was very uneconomical.

By the mid 1850s when the Crimean War showed that wooden ships could not resist the penetrative effects of shellfire, the problems of fouling, compasses, iron quality, and other minor matters were in a fair way to being resolved. So, when the French built the wooden, armour-plated, steam-propelled *Gloire* in 1858, Great Britain was ready to usher in the modern battleship era with the *Warrior* and *Black Prince*, iron-hulled, iron-armoured and steam-propelled: the first modern battleships.

Left: *The paddle steamer Alecto is seen towing schooners past the batteries of San Lorenzo in Argentina. Alecto was convincingly beaten by the screw-propelled Rattler in an influential series of trials held in 1845. The writing was on the wall for paddle ships.*

which included armed paddle steamers, under Admiral The Hon Sir Robert Stopford in the *Princess Charlotte*, and Commodore 'Mad Charley' Napier in the *Powerful*, captured Mehemet Ali's fortress of St Jean d'Acre after a heavy bombardment. Steam ships came under enemy fire for the first time and Admiral Stopford shifted his flag to the steam-frigate *Phoenix*, commanded by his son, to get closer to the action – the first time a C-in-C had flown his flag in a steamer in action.

Apart from the war in Syria, there was also an Opium War in China, the beginning of a protracted campaign there, and a third war, in New Zealand, the first of several against the warlike Maoris. The Navy also maintained ships on over a dozen stations at home and abroad, each with its Commander-in-Chief, and was fully engaged in patrols against piracy off Borneo and Malaya, against slavery off the coast of Africa and in the West Indies, besides mounting explorations to polar regions, and continuing surveys of the world's seas, rivers and coastlines.

The Syrian War was the first time the Navy experienced a real shortage of men. It was the first practical proof that the old methods of manning were no longer enough. This had been to a certain extent foreseen. The Register of Seamen, introduced in 1835 by the then First Lord, Sir James Graham, was essentially a vast service roster. When a man's name reached the top of the list he was required to undertake five years' service, at the end of which time he was replaced by others on the Register. (In practice, few served the full five years: most were released after the end of the ship's commission, in three or four years.) However, no long-term arrangements to retain men on a more permanent basis were yet under consideration. There were no long-term engagements, and no barracks to house men ashore, merely lodgings in hulks while they waited for their ships. In 1846, when Lord Auckland was First Lord, a naval reserve was created from the Dockyard Service and the Coastguard, but it provided very small numbers of men compared with the nation's total need.

THE CURSE OF SLAVERY

'Slaves cannot breathe in England; if
  their lungs
Receive our air, that moment they are
  free;
They touch our country, and their
  shackles fall.'

So wrote William Cowper in 'The Task' in 1785. But, with an enthusiasm which Lecky called 'among the three or four perfectly virtuous pages in the history of nations', Britain pursued the freedom of slaves at sea as well as on land. The carriage of slaves in British vessels was abolished in 1807. In 1811, slave trading was made a felony, punishable by 14 years' imprisonment. In 1824, slaving was made a felony, punishable by death (a penalty changed to transportation for life in 1837), in 1833 the great Act of Emancipation was passed. From 1 August 1834 all slave children under six years were free at once. Adult slaves served some years longer before they too were free.

By 1815, most civilised countries had declared the slave trade illegal. In theory, the trade should have been extinct. In practice, it flourished, and 30 years after slavery was 'abolished' nearly twice

Above: *Chinese war junks being destroyed in Anson's Bay near Canton on 7 January 1841 by* Nemesis, *an iron steamship of the Honourable East India Company under the command of Lt W.H. Hall. Such hostilities were part of the First Opium War which broke out when China attempted to restrict the activities of British traders who were importing opium into China. The painting is by E. Duncan.*

Right: The trade in slaves reached its ignoble peak in the 18th century when more than six million captives were shipped to the Americas. The west African trade came to an end in 1870, thanks in no small measure to the work of the Navy's anti-slavery squadrons. The east coast trade, however, persisted into the 20th century.

Right: The trade in slaves reached its ignoble peak in the 18th century when more than six million captives were shipped to the Americas. The west African trade came to an end in 1870, thanks in no small measure to the work of the Navy's anti-slavery squadrons. The east coast trade, however, persisted into the 20th century.

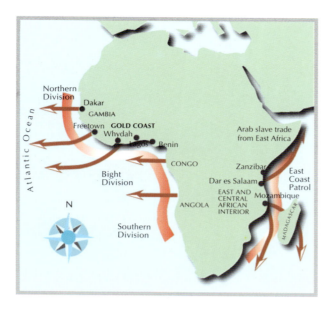

as many slaves were being exported from West Africa as before. For political and legal reasons it was impossible for British ships to stop and search ships of the United States, Spain, Portugal and France. As countries signed Right of Search treaties, so slaving captains sailed under other flags and carried false sets of papers.

Britain not only freed her own slaves but, largely through the agency of the Royal Navy, waged a campaign lasting most of the 19th century to free all slaves. The Navy maintained patrolling ships off both coasts of Africa, the Cape of Good Hope, the coasts of Brazil, and the islands of the Caribbean, especially Cuba. The Navy's main instrument against slavers in the first half of the 19th century was the West African Squadron. Liberia, the state established in Africa by freed slaves in 1822, would soon have been overrun by hostile neighbouring native tribes but for the Squadron's protection.

Once rescued, the slaves were taken to Freetown (hence the name) where there was an Admiralty Court empowered to condemn prizes, and there were facilities for watering ships and obtaining fresh food. But Freetown had one of the worst climates for the health of Europeans on the whole coast. The sailors made macabre jokes about the place, saying that ships' standing orders permanently detailed one party 'employed digging graves as usual', and another 'making coffins until further orders'.

Freetown was one of the few places where ships gave leave. After months on board, the sailors flocked ashore to drink the fiery native spirit, and then to lie about in the gutters, to be attacked by mosquitoes, until the morning. Thus the sickness rate on the Station was appalling. The old rhyme, 'Beware and take care of the Bight of Benin, There's one comes out for forty goes in', was not much of an exaggeration. Malaria, yellow fever and blackwater fever were all endemic on the coast. Whole ship's companies were reduced to skeleton crews by sickness, and some ships were actually forced to leave the Station. The best prophylactic was a visit to Ascension Island or St

1845–46 Operations in New Zealand.

1845–48 First French invasion scare.

1849 Anti-slavery operations against junks at Kua Kum, Indochina. Navigation Laws repealed.

Helena, where the cooler climate, fresh meat, fruit, fish, turtles, eggs and fresh water worked wonders for the sailors' health.

The West African Squadron increased from about seven cruisers and 700 men in the 1820s, to about 30 cruisers and 3,000 men in the 1840s. This led to an outcry at home about the expense of keeping so many ships and men on the Station, and the Squadron's efficiency was also frequently questioned and debated. Nevertheless, by 1848, the Navy had 24 cruisers off West Africa, nine off the Cape, 12 off Brazil and another ten in the West Indies or off North America.

The greatest technological advance for the Squadron was, of course, the coming of steam. At last, the elusive slavers could be run down and captured, whether or not the wind failed at the critical time. The large sailing frigate *Penelope* (16), which had had engines and paddlewheels fitted in 1842, arrived on the Station in 1845. The slavers themselves soon began to use steamships and one of *Penelope*'s most notable *coups* was the pursuit and capture of the large slave steamer *Cacique*, with 1,500 slaves on board, in March 1846. In March 1848 Captain Hotham, then commanding *Penelope*, reported that of 59 slavers captured in the previous year, 23 were taken by steamers.

In December 1851, a British squadron under Commodore Jones, flying his broad pennant in *Penelope*, assaulted and stormed Lagos, destroyed the slave barracks, and turned the port over to legitimate commerce. After the inauguration in 1861 of President Lincoln, who was whole-

THE STRUGGLE AGAINST SLAVERY

The main slaving territory stretched for some 3,000 miles (4,800km) down the west coast of Africa, from the Gambia to the Congo. Slavers operated from every river mouth and creek. There were almost no harbours, and very few anchorages which could shelter a fair-sized warship. The principal slaving ports were Lagos and Whydah, in the Bight of Benin, where the rivers of the coast, the Bonny, the Calabar, the Cameroons and the Oil River branches of the Niger, had been slaving posts since time immemorial.

The task of intercepting slavers was very difficult. The slavers were fast and very manoeuvrable. The slaving captains knew the coast and used darkness and local weather conditions skilfully. Even when

Left: A chain and shackle used to secure a captive slave and African currency confiscated by the Navy during anti-slavery operations.

Right and above right: Axes and pikes used for close-quarters shipboard fighting.

heartedly against the slave trade, slavers could no longer use the American flag. By 1865, the slave trade had diminished to the point where no ships at all were brought into Freetown for adjudication that year. By 1870, the West African slave trade was virtually extinct.

THE EAST COAST TRADE

The slave trade on the east coast of Africa continued to thrive, lasting well into the 20th century, and is not entirely extinct even today. There were two main slaving routes, one from the

they had been overhauled, captains produced their false papers and documents to prove that all the blacks on board were indentured household servants. Sometimes, chains and shackles were thrown overboard beforehand. Sometimes, even the slaves themselves were jettisoned.

When a slaver had been captured, the prize crew put on board had to take the greatest care they were not themselves surprised and overtaken. Man-of-war captains were often misled by officials ashore who were profiting from the slave trade, passing false information to the ship's captains, and accurate intelligence of the Navy's movements to the slavers. Ashore, the Navy had to patrol river estuaries in small boats, destroy the depots or barracoons where the slaves were kept after their journey down from the interior and before they were taken on board, and, not least important, continue to supervise native chiefs who had agreed to give up slaving.

The officers and men of the Navy were themselves accused of being hypocrites and taunted with greed, because they were given prize money for slaves captured. The rules for arresting slavers were so complicated that a captain could easily make an error. But any captain who did so found that he had to defend himself at law, at his own expense. Often proceedings were bureaucratically delayed until the captain concerned had left the Station, and the case then lapsed for lack of evidence.

northern part of Central Africa through Zanzibar to Arabia and southern Asia, and the other from the southern regions of Central Africa across to Madagascar.

The trade was seasonal, depending upon changes in the prevailing winds and currents of the Indian Ocean. The slaving dhows made two voyages a year, one on each monsoon, sailing southwards with the stream of legitimate traffic to Zanzibar on the north-east monsoon which lasted from November to April. Having embarked slaves, they sailed northwards again on the south-west monsoon, between April and September.

Knowledge of these climatic limitations was very useful to the naval squadron, but it was about their only advantage. Slavery was legal in all Muslim countries, and HM ships could only become involved with slaving when it took place on the high seas. Treaties and rights of search were negotiated as time went on with local potentates such as the Sultan of Oman and the Sultan of Zanzibar, and the governments of Persia and Turkey, but in practice the captain of a British man-of-war was very much his own judge and jury. The only port to which he could take prizes and release slaves was Bombay, and to go there meant his ship being off station for a long time.

The largest dhows were about 300 tons, but most were very much smaller. None of them left the sight of land if they could avoid it. With their very shallow draught, high poops and low freeboard forward, they looked like delicate ladies' slippers skimming swiftly over the water. Their large white cotton lateen sails were very conspicuous, but the dhows were very fast sailers, often faster than the naval brigs pursuing them.

The essence of east coast slaver-catching was boatwork. A ship's boats were kept at five minutes notice, ready equipped with water barricoes, salt pork, biscuits, arms, local currency and a small cask of rum with a lock on it. Manned by eight or

Above left: After a chase lasting 14 hours and an action of 80 minutes, HMS Pickle is seen capturing the slave schooner Bolodora on 6 June 1829. The engraving is by E. Duncan after a painting by W.J. Huggins.

Above: The capture of the slave brig Borboleta by the boats of HMS Pantaloon off Lagos on 26 May 1845. The boats from the brig Pantaloon are alongside and a fierce action is taking place.

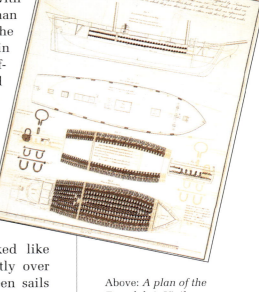

Above: A plan of the French brig Vigilante that was employed in the slave trade and captured on 15 April 1822. 345 slaves were found on board, crammed (mostly on their backs) into the lower decks in the manner illustrated.

Right: HMS Dryad *firing on an Arab dhow suspected of having slaves on board near Aden. The engraving, after a picture by Lt W. Henn, first appeared in* Slave Catching in the Indian Ocean *by Captain Colomb which was published in 1873.*

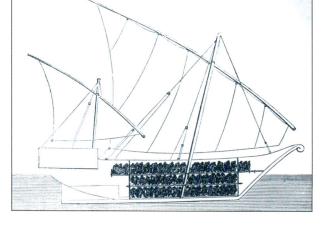

Right: A diagram that appeared in Dhow Chasing in Zanzibar Waters *(1873) by Captain G.L. Sulivan showing how slaves were stowed below the decks of a dhow in appallingly inhumane conditions.*

1852 Committee on Navy manning appointed under Admiral Parker.

1852–53 Second French invasion scare. Second Burmese War.

1853 Continuous Service Act passed in Parliament.

nine sailors, with a midshipman or junior lieutenant in command, a boat was often away from the ship for two or three weeks, normally anchoring every night, the men off watch sleeping along the thwarts.

In all the reports and reminiscences of the Navy's battle against slavery, the moral certainty of the officers and sailors taking part is evident. To them, slaving was not only a legal but a moral crime, a sin against humanity. The deaths, the ruined constitutions, the hardships and diseases, the ill-informed criticisms, the boredom, were all worth enduring in the long run. Every sailor involved was quite certain in his own mind that what he was doing was absolutely right and the slavers were utterly wrong, offenders against God as well as man.

PROBLEMS OF RECRUITMENT

The problem of manning the Navy at an acceptable level in peacetime, and boosting numbers in wartime by means other than the press gang, remained to be tackled. During the

1840s some 1,000 men were leaving the Navy each year, and the list of names on the Register of Seamen had dropped from 175,000 (plus about 22,900 apprentices) in 1839 to 150,000 by 1852, of whom 50,000 were exempt from service. In fact, only four percent of the men on the lists had ever served in the Navy. Fewer than 3,000 men had passed through the training establishment *Excellent* in more than 20 years.

Action had to be taken to review recruitment, and in 1852 Admiral Sir William Parker headed a committee of naval officers appointed for this purpose by Lord Derby's government. During the course of its considerations, Lord Derby's government fell and the committee's final report was made to Lord Aberdeen's First Lord, Sir James Graham, and the Second Sea Lord, Rear Admiral Maurice Berkeley, a key figure in the reformation of the Victorian Navy.

The committee's main recommendations were embodied in an Order in Council dated 1 April 1853 and the Continuous Service Act later that year, taking effect from 1 July 1853. Tighter standards of entry were introduced. New boy entrants started their 'time' at the age of 18, and engaged for a ten-year term of service: those already serving, both boys and seamen, were encouraged to transfer to the new engagements.

The terms of service were considerably improved. Pay was raised in general. An ordinary seaman's monthly pay increased by 7s. 7d. (38p) to £1 13s. 7d. (£1.68), and an able seaman's by 7s. 4d. (37p) to £2 1s. 4d. (£2.07). The new rate of leading seaman earned an extra 2d. per day, and senior ratings could look forward to an extra 3d. per day if they achieved advancement to chief petty officer. Men who had passed the *Excellent* were eligible to qualify for warrant gunners or 'captains of guns'. Career prospects were also enhanced by increasing the opportunities for promotion from boy to ordinary seaman. Pension

rights improved: instead of serving 21 years from the age of 20, seamen were now eligible for a pension after 20 years from the age of 18.

In terms of conditions of service, the Act laid down the broad foundations of the system still used by the Navy today. Sailors were granted paid leave between commissions, better sick pay conditions, a more uniform and restrained scale of punishment and – a matter of importance particularly for older seamen – they retained their right to choose their ship.

TRAINING AFLOAT

Opportunities for training afloat were extended. For many years a number of training brigs had been in commission, undertaking low-key but useful recruiting in home waters. Now, in 1854, a boys' training base was set up at Portsmouth on the old two-decker *Illustrious*, commanded by Captain Robert Harris. Under Harris, entrants followed a year's course in seamanship as well as general education. The next year, a second training base was established at Devonport on the *Implacable*.

John Arbuthnot Fisher, the future Admiral of the Fleet and First Sea Lord, and one of the most charismatic and influential reforming personalities in the Royal Navy's history, said that 'My examination [on board *Victory*] to enter the Navy was very simple, but it was adequate. I wrote out the Lord's prayer and the doctor made me jump over a chair naked, and I was given a glass of sherry on being in the Navy.'

In fact, Fisher did pass a full medical, and a written examination, as required by a circular of 1851, when the Admiralty was at last beginning to reform officers' entry into the Navy, after it had

remained haphazardly defined for years. In 1838, an Admiralty circular laid down that a Volunteer First Class 'must not be under twelve years of age. He must be in good health, fit for service, and able to write English correctly from dictation, and be acquainted with the first four rules of arithmetic, reduction and rule of three'. New entrants were termed 'Volunteers' until 'Naval Cadet' was introduced in 1843.

When Fisher joined the Navy in June 1854, aged 13, nominations for cadets were usually made by the Admiralty. However, a certain number of nominations were in the gift of admirals on hoisting their flags, and captains on their appointments in command. In June 1854 the 13-year-old Fisher was a nominee of Admiral Sir William Parker, who hoisted his flag as Commander-in-Chief Plymouth in that year.

Since the closure of the Naval College in 1837, cadets' education had been carried out by the Schoolmaster, a title that was changed to Naval Instructor in 1842. The Naval Instructor received the light blue distinctive colour on his sleeve in 1879, and was officially designated 'Instructor Officer' in 1919.

Captain Harris of the *Illustrious* was sufficiently impressed by the success of the novice-training scheme to recommend that another training ship should be set up for naval cadets. There was some opposition from traditionalist officers who saw no reason to change the system whereby boys progressed directly from school to sea. However, Harris demonstrated his faith in his scheme in January 1856 when he enrolled his own son Robert Hastings Harris (later Admiral Harris) on *Illustrious*'s books. The young Harris studied navigation and nautical astronomy under the Rev. Robert Inskip on board *Victory*, and seamanship alongside the *Illustrious* novices. Admiralty opinion swung round in favour of Harris's proposal, and a few weeks after his son had

completed his year's training, a new approach to the education of young naval officers was agreed. From now on, before proceeding to sea, there would be a compulsory period of training aboard a stationary ship.

In August 1857, *Illustrious*, moored off Haslar Creek in Portsmouth Harbour, received the first batch of 23 naval cadets. Soon it was decided to separate the training of officer cadets and seamen. At the end of the year the boy seamen were moved to a different base, and *Illustrious* became a dedicated cadet training centre. A year later the scheme had expanded to the point where a bigger ship was needed, and on 1 January 1859 Captain Harris shifted his pennant to the three-decker *Britannia* in Portsmouth. The *Britannia* was moved to Portland in February 1862, and moved again in September 1863 to her permanent base in the river Dart, moored half a mile above the town of Dartmouth.

> *HMS* Queen
> *Spithead*
> *February 7th 1842*
>
> *My dear Bessie,*
> *...I had first watch, from four to eight, (AM) after which I bundled down into the cock-pit, and washed and rigged out in full uniform, sword and all. In the next place, the most important proceeding of the whole day, breakfast – Then the drum beat to divisions, and away we all marched on deck, to muster the men....*
>
> LETTER FROM VOLUNTEER 1ST CLASS THOMAS ATKINSON

WAR WITH RUSSIA

The Navy's peacetime manning problems had been partially solved by the 1852 Committee's reforms. How to increase its strength rapidly in time of war remained problematic, as was apparent when the war against Russia broke out in 1854. Suddenly the Navy required enough seamen to man two fleets, in the Black Sea and in the Baltic. It found itself relying heavily on a small core of trained men, including many coastguards, considerably older than normal lower-deck contingents. There was much resentment among these men at being rushed back to sea at short notice, and they were no happier about the requirement to wear 'pusser's slops' (service clothing) instead of their own gear.

To supplement this core, an energetic recruiting drive took place. As far away as Stockholm, Norwegian and Swedish volunteers were signed on. The need for men was so great that the *Cumberland* (70), arriving home after three years on the North America Station, found itself sent direct to the Baltic. Its men, denied any leave (or indeed any information on their new destination) at the end of their term of duty were redistributed as petty officers among other ships because of their experience.

While the Russian War was in progress, Queen Victoria herself conceived the idea of a new award for valour, which was to be named after her – the Victoria Cross. She had realised, as the preamble to the original Royal Warrant of 29 January 1856 stated, that there was no way of 'adequately

---

QUEEN VICTORIA'S 'GUNBOAT NAVY'

From 1815 to 1914, the Royal Navy was never seriously challenged at sea. Its major task was to guard a far-flung and ever-expanding Empire, to which Victoria's reign saw the addition of such territories as Cyprus, Ceylon (Sri Lanka), Singapore, Hong Kong and Aden. The advent of steam necessitated the establishment and maintenance of a world-wide network of coaling stations (where 'coaling ship', especially in the tropics, became the seaman's most arduous and dreaded task). The Navy's preservation of order in often remote localities lends some truth to the often-quoted remark that British foreign policy in the 19th century boiled down to 'Send a Gunboat!'.

The ordinary seaman might have little chance to savour exotic places. Until 1890, shore leave was a privilege, not a right. A seaman in HMS *Leander* recorded that when she put in at Valparaiso in 1863 men who had not been ashore for 16 months were refused leave, while 'the officers have been ashore every day...but as we are not flesh and blood the same as them we could not get leave....' The result was a minor mutiny, for which a ringleader received 48 lashes. He had not risked being hanged at the yardarm – the last was in 1860 – but flogging in peacetime was not forbidden by the Admiralty until 1871, and in

Above: *George Cruikshank's cartoon of 1835 'Master B finding things not exactly what he expected...' paints a comic picture of conditions below decks on a warship.*

wartime until 1879. (It has never been formally abolished.)

The risks of desertion, drunkenness and disease were the usual reasons for denying leave. Desertion was, in fact, found to decrease with fairer treatment. Drunkenness, although a real problem ashore, was abated on board by the halving of the rum ration in 1824, the payment of an extra 7s. 6d. (37p) a month to men contracting to take no ration, and the institution in 1849 of the good conduct badge, worth an extra 3d. (1¼p) a day, for five years' crime-free service. These rewards were worth having when an ordinary seaman's pay was 38s. 9d. (£1.94) per month. Venereal disease decreased after the custom of allowing prostitutes aboard when in port was stamped out from 1840.

Left: *A Scene on the Main Deck, a cartoon dating from 1841. Women were frequently allowed aboard when ships were in port. Other popular leisure pursuits evidently included gaming, drinking and dancing!*

rewarding the individual gallant services either of officers of the lower grades in Our naval and military service, or of warrant and petty officers, seamen and marines in Our navy, and non-commissioned officers and soldiers in Our army'. Thus, from its first inception, the Victoria Cross was an award for everyman; it was open to any officer or man who served the Queen in the presence of the enemy and then performed some signal act of valour or devotion to his country. All persons were on an equal footing – 'neither rank, nor long service, nor wounds, nor any other circumstance or condition whatsoever, save the merit of conspicuous bravery' would qualify a man for the VC.

THE FIRST VCS

The first awards of the Victoria Cross to officers and men of the Navy fairly reflect the part the Navy played in the Russian War, afloat and ashore. The earliest act to win a Victoria Cross was carried out by a twenty-year-old Mate, Charles Davis Lucas, serving in the 6-gun steam paddle sloop *Hecla* in the Baltic Fleet, under Admiral Sir Charles Napier, in the summer of 1854.

On 21 June, *Hecla* (Captain W.H. Hall) was bombarding the coastal fortress at Bomarsund, in the Åland Islands, guarding the entrance to the Gulf of Bothnia, when a live enemy shell landed on *Hecla*'s upper deck. All hands were ordered to fling themselves flat on the deck but Lucas, with what Hall called 'great coolness and presence of mind', ran forward, picked up the shell and tossed it overboard. It exploded with a roar before it hit the water. Some minor damage was done to the ship's side and two men were slightly hurt but, thanks to Lucas, nobody was killed or seriously wounded. He was immediately promoted to Acting Lieutenant and, in due course, gazetted for the Victoria Cross in the first list.

The first lower-deck winner of the Victoria Cross was a stoker called William Johnstone. He was almost certainly not a British national, but very probably one of the Swedes recruited in Stockholm. He won his VC in an exploit which might have come straight out of the pages of the *Boys Own Paper*. In August 1854, Captain Hastings Yelverton, commanding the 47-gun screw frigate *Arrogant*, came back from a call on Admiral Napier saying that the Admiral had told him that important despatches from the Czar of Russia were being landed at Wardo Island and forwarded to Bomarsund. The Admiral was surprised that nobody had sufficient enterprise to 'stop this kind of thing'.

Hearing this, *Arrogant*'s officer of the watch, Lieutenant John Bythesea, went down to the ship's office to ask whether anyone on board spoke Swedish. He was told that Johnstone was a native of the country. Bythesea proposed that he and Johnstone land and intercept the Czar's despatches. Yelverton thought that two men were not enough, but was persuaded that a larger party would attract attention.

Bythesea and Johnstone rowed ashore to a small, remote bay on Wardo Island on 9 August. At a nearby farm they were well received by the farmer, whose horses had recently been commandeered by the Russians, and who was anxious to assist in any way he could. While the farmer and his daughter sheltered them, on one occasion concealing them from a Russian search party by dressing them as local peasants, Bythesea and Johnstone spent two nights reconnoitring the coastline in their boat, returning before dawn.

On 12 August, the farmer said the despatches were due. That night Bythesea and Johnstone hid in ambush beside the road. When the military escort turned back and the five Russians carrying the mails came on by themselves, Bythesea and Johnstone jumped out into the road and challenged them with their pistols. Two of the carriers dropped their mail-bags and ran. The other three surrendered, believing themselves to

Above left: *The British and French fleets in the Baltic provisioning at sea in 1854. The ship in the centre right foreground in HMS* Cumberland.

Above: *Naval Brigade gun batteries played an important part in the bombardment of Sevastopol in 1854. Here we see the 'Bellerophon Doves' in their encampment.*

Above: *Charles Lucas, the first Naval VC.*

Above: *John Bythesea won his VC by intercepting Russian despatches on Wardo Island in August 1854.*

Right: *The small port of Balaklava on the northern coast of the Black Sea. The naval guns used in the siege of Sevastopol were unloaded here and the British, French and Turkish troops were kept provisioned by ships that were able to use the harbour to unload stores.*

Above: *A man of extraordinary courage – William Peel who won a Victoria Cross for three separate acts of bravery.*

Below: *Diamond Battery at the siege of Sevastopol. The heavy guns from the frigate* Diamond *were under the command of Captain William Peel.*

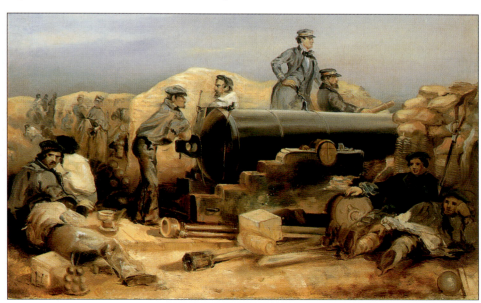

be surrounded by a large force. They were taken down to their own boat, where Bythesea made them row back to *Arrogant*. Bythesea's and Johnstone's VCs were gazetted in the first list.

In the Crimea, soon after the Allied landing on the coast and the battle of the Alma in September 1854, the British Commander-in-Chief, Lord Raglan, asked for the Navy's assistance. On 1 October, over a thousand bluejackets and officers with over a thousand marines began to disembark with their guns and equipment in Balaklava. Among them were sailors and heavy guns from the 28-gun frigate *Diamond*, under their Captain, William Peel.

WILLIAM PEEL'S GALLANTRY

The third, and favourite, son of Sir Robert Peel, the celebrated Prime Minister, William Peel was one of the most remarkable men ever to serve in the Navy. He won his Victoria Cross three times

over, and but for his premature death from smallpox at Cawnpore, aged only 33, he would have reached the highest ranks in the Service. By 7 October, the Naval Brigade had constructed and manned two gun batteries facing the city of Sevastopol, mounting 32-pounder, 68-pounder and Lancaster guns from the ships, having dragged them by hand up the hillsides from Balaklava harbour. These naval guns took part in the great bombardment of Sevastopol which began on 17 October. The next day, the horses drawing the ammunition wagon for the *Diamond*'s Battery refused to face the heavy Russian fire. Volunteers went to clear the wagon and bring up the ammunition. Before the powder could be stowed in the magazine, a 42-pounder Russian shell with its fuse burning fell in the middle of the powder cases and the volunteers unloading them. Hearing the shout of alarm, Peel sprang to the shell, clasped it against his chest and carried it until he could throw it over the parapet. The shell burst almost as soon as it left Peel's hands but fortunately nobody was injured.

On 5 November, during the battle of Inkerman, when the Russians made a determined effort to seize the commanding heights above Sevastopol, the Duke of Cambridge with some of his staff and about 100 men were grouped around the colours of the Grenadier Guards in the Sandbag Battery, an emplacement some 30 feet (9m) wide, with embrasures for two guns. Unknown to them, they had been cut off by the enemy, and two more Russian battalions were advancing on the position from their left. Peel saw the danger through his field-glasses and at great risk to himself made his way through the smoke and mist to warn the Duke's party, who then managed to make a fighting retreat out to safety.

On 18 June 1855, the anniversary of the Battle of Waterloo, the British and French attempted to storm the massive and strongly defended fortress of the Redan at Sevastopol. But the attacks were not properly coordinated and the attackers, including many of the Naval Brigade with scaling ladders, had to cross open ground under heavy fire. There were many casualties amongst the sailors and Peel, who led the first scaling party to the very foot of the Redan wall, was himself severely wounded in the arm, and had to withdraw with the other survivors. For these three separate acts of gallantry, William Peel won the Victoria Cross.

Inkerman, fought in fog, thick mist and drizzling rain, with visibility seldom more than a few yards, so that commanding officers could see nothing of the action, has been called the 'Soldiers' Battle'. It was also the Sailors' Battle, for there were 600 of the Naval Brigade in the field and as many more manning the batteries.

In one battery, the soldiers suffered many casualties under a fierce Russian attack. Five sailors who were also in that battery mounted a rapid repulsing fire. Wounded soldiers, lying in the trench below them, reloaded rifles and passed them up until eventually the Russians fell back. Two sailors were killed by the withering enemy fire which constantly swept the top of the parapet, but the remaining three, James Gorman, Thomas Reeves and Mark Scholefield, all seamen from the line of battleship *Albion* (90), survived to win the Victoria Cross. At that time there were no posthumous Victoria Crosses, so the two sailors who were killed got no mention and no medal. Their names were not recorded and are now regrettably forgotten.

RUSSIA IN RETREAT

In May 1855, a strong expedition of some 15,000 infantry and 56 ships – frigates, light draught steamers, gun boats, and launches armed with 24-pounder howitzers and rockets – was sent eastwards across the Black Sea to seize the Straits of Kertsch, and operate in the Sea of Azov beyond, with the object of cutting the Russian supply line by sea.

The Russians blew up their forts and retreated from the Straits, so that the objectives were captured without the loss of a man. A steam flotilla went through the Straits and within a week had sunk four steam warships and 246 merchant vessels of various kinds, captured corn, flour and powder magazines to the value of £50,000 and seized over 17,000 tons of coal.

The Azov operations encountered no seaborne opposition, so all the actions were therefore daring commando-like raids by small parties to destroy enemy *matériel* ashore, in which the Navy won several more VCs.

The last bluejacket's VC at Sevastopol was won by Boatswain's Mate John Sheppard, of the screw line-of-battleship *St Jean d'Acre* (101). He built a

Above: The interior of the strongly defended Redan at Sevastopol. It eventually fell to British and French forces in September 1855 after a campaign lasting almost a year.

canvas duck punt, which floated only three inches above the water and would be virtually invisible at night. The punt held an explosive charge in a light iron case, fitted with a Bickford fuse which burned under water. Sheppard himself would sit in the stern sheets and steer with his paddle. His plan was to penetrate Sevastopol harbour, paddle silently up to a Russian man-of-war, fix his explosive charge to her side, and paddle away again.

He made his first attempt on the dark night, specially chosen, of 15/16 July 1855. He got amongst the Russian warships, but when he was approaching the great three-deckers which were his objectives, he was frustrated by an unbroken line of boats, carrying troop reinforcements to Sevastopol, which formed a barrier across the harbour. After waiting for over an hour, he finally had to abandon his venture, and return to the Allied shore as dawn was breaking. He made a second attempt on 16 August, but was no more successful. However, Boatswain's Mate John Sheppard could justifiably claim to be the common ancestor of the midget submarine crews, the charioteers, the 'cockleshell heroes', and all the special boat parties of the Second World War.

The first Victoria Cross awards, made retrospective to cover the Russian War just ended, appeared in *The London Gazette* of 24 February 1857. There were 85 names in that first list, 27 from the Navy and the Marines. Queen Victoria herself held the first Investiture of VCs, in Hyde Park on Friday 26 June 1857. Of the 62 VCs invested that day, 12 were from the Navy, and two from the Marines. The first man ever to wear a VC was Commander Henry Raby, who had won his Cross at the Redan in June 1855, and was invested first, as the senior officer of the Senior Service present. It was said that the Queen inadvertently dug the point of the pin holding the VC ribbon deep into Raby's shoulder, but he said not a word and flinched not a muscle.

Above: John Sheppard who won the last bluejacket VC of the Crimean War.

Above: Seaman Joseph Trewavas who won a VC for his action in the Sea of Azov on 3 July 1855 when he destroyed a pontoon bridge, so cutting a Russian supply route.

CHAPTER SIX

FROM WARRIOR
TO
DREADNOUGHT

Previous pages: *HMS
Illustrious of the
Majestic class, 'the
epitome of Victorian
battleship splendour',
is seen off Corfu in
1899. The artist, Ian
Marshall, records such
details as the booms
along the hull for anti-
torpedo netting and
the 3-pounder quick-
firers in the fighting
tops.*

Below: *A cutaway
view of the broadside
ironclad HMS Warrior,
the first true battleship
in the modern sense.
Her main gun deck
and machinery are
protected by a 210ft
(64.6m) long 'citadel'
of 4.5in (11.4cm)
wrought iron plate
backed by 18in
(45.7cm) of teak.*

Warrior was the most revolutionary
warship of her time, perhaps of all
time. She was the largest, fastest, most
powerful warship of her day. She made
everything else obsolete overnight. She was not
the first ironclad in the Royal Navy, and the
original design concept was that she should be a
frigate. Nevertheless, as built, *Warrior* was certainly the first ocean-
going, iron-hulled *battleship*, in the modern sense
of the word.

The first impulse to
build *Warrior* did not
come from the Admiralty.
As the world's greatest
naval power, Britain did
not need to innovate.
'New-fangled' inventions
could safely be left to
weaker nations, who had
to try and make up in
ingenuity for what they
lacked in sheer brute
naval strength. Even if an
innovation proved suc-
cessful, Britain had the
industrial resources to
outstrip the original inno-
vators with ease.

The pressure to build a
British ironclad arose from
one of the 'invasion scares'
which swept Victorian
England from time to time. Relations with France,
always prickly, deteriorated sharply towards the
end of the 1850s, when the Emperor Napoleon III
showed clear signs of wanting to emulate and
even to surpass the military prowess of his famous
namesake. Rumours, press stories and intelli-

Above: HMS Warrior *after restoration that was
carried out in 1979–87. Note that she is ship-rigged –
and that she once recorded 13 knots under full sail.*

gence reports reached England that the French
were building a new type of warship.

Completed in August 1860, and called the
Gloire, the new ship was literally an ironclad – a
wooden ship with wrought iron plates overlaid on
her sides. The Admiralty's first proposal was
simply to follow this French example and fit iron
plates on a wooden hull. Fortunately for the Navy
and the country, the First
Lord, Sir John Pakington,
adopted a much bolder
concept: an iron-*hulled*
ship, proposed by Captain
Sir Baldwin Walker, the
Surveyor of the Navy, to
the broad design of the
Chief Constructor, Isaac
Watts, assisted by the ship
designer John Scott
Russell.

The specification was
for a frigate, with 4 inches
(10.2cm) of iron
protection on her sides
extending from the upper
deck to five feet (1.5m)
below the waterline, over
a length of 200 feet (61m)
amidships, with protected
bulkheads at each end, so
as to form the middle of
the ship into an armoured
box, or 'citadel'. The bow
and stern sections were to
be unarmoured, but sub-divided into watertight
compartments. The hull would have 34 gun ports
on the main deck, the ports to be at least nine feet
(2.75m) above the waterline in the midships
section, with two upper deck guns as bow and
stern chasers. The top speed was to be 13½ knots.

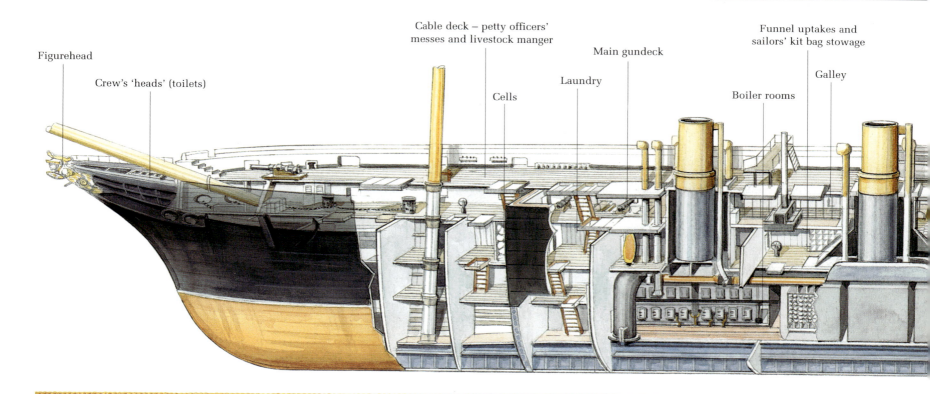

Figurehead

Crew's 'heads' (toilets)

Cable deck – petty officers'
messes and livestock manger

Cells

Laundry

Main gundeck

Boiler rooms

Funnel uptakes and
sailors' kit bag stowage

Galley

Under sail, the ship would be rigged as for an 80-gun ship.

Launched (by Sir John Pakington) on the Thames on 29 December 1860, so new and revolutionary a ship naturally aroused die-hard criticism. 'This miserable, peg-topped leangutted model,' said Admiral Sir Edward Belcher, speaking for the older generation. However, *Warrior* was the first ship to incorporate four of the great Victorian advances in warship building: armour protection; an iron structure in both frame and plating; a ratio of length to beam of 6.5. to 1; and a system of subdivision in her compartments (92 in all) to give much improved watertight integrity. As completed, she displaced 9,210 tons (hull 6,150 tons, equipment 3,060), with an overall length of 418 feet (127.4m) – 380 feet (116m) between perpendiculars – a beam of 58¼ feet (17.75m) and a draught of 26 feet (7.9m). She cost £377,000, including the guns and 850 tons of coal.

As first commissioned on 1 August 1861, *Warrior* had a main deck armament of nine 68-pounder Muzzle Loading Smooth Bore (MLSB) guns and four 110-pounder Armstrong 7-inch 82-cwt Breech Loading Rifled (BLR) guns on each side within the citadel. She also had four guns (two MLSB, two BLR) forward of the citadel and four more aft. This gave a broadside of 17 guns a side – 34 guns in all. On the upper deck were two 110-pounder BLR chasers, one forward and one aft, and four 40-pounder BLRs. The total armament was therefore 40 guns, and as a result *Warrior* was first officially designated as a 40-gun Screw Ship, Iron.

Warrior's first captain was The Hon. Arthur Cochrane, third son of the famous Lord Cochrane, hero of the Napoleonic Wars. Her wardroom had a hand-picked look about it. Her commander, George Tryon, was one of the ablest officers of his generation, and one of her gunnery lieutenants

Above: *HMS* Warrior *is seen sometime after 1863 when the height of her funnels was increased by 6ft (1.8m) to provide better draught for the boilers. She and her sister-ship* Black Prince *were the among the last British capital ships to have figureheads.*

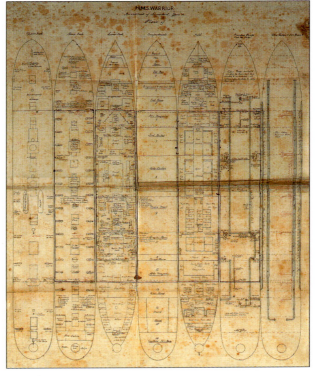

Left: *This plan of HMS* Warrior *appears in the log of Midshipman H.A.K. Murray, compiled between June 1861 and March 1863. The ends of the warship were not protected by armour, but featured 92 watertight compartments. She had a complement of just over 700 men.*

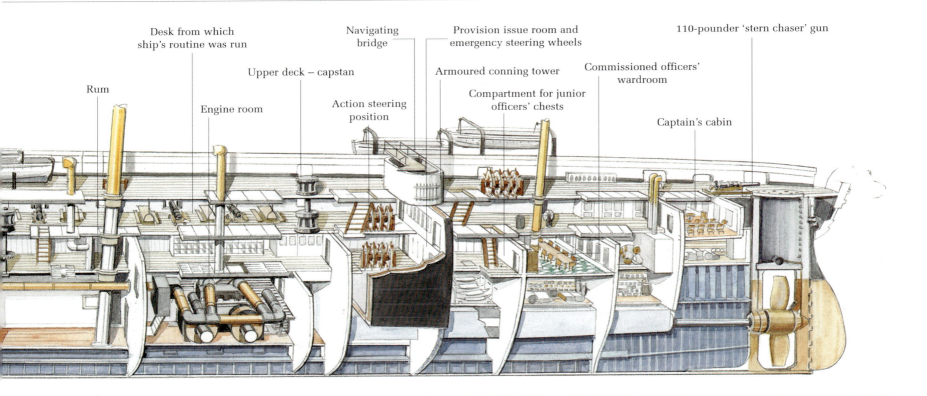

Rum

Desk from which ship's routine was run

Engine room

Upper deck – capstan

Action steering position

Navigating bridge

Provision issue room and emergency steering wheels

Armoured conning tower

Compartment for junior officers' chests

110-pounder 'stern chaser' gun

Commissioned officers' wardroom

Captain's cabin

Right: *Continuous
Service was
introduced into the
Royal Navy in 1853.
Above is the
Certificate of Service
of Henry Davis; below,
the Continuous
Service Certificate
(1855–60) of William
Wright.*

▶ **1859** Statute
authorizing Royal
Naval Reserve passed.
Warrior laid down at
the Thames Ironworks
slipway.

1860 Naval Discipline
Act passed.

1861 HMS *Warrior*
commissioned.

1863 Engineers' purple
stripe introduced.

1863–64 Operations at
Kagoshima, Japan.
Maori War.

Below: *The uniform
and accoutrements of
Captain The Hon.
Arthur A. Cochrane,
first captain of HMS
Warrior. Shown here
are his sword, dressing
case and medals,
including the Breast
Star of a Knight
Commander of the
Order of the Bath
(KCB) and campaign
and Naval General
Service medals.*

was Jackie Fisher, a future First Sea Lord. Her complement, as given in the Ship's Book, was 51 officers, 83 petty officers, 382 seamen, stokers and idlers, 63 boys, and 125 Marines.

Like all the early ironclads, *Warrior* suffered from a shortage of men, because a conservative Admiralty refused to acknowledge that ironclads needed new manning scales. Warships had always been graded in 'rates', according to the number of guns they carried, and their complements were rigidly fixed, being assessed on the watch and quarter bill of a ship of that rate.

'Rates' did not apply to ironclads. Simply to count the number of guns, as in the old days, was absurd. That would put *Warrior*, the most powerful warship afloat, down among the frigates. But Admiralty bureaucrats, then as now, stuck rigidly to their rules. *Warrior* had 40 guns. Therefore she must be a frigate. However, the Gunnery branch calculated that *Warrior* needed 740 men, close to the number in a third-rate ship of the line, which was 705. Therefore *Warrior*, for manning purposes, was classed as a third-rate, with a complement of 705.

Warrior's engines, boilers, and propeller hoisting gear (when proceeding under sail alone) were made by John Penn & Sons of Greenwich. The 1,250 nominal horsepower engines were jet-condensing, horizontal-trunk, single expansion, with a piston stroke of four feet (1.2m) and a cylinder bore of 9 feet 4 inches (2.84m) (the largest in diameter ever cast for a marine engine). There were ten rectangular multi-tube (440 brass tubes per boiler) fire-tube wrought iron boilers, four in the forward and six in the after boiler room. Each boiler had four furnaces, and contained 29 tons of water. Normal steam pressure was 20-22 psi. *Warrior* could officially make 14.3 knots at 55 shaft revolutions/minute under steam, 13 knots under sail. She once logged 17.7. knots (a figure never surpassed) under both.

The invasion 'scare' which gave *Warrior*'s

advent such impetus also led to another manning crisis. The end of the Russian War left the Navy, in April 1856, with a complement of more than 26,000 men manning a fleet of 25 sail of the line and some 200 ships of other classes at Spithead. More than half these ships were paid off, and 15,000 crew members discharged to shore, within the next two months.

In May 1857 the Admiralty took a further step to reduce numbers. All petty officers, seamen and boys whose ships were in or returning to home waters were offered discharge (without payment) from their continuous service engagements. The physically unfit and men of poor character received compulsory discharge.

Considerable resentment was aroused by this apparent return to the bad old days of casual recruitment, particularly among the many sailors who accepted their discharge in haste only to repent it at their leisure. It seemed that the Admiralty's vaunted new deal for seamen, with its promise of permanent naval careers, was still some way from fruition.

THE ROYAL NAVAL RESERVE

The manning crisis was addressed by a Royal Commission set up by Sir John Pakington in June 1858. In January 1859, the Commission made its recommendations, including better pay for seamen gunners, better victualling, free bedding and mess utensils for new recruits and free uniforms for continuous service entrants. It also urged more training ships and brigs for boy seamen. The *Illustrious*, paid off in 1859, was succeeded in 1862 by the *St Vincent* at Portsmouth and the *Impregnable* at Devonport, the *Boscawen*, in Southampton Water until about 1867 when it moved to Portland, the *Ganges* at Falmouth in 1866, and the *Wellesley* at Chatham. But the Commission's key recommendation was the formation of a Royal Naval Reserve.

In August 1859, the creation of the Reserve was authorized by Statute. It targeted the thousands of experienced merchant marine sailors who made three or four short voyages a year. They were invited to enlist for an initial five years, with 28 days training a year. They would be called out only by a Royal Proclamation, and at times of 'sudden emergency' for an initial three-year period. They were paid naval rates, and would qualify for a pension from the age of 60. The qualifying requirements were rigorous. Only seamen of British descent were eligible, if under 35 years of age (although until 1860 they could join up to 40), physically fit, having served five years in the previous ten (at least one at AB rate), preferably of fixed abode, selected by a shipping master to whom they were personally known, and approved by their local coastguard.

The Admiralty envisaged the recruitment of some 20,000 men, but initial response was almost nil. Recent memories of the Admiralty's discharge of continuous service men in 1857, combined with lingering suspicions of the press gang, fears of being shanghaied to the China Station and doubts of how a 'sudden emergency' would be defined, left merchant seamen mistrustful. However, eventually the Reserve built up its numbers, and by 1865 it comprised some 17,000 men.

Events had already overtaken the Admiralty's plans by that time. In 1859, the anti-French 'scare' found the Navy under-manned. Numbers had to be raised hastily by offering a bounty: £10 for ABs, £5 for ordinary seamen and £2 for landsmen. As in the days of the old 'Quota men', the majority of 'bounty men' were undesirables – criminals, debtors, mental defectives, unemployables and family black sheep. Many ships found themselves with what amounted to two ship's companies, the 'bounty men' and the unfortunate regulars who found themselves – for the same pay – having to cover the deficiencies of the former group as well as carrying out their own jobs.

Understandably, there was considerable discontent on the lower decks, sometimes leading to serious unrest. All too often matters were made worse by officers' harsh, old-fashioned (sometimes downright stupid) approach. A major grievance concerned leave. In the late 1850s, it became clear that a more regular and more humane allotment of leave was vital to tackling the crisis of discipline in the fleet.

In April 1860, new regulations authorized captains to grant regular leave: 48 hours or four days, depending on circumstances and on the

recipient. Senior officers watched the first grants of leave 'in an agony of suspense' – and initially their fears were justified by mass leave-breaking and a near-epidemic of desertions.

In 1860, the Naval Discipline Act provided the first definition of desertion: after 21 days unauthorized absence from his ship, a seaman had his papers marked 'Run' and an 'R' entered on the ship's books. Once classed as a deserter, he forfeited his pay, prize money, bounty, pensions, medals, decorations and even any clothes and effects left on board. Even this stringent penalty failed to deter some 2,000-2,500 men a year from deserting.

In 1866, three categories of leave were classified: 'special' for men of good character, 'privileged', given when convenient, for the less reliable, and 'regular' for all others, including

Above: *HMS* St Vincent, *a 120-gun ship completed in 1815, was established at Portsmouth in 1862 as a training ship for boy seamen, one of five such vessels thus designated around that time. Seen below is her badge.*

1866 Prototype of Whitehead torpedo produced. Establishment of the Albert Medal for Gallantry in saving life at sea.

1870 Trials of Whitehead torpedo at Sheerness. HMS *Captain* capsizes off coast of Spain with loss of 472 lives.

1872 HMS *Vernon* fitted out as torpedo instructional ship. First British Whitehead torpedo built.

> '*The bare bleakness of the mess-deck with its long range of plank tables and stools had as little suggestion of physical ease as a prison cell. It was damp and chilly in a cold climate, and damp and hot in the tropics. It was swept by searching draughts if the ports were open, and nearly pitch dark if they were closed, glass scuttles not having been invented. It was dimly lit at night by tallow candles inside lamps at long intervals, and as there were no drying rooms it reeked of wet serge and flannel. In short the living quarters of the mid-Victorian bluejacket, stoker, or marine were as widely dissociated from any ideal of a home in the usual sense as could be imagined.*'
>
> ADMIRAL GEORGE BALLARD, WHO JOINED THE
> BATTLESHIP *RESISTANCE* IN 1877

those in the Second Class for Conduct. Leave was a privilege rather than a right until 1890.

1859 saw the introduction of the First Class for Conduct. Sailors and marines in this class were exempt from flogging except by court martial sentence. Parliamentary surveillance over the numbers of men flogged, and frequent strict injunctions from the Admiralty to captains to curtail excessive punishment, began to have their effect. Changing social attitudes to flogging and adverse publicity persuaded the Navy in 1871 to suspend flogging in peacetime, and in 1879 it was suspended altogether. To this day it remains suspended rather than banned outright: strange as it may seem, in theory at least, it could be brought back in wartime.

THE VICTORIA CROSS

Thirteen naval winners of the VC in that first list of February 1857 were not present at the first Investiture in June because they were serving abroad. The Admiralty sent off the Victoria Crosses for those naval winners so that they could be invested on their foreign stations.

Amongst those Victoria Crosses sent abroad was William Peel's. At the time of the Investiture, he was in command of the new and experimental 51-gun steam frigate *Shannon*, on the way to the China Station. *Shannon* was at Singapore when the news of the Indian Mutiny arrived in June 1857. She sailed for Hong Kong to embark troops and then for Calcutta, where she arrived in August. Peel formed a Naval Brigade of nearly 400 officers and men and ten 8-inch guns from *Shannon* and took them up the river Ganges by steamer to Allahabad.

Shannon's sailors, 'Peel's Jacks', as they were called, served with great distinction in the Indian Mutiny, taking part with the army in operations in Cawnpore and Lucknow, and winning five Victoria Crosses. They were superb campaigners, able to march, fight, march again, fight again, live off the land, handle horses and bullocks with the same ease as they handled their heavy guns which they moved about as though they were light field pieces, while enduring heat, short rations, disease and fatigue with courage and good humour. They soon won a fearsome reputation amongst the sepoys, who firmly believed that the Jacks were

Left: *Admiral of the Fleet Sir Arthur Knyvet Wilson won the VC for gallantry ashore.*

DEVOTION TO DUTY

Field Marshal Slim opined in 1957 that the Victoria Cross was won by men of two kinds: 'those who live on their nerves and those who have not got any nerves.' Into which category Admiral Sir Arthur Knyvet Wilson, whose VC and other decorations are seen here, fell we cannot know. He won it in hand-to-hand combat, saving a gun from Arab attack while serving ashore with the Naval Brigade at the battle of El Teb (1884). Wilson's decorations include the Grand Cross of the Bath (GCB). Naval officers too junior to merit the Companionship of the Bath (CB) were rewarded from 1874 with the Conspicuous Service Medal, or from 1886 with the Distinguished Service Order (DSO); ratings might win the Conspicuous Gallantry Medal (CGM).

The origins of the VC and early naval recipients are described in Chapter 5. From 1856, all non-commissioned holders received a pension of £10 per

Below: *In winning his VC at El Teb in 1884, Wilson broke the sword shown in the centre. The upper weapon was presented to him by the ladies of Malta as a replacement; the lower was presented in admiration of his bravery by the officers and men of HMS* Vernon.

all four foot high by five foot wide from snout to tail, carried 9-pounder guns over their heads, and ate human flesh as much as they could, salting down the rest for future consumption.

A second Naval Brigade, from the 21-gun steam corvette *Pearl*, also served in the Indian Mutiny. Led by their Captain, E.S. Sotheby, the *Pearl*'s Brigade went up river from Calcutta in September 1857 to fight in open country warfare in north-west Bengal. They won no VCs although they served longer in the field than *Shannon*'s Brigade. At the outset of the Mutiny, there were so few British troops in India that *Pearl*'s were the only white troops north of the Ganges, responsible for the defence of a huge area of the sub-continent, from the Ganges north to the Nepalese border.

Although the Admiralty did not encourage the use of Naval Brigades, always being very reluctant to have highly-trained bluejackets serving ashore as infantry and artillery, and always eager for them to re-embark in their ships as soon as possible, there were very few years in the 19th century when sailors were not serving in Naval Brigades somewhere in the world. Between the end of the Indian Mutiny and the Boxer Rising in 1900–1, sailors served ashore in China, in Burma, New Zealand, Japan, Abyssinia, in the Ashanti and Zulu Wars, the Sudan, in Crete and in both Boer Wars.

Having once made every other ship out-of-date, *Warrior* was herself out-of-date within a few years and began to slip down the Navy List, from the Channel Squadron, to the Reserve, to stationary depot ship and, finally, to hulk, having never fired a shot in anger. She would have been broken up

Above: 'Blue Jackets to the Front!': men of the Naval Brigade rush a light gun into action in the Sudan in 1884. The incident was recorded on the spot by the war artist Melton Prior. His sketches were worked up by artists at home – as was this, by W.H. Overend.

Left: The Naval Brigades at Tel-El-Kebir (1882), a plan from the papers of Rear-Admiral Edward Pitcairn-Jones.

year (raised to £100, regardless of rank, in 1959). Unhappily, one early naval recipient did not long enjoy this benefit. In 1861, Midshipman E. St.J. Daniel, who won his medal during the Indian Mutiny (which saw the award of a prolific 182 VCs, as many as were awarded in the entire Second World War), became the first of only eight men (and the only sailor) to forfeit the VC, in his case for desertion.

'He who does what he ought to do is brave,' wrote Tolstoy. His aphorism fits Boy First Class John Cornwell, the Navy's youngest (16 years and 4 months) VC. A sight-setter at a 5.5-inch gun on the light cruiser HMS *Chester* at Jutland, Cornwell, mortally wounded, remained at his post although all his companions were killed or disabled. On Admiral Beatty's recommendation he was awarded a posthumous VC – although such awards were not officially sanctioned until 1920.

Since then the VC has frequently been awarded posthumously, as it has now been in some 300 cases out of a total of 1,356 awards, of which 119 have gone to the RN, RNR, RNVR and RM.

Left and below: Admiral Wilson's Mantle of a Knight Grand Cross of the Bath, and his medals and orders. The Victoria Cross takes first place among his medals; the orders are KGCB; Order of Merit; Knight Grand Cross of the Royal Victorian Order; French Legion of Honour; Spanish Order of Naval Merit; Turkish Order of the Medijie.

Above: HMS Black Prince *in 1878 – when she and* Warrior *were already obsolescent. Problems with the original breech-loading guns led to their replacement by rifled muzzle loaders in the later 1860s.*

▶ **1873** Opening of Royal Naval College, Greenwich, the 'university of the Navy'. HMS *Devastation*, the first true mastless capital ship in the Navy, completed. Compound engines introduced.

Below: HMS Monarch *(1868) was the first ocean-going turret ship. Her two turrets, forward and aft of the funnel, each mounted two 12-inch muzzle loaders.*

years ago if anybody had been willing to buy her. Miraculously, she survived to undergo a marvellous renaissance and return to Portsmouth, restored to her authentic Victorian splendour, in June 1987.

The reason for *Warrior's* rapid obsolescence was, of course, the sheer speed of technological advances in the Royal Navy. By 1870, the Navy had some 30 ironclad ships of the line, and all of them, because of the rapidity of change, were unintentionally experimental. Not all were made of iron: in 1862, the Admiralty decided to use up half-built wooden hulls, cladding them with armour, cutting down their top hamper and altering their lengths. This produced *Caledonia, Royal Alfred, Lord Warden, Lord Clyde,* and others. Of the iron-hulled ships some, like *Warrior,* her sister ship *Black Prince* and the three five-masted giants *Minotaur, Agincourt* and *Northumberland,* fired their guns in broadsides, as in Nelson's day. Some were central battery ships, like *Bellerophon* and the four Invincible class, and some were turret ships, like *Monarch* and the ill-fated *Captain.*

There were 18 different hull shapes, eight different thicknesses of armour, and five designs of bow: *Warrior* and *Black Prince* had the old-fashioned knee bows; *Achilles* had a stem with a slight outward curve, the five-masted ships, *Defence* and some others, had rounded underwater rams; *Captain* and *Favorite* had straight stems; and the rest had pointed wooden rams. There were three types of stern: *Warrior, Black Prince, Resistance,* and the Invincible class had regular frigate sterns, with wide taffrails, quarter galleries and ornamentation; the five-masters and *Achilles* had plain round sterns, rising vertically from a low counter; the rest had a blunted form of the modern so-called 'cruiser' stern. As for machinery, some ships had trunk engines, some direct acting engines, some return connecting-rod engines, with single screws, twin screws, disconnecting screws, or hoistable screws.

ADVANCES IN GUNNERY

Through the use of forged iron and steel instead of cast iron, the weight of the largest naval guns increased by nearly three times between 1860 and 1865. There were 20 different scales of armament. Breech loaders were discarded, after a disappointing performance in the bombardment of Shimonoseki in 1863, and by 1870 the Navy had reverted to rifled muzzle loaders, of up to six different calibres. Most ships mounted guns of two calibres, some even three. There were 6-inch guns mounted on wooden trucks and trained by handspike; 7-inch guns on iron carriages and slide mountings, trained by tackles; 8-, 9-, and 10-inch guns trained by winches; and 12-inch guns in turrets trained by steam. 6 and 7-inch projectiles were lifted to the muzzles by hand, the larger calibres by shell whips. 10- and 12-inch calibre shells were rammed home by the whole gun's crew manning bell-ropes on the rammer staff, the smaller calibres being rammed home by the loading numbers only. All calibres were laid for elevation by hand-lever, and fired by lanyard and friction tube.

At a time of such rapid change, when almost every new ship had different guns, different machinery and different armour to her predecessors, there was always the danger that sooner or later invention would outrun discretion. Over-confidence, compounded by the flouting of some basic principles of ship stability, undoubtedly contributed to the greatest disaster of the mid-Victorian Navy, the capsizing of *Captain* with the loss of 472 lives in the Bay of Biscay in September 1870.

Captain's designer, Captain Cowper Coles, was a brave, inventive and persistent officer, who knew how to marshal what would now be called the media on his side. He had served in the

Crimea where, on his own initiative, he had built primitive forms of monitor for shore bombardment. One version had a 68-pounder gun mounted on a centrally-pivoted platform, so that the gun could be trained.

Coles strongly urged this concept of a turret ship – in which the *gun*, not the ship, was trained – upon the Admiralty, who were sufficiently impressed to appoint a committee led by Edward James Lyon, the Chief Constructor, who produced the *Monarch*.

In all the furore over *Captain*'s fate, *Monarch*'s excellence has unfortunately been somewhat obscured. She was the first ocean-going warship to embody all the three great changes in Victorian fighting ship design – she was constructed of metal and not timber, she was designed to fight under steam instead of sail, and she carried her main armament outside, rather than inside, her hull – in turrets.

The Admiralty deeply mistrusted Cowper Coles' design, but as a result of intense pressure from Coles and his partisans, including *The Times*, they took the amazing and unprecedented step of commissioning a ship of Coles' design, to be built at Cammell Lairds, a private yard, at Birkenhead. They even gave the ship a name with Nelsonian resonances.

Captain's designed freeboard was 8½ feet (2.6m) but when all coal, ammunition and stores were on board, her freeboard was only 6½ feet (2m). Coles intended her to be a mastless hull, with two propellers. But the Admiralty insisted that if she was to serve in a deep-water fleet she must carry enough canvas for a moderate speed without steam. Confidently, Coles added the maximum spar and sail plan for a first-rate, with a sail area of nearly 40,000 feet, and three masts. Normal staying would have interfered with the

Above: *Main armament of the ironclad ram HMS Hotspur: one 25-ton, 12-inch rifled muzzle loader, mounted on a turntable in a fixed, armoured gun house.*

Below: *The central battery ironclad HMS Sultan. The inset shows her sinking after striking a rock off Malta in March 1889. She was salvaged.*

Above: *HMS* Captain *carries much of the spread of sail (a total area of nearly 40,000 square feet, 3,700m²) that led to her loss. Cowper Coles, her designer, intended her to be mastless, but the Admiralty insisted she be able to operate under sail. Tripod masts increased her top weight, and she had a low freeboard. She capsized and sank in a squall; among the 472 lost was Cowper Coles himself.*

Below: *The steel corvette (or sloop) HMS* Calypso – *one of the first warships to feature a protective steel deck – and the iron screw corvette HMS* Volage *at sea in 1890.*

arcs of fire of the two turrets, so tripod masts had to be fitted, adding to top weight and wind resistance. Thus everything seemed to conspire to make *Captain* top-heavy and cranky.

Captain commissioned on 30 April 1870 at Portsmouth (lower deck legend said the signal-man hoisted her ensign upside down by mistake that day). To many, she 'looked all wrong', but they were mostly being wise after the event. Her Captain, Hugh Burgoyne VC, professed himself entirely satisfied with her.

Her armament was almost equal to *Monarch's*. Both mounted four 12-inch MLR (muzzle loading rifled) guns in two turrets. *Monarch* had three 7-inch MLRs, to *Captain's* two. But *Captain* was inferior in every other respect: she was less economical in coal consumption, her turning circle was larger, her speed lower at every point of sailing, she was less able to fire her guns in heavy weather and, crucially, her maximum safe heeling angle was 21°, less than a third of normal for that time, while *Monarch's* was over 70°.

On 6 September 1870, *Captain* was with the combined Channel and Mediterranean Fleets on an exercise cruise in the Bay of Biscay. The weather worsened throughout the day, and that evening the wind steadily strengthened as the barometer dropped. Upper sails were furled and topsails double reefed in the fleets, but by eleven o'clock proper station keeping was no longer possible and the flagship *Lord Warden* signalled 'open order'.

Captain acknowledged the signal. Shortly after midnight, there was a sudden fierce squall in which every ship lost sails and had rigging damaged. It was almost certainly this squall which caused *Captain* to heel over, turn turtle, and sink. The Gunner and 17 sailors reached the Spanish shore in a pinnace the next day. Everyone else was lost, including Cowper Coles, who was taking passage on board.

Cowper Coles may have drowned, but his ideas of guns in turrets and ships with two propellors lived on. When the first true mastless capital ship in the Navy's history, the 9,330 ton *Devastation*, completed for sea in 1873, she had two propellers, and her four 12-inch 35-ton MLR guns were mounted in two huge turrets, 31 feet (9.4m) in diameter and capable of training through arcs of 280°. Her accommodation, like *Captain's*, was not so impressive. The sailors called her, and the seven Cyclops defence ships of about the same period, 'rat-holes with tinned air'.

THE LOSS OF THE *EURYDICE*

By the late 1870s, there were fewer than a dozen pure sailing ships in the Navy List, and they were all employed training officers and men. One was *Eurydice*, a so-called 'Jackass' frigate of 900 tons,

built in 1842, and commissioned as a training ship for young seamen in February 1877.

In November 1877, *Eurydice* went on a cruise to the West Indies, and left Bermuda for Portsmouth on 6 March 1878. By noon on 24 March, she was off the Isle of Wight, carrying all plain sail with studding sails, making about seven knots against an ebb tide, and expecting to anchor at Spithead that evening.

The Isle of Wight, and its steep cliffs split by deep chines running down to the sea, is particularly dangerous for squalls. That afternoon, merchantmen further out could be seen shortening sail, but they had far fewer hands than *Eurydice*, whose crew were numerous, superbly trained and fit, and could be relied upon to have everything off her in double quick time.

At about 3.30 p.m., hands were ordered aloft to shorten sail, but evidently the captain, Marcus Hare, then decided there was not time before the squall arrived, and the men were ordered down again. Sheets and halliards were cut, but it was too late. A snow squall overwhelmed *Eurydice*,

pushing her over on to her starboard beam ends. Her main deck gun ports were open, the main deck flooded, and *Eurydice* sank, righting herself as she went down, in seven fathoms of water.

The schooner *Emma* closed the spot, where *Eurydice*'s royals could be seen still flapping above the water. *Emma* picked up five men, of over 300 on board, but only two of them lived. The other three, and everybody else, died.

The loss of *Eurydice*, with all those young lives, sent a current of horror round the whole nation. It was a tragedy which made people remember where they were and what they were doing when they heard of it. Two years later, in one of those eerie coincidences which occur at sea, *Atalanta*, another training ship similar to *Eurydice*, also coming home from a cruise in the West Indies with young seamen on board, was lost with all hands somewhere between Bermuda and Portsmouth.

In the late 1860s, Mr Robert Whitehead, manager of an engineering factory in Fiume, developed a self-propelling, depth-keeping tor-

▶ **1873–74** Ashanti War.

1875 Expedition to Perak in Malay Peninsula.

1876 World's first torpedo boat, HMS *Lightning*, launched.

Below: *The sail training frigate HMS* Eurydice *sank in a snow squall off the Isle of Wight in 1878.*

Below left: *More than 300 young seamen died aboard the* Eurydice; *a photograph of the only two survivors is shown among objects and relics commemorating the disaster. The salvage operation is depicted (bottom) in an oil painting by William Lionel Wyllie.*

Above: *In 1872, the old sailing frigate HMS* Vernon *was established as a torpedo training school at Portsmouth. She is seen here in c.1908, partially obscured by HMS* Warrior *(centre) and HMS* Marlborough *(left) and HMS* Donegal, *vessels that were also part of the training establishment.*

Below: *The torpedo cruiser HMS* Porpoise *had one fixed bow torpedo tube and two traversing upper deck torpedo carriages.*

Below right: *Completed in 1894, HMS* Havock *was the world's first destroyer. She originally mounted three 18-inch torpedo tubes, one 12-pounder gun and three 6-pounders.*

pedo. His design, which was ahead of all its contemporaries, had a hydrostatic balance chamber which responded to increasing or decreasing water pressure by operating elevator flaps on the torpedo's side, causing it to self-correct its running depth, and thus maintain an average depth. A pendulum device compensated for any tilt, fore or aft, of the torpedo while it was running.

In one of the best bargains in British naval history, contracts were exchanged by which the British Government paid Whitehead the comparatively modest sums of £15,000 and expenses of £2,000 for the licence to build Whitehead torpedoes in England, to purchase further models from Whitehead's own works at Fiume, and permission for a certain number of officers to be trained in the mysteries of Whitehead's depth-keeping devices. The most successful of all subsequent British torpedoes, the 21-inch Mark VIII, used in earnest as recently as the Falklands conflict of 1982, was a development of Robert Whitehead's original basic design.

1872 saw the frigate *Vernon*, a hulk serving as a coaling jetty, brought from Portland to Portsmouth to be converted into a torpedo instructional ship. In September that year Commander Jackie Fisher, who had been a key figure in the formation of the new Torpedo Branch, was appointed to the *Excellent* for 'torpedo instruction'. Initially a tender to the *Excellent* and a branch of the gunnery school, *Vernon* broke away in 1876, to be commissioned as an independent command.

Over the years, various other hulks collected around *Vernon* as bases for accommodation and instruction (see photograph at left), and in 1895 all were moved to Portchester Creek. The next move was in 1923, when *Vernon* moved ashore to the Gunwharf in Portsmouth Harbour, already the site of the Mining School. Both officers and ratings, including (from 1944) ships' divers, received their training and instruction at *Vernon*. The Torpedo Branch took on responsibility for all aspects of torpedo and mine warfare, as well as for the supply and installation of electricity on the Navy's ships.

THE ADVENT OF DESTROYERS

The world's first torpedo-boat, *Lightning*, 19 tons, 19 knots, was launched in 1876 to carry spar torpedoes (which had the explosive charge on the end of a long pole, to detonate on impact). She was converted in 1879 to have two above-water tubes, to fire Whitehead torpedoes. Renamed *Torpedo-boat No.1* in 1880, she was so successful that other foreign navies began to build torpedo-boats in such large numbers that the Admiralty built torpedo-boat *destroyers* to combat them. *Havock* and *Hornet*, 250 tons, 27 knots, with four guns and three torpedo tubes, launched in 1893, were not only too fast and powerful for any torpedo-boat but took over their function. Thus *Havock* was, in fact, the world's first destroyer.

For some 20 years from the 1860s onwards, much faith was placed in the ram as the para-

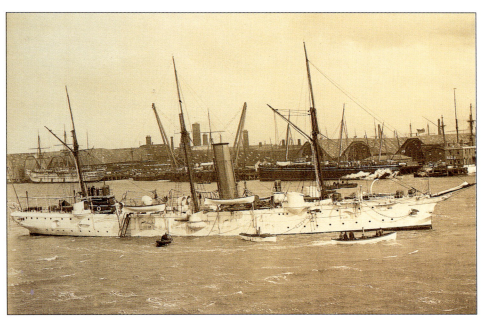

mount weapon at sea. The first British ships to be designed specifically for ramming were the 3,700 ton armoured corvette *Pallas*, and the 7,550 ton battleship *Bellerophon*, both commissioned in 1866, and both having their main armament (*Pallas* four 7-inch MLRs, *Bellerophon* ten 9-inch MLRs) mounted in armoured central 'box' batteries

In practice, the ram was more of a menace to friend than foe. On 1 September 1875, the 6,000 ton ironclad *Iron Duke* rammed her sister ship *Vanguard* in fog off Dublin Bay, hitting her between the boiler and engine rooms. Both compartments flooded, and *Vanguard* sank 70 minutes later.

No lives were lost on that occasion. A much more serious ramming accident, the worst naval disaster of the 1890s, occurred off Tripoli on the Lebanese coast, on 22 June 1893. That afternoon, eight battleships, three armoured cruisers, and two third-class cruisers of the Mediterranean Fleet were steaming in two columns, the starboard column led by the 10,500 ton battleship *Victoria*, flagship of the C-in-C, Vice Admiral Sir George Tryon, and the port column by the 10,500 ton battleship *Camperdown*, flagship of Rear Admiral Hastings Markham, Tryon's second-in-command,

George Tryon was one of the ablest and best-known flag officers of his day. Although he was also one of the most autocratic and powerful personalities ever to serve in the Navy, delighting in intricate fleet manoeuvres, at times so intricate that Markham sometimes confessed he could not understand them, Tryon was no dictator demanding slavish obedience. He expected his subordinates to show initiative.

To get his fleet into proper position for anchoring that evening, Tryon ordered the two columns to turn inwards. They were steaming six cables

(1,200 yards, 1,100m) apart. The minimum turning circle of the ships was eight cables (1,600 yards, 1,460m). With hindsight, it seems that in a moment of mental aberration Tryon simply mistook the fleet's turning circle diameter for its radius. But such was the sledgehammer force of his personality (and so unusual was it in the Victorian navy even to breathe the slightest question about an admiral's orders) that, after some hesitation on Markham's part, *Victoria* and *Camperdown* put their helms hard over and headed inwards towards each other

Although *Victoria*'s engines were put 'full speed astern', she was turning in a tighter circle than *Camperdown*, whose stem hit her on the starboard bow about ten feet (3m) abaft the anchor, at an angle of about 68°, both ships steaming at five to six knots. The order to shut watertight doors and hatches had only been given a

Above: *The ironclad ram HMS* Hotspur *with her anti-torpedo netting deployed.*

Below left: *The central battery ironclad HMS* Vanguard *sank after being accidentally rammed by HMS* Iron Duke *in June 1893. Inset: HMS* Triumph, *another central battery ironclad, was ship-rigged, with a total sail area of some 40,000 square feet (3,700m²).*

Below and right: *On 22 June 1893, Admiral Tryon's liking for complex manoeuvres and the unquestioning obedience of his subordinates resulted in disaster. His flagship HMS* Victoria, *rammed by HMS* Camperdown, *sank with great loss of life, including his own. The 365 officers and men lost are listed on a scroll of honour.*

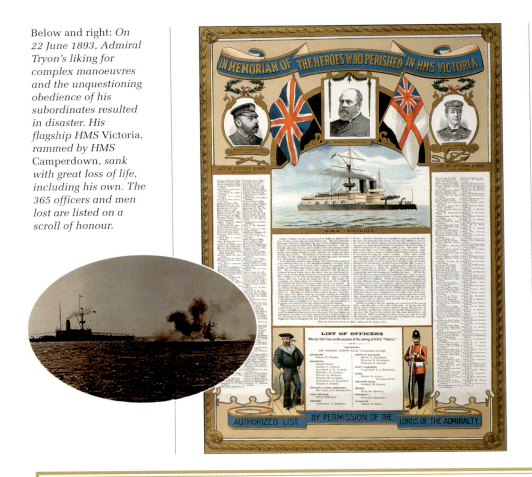

minute earlier, so many were still open at the time of the collision. Water flooded in from forward, and *Victoria*'s fo'c'sle was awash within minutes. She went down by the bow, lurched over onto her side, then rapidly turned bottom up and sank by the head at an angle of about 30° to the vertical. Three hundred and sixty-five officers and men, including Tryon himself, were lost.

A TIME OF INNOVATION

The mid-decades of the last half of the 19th century, the so-called 'Dark Ages', were still a period of intense innovation and development in warship design. It was not unusual to have a squadron of six ironclads in which not one was a sister ship of any of the others. Steel was used to a much greater extent in warship construction. The 3,700 ton despatch vessel *Iris* of 1877 was the first warship of any size to be built entirely of steel (although torpedo-boats were built of steel from the outset). Steel combined with wrought iron was also extensively used in armour, which

GREAT GUNS AND QUICK-FIRERS

On 11 July 1882 the Navy's biggest guns—the four 16-inch MLRs of the masted turret ship HMS *Inflexible* – opened fire on Alexandria to quell the Egyptian nationalist forces of Arabi Pasha. The 10-inch MLRs of the central battery ironclad *Superb*, 10- and 11-inch MLRs of the central battery/barbette hybrid *Temeraire*, 10- and 11-inch MLRs of the central battery ironclad *Alexandra*, 12-inch and 7-inch MLRs of the masted turret ship *Monarch*, and 9- and 10-inch MLRs of the central battery ironclad *Sultan* all added their weight to the day-long bombardment. The rebels had to retreat— but it was claimed that of some 3,000 shells fired (not

all from the big guns), less than 10 per cent hit the fortifications at which they were aimed.

Only seven years after that motley fleet's haphazard Alexandrian bombardment, the Royal Navy's transition from ML to BL guns of improved design, the introduction of more effective 'smokeless' powder, and other technical advances described in this chapter, saw the beginning of a far more homogenous fleet of 'pre-dreadnought' battleships. This marked the end of a period of experimentation that saw such aberrations as the 'turret ram' *Conqueror* (launched 1881). HMS *Royal Sovereign* (launched 1891) and her six sisters each had a main armament of four 13.5-inch BLs; in the *Majestic* (launched 1895; first of a class of ten) the main armament consisted of four 12-inch, wire-wound, Mk

Below left: *The ironclad HMS* Alexandra *wears the flag of Admiral Beauchamp Seymour at the fore.*

Below: *Seymour's fleet suffered only ten men killed and 27 wounded, but Egyptian gunners hit the* Alexandra, *seen here after the action, and other vessels.*

Below right: *The Lighthouse Fort after the bombardment.*

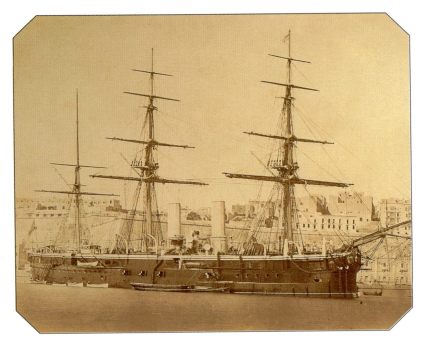

rapidly increased in thickness, from 4½ inches (11.4cm) in *Warrior* to 24 inches (61cm) in the battleship *Inflexible*, launched in 1876 and completed in 1881.

By the 1880s the 'box battery' was obsolete, and the next step was the barbette, where the guns were mounted upon an armoured platform. The Navy's first barbette ship was *Collingwood*, laid down in 1880 and completed in 1887. In *Collingwood* the Navy finally reverted to the breech-loading gun. Until then muzzle loaders were retained, which eventually reached monster sizes, of 16-inch with hydraulic loading gear in *Inflexible*, and 16.25-inch, weighing 110 tons, in *Benbow*, commissioned in 1888.

The design and construction of the big guns were greatly improved. No longer were the barrels bored out from solid castings, but were built up by tubes shrunk on top of each other. This permitted guns of much greater size and range (although *Benbow*'s two huge 16.25-inch barbette guns, firing a projectile of 1,800lb (816kg), tended to 'droop' at their muzzles and proved to have a very short effective service life).

There were also significant advances in explosives. The old black gunpowder was

Left: *The masted turret ship HMS* Inflexible, *seen at Malta in 1883, was protected by 'compound' armour (a first use) on her central citadel. It consisted of two layers each of iron and wood, with a maximum thickness of 41 inches (104cm).*

replaced first by prismatic powder, followed by nitro-cellulose (gun cotton) and then, eventually, by cordite. These propellants, which burned more slowly and more accurately, enabled the barrel lengths and ranges of guns to be greatly increased.

Collingwood and the similar Admiral class, of *Anson*, *Camperdown*, *Howe* and *Rodney*, launched between 1882 and 1883, and completed between 1888 and 1889, were a major step along the evolution from the ironclad to the true battleship. They were 10,600 tons, with four 13.5 inch 67-ton BLs in barbettes, numerous smaller guns, torpedo tubes, a high speed for that time of 17½ knots, and a single mast. Apart from their low freeboard forward, which affected their sea-keeping, they were the first 19th century ships to begin to look like the 20th century image of a battleship.

To achieve their 17 knots, the 'Admirals' had two sets of compound inverted reciprocating steam engines, each with one high pressure and two low pressure cylinders, and a stroke of three and half feet (1.1m), driving two 18½ foot (5.6m) diameter propellers at 100rpm. The steam was provided at 90lb/sq in by 12 cylindrical boilers, with a total of 36 furnaces.

These higher speeds, requiring ever larger, more powerful and more complicated main engines, also required personnel with the proper engineering expertise to maintain them. The Navy's demand for engineers has always greatly exceeded their regard for them, and for most of the 19th century the Admiralty had to grapple with the problems of manning the engine-rooms of the fleet, which meant having to resolve successive crises over engineers' recruiting.

Above: *HMS* Collingwood, *the Navy's first barbette ship, had two 12 inch breech loaders in each of two barbettes protected by 10-11 inch (254-280mm) armour. The lighter barbettes could be mounted higher than turrets, so permitting more effective gunnery.*

▶ **1877** HMS *Marlborough* commissioned as training ship for engineer students. HMS *Iris*, first steel-hulled warship for the Navy, completed. First time torpedo used in action, by HMS *Shah* against Peruvian *Huascar*.

1878 Fear of war with Russia. Training ship *Eurydice* lost off the Isle of Wight.

VIII BLs of a type that remained standard for 16 years (*Dreadnought* had Mk 10s).

The Royal Sovereigns and Majestics also mounted powerful secondary armament. From around 1870, capital ships faced the threat of small, fast torpedo boats. Machine guns like the Gardner and Nordenfelt had insufficient 'stopping power', and from about 1880 French-designed Hotchkiss 3- and 6-pounder quick firers (QF) were carried. From these, Armstrong developed larger QFs – and in 1887 demonstrated an Elswick 4.7-inch QF that could fire 10 rounds in 47.5 seconds (about eight times the rate of the *Inflexible*'s secondary 20-pounder BLs at Alexandria). The Royal Sovereigns each carried ten 6-inch QF, 16 6-pounder QF and 12 3-pounder QF; the *Majestic* mounted 12 6-inch, 16 12-pounder and 12 3-pounder QFs.

1879 Punishment of flogging suspended. Zulu War.

1879–81 First Boer War.

1880 First students transfer from HMS *Marlborough* to Royal Naval Engineering College, Keyham.

1882 Bombardment of Alexandria. Defeat of Egyptian forces by Wolseley's troops at Tel-el-Kebir (12-13 September).

1884 Battle of El-Teb, Sudan (29 February).

1885 Triple expansion engines introduced in HMS *Victoria*.

Engineers continued to have a low status in the Navy. The 'curl' for executive officers was introduced in 1860 and the purple distinguishing stripe for engineers in 1863. Chief Engineers with 15 years seniority were equal to a Commander in rank, but until 1883 only Chief Engineers could mess in the wardroom.

At times, it seemed that whatever the Admiralty did to try to raise engineers' status was wrong. When in 1868 they introduced 'engine-room artificers' in an attempt to establish a supervisory role for engineer officers, elevating them above manual work, junior engineer officers took it as a threat to their livelihoods. Feelings on this and other matters ran so high that in the 1870s the Admiralty faced another crisis over engineers' recruiting.

In 1875 a committee was set up to examine the position, but their recommendations on pay, rank, promotion and 'military status' were all turned down. However, in 1877, an old 121-gun screw line of battle ship, the *Marlborough*, was allocated as an accommodation ship for engineer students in Portsmouth. The main training of engineers

was still carried out in the dockyards until a training school for engineer students, known later as the Royal Naval Engineering College, was built at Keyham, Devonport. The first students transferred to it from the old *Marlborough* in 1880.

Keyham and *Marlborough* existed together until 1888, when classrooms and studies were built at Keyham, and *Marlborough* closed down. Students entered Keyham aged between 14 and 17 years, and entry was by competition. The students undertook a six year course, with lectures on mathematics and mechanics in the College, and practical work in the dockyard workshops, foundry, pattern-makers' and boiler-makers' shops. The students built auxiliary machinery and carried out steam engine trials. From time to time, they went to sea in the torpedo gunboat *Sharpshooter* for practical steaming experience, cruising along the Devon and Cornish coasts

At Dartmouth, the number of cadets in the old *Britannia* had risen from 230 to over 300 over a few terms. In 1864 the old two-decker *Hindostan* was moored upstream of the *Britannia* to provide

DAILY LIFE ABOARD *BRITANNIA*

Hard exercise and fierce discipline were the hallmarks of the cadets' life. They began each day with a swim in a cold salt-water bath and proceeded through a rigid timetable of prayers, inspection, classes, meals, boatwork and exercise, the sessions punctuated by the ship's bell. Their studies fell into three broad areas. Sailing lore and signals came under the heading of seamanship. In addition to this, there were 'study', comprising mathematics and navigation, and 'out of study' comprising French and drawing (the latter to enable naval officers to sketch navigational landmarks as they sailed past them).

Instruction was followed by sport – football or cricket, walks and cross-country runs. Cadets had access to a flotilla of four-oared gigs and pair-oared skiffs (known today at Dartmouth, as then, as 'blueboats') and to launches and cutters for sailing.

A Captain RN was in charge of discipline and the general non-academic ruling of the ship. He was supported by a Commander, three Lieutenants, a master at arms, four ship's corporals, and six cadet captains and chief captains picked from the senior term. No disciplinary powers were allotted to academic staff, but if they reported poor or careless

work the cadet was punished, without appeal.

The severe scale of punishment included caning with trousers on, birching with trousers off, and confinement to cells on bread and water. Cadets who were graded in the third (worst) class for conduct were marked out with a white stripe on the arm and had extra drill, using heavy Brown Bess muskets or bar-bells. They were fed apart from other cadets, in the cockpit or a separate messroom. Offenders under punishment served a longer day, rising early in the morning, and being kept on their feet after other cadets had turned in. They were also required to stand to attention for an hour facing the main deck bulkhead, a lower-deck punishment which survived until its abolition in 1912.

Below left: *The training ship HMS* Britannia *was established in 1863. The* Britannia *seen here, in 1875, is the former 131-gun HMS* Prince of Wales, *which replaced the first ship in 1869. A walkway connects her to the two-decker HMS* Hindostan.

Above: *The foundry. As on* Britannia, *training at the junior naval college at Osborne, Isle of Wight, which opened in 1903, was practical.*

Below right: *Sport was not neglected – cadets at the Royal Naval College, Dartmouth, 1906.*

extra accommodation, her stern connected with the *Britannia*'s bow by a walkway. In July 1869, a much larger *Britannia* succeeded the old vessel, in the form of a 131-gun screw ship launched in 1860 as the *Prince of Wales*.

LIFE ON *BRITANNIA*

Although Admiralty circulars from time to time changed the syllabus, made the entrance examination competitive and defined the age limits for entry, life on board the *Britannia* followed much the same pattern into the next century. Her foremast was rigged, with a safety net beneath, for the cadets to practise on, but her other masts and rigging had been removed. Class rooms, model rooms and cabins for the ship's officers took up almost the whole of the upper deck. The guns were removed from the gundecks to make room for dormitories, bathrooms and mess rooms.

Each year two terms of cadets joined, to spend two years aboard. They slept in hammocks, and kept their belongings in sea-chests. The large cadets' messroom served for morning prayers, inspections and evening preparation. Meals were served there on four long tables for all four terms, and the same room served as a mess where cadets' spare time was spent in reading, writing letters and amusing themselves.

The *Britannia* comprised an almost completely enclosed world where cadets led an insular existence, shut off from real-life naval business – as was more or less the case until the outbreak of the Second World War. The small sailing brigs attached to the seamen's training ships at Plymouth and Portsmouth, which sometimes anchored briefly near the harbour entrance, were the only seagoing men-of-war they ever saw. Dartmouth harbour was not the place to excite a cadet's interest in naval affairs.

Their examinations passed, cadets progressed to sea as midshipmen. Life in the fleet's gun-rooms was even tougher, and the conditions more spartan, than aboard the *Britannia*. Midshipmen were kept busy running the ship's boats, watch-keeping at sea and in harbour, and learning how to take sights, to handle groups of men and to deal with all manner of shipboard events and emergencies. All this practical work took priority over theory in the

form of navigation lessons from the naval instructor, which were scheduled for every forenoon as well as the occasional afternoon. Their demanding duties, the various commitments and distractions of shipboard life, and the loss of sleep during watchkeeping rotas, all made it hard for midshipmen to concentrate on their studies, and they took advantage of every pretext to avoid school whenever possible.

After serving five years at sea, midshipmen took an examination in seamanship before a board of captains. A first-class pass gave advancement in seniority. Now aged about 20, the young men proceeded as sub-lieutenants to the Royal Naval College, Greenwich. Founded in 1873 as the 'university of the Navy', the College absorbed both the Royal Naval College, Portsmouth, and the Royal School of Naval Architecture and Marine Engineering, South Kensington. Its aim, to cultivate 'the general intelligence of officers, to improve their aptitude for the various duties which a naval officer is called upon to perform', took some years to achieve. After five years at sea, sub-lieutenants were often reluctant to return to academic studies and had forgotten much of their lessons.

The last great reform the Victorian Navy needed – and the hardest to achieve – was promotion from the lower deck to the quarterdeck. Officer recruitment was still restricted almost entirely to the same self-defining and self-perpetuating section of society, almost like an exclusive club, rather than being simply based on merit or achievement. In the late 19th century, for all its impressive technological progress, the Navy remained at its most reactionary with regard to personnel policies.

Above: Cadets' quarters may have been Spartan; their instructors fared better. These were the Commander's quarters on HMS Marlborough, *which became an accommodation ship for engineer students at Portsmouth in 1877.*

Below left and right: The uniforms of a Captain (left) and Seaman (right) in the Royal Navy in 1880, shown in watercolours by Richard Simkin. The officer's cocked hat is little changed from Nelson's time; the seaman's straw hat was introduced in 1857.

Above: *A membership certificate for the Royal Naval Fireman's Benefit Society. 'Fireman' here refers to a stoker. From around 1900, Benefit Societies – distrusted by the Admiralty as 'trades unions' – with members including pensioners and civilians, sought better pay and conditions.*

As early as 1852, the Manning Committee had recommended the promotion of warrant officers to the rank of lieutenant on the grounds of gallantry or daring in action. However, only two such promotions (the 'Jubilee Memorials') were made, and those not until the time of Queen Victoria's Golden Jubilee honours list. No more followed until the end of the century.

The system was challenged by one man, Henry Capper. He had joined the *St Vincent* as a boy seaman in 1869, qualifying as a gunner in 1879. In 1881, as a young and ambitious warrant gunner, he attended his first dinner in *Excellent* and was warmly applauded by the 60 officers present when the president announced him as a new member. His acknowledgement of this welcome was well received, but his comment that he 'had done my best to reach this mess only as a halfway house to a commission', which was greeted with derisive laughter. The president made it clear that no further promotion was open to him for some 30 years, when he might receive a chief gunner's stripe just before retirement. 'No naval warrant officer has had a commission these last 70 years: if you want one you must get the system changed first.'

Undeterred, Capper resolved to do just that. After contributing anonymously (though with the Admiralty's knowledge) to the press for some years, in 1888 he founded the monthly *Naval Warrant Officers' Journal* to publicize their case. Two years later, the First Lord, Lord George Hamilton, declared that 100 more lieutenants were needed urgently. The warrant officers responded with 'An Earnest Appeal for Promotion from the Ranks, Royal Navy', noting that they already performed lieutenants' and sub-lieutenants' duties and that some of them were prepared to sit the lieutenant's examination.

There was strong support for their case from the press and Parliament, and a motion was raised in the House. However, the government – and some serving officers, who preferred to keep the status quo – opposed change, and the extra lieutenants ('The Hungry Hundred') were created by transferring RNR officers from the Merchant Marines. Promotion for warrant officers had to wait until the next century.

JUBILEE REVIEW

In July 1887, there was a fleet review at Spithead to celebrate Queen Victoria's Golden Jubilee. There were 128 warships on view, with visitors from France, Germany and the Netherlands. Every ship was from home waters. Not one had come from a foreign station. But to experienced eyes (including those of the French naval attaché) the review showed the Navy's weakness as well as its strength. To make the numbers more impressive, the Navy had commissioned all manner of warships, some of which had not seen service for years, and to get them to sea at all had had to man them with inexperienced crews, There were several collisions, so that the *Daily News* advised the Navy to keep foreign visitors out of the way 'until our bumping races of ironclads have come to an end'.

Nevertheless, the review contributed to a growing national awareness of the Navy (just as Lord Charles Beresford, one of its chief organisers, hoped it would). There were a number of naval 'panics' in the 1880s, Mr W. T. Stead, editor of the *Pall Mall Gazette*, caused a 'panic' of his own in 1884 when he published anonymously 'The truth about the Navy by one who knows the facts'. In 1885, the Poet Laureate Lord Tennyson published his celebrated accusatory poem 'The Fleet' addressed to the Sea Lords. The general discovery of the Government's and Their Lordships' complacency towards the Navy caused public and press outrage, so that Gladstone's Government was driven into a ship building programme of £3,100,000 and expenditure of £2,400,000 on coaling stations and buildings.

Even this was not enough. In 1888, Lord Salisbury's Government was found to be backsliding on its undertakings and, with rumours of a possible Franco-Russian alliance, there was another 'panic', which led to the Naval Defence Act of 1889, with authorised expenditure of £21,500,000 on the building of 70 new warships, including ten battleships. The Navy, henceforth, was to be on a scale 'at least equal to the naval strength of any other two countries'.

Since the early 19th century there had been a marked change in the public perception of sailors. Barracks were built ashore to replace the insanitary hulks. The sailor's public image was improved, and his self-esteem raised, by the work of Agnes Weston and her helpers in the Royal Naval Temperance Society and in her Sailors' Rests, the first of which opened in 1876 in Devonport. No longer 'poor Jack' or the drunken 'common sailor' of 1815, the bluejacket ashore was now 'The Handyman', celebrated in songs, verses and plays as the hero of many Naval Brigade campaigns. A great naval exhibition on the Thames embankment, opened in May 1891, was a huge success, attracting more than two and a half million visitors by the time it closed in October.

After many years of public indifference and unresponsive internal administration, in the 1890s the Royal Navy suddenly became fashionable. The sailor became a marketing icon, notably in soap and tobacco advertisements, while toy manufacturers produced naval tactics board games, using squares and counters. 1893

Above: 'The Sailor's Return', a Staffordshire pottery figure from the collection assembled by Captain Kenneth Douglas-Morris, RN. In the later 19th century, the sailor's public image changed from that of 'Jack Nastyface' to that of a jovial, popular hero.

FROM 'JACK NASTYFACE' TO JACK TAR'

'No man will be a sailor who has contrivance enough to get himself into a jail...,' said Dr Johnson, and the writings of 'Jack Nastyface' (William Robinson, a purser's steward and Trafalgar veteran, who deserted in 1811 and published his *Nautical Economy...* in 1836) paint a hellish picture of life on the lower deck. By the later 19th century, seamen's conditions had much improved, and the public image of 'Jolly Jack Tar' changed accordingly. Not everyone welcomed the 'new sailor'. Writing in 1871, an anonymous officer lamented that 'the old seaman has vanished', and told how 'In the old days...full of frolicsome fun' the men of a paid-off crew 'each with 50 and 60 pounds in his pocket...roamed the streets of Portsmouth the next night without a penny left them.' The establishment of Naval Savings Banks afloat in 1866 helped end such spendthrift habits.

Above: All hands to the shovels in the stokehold of HMS Majestic in 1895. The photograph vividly illustrates the dirt, dust and general gloom in which the stokers worked.

Ashore, 'Aggie Weston's Sailors' Rests' helped keep men out of bars and brothels. In foreign ports, wise captains – as Jackie Fisher prescribed – kept men entertained with football and boxing competitions, sailing and rowing regattas, even guided tours of the sights of China and other exotic stations. Afloat, the call for 'All hands to dance and skylark' might herald the ship's banjo band: this relatively simple instrument, popularized by minstrel shows from around 1850, became so popular that Kipling called it 'the war drum of the white man round the world'. Sailors had not made their own clothing since the advent of 'slops' before 1700, but the 'Make and mend' half-day saw 'housewifes' – containers for needles, thread and the like – employed in tailoring 'tiddly suits' (smart going-ashore uniforms).

Coaling, although much dreaded, was not an everyday task, unlike holystoning, scrubbing the decks with 'prayer books' (since they were used kneeling) of soft sandstone: '...Poor Jack awoke/Before the dawn of day had broke.../He bent his knee but not in prayer/And cursed the man who sent him there.' Sailors were wont to say that on arrival in Heaven they would be employed in daily holystoning of the Holy Ghost!

Left and far left: Two contrasting incidents in the daily routine. Seamen aboard HMS Crescent assemble for their grog in c.1900, while less happy hands aboard HMS Calliope (left) undertake the morning chore of swabbing the deck.

Right: *The Empire upon which the Sun never set. The extent of Queen Victoria's rule, largely won and maintained by maritime power, is seen in a map showing the Royal Navy's worldwide network of coaling stations and docks. It is adapted from a map that was originally issued as a supplement to the* Pall Mall Gazette *in 1884.*

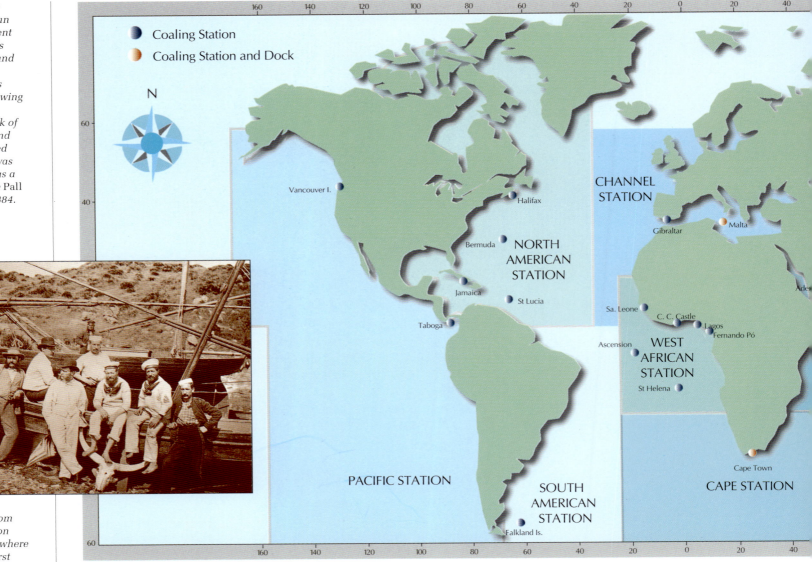

● Coaling Station
● Coaling Station and Dock

N

Vancouver I.

Halifax

CHANNEL STATION

Gibraltar   Malta

Bermuda   NORTH AMERICAN STATION

Jamaica

St Lucia

Sa. Leone   Aden

C. C. Castle

Lagos

Fernando Pó

Taboga

Ascension   WEST AFRICAN STATION

St Helena

PACIFIC STATION

SOUTH AMERICAN STATION

Cape Town

CAPE STATION

Falkland Is.

Above: *Sailors from* HMS Endymion *on shore leave somewhere in the Empire. First class protected cruisers like the 7,350-ton* Endymion, *one of nine Edgar-class ships, were the 'policemen' of the Imperial seaways.*

'*S*o we were served out, if you please – and which you won't believe – with cutlasses which had been used for several hundred years, round our waists, and of course a revolver, a very heavy one, the ordinary 45 of the day, and beyond that I had a whistle around my neck. We did not have, I may mention, the Hale War Rocket, which, as you know, was labelled "not to be used in civilised warfare".'

COMMANDER C.R. SHARP, DURING THE SIEGE OF LADYSMITH, 1899–1900

1897 Diamond Jubilee Review at Spithead. Charles Parsons' *Turbinia*, the first vessel driven by steam turbines, is a sensation.

1899-1902 Second Boer War. Navy's first turbine-driven destroyer, HMS *Viper*, launched.

1900 Boxer Rising, China.

1901 Death of Queen Victoria.

saw the creation of the Navy Records Society, specifically to print papers and documents of naval biography, history and archaeology. The next year the Navy League was founded to secure, 'as the primary national policy, the command of the sea'. Naval history entered the curriculum at Oxford and Cambridge (though not in *Britannia*), and key works of naval history were published by A.T. Mahan and P.H. Colomb. In 1898 Kipling, having gone to sea with the Channel squadron, published *A Fleet in Being*, and that same year saw the first edition of Fred T. Jane's *All the World's Fighting Ships*.

On 26 June 1897, another review was held at Spithead, to honour the Queen's Diamond Jubilee.

But this review was a show of real strength. There were 165 warships of all kinds, spread out over 30 miles (50km), in five lines. As in 1887, not one ship had been drawn from abroad, all were from the home station.

WILLIAM WHITE

The 1897 Diamond Jubilee Review, the greatest display of naval force the world had ever seen, was very largely the work of one man. William White was born in 1845 and apprenticed as a shipwright in the Royal Dockyard, Devonport. In 1864 he went to the newly-founded Royal School of Naval Architecture in South Kensington, passing out in 1867 with its highest honours. He joined the Admiralty as professional secretary to Sir Edward Reed, the chief constructor of the Navy, and was closely involved in the *Inflexible* and *Collingwood* designs.

In 1883, the year he devised the organisation of the Royal Corps of Naval Constructors, White left the Admiralty to join Armstrong & Co as designer and manager at their warship-yard being constructed at Elswick-on-Tyne. He returned in

Above: *A pay muster aboard HMS Royal Sovereign in 1895. At this time, an Able Seaman's pay was 1s 7d (8p) per day – and it remained so until 1913.*

Above left and above: *Chief Stoker Walter Grainger, serving in the sloop HMS Daphne in 1895–1901, wrote these loving letters to his fiancée (later wife), Edith Townsend, from the China Station. Illustrated with watercolour paintings, they came from Hong Kong (above left) and Shanghai (above).*

Far left: *Stalwarts of the pre-1914 fleet: the battleship HMS Royal Sovereign and armoured cruiser HMS Kent (foreground).*

1885 to succeed Sir Nathaniel Barnaby as Director of Naval Construction. In his 17 years in the post, White revolutionised battleship design, starting with the seven ships of the superb Royal Sovereign class of 1889: 14,400 tons, 17½ knots, four 13.5-inch guns, secondary armament, and torpedo tubes, they were the first truly seaworthy 'mastless' battleships in the fleet. They were followed by the nine ships of the Majestic class of 1893: 14,800 tons, 17½ knots, four 12-inch guns, secondary armament and torpedo tubes. With their black hulls, red boot-topping, white superstructure with distinctive stripes, and two yellow funnels and masts, the Majestics looked the very epitome of Victorian battleship splendour.

By the time he retired because of ill-health in 1902, Sir William White (he was appointed KCB in 1895) had designed a total of 42 battleships, ending with the eight King Edward VII class, which began building in 1902: 16,500 tons, armed with four 12-inch, four 9.2-inch and ten 6-inch guns, and a speed of 18½ knots. He also designed twenty 'protected' (without side armour) cruisers, ranging from *Crescent* of 7,700 tons and a speed of 19½ knots, to *Powerful* and *Terrible*, 14,200 tons, 22 knots; 28 large armoured cruisers, including the four Drake class of 14,100 tons, 23½ knots; and many smaller cruisers, destroyers and miscellaneous vessels.

Sir William White's successor as DNC was Philip Watts, whose first design for which he was entirely responsible, was *Lord Nelson* and *Agamemnon*: 16,500 tons, armed with four 12-inch and ten 9.2-inch, with a speed of 18 knots. Laid down in 1905, and known later as the last of the pre-Dreadnoughts, *Lord Nelson* and *Agamemnon* were both considerably delayed, and did not commission until 1908, because some of their 12-inch guns were appropriated to expedite the completion of *Dreadnought*.

Dreadnought: the name of a new ship, and a new battleship concept.

CHAPTER SEVEN

THE DREADNOUGHT ERA

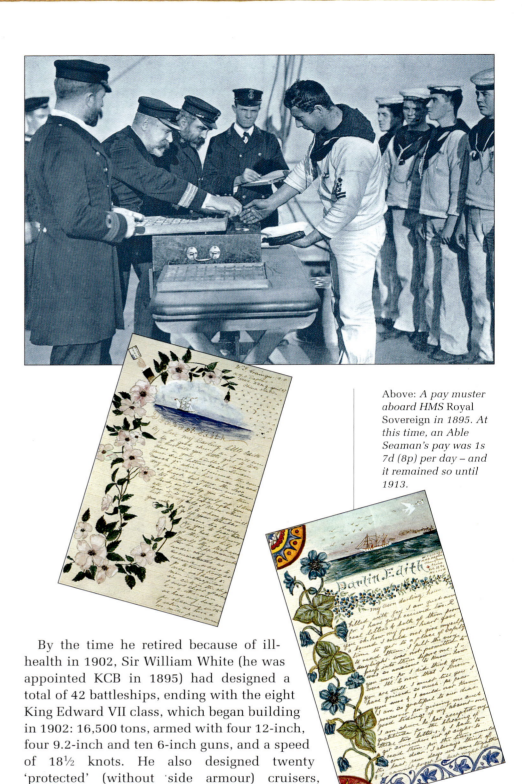

Above: *A pay muster aboard HMS* Royal Sovereign *in 1895. At this time, an Able Seaman's pay was 1s 7d (8p) per day – and it remained so until 1913.*

1885 to succeed Sir Nathaniel Barnaby as Director of Naval Construction. In his 17 years in the post, White revolutionised battleship design, starting with the seven ships of the superb Royal Sovereign class of 1889: 14,400 tons, 17½ knots, four 13.5-inch guns, secondary armament, and torpedo tubes, they were the first truly seaworthy 'mastless' battleships in the fleet. They were followed by the nine ships of the Majestic class of 1893: 14,800 tons, 17½ knots, four 12-inch guns, secondary armament and torpedo tubes. With their black hulls, red boot-topping, white superstructure with distinctive stripes, and two yellow funnels and masts, the Majestics looked the very epitome of Victorian battleship splendour.

By the time he retired because of ill-health in 1902, Sir William White (he was appointed KCB in 1895) had designed a total of 42 battleships, ending with the eight King Edward VII class, which began building in 1902: 16,500 tons, armed with four 12-inch, four 9.2-inch and ten 6-inch guns, and a speed of 18½ knots. He also designed twenty 'protected' (without side armour) cruisers, ranging from *Crescent* of 7,700 tons and a speed of 19½ knots, to *Powerful* and *Terrible*, 14,200 tons, 22 knots; 28 large armoured cruisers, including the four Drake class of 14,100 tons, 23½ knots; and many smaller cruisers, destroyers and miscellaneous vessels.

Sir William White's successor as DNC was Philip Watts, whose first design for which he was entirely responsible, was *Lord Nelson* and *Agamemnon*: 16,500 tons, armed with four 12-inch and ten 9.2-inch, with a speed of 18 knots. Laid down in 1905, and known later as the last of the pre-Dreadnoughts, *Lord Nelson* and *Agamemnon* were both considerably delayed, and did not commission until 1908, because some of their 12-inch guns were appropriated to expedite the completion of *Dreadnought*.

Dreadnought: the name of a new ship, and a new battleship concept.

Above left and above: *Chief Stoker Walter Grainger, serving in the sloop HMS Daphne in 1895–1901, wrote these loving letters to his fiancée (later wife), Edith Townsend, from the China Station. Illustrated with watercolour paintings, they came from Hong Kong (above left) and Shanghai (above).*

Far left: *Stalwarts of the pre-1914 fleet: the battleship HMS* Royal Sovereign *and armoured cruiser HMS* Kent *(foreground).*

Previous pages: *An armoured cruiser squadron of 1914 vintage is escorted by Sopwith seaplanes and a submarine during 'Fleet Manoeuvres', a watercolour by Frederick Gordon Crosby (1885–1943).*

Below: *(Left) The first class cruiser HMS* Terrible *and (inset) a photograph autographed by her officers. (Right) The* Terrible's *Naval Brigade during the Boer War, c.1899.*

The Old Queen died at her favourite Osborne House, on the Isle of Wight, with many of her children and grandchildren around her, on the evening of 22 January 1901. On 1 February, bluejackets drew the gun carriage bearing the Queen's coffin through the streets of Cowes to Trinity Pier and carried the coffin on board the Royal Yacht *Alberta* lying alongside.

While those bluejackets were drawing Queen Victoria to her last resting place, others were serving ashore at opposite ends of the world, in southern Africa and in northern China. Service in the Naval Brigades at the turn of the century was well exemplified by the experiences of the officers and men of the large armoured cruiser *Terrible*, which first commissioned at Portsmouth under Captain Charles Robinson in March 1898.

After 18 months spent largely on experimental trials and working up in the Mediterranean, *Terrible* sailed from Spithead, now commanded by Captain Percy Scott, the most inventive and resourceful gunnery officer of his day, in September 1899, bound for the Cape of Good Hope. She arrived at Simonstown on 12 October, two days after Boer Commandos from the Transvaal and the Orange Free State crossed the border of the British province of Natal, to begin the second Boer War.

At Simonstown, *Terrible* joined her sister ship *Powerful*, on her way

Above: *A recruitment poster showing men of the Royal Marine Artillery (RMA) and Light Infantry (RMLI) – the two did not amalgamate until 1923 – on active service at sea,*

home from China, the 2nd Class cruiser *Doris*, flagship on the Station, the battleship *Monarch*, the gunboat *Thrush*, and some torpedo boats. Other ships were at Durban, Delagoa Bay and other ports along the coast.

In the Boer War, as in most wars of that century, the Naval Brigade supported the army, providing artillery, machine guns, transport and, not least, inventive ingenuity. A Naval Brigade of sailors and marines from *Terrible, Powerful, Monarch* and *Doris* left Simonstown by train on 20 October. The officers and men from *Terrible* in particular took part in the battles of Graspan in November and Colenso in December 1899, in operations at Stormberg and Magersfontein, at Spion Kop in January 1900, and in the defence and relief of Ladysmith.

Percy Scott devised carriages and mountings to enable 4.7-inch quick-firing naval guns, long 12-pounders, and even a 6-inch gun, to be used in the field. He designed an armoured train, fitted with Maxims and a 7-pounder gun, manned by sailors, and drawing armoured trucks to carry infantry, and mounted two mobile searchlights on railway trucks, one near Kimberley, the other near Ladysmith, for long-range signalling.

On 29 October, *Powerful* took naval guns to Durban, where within five hours a Naval Brigade entrained for Ladysmith, taking with them two 4.7s, three long 12-pounders, a short 12-pounder and four Maxims, which were all to play a crucial

part in the defence of Ladysmith. In November 1899, *Terrible* also went to Durban, where Percy Scott was appointed Military Commandant, responsible for the city's defences. Within days, he had all roads into Durban guarded by batteries of guns.

In all, there were three Naval Brigades: one, with General Sir George White, was besieged in Ladysmith; another was part of the force under General Sir Redvers Buller which eventually relieved Ladysmith, after a siege of 118 days, at the end of February 1900; a third, serving under Field Marshal Lord Roberts, fought and marched from the Cape to Bloemfontein and Pretoria and finally to the borders of Portuguese East Africa (Mozambique) on the eastern coast.

The sailors were tremendous campaigners, capable of prodigious feats of endurance. One detachment under Lieutenant Grant of *Doris*, with two 4.7s, marched over 1,000 miles (1,600km), including a 17-day chase of De Wet in which 'Grant's guns', as the army called them, covered 250 miles (400km) in 15 days, an average of 16.7 miles (26.8km) a day, and made two forced marches of 37 miles (60km), one completed in 13 hours, the other in 25. They were in action 25 times (counting as one action an engagement at Paardeberg which lasted over eight days) and fired between 500 and 600 rounds.

The *Terribles* rejoined their ship at Durban in March 1900, and the ship sailed on 27th for the Far East which had been her original destination when she was diverted via the Cape of Good Hope. *Terrible* was an excellent steamer, capable of maintaining high speeds for long periods. She had 48 Belleville boilers, the first type of water-tube boiler to be fitted in the Navy's larger ships. They had their critics, and inexperienced handling sometimes caused difficulties and high coal consumption. *Terrible* herself had a serious accident while returning from the Mediterranean in March 1899, when a tube burst and a stoker was fatally scalded.

Terrible arrived in Hong Kong in May 1900, by which time the Boxer Rising had already broken out in China. Its root cause, as in the Boer War, was hostility towards foreigners – 'uitlanders' in the Transvaal, 'gweilos' in China. In 1896, a Chinese secret society in the northern provinces, I Ho Ch'uan (the Society of Righteous and Harmonious Fists) had begun to murder Christian

Above: *Scenes from HMS* Terrible's *commission of 1899–1902. (Top) The crew of a 4.7-inch gun; (centre left) a 4.7in gun; (centre right) a 6in gun; (bottom) 4.7in guns in action with the Naval Brigade at the Battle of Colenso, South Africa, 1899.*

'HANDYMEN' OF THE NAVAL BRIGADES

Sailors serving in the Naval Brigades during Victoria's 'Little Wars', described in Chapters 5 and 6, were nicknamed 'Handymen' – and from 1907 the Interport Field Gun competition (1907–98) of the Royal Tournament commemorated the handiness of HMS *Terrible*'s gunners ashore during the Boer War. Among the handiest were Captains Arthur Wilson and Jackie Fisher – both future First Sea Lords. On 26 July 1882, during the campaign against Arabi Pasha's Egyptian rebels, they commissioned the RN's first armoured train: a locomotive with sand-bagged boilers hauling two wagons on which light armour plate protected machine guns manned by bluejackets. The end of the campaign saw wagons mounting 40-pounder guns.

During the Boer War, Winston Churchill noted that 'that forlorn military machine' the Estcourt armoured train 'was nicknamed 'Wilson's death trap''. The major armament of this vehicle, whose destruction by Boer field guns led to Churchill's capture, was 'a 7-pounder muzzle-loading gun, served by four sailors from the *Tartar*...'. The trains designed by Percy Scott were far more effective: he even anticipated the heavy rail-borne artillery of later wars with his mounting for a 9.2-inch naval gun.

The task of the Naval Brigades was largely to provide specialist help with transport, machine guns,

artillery, and signalling. The Naval Division formed at the outset of the First World War – to absorb some 25,000 naval reservists in excess of seagoing needs – was a much larger, less special force. The men of its 12 battalions (eight RN and four RM) originally wore naval uniform, but were soon outfitted in khaki, with only a cap badge to show their naval origin, and used as conventional infantry.

Traditional handiness lingered, however, in the buccaneering activities around Dunkirk in 1914 of Commander C.R. Samson's RNAS armoured car squadrons, in their sheet-steel-plated Rolls-Royce Silver Ghosts, each mounting a Vickers machine gun in a stubby turret. Nor should it be forgotten that 'Little Willie', ancestor of all tanks, was the child of the Naval Landship Committee established in February 1915 by First Lord of the Admiralty Winston Churchill, and that its co-designer was the then Lieutenant W.G. Wilson, RNAS.

Above: *Admiral Percy Scott's innovations included an improved telescopic sight for a 12-inch gun (left) and an aiming rifle (right).*

Left: *Boer War memorabilia: a model Ladysmith gun; a plate; an egg cup made from the wood of HMS* Terrible; *and Queen Victoria's gift box for servicemen.*

Right: *A memento of HMS* Powerful's *return to Portsmouth in 1900 celebrates her crew's part in the Relief of Ladysmith.*

Above: *Men of the Naval Brigade during the Boer War parade before the Battle of Graspan, November 1899. The Brigade was formed by sailors and marines from the battleship HMS* Monarch *and the cruisers HMS* Terrible, Powerful *and* Doris.

1904 Fisher appointed First Sea Lord. Home Fleet created. Submarines take part in naval manoeuvres for first time.

1905 Royal Naval College, Dartmouth, opened. HMS *Dreadnought*, the first all-big-gun battleship, powered by turbines, laid down.

1906 HMS *Dreadnought* commissioned. Rival navies rush to build their own Dreadnought-type battleships.

converts and destroy Christian property, with the aim of expelling all foreigners from China.

The situation rapidly deteriorated, and the capital, Peking, was besieged by the Boxers, with the help of Imperial Chinese troops. But it was mid-June before *Terrible* received orders to sail for China. She arrived on 21st, to join a large fleet of British, German, Russian, American, Austrian, Italian and Japanese warships off the entrance to the Peiho river (guarded by the Taku forts, famous scene of two earlier 19th century wars against the Chinese).

Anticipating that artillery would be needed, Percy Scott had prepared four long 12-pounders on their carriages. But to his amazement and fury, the C-in-C, Admiral Sir Edward Seymour, would take only one, while *Terrible* herself was ordered down the coast to Chefu and then to Wei-Hai-Wei, taking the other three guns with her.

The relief force for Peking, of 2,000 officers and men, including 900 British seamen and marines, led by Seymour himself, ran into difficulties and had to retreat, with casualties. The town of Tientsin was besieged, bombarded and finally burned by the Boxers. At last, *Terrible* and her three 12-pounders were sent for in haste, and all four guns went with the international relief force of 12,000 men to Tientsin in July and on to Peking in August. *Terrible*'s officers and men who had been to Peking returned to the ship, with the guns, on 7 September 1900. The fleet won two VCs in China: Captain Lewis Halliday RMLI, of the cruiser *Orlando*, in Peking in June, and Midshipman Basil Guy, of the battleship *Barfleur*, in Tientsin in July.

At the turn of the century, there was yet another recruiting crisis in the engineering branch. The 1875 Committee had had the view that 'too many engineer students are being taken from the sons of dockyard artificers, of seamen and marines and of others belonging to the same class of society'. This had become markedly less true as the years passed, but there was still an attitude amongst seamen officers that an engineer was really no better than 'a lascar with a bottle of oil'.

A drop in recruitment forced the Admiralty to take urgent steps again, filling the gaps with 'emergency engineers'. The officers of the Board of Admiralty had apparently learned nothing in the nearly 80 years since the Navy's first steamships. The new arrivals had even less in common with the wardroom than those officers who had progressed through Keyham, and consequently the same old vicious circle continued, with a further fall in recruitment.

EDUCATION AND TRAINING

In 1903 Admiral 'Jackie' Fisher, then Second Sea Lord, and Lord Selborne, First Lord of the Admiralty, jointly devised a solution to this unhappy state of affairs. Engineering was henceforth to become an area of specialization in the same way as gunnery, torpedoes and navigation. All officers would join and be educated and trained together, as a single company.

There was no intention originally to provide cadets with the equivalent of a public school education. 'Nothing is worse,' Fisher stated, 'nothing is more retrograde than trying to ape the Public School system for the Navy', and he considered that officers should, like himself, go to sea at 12 or 13. However, plans were announced

NEW SKILLS AND NEW VALUES

'We are the one Navy where man is so valuable and so scarce...as we have no conscription...', wrote Admiral Fisher to Lord Selborne, First Lord of the Admiralty, in 1902. Both were determined to forge a Navy in which seamen were no longer just 'the ship's people', but individuals skilled in the many new techniques of warfare: torpedoes, submarines and anti-submarine warfare, oil-fuelled machinery (introduced from around the beginning of the First World War); mines and mine-sweeping; airships, aircraft and the ships that handled them; and electrical equipment.

The last-named category was particularly important. Not only were warships now beginning to be fitted with wireless – giving commanders greater tactical control of fleets in battle, and also (not an unmixed blessing, felt many sea officers) permitting speedy Admiralty intervention; electricity also revolutionized gunnery. Percy Scott, Inspector of Target Practice from 1905, worked closely with the firm of Vickers in the development of 'Director Firing'. In his post high on the superstructure, where he was above the gun smoke and well placed to observe the fall of shot, the Director received updates of ranges, speeds, and positions of targets. At the ideal moment, he could fire all guns that bore on the target by pressing a single switch.

As well as advancing technical education, as Chapter 6 shows, Fisher sought to make the Navy a in 1896 for a new shore-based college to replace the old *Britannia*, chiefly for reasons of sanitation and discipline.

Nonetheless, as naval historian Julian Corbett put it, 'You cannot train except at sea and at sea you cannot teach'. This problem was dealt with by the creation of the Dartmouth scheme: cadets entered at 13 years of age to receive a four-year general education (actually 11 terms), equivalent to that provided by a public school.

In March 1902, Edward VII laid the foundation stone of Aston Webb's new building at Dartmouth, the Royal Naval College, HMS *Britannia*. Pending the completion of the new College in September 1905, a 'junior' College was opened on the Isle of Wight at Queen Victoria's house, Osborne, and in September 1903 it received the first cadets.

Entry was by nomination subject to interview, qualifying examination and medical examination. Training for cadets comprised two years at Osborne, a further two years at Dartmouth, and six months at sea in a training cruiser. Then they joined the fleet as midshipmen.

Admiral Sir John Fisher was appointed First Sea Lord in October 1904. A month later, an Admiralty Committee on Designs appointed by him considered a proposal and a design for an 'all big gun ship', an idea first mooted in the 1903 edition of *Jane's Fighting Ships* by an Italian naval architect, Vittorio Cuniberti. A sketch design was approved on 15 January 1905, and the keel was laid on 2 October. Time was saved by obtaining material well in advance, ordering large numbers of plates of standard size and thickness, and by using the 12-inch guns and spares for *Lord Nelson* and *Agamemnon*. As a result, the ship, named *Dreadnought*, was launched at Portsmouth by King Edward VII on 10 February 1906, after only 130 days on the building slip, and was ready for trials, after a year and a day, on 3 October.

Dreadnought, who gave her name to a whole generation of capital ships, cost £1,783,883, mounted ten 12-inch guns in five turrets, had 11-inch armour, and displaced 17,250 tons. She rendered obsolete at a stroke every other battleship in every other navy, including the German Navy, which was fast becoming the principal challenger to British naval supremacy.

Below: *The 'all big gun ship' HMS* Dreadnought *under construction early in 1906. Her speed and firepower rendered all other battleships obsolete. Other navies quickly joined a race to build their own 'dreadnoughts'.*

Above: *Admiral Sir Percy Moreton Scott (1853–1924), one of the greatest gunnery experts in naval history, is seen here as Captain of HMS* Terrible *in 1895.*

Below: *The main house at Osborne, Isle of Wight, a former royal residence. The 'junior' Royal Naval College was opened here in September 1903.*

Right and above: *The training hulk HMS* Impregnable *(right, c.1900) was replaced by a shore establishment (above, c.1910).*

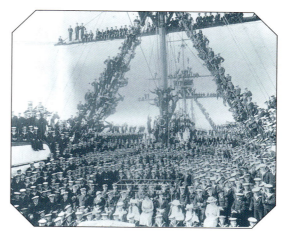

less rigid society. The attitude he opposed is summed up in a supposed exchange between two cadets at the Royal Naval College. 'I don't care what the Admiralty says,' states the potential executive officer to the potential engineer, 'my Mama would not have your Mama to tea.' For the training of boy seamen, Fisher supplemented the old floating schools like HMS *Impregnable* with shore establishments teaching modern curricula. Even so, tough training for boys was the rule – but perhaps rigid discipline was sometimes necessary, if irksome. A 16-year-old naval volunteer in 1916 remembered that 'any boy who got sent before the magistrates used to be offered the chance of going to prison or joining the Navy. …we volunteers got fed up with being treated as if we were criminals.'

1911 Winston Churchill becomes First Lord of the Admiralty

1912 First flight of a British aircraft from a ship's deck at anchor (HMS *Africa*), and first aircraft to take off from a ship underway at sea, HMS *Hibernia*. HMS *Queen Elizabeth*, first oil-fuelled capital ship, laid down. Naval Staff instituted in the Admiralty.

Right: *A view of HMS Dreadnought from the stern. She was the first large naval warship to be powered by turbines. Note the fire control platform, or spotting top, on her tripod mast.*

Below: *HMS* Viper, *the Navy's first turbine-powered destroyer, could make more than 36 knots. Her loss, and that of the similar HMS* Cobra, *in 1901 had no connection with her Parsons' turbines.*

Dreadnought had 18 Babcock and Wilcox water tube boilers, and two sets of Parsons direct drive turbines. Each set had a high pressure and a low pressure turbine, each of which drove one shaft, to give a speed of 21 knots (21.6 on trials). She was the first 'all big gun battleship' to have four shafts and twin rudders. She was a handsome and striking ship, and actually looked the part of the most powerful warship of her time, superior in fire power and speed to any other capital ship then afloat.

She was also the first large naval ship to be powered by turbines. The sensation of the 1897 Diamond Jubilee Review had been the appearance of the tiny *Turbinia*, designed by the celebrated marine engineer Charles Parsons. The first vessel driven by steam turbines, *Turbinia* had three shafts, each with three propellers and had shot through the Review lines at 34 knots, four more than the fastest destroyers of that time.

As a result, the Admiralty ordered from the Parsons Steam Turbine Co (with the hull sub-contracted to Hawthorn Leslie) the Navy's first turbine-driven destroyer, *Viper*, launched in 1899. She and her successor, *Cobra*, built by Armstrong Whitworth, both achieved speeds of nearly 37 knots. But *Viper* ran aground on the Casquets, Alderney, during the Naval Manoeuvres on 3 August 1901, and became a total loss. Six weeks later, on 18 September, *Cobra* broke in half and foundered in heavy weather whilst on passage from the Tyne to Portsmouth. These two accidents caused a reaction against turbines and, coupled with the wreck of the torpedo cruiser *Serpent* on the coast of Spain in November 1890, a lasting prejudice against 'snake' names.

Dreadnought and Fisher had their critics, who argued that by building such a ship the Royal Navy had wilfully forfeited its advantages over other navies. But the sincerest tribute to *Dreadnought* was paid by those other navies, who began furiously to build their own Dreadnoughts. However, Britain was able to outstrip the rest and built 30 Dreadnoughts, including the faster, more lightly armoured battlecruisers, in the eight years between 1906 and the outbreak of war in 1914.

Fisher incurred more criticism when he embarked upon a five-year programme of sweeping changes. He amalgamated the Nore, Portsmouth and Devonport divisions into one Home Fleet. He radically modified the worldwide strategy the Navy had pursued since the Crimean War and concentrated the main fleet in the North Sea. He scrapped no less than 154 ships, including 17 pre-Dreadnought battleships, which he said were too weak to fight and too slow to run away, and were therefore mere devices for wasting manpower. In Fisher's view, four kinds of warship were needed for his type of warfare: 21-knot battleships, 25-knot armoured cruisers, 36-knot destroyers, and submarines – of which he was one of the earliest and most vehement advocates.

THE FIRST SUBMARINES

The Royal Navy's first five submarines, *Hollands 1-5*, were built in secret and officially as experiments, using the design of the American submarine pioneer John P. Holland. *Holland 1* was launched by Vickers, Son & Maxim at Barrow-in-Furness on 2 October 1901 when the general feeling in the Navy, succinctly expressed by

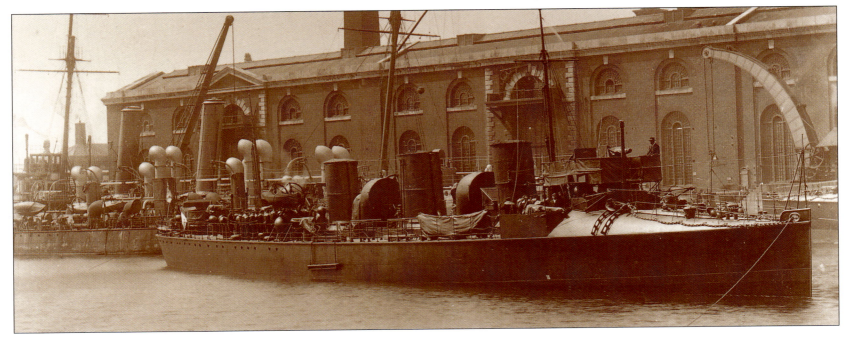

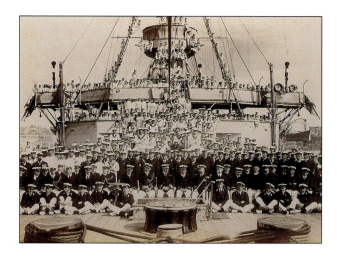

Left: *Battlecruiser HMS* Indomitable. *Built for speed, to counter commerce raiders and act as scouts, Invincible class battlecruisers were larger than all the pre-Dreadnought battleships, and this increase in size meant that dry docks had to be enlarged to accommodate them.*

Far left: *The ships's company of HMS Duncan, a pre-Dreadnought completed in 1903. There were 750 men in* Duncan, *compared to 862 in* Dreadnought, *so that the new ships meant that the Navy needed more men.*

Below left: *HMS* Zealandia *leads the Third Battle Squadron into Malta, 1912. One of a class of eight pre-Dreadnoughts completed in 1905, and originally named New Zealand, she was renamed in 1911 so that her name could be given to a new battlecruiser paid for by the Dominion.*

Below: *The pre-Dreadnought battleship HMS Formidable is seen in 1908. On 1 January 1915, she was torpedoed and sunk off Portland by the German submarine U.24.*

Admiral Sir Arthur Knyvet Wilson VC, was that submarines were somehow 'underhand' and 'damned un-English weapons' whose crews, when captured, should be hung as pirates.

The Holland boats were tiny, 63 feet (19.2m) long, 104 tons surfaced, 122 dived. They were armed with one 18-inch torpedo tube, and had one propeller, driven by a petrol engine on the surface and by an electric motor dived. The complement was two officers and five ratings. The earlier boats had no periscope, so the boat had to break surface to allow the Captain to look through one of the scuttles in the small conning tower.

A primitive but effective periscope, which projected its image on a mirror in the control room, was designed by Captain Reginald Bacon, the first Inspecting Captain of Submarines, and one of the Navy's chief pioneering spirits in submarines, who also designed the first British submarines, the A class of 1903, with higher conning towers than the Hollands and Captain Bacon's periscope.

At first, submarines were regarded as no more than an advanced form of defensive mining. The Naval Manoeuvres of 1904, the first in which submarines took part, changed all that. *Holland 3* scored a hit with a dummy torpedo on the cruiser *Juno* and another *Holland* closed to within 80

yards (73m) and torpedoed the flagship. Although Admiral Wilson could personally semaphore 'You be damned' to a submarine which claimed to have sunk his flagship, those 1904 Manoeuvres showed those who had eyes to see it that here was a new weapon with terrible potential.

The 1904 Manoeuvres also saw the first British submarine disaster. On the final day, 18 March, *A.1* was carrying out an attack on *Juno* in the Solent when she was run down and sunk with all hands by ss *Berwick Castle*.

The A class were followed by the B (1905) and C (1906) classes, which were progressively bigger and faster, with larger complements and longer ranges, more efficient periscopes and two torpedo tubes. The Bs were the first British submarines to be fitted with fore hydroplanes. The Cs were officially designated 'Coastal submarines', but three of them made a voyage to Hong Kong in 1911.

The first British 'Patrol submarines' were the D class. Built between 1908 and 1911, they were a tremendous advance in submarine design, with a surface range of 2,500 miles (4,000km) at 10 knots, a top surface speed of 16 knots, and 9 knots dived, three 18-inch torpedo tubes (two bow and one stern), larger conning towers and greatly improved living accommodation. They were the

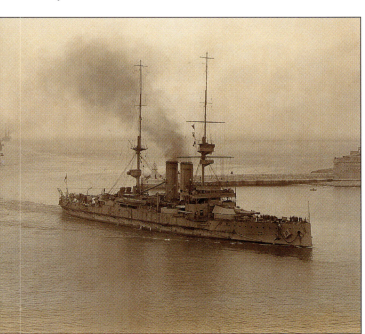

1914 RNAS formed from RFC Naval Wing. Grand Fleet Review at Spithead (July). Outbreak of First World War (August). Battle of Heligoland Bight (28 August). HMS *Pathfinder* sunk by torpedo from *U.21*, first warship to be sunk by a self-propelled torpedo fired by a submarine at sea (5 September). First German warship, *Hela*, sunk by British submarine, *E.9* (13 September). Battle of Coronel (1 November). Raids on East coast of England by German High Seas Fleet (November). Falklands defeat of Graf von Spee by Sturdee (8 December). Seaplane carriers launch first shipborne aircraft raid on a shore target, Cuxhaven (December).

Right: *A page from a photograph album showing D class submarines in Cromarty Firth, one of the new bases built to support the fleet against the German threat. The D class of 1908–11, seen here on manoeuvres in 1913, were the Royal Navy's first 'Patrol submarines'. (Above left) D.3 and D.6 secured alongside; (above and centre right) D.6 under way; (below left) D.3 leaves the depot ship; (below right) at the Nigg Sands beacon.*

Right: *Like his bulldog, Admiral Lord Charles Beresford (1846–1919) looks a tough customer. Fisher found him so, when the powerful 'Charlie B' fiercely opposed his policy and reforms of 1904–10.*

first to have diesel engines and twin shafts, to have saddle tanks outside the pressure hull instead of internal ballast tanks, and to be fitted with wireless. *D.4* was the first British submarine to be fitted with a gun. In exercises in 1910, *D.1* torpedoed two 'Blue Fleet' cruisers, after remaining undetected off the coast of Scotland for three days.

Fisher was elevated to the peerage as Baron Fisher of Kilverstone in November 1909 and retired, reluctantly, from the Admiralty on 25 January 1910, his sixty-ninth birthday, after five tumultuous years in which he had made many enemies and carried on one disastrous feud, with Admiral Lord Charles Beresford, C-in-C of the Channel Fleet, who disapproved of Fisher and his methods. It was a disastrous quarrel which split the senior ranks of the Navy and in April 1909 caused the Asquith government to investigate it. However, Fisher's daemonic energy had shaken the Navy out of its lethargic post-Nelsonic Victorian complacency, when paintwork was much more important than gunnery, and transformed it into the formidable modern weapon with which Britain entered the First World War.

Fisher was replaced by Admiral Sir Arthur Wilson. But though he was gone, his influence continued. Winston Churchill became First Lord of the Admiralty in October 1911, believing that 'Fisher was right in nine-tenths of what he fought for'. Churchill also believed in the necessity of instituting a naval staff, which both Reginald McKenna, Churchill's predecessor, and Wilson did not. Thus Arthur Wilson was in turn relieved, by Sir Francis Bridgeman, C-in-C of the Home Fleet.

Churchill was a reformer as zealous as Fisher. He increased sailors' pay, set up Naval Detention Quarters instead of civil prisons for naval offenders, and in 1912, to the disapproval of tradionalists such as Sir Arthur Wilson, instituted a Naval Staff in the Admiralty, the first in the Navy's history. His other institution that year was the 'Mate Scheme' by which young warrant and petty officers could be given educational training ashore and then sent to sea as officers. This long awaited and much needed reform, warmly welcomed by the lower deck, was an immediate success.

THE NAVY'S AIR WING

The first flight from a Royal Navy ship was made by Lt C.R. Samson, who took off in a Short S27 box-kite from a track built on the bows of the old battleship *Africa* at Sheerness on 12 January 1912. Churchill himself was learning to fly with the first naval pilots and he enthusiastically supported the Naval Wing, the Navy's own air wing, formed unofficially in May 1912, when it broke away to develop independently of the Royal Flying Corps, itself formed only a month earlier.

In the same year, Churchill and the Admiralty decided to build a new fast squadron of five battleships, *Queen Elizabeth, Warspite, Barham, Malaya* and *Valiant* (one suggested name was *Oliver Cromwell* but the King, understandably, objected). They displaced 27,500 tons, and were one of the most successful classes of battleship ever built. They were the first battleships to be armed with 15-inch guns, the first to have a top speed of 24 knots, and the first to use oil instead of coal. This too was controversial because, critics argued, Britain had coal in abundance but no oil, which had to be brought from great distances overseas. A controlling share in the Anglo-Persian Oil Company was bought to safeguard supplies.

Churchill's reforms continued in 1913, when he introduced the 'special entry' scheme, by which public-school-educated cadets joined Keyham at the age of 18, and had two cruises in the cruiser *Highflyer* to learn some seamanship and navigation, before joining gunrooms in the fleet.

There was a Grand Fleet Review at Spithead on 16 July 1914, a fortnight before the outbreak of war. Ostensibly, it was held to test the efficiency

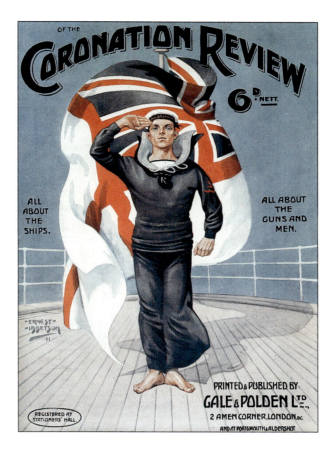

of the system for mobilising the feet and calling up reservists, but it was equally a response to the deepening political crisis.

The fleets were to have dispersed after exercises that week, but Churchill placed the Navy on a 'preparatory and precautionary basis' on 28 July. Next day, the First Fleet left Portland and on the night of 29/30 July passed at high speed and with lights out through the Straits of Dover, heading up the North Sea to Scapa Flow. As Churchill said, 'the King's ships were at sea'. On 4 August, the country was at war with Germany.

Left: A Bluejacket painted by Ernest Ibbetson graces the programme for the Naval Review celebrating the Coronation of King George V, himself a professional naval officer, in 1911.

Below: A watercolour by Richard Simkin shows the imposing dress uniform of a Flag Captain, Royal Navy, in 1913.

Below: HMS Queen Elizabeth, *the name ship of a class of five battleships. They were the first to mount 15-inch guns and to be oil-fuelled. She is seen after her first rebuild in the late 1920s.*

Above: *The 13.5-inch guns of the battleships HMS* Orion *(leading ship),* Conqueror, Monarch *and* Thunderer *are trained to starboard as the Third Battle Squadron steams in line ahead.*

THE OUTBREAK OF WAR

The first months of the war were naturally a time of 'firsts'. The first enemy warship, the minelayer *Konigin Luise*, was sunk by the destroyers *Lance* and *Landrail* of the 3rd Flotilla 30 miles (50km) east of Aldeburgh on 5 August, but one of her mines sank the flotilla leader, the cruiser *Amphion*, the following day.

The first controversy of the war began on 5 August when the cruiser *Gloucester* detected the German battlecruiser *Goeben* in Messina by wireless interception (the first use of this technique by the Royal Navy in wartime). *Goeben* and the light cruiser *Breslau* evaded the Mediterranean Fleet and passed through the Dardanelles on 9 August, thereby much enhancing Germany's prestige in Turkey. Rear Admiral Troubridge, commanding the battlecruiser squadron, who avoided action because he believed *Goeben* could outgun his ships and the Admiralty had ordered him not to engage a superior force, was subsequently court-martialled.

On 8 August, *U.15* made the first submerged attack of the war, firing a torpedo which missed the battleship *Monarch* off Fair Isle. On the following day, the Royal Navy had their first U-boat kill, when the cruiser *Birmingham* rammed and sank *U.15* 120 miles (190km) south-east of the Orkneys.

On 20 August there was an event which cast a long shadow down the years, when the German light cruiser *Magdeburg* ran aground in fog during an engagement between German and Russian ships off the Gulf of Finland. Her code books were recovered by divers and passed to the Naval Intelligence Department in Room 40 at the Admiralty, who were then able for a time to read

German messages – the first such intelligence *coup* of the century.

August 1914 saw the first major surface ship action of the war: a raid on German patrols whose positions and movements were being reported by British submarines in the Heligoland Bight. The Harwich Force, of the light cruisers *Arethusa* and *Fearless*, and two flotillas of destroyers, commanded by Commodore R.Y. Tyrwhitt, covered by the Battle Cruiser Force, under Rear Admiral David Beatty, and the 1st Cruiser Squadron, under Commodore W.R. Goodenough, entered the Bight at dawn on 28 August.

Just after 7 a.m. Tyrwhitt's cruisers sighted two German torpedo boats, and sank one of them. The German light cruisers *Stettin, Frauenlob,* and *Mainz* came up in support and were later joined

Left: *Thanks to the initiative of First Lord of the Admiralty Winston Churchill, 'the King's ships were at sea' from the first moment of the First World War. Here, a cruiser escorts troopships from Port Said to the French port of Marseilles in 1914.*

Above: *A battleship of the Iron Duke class in dry dock. The name ship of the class, each of which mounted ten 13.5-inch guns, was the flagship of Admiral Sir John Jellicoe at the Battle of Jutland in 1916.*

by the light cruisers *Köln* (Rear Admiral Maas), *Stralsund*, and *Ariadne*. Now outgunned, and entangled by what Tyrwhitt called 'a hornet's nest' of opponents, the Harwich Force withdrew at high speed after a series of confused actions, but might well have been overwhelmed had not Beatty's five battlecruisers arrived, belatedly but in time, The German ships then also withdrew under cover of mist, but lost *Mainz, Köln*, and *Ariadne*. British casualties were 35 killed and 40 men wounded, and one cruiser and a destroyer damaged. The Germans lost over 1,200 killed, wounded and taken prisoner.

Although there had been serious failures in communication and coordination on the British side, Heligoland Bight was a definite victory, and it made heroes of Tyrwhitt and Beatty.

U- BOAT SUCCESSES

In September 1914 submarines began to show their true potential as weapons of war. On the afternoon of 5 September, the light cruiser *Pathfinder* was on anti-submarine patrol off the Firth of Forth when Lt Otto Hersing sighted her through the periscope of *U.21*. *U.21* fired one Type 'G' (Whitehead) torpedo which hit *Pathfinder* on her starboard side, below the bridge, and counter-mined ammunition in the forward magazine. *Pathfinder*'s forward half virtually disintegrated and she sank with great loss of life. This was the first time in naval history that a warship had been sunk by a self-propelled torpedo fired from a genuine submarine in the open sea.

The first sinking of a German warship by a British submarine followed on 13 September, off Heligoland, where Lt Max Horton was on patrol in *E.9*, one of a numerous (57 of them were built) and successful class of submarine. Armed with five torpedo tubes (two bow, two beam, one stern), 660 tons surfaced, 800 dived, capable of 16 knots on the surface and 10 dived, and having a range of 3,000 miles (4,800km) at 10 knots, the E class were essentially the submarine workhorses of the First World War.

Horton sighted the German cruiser *Hela* through *E.9*'s periscope early that morning and fired two torpedoes from a range of 600 yards (550m). One hit, and when Horton looked through his periscope again he could see only trawlers where the cruiser had been.

On 20 September, in the 'Broad Fourteens' off the Dutch coast, three elderly British cruisers, *Aboukir, Cressy* and *Hogue*, nicknamed with somewhat macabre humour the 'Live Bait Squadron', were patrolling in support of the destroyer flotillas at Harwich. Bad weather had forced the destroyers to return to base and the three ancients were alone when, at 6.30 that morning, *U.9* (Lt Otto Weddigen) fired a single torpedo at *Aboukir*.

One was enough. *Aboukir* listed heavily to starboard and then sank. The others thought she had struck a mine, and *Hogue* had stopped to pick up survivors when she herself was hit and sunk by two torpedoes. *Cressy* carried on picking up survivors, giving *U.9* time to reload. *Cressy* was also hit and sunk by two more torpedoes. Nearly 1,400 officers and men, most of them newly-joined naval reservists, were lost.

A month later, on 20 October, there was an event which had the most ominous portents for the future. The small British steamer *Glitra*,

making her way across the North Sea, encountered *U.17* which fired a shot across her bows and sent an armed boarding party on board. *Glitra*'s Captain and crew were hustled down into a lifeboat, and her seacocks were opened. She was thus the first merchant ship to be sunk by a U-boat, albeit scuttled and not torpedoed.

U.17's Captain had behaved perfectly properly, according to current German Naval Prize Regulations, but with the sinkings of *Pathfinder*, the 'Live Bait' Squadron and *Glitra*, the true and savage nature of U-boat warfare had begun to emerge. Whatever international law and regulations might say in theory, from 1914 onwards in practical terms the U-boat became its own arbiter.

The First Sea Lord, Prince Louis of Battenberg, was forced to resign on 29 October because of his German antecedents, after a period of fierce public hostility towards anything German, including dachshunds and shop-keepers with German surnames. Churchill replaced him with Fisher, who was at once faced with the first naval defeat of the war.

Vice Admiral Graf von Spee, commanding the German East Asiatic Squadron, of the armoured cruisers *Scharnhorst* (flagship) and *Gneisenau* and the light cruiser *Nürnberg*, had been forced to leave Chinese waters because of British and Japanese superiority there, and headed across the Pacific towards South America, being reinforced at Easter Island by the light cruisers *Dresden* and *Leipzig*.

CORONEL AND THE FALKLANDS

Von Spee's ships were brought to action off Coronel, on the coast of Chile, by the British South American squadron, an ill-assorted force of the old armoured cruisers *Good Hope* (flagship) and *Monmouth*, the light cruiser *Glasgow* and the armed merchant cruiser *Otranto*, under Rear Admiral Sir Christopher Cradock.

At first, both sides thought that only a single enemy ship was present, but when *Glasgow* informed Cradock of his opponent's true strength, the wiser course would have been to retire, as he could have done. To an officer with Cradock's sense of honour and duty that was unthinkable.

Von Spee, for his part, held off until the British ships were silhouetted against the setting sun, whilst his own ships were almost invisible against the gathering gloom. When his ships opened fire, at a range of 12,000 yards (11,000m), their gunnery was devastatingly accurate, while *Monmouth*'s 6-inch and *Good Hope*'s 9.2-inch were ineffective. *Good Hope*'s 6-inch, in the lower batteries nearer the waterline, could not be used at all because of the heavy sea and swell running. The upshot was that *Good Hope* and *Monmouth*

Below: *Ships of Admiral Cradock's South American squadron which took part in the Battle of Coronel, 1 November 1914. Cradock's ill-assorted force was defeated by von Spee's cruisers and the armoured cruisers* Good Hope *and* Monmouth *were sunk with all hands.*

were both sunk with all hands. *Glasgow* and *Otranto* managed to escape in the darkness. Von Spee's ships had no casualties or damage

Such a defeat demanded vengeance. Fisher at once despatched the battlecruisers *Invincible* and *Inflexible*, under Vice Admiral Sir Doveton Sturdee, to the South Atlantic. Sturdee rendezvoused with Rear Admiral Stoddard, who had assembled the cruisers *Glasgow*, *Cornwall* and *Kent* at Montevideo, and the whole force arrived at Port Stanley in the Falklands on 7 December.

Meanwhile, Graf Spee had decided to attack and destroy the base facilities at Port Stanley, which he believed were undefended, and then go on into the Atlantic, break through the British blockade, and so return home to Germany. He sent *Gneisenau* and *Nürnberg* on ahead to reconnoitre the position at Port Stanley. *Gneisenau*'s officers were horrified to see, on the morning of 8 December, the distinctive tripod masts and fighting tops of two battlecruisers in the anchorage. Von Spee turned and fled south-east at full speed.

Sturdee had also been caught by surprise, with several of his ships coaling. However, all his ships had steam up in two hours and set off on what was to be a long chase. The action began at 1 p.m. when *Leipzig*, lagging behind the rest, came under fire. Von Spee ordered his light cruisers to scatter, while *Scharnhorst* and *Gneisenau* engaged the enemy. It was von Spee's turn to be outranged and outgunned. *Scharnhorst* sank with all hands at 4.15 p.m. and *Gneisenau* followed, leaving a handful of survivors, at 6 p.m.

Glasgow and *Cornwall* pursued and sank *Leipzig*, and *Kent* sank *Nürnberg* after a prolonged and furious chase when at one point *Kent*'s sailors were ordered to assemble on the quarterdeck so as to weigh the

Above: *The light cruiser SMS* Dresden *was the sole survivor of von Spee's defeat in the Battle of the Falklands.*

Left: *Men from the armoured cruiser HMS* Kent *man a shore emplacement in the Falkland Islands.*

Above: *Admiral Sir Doveton Sturdee (1859–1925), whose battlecruisers avenged Coronel.*

Left: *A watercolour by Ian Marshall shows battlecruisers HMS* Invincible *and* Inflexible *in the fight off the Falklands.*

Right: *The end of SMS* Dresden. *She fled from the Falklands to hide among the islands off Chile. On 15 March 1915, she was run to earth by British warships at San Ambrosio Island, and blew herself up.*

Below: *A Parseval airship at Farnborough, April 1914. This German-designed, non-rigid airship, 301ft (92m) long, was Naval Airship No. 4 in Royal Naval Air Service (RNAS) use. (Bottom) A B.E.2c biplane developed by the Royal Aircraft Factory at Farnborough.*

stern down and give the ship extra speed. Only *Dresden* escaped but in March 1915 she was found by *Kent, Glasgow* and *Orama* at San Ambrosio Island, off the Chilean coast, where without coal or friends she blew herself up. Cradock and his men had been avenged.

The year 1914 ended with a 'first' for the RNAS. German army Zeppelin hangars at Cologne and Düsseldorf had been attacked by land-based RNAS aircraft until the German advance through Belgium and northern France put them out of range, but the German fleet's Zeppelin bases had been out of range since the start of the war. They could only be attacked by aircraft taken by sea to within striking range.

Three cross-Channel passenger ships, *Engadine, Riviera* and *Empress,* had been converted into seaplane carriers by fitting them with fore and aft canvas shelters and seaplane-handling booms, Escorted by the cruisers *Arethusa* and *Undaunted* and the destroyer *Lurcher,* the seaplane-carriers sailed from Harwich on Christmas Day and launched seven seaplanes to attack a Zeppelin base believed to be at Cuxhaven (but actually some distance away).

The attack failed, but this was the first seaborne air strike in naval history and the first open-water naval battle in which aircraft were the only striking weapons on both sides. Opposing surface warships did not exchange a shot. *D.6* and *E.11,* and U-boats, also took no part.

THE DOGGER BANK

Signalling errors at the Heligoland Bight had not prevented a clear victory. Similar errors at the Dogger Bank in January 1915 had a much more serious result. A German force of the First

Scouting Group, of the battlecruisers *Seydlitz* (flag of Rear Admiral Franz von Hipper), *Moltke*, and *Derfflinger*, and the armoured cruiser *Blücher*, four light cruisers and two flotillas of destroyers, sailed from the Jade river on 23 January to attack British patrols and fishing vessels in the area of the Dogger Bank.

Forewarned by intelligence, the British Battlecruiser Force, of *Lion* (flagship of Vice Admiral David Beatty), *Tiger, Princess Royal, New Zealand* (flagship of Rear Admiral Arthur Moore) and *Indomitable*, with the 1st Light Cruiser Squadron, were ordered to rendezvous with the Harwich cruiser and destroyer force under Commodore R.Y. Tyrwhitt north-east of the Dogger Bank at dawn on 24 January.

The enemy ships were soon sighted, steaming westward at high speed. Believing he faced a superior force, Hipper turned back but was overhauled by Beatty's battlecruisers who opened fire at extreme range. In a running high speed battle, *Lion* was badly damaged and dropped astern. *Seydlitz* and *Blücher* were also damaged, but while *Seydlitz* managed to keep station, *Blücher* had to slow down.

With Beatty in *Lion* now far astern, Moore took over command of the British force. Unfortunately Moore misunderstood Beatty's signal, to leave *Blücher* to be finished off by *Indomitable* while he himself continued to pursue the enemy, and broke off the chase. Beatty transferred his flag to a destroyer but by the time he had caught up, it was too late. *Blücher* was sunk with only 189 survivors, but the rest of the German ships escaped. The crippled *Lion* was towed back to harbour by *Indomitable*.

British casualties were 15 killed and 80 wounded. The Germans lost 954 killed and 80 wounded, but they learned a valuable lesson from the action: that magazines were vulnerable to flash from bursting shells and burning cordite. They took steps to make their ships safer by fitting anti-flash shutters in the ammunition hoist trunkings. These were to serve them well at Jutland (in dramatic contrast to the fate of British ships).

On 29 January 1915, the steamer *Oriole* disappeared, believed torpedoed, with all hands in the Channel – the first British merchant seamen to be lost in the war. On 4 February, the German Admiralty declared all the waters surrounding Great Britain and Ireland to be a war zone. From 18 February, every merchant vessel found within this war zone would be destroyed 'without it always being possible to avoid danger to the crews and passengers'.

By February 1915 Germany had lost seven of the 28 U-boats with which it had entered the war. By then U-boats had sunk ten British merchantmen of 20,000 tons aggregate, which was less than ten per cent of the total tonnage lost from all causes in the first six months of the war. To February 1915, surface raiders had sunk 51 vessels of 215,000 tons, while 14 merchant ships of 37,000 tons had been sunk by mines.

But by April 1915 all the German surface raiders had been sunk or accounted for and the U-boats had sunk another 38 vessels of 105,000 tons since February. The pattern of sinkings for the future had been set. Losses to U-boats far outweighed losses to any other weapon.

THE DARDANELLES CAMPAIGN

On 3 November 1914, an Anglo-French squadron bombarded the outer forts at the Dardanelles, the narrow strait which separates Turkey in Europe from Turkey in Asia and leads to the Sea of Marmara, the object being to discover the amount of damage that could be inflicted on the forts by ships' guns. It was the first move in what was to be a long and terrible saga.

1915 Battle of Dogger Bank (24 January). Bombardment of Dardanelles forts (February–March). First unrestricted U-boat campaign begins (February). Landings at Gallipoli (April). Suvla landings (August). End of unrestricted U-boat campaign in Atlantic after protests by United States (September). Evacuation from Anzac and Suvla beachheads begins (December).

Below: *Jack ashore – but not at liberty. In assorted uniforms, men of the Naval Division face the camera while interned in Holland in 1917.*

Left: *The tunic of an officer of the Royal Naval Division who served in the First World War. Only the sleeve insignia of rank and the cap badge differ markedly from an Army officer's tunic.*

Above: *Logistical preparation for the Gallipoli campaign. A mule is hoisted ashore at Mudros Bay, the Allied base on the Aegean island of Lemnos, in 1915.*

Above right: *British Forces landing at the Dardanelles, April 1915, a photogravure by Walter Thomas. The landings were fiercely opposed.*

Below: *'W' beach, near Cape Tekke, after the British landing. On crowded beachheads, Allied forces were subjected to Turkish fire from commanding heights.*

Inspired by Mr Churchill, but only very reluctantly supported by Fisher, the plan was first to silence the Dardanelles forts by bombardment by old (and presumably expendable) battleships, clear the minefields in the Narrows with minesweeping trawlers, enter the Sea of Marmara and proceed to Constantinople, thus forcing the Turks to seek an armistice. With Turkey out of the war, a vital sea route would be opened to Russia.

Unfortunately, the earlier bombardments in November and December 1914 alerted the Turks, who greatly improved their defences, built new forts, brought up mobile batteries, and laid more minefields. Attempts to force the Narrows in February and March 1915 failed. It became clear that warships could not succeed alone. It was impossible to sweep the minefields without first silencing the shore batteries and this could only be achieved for short periods.

On 18 March, a final attempt was made to break through by an Anglo-French bombarding

'It wasn't just the rifle fire that was so hard to endure but the heavy Turkish artillery from Kum Kale. That was constant – there was no peace. All the time we were kept busy: it was semaphore or morse flag by day, box lamp with dry batteries, or boats' flashing lamp at night. Later, when we got more established, we used a heliograph for hourly communication with Tenedos, which was about 12 miles away…

Rumours of a possible evacuation came through to us before anyone else. Units began to disappear. We then heard that Suvla and Anzac beaches had been successfully evacuated with no casualties. By now, December, the weather was raw cold. Yet we couldn't believe that the Turks would let us simply slip away. But they did, and on 8 January 1916 we left from the pierhead. Of that 20-man naval party I was one of the first on to the beach on 25 April 1915 and one of the last to leave. I was ten days off my eighteenth birthday.'

SIGNALMAN ERIC PEACOCK WHO LANDED AT 'W' BEACH,
CAPE HELLES IN THE DARDANELLES, 1915

squadron of 16 battleships, including the new *Queen Elizabeth.* The French battleship *Bouvet* hit a mine and sank in three minutes. She was followed by *Ocean* and *Irresistible,* also mined and sunk. *Inflexible* was damaged by shore batteries, struck a mine, and only just managed to reach Tenedos safely. This was the end of any naval attempt to force the Dardanelles.

It was then decided to mount an amphibious operation in April 1915 to land the army on the Gallipoli peninsula at four beaches, 'V' on the southern tip of Cape Helles and at 'W', 'X' and 'Y' beaches, further up the coast.

At 'V' beach, the plan was for the battleship *Albion* to bombard the defences early on Sunday 25th and keep Turkish heads down, while the converted collier ss *River Clyde,* with a small hopper and three lighters to form a floating bridge, ran in to the shore and grounded. The 2,000 soldiers on board *River Clyde* would then disembark through ports cut in her sides and cross the floating bridge to the beach.

When the bombardment lifted, the Turkish defenders returned to their hardly damaged trenches and, just as the disembarkation began, opened fire. In a moment *River Clyde's* gangways were strewn and choked with dead and dying. The soldiers in the lighters were cut down where they stood.

After three hours, 1,500 men had tried to land, and only 200 had done so. That anybody got ashore at all was almost entirely due to the great gallantry and physical stamina of *River Clyde's* officers and men working in the lighters. *River Clyde's* captain, Commander Edward Unwin, two of her midshipmen, George Drewry and Wilfred Malleson, and Able Seamen Williams and Samson, all won the Victoria Cross, Williams posthumously.

At Gallipoli, the original plan had been for the troops from the four beaches to press on inland and take the heights of Achi Baba to the north-

west. Instead, the troops became embroiled in bitter close-quarter trench warfare, in appalling conditions of heat, dust, flies and water shortage. Disasters continued at sea. *U.21* sank the battleship *Triumph* outside the Dardanelles on 25 May and the battleship *Majestic* off Cape Helles two days later.

NASMITH AND E.11

All was not gloom and failure. 'Go and run amuck in the Marmara' was the order Commodore Roger Keyes, the C-in-C's chief of staff, gave Lt Cdr Nasmith, CO of *E.11*. Nasmith needed no second urging, and set off on 19 May 1915 on a 20-day patrol which was the stuff of legend.

In cold figures, *E.11* sank 11 ships: a large gunboat, two transports, three store ships, an

Above: *Cheers greet E.11 as Lt Cdr Nasmith, a VC winner in an earlier patrol, brings her back from the Marmara cruise during which she sank the Turkish battleship Haireddin Barbarossa.*

▶ **1916** Gallipoli evacuation complete (January). Second unrestricted U-boat campaign begins (February) and ends after further protests from United States (April). Battle of Jutland (31 May). HMS *Hampshire* sunk and Lord Kitchener drowned (5 June). German U-boat offensive intensifies.

Left: *A landing party from the battleship HMS Queen Elizabeth photographed on 'X' beach, Cape Helles, March 1915. Unlike the men of the Naval Division, who fought in khaki at Gallipoli, they retained their naval dress.*

he was in the narrowest part of the channel, covered by shore batteries. So *E.11* towed the mine for 11 miles (18km), until Nasmith could order full astern and surfaced stern first, when the mine floated free. He did not mention the mine to anyone else on board. Not surprisingly, Nasmith was gazetted for the Victoria Cross in June.

In the same month, the RNAS won their first VC. Of some men it could be said that they would either be killed, or win the VC, or both. For Flight Sub Lt 'Rex' Warneford of No. 1 Squadron it was both, and in the most spectacular manner. On the night of 6/7 June 1915, he singlehandedly destroyed a Zeppelin over Ghent. He became a national hero overnight and was awarded the Victoria Cross on 8 June; this was by far the shortest interval in the VC's history between the deed and the award. On 17 June, Warneford took an American journalist up for a flight near Versailles. The aircraft turned over, and both men were thrown out and killed.

By December 1915, it had been recognised that the Gallipoli venture had comprehensively failed. Evacuation of the beachheads began on 19 December and was finally completed on 8 January 1916. There were no casualties, and the enemy suspected nothing. It was ironic that the most successful operation of the whole Gallipoli campaign was the leaving of it. Churchill and Fisher both resigned, and were replaced by Arthur James Balfour and Admiral Sir Henry Jackson.

JELLICOE AND JUTLAND

Since long before the war, the Royal Navy had looked forward to, and trained for, the one great decisive naval engagement, in which the enemy would be comprehensively defeated. Many had expected such an encounter to take place as soon as war was declared. As months turned to years, and still the naval Armageddon was delayed, the Grand Fleet at Scapa Flow continued to train for it, hoping it would come about any day. That the fleet's morale stayed so high, despite the frustrating wait, was largely due to the loyalty and respect they had for the C-in-C, Admiral Sir John Jellicoe.

John Jellicoe joined the *Britannia* as a cadet, aged thirteen, in 1872 and qualified as a gunnery officer at *Excellent* in 1884. He was commander of *Victoria* when she was rammed and sunk by *Camperdown* in 1893. He commanded the battleship *Centurion* as flag captain to Admiral Seymour and served in China during the Boxer Rising, when he was shot and badly wounded in one lung. He had been

ammunition ship and four other vessels. But the patrol's effect on the enemy was as much psychological as physical. *E.11* twice penetrated Constantinople harbour (like a Turkish submarine appearing in the Pool of London) to sink a troop-carrying barge and throw the population into a panic. Many were convinced that the Allied fleet was off the Bosphorus and fled into the countryside. Nasmith improved the moment by taking the first-ever photographs shot through a periscope.

Bringing *E.11* back through the Dardanelles, Nasmith had reserved two torpedoes for a battleship he hoped he would find in the Straits. The battleship was not there. A lesser man would not have pressed his luck, but Nasmith remembered a large transport he had passed further up the passage. He turned *E.11* through 180° (itself a fine feat of seamanship in the Dardanelles currents), went back and sank the transport.

Nasmith heard a grating sound forward and saw through the periscope a mine entangled by its cable in the port forward hydroplane. He could not slow down, for fear the mine would swing against *E.11*'s side. He could not surface, because earmarked by Fisher to be 'admiralissimo when Armageddon comes' and was appointed C-in-C of the Grand Fleet on the first day of the war in 1914. He was a cautious man, quite the opposite of the traditional dashing sea-dog, who believed that a naval action should be a gunnery duel fought in a strictly controlled line of battle.

By 1916, German bombardment raids on East Coast towns and the success of the U-boat campaign in 1915 increased the pressure on Jellicoe to bring the German High Seas Fleet to action. In May, he therefore planned to despatch two squadrons of light cruisers supported by a battle squadron into the Kattegat as a decoy and so to lure the enemy out to sea, where the Grand Fleet would be waiting.

Across the North Sea, Admiral Reinhard Scheer, commanding the High Seas Fleet, was facing remarkably similar problems. He knew that he was not strong enough to take on the entire Grand Fleet. Therefore he sought to create a situation where the whole High Seas Fleet could be brought to bear upon part of the Grand Fleet, thus defeating his enemy in detail.

Because of bad weather and other reasons Scheer's plan could not be put into effect until 30 May, when the fleet was to carry out a raid on Allied shipping in the Skagerrak and along the Norwegian coast. This might still tempt part of the Grand Fleet to sea. Hipper's advance Scouting Force of battlecruisers, cruisers and destroyers sailed on 30 May, with Scheer's battleships some 60 nautical miles (110km) astern.

Scheer's sailing signal was intercepted and read in the Admiralty and passed to Jellicoe. The Grand Fleet sailed late on 30 May, while Beatty's battlecruisers and the fast battleships of the 5th Battle Squadron sailed from Rosyth to join them. Unfortunately, the Admiralty overlooked the important fact that the German navy normally transferred the Flagship's call sign to a shore base when the fleet sailed. Thus, Jellicoe thought that Scheer and the major part of the High Seas Fleet were still in harbour.

The forthcoming battle of Jutland, the greatest naval engagement of the First World War, involved a huge number of warships. Jellicoe, flying his flag in *Iron Duke*, had 24 Dreadnoughts in three Battle Squadrons, three battlecruisers in the Third Battlecruiser Squadron, commanded by Rear Admiral The Hon. H.L.A. Hood, eight armoured cruisers, 12 light cruisers, 51 destroyers, and the minelayer *Abdiel*.

Beatty, flying his flag in the battle-cruiser *Lion*, had six more battlecruisers, four fast battleships of the Fifth Battle Squadron, 14 light cruisers, 27 destroyers and the seaplane carrier *Engadine*.

Scheer, flying his flag in *Friedrich der Grosse*, had 16 Dreadnoughts and six pre-Dreadnoughts,

Above: *Approaches to Jutland. Late on 30 May 1916, the Grand Fleet sailed from Scapa Flow and the Battlecruiser Fleet and Battle Squadrons from Cromarty Firth and Rosyth. The German High Seas Fleet left Wilhelmshaven early on 31 May.*

six light cruisers, and 31 torpedo-boats. Hipper, flying his flag in *Lützow*, had five battlecruisers, five light cruisers and 30 torpedo-boats.

The two great fleets approached each other on the fine summer's afternoon of 31 May 1916, with good visibility and a calm sea, Beatty's ships steaming some 60 nautical miles (110km) ahead of Jellicoe's, as Hipper's were ahead of Scheer's, and neither Jellicoe nor Scheer aware that the other was at sea.

The action began by accident. The light cruiser *Galatea*, in Beatty's advanced screen, sighted the small Danish merchant ship *N.J.Fjord* to the east and turned to port to investigate. At the same time, *N.J.Fjord* was sighted by the German light cruiser *Elbing*, the port wing ship of Hipper's force, who also turned to investigate. In a moment, the signal 'Enemy in sight' was being flashed around both fleets. *Galatea* opened fire at 2.28 p.m. to begin the battle of Jutland.

There was some initial confusion and muddled signalling on both sides. The British light cruisers were first reported as battlecruisers and then as battleships. Beatty's flag signal to steer south-east

Left: *Seen here with his cap at its usual rakish angle, Vice Admiral Sir David Beatty (1871–1936) commanded the Battlecruiser Fleet and battleships of the Fifth Battle Squadron at Jutland.*

22ⁿᵈ. B.S. ᴳᴰ ACTION. BATTLE OF JUTLAND MAY. 31ˢᵀ 191⸳

Above: *The Second Battle Squadron steams into action at Jutland. This force of eight battleships was commanded by Vice-Admiral Sir Martyn Jerram, flying his flag in HMS* King George V.

Right: *The battleship HMS* Royal Oak, *seen here at Malta between the wars, added the might of her 15-inch guns to the enormous firepower deployed at Jutland. Early in the Second World War, she was torpedoed and sunk in Scapa Flow by U.47.*

at about 4 p.m. *Lion* was hit by a shell which penetrated into her midships 'Q' turret and exploded, killing the turret crew and setting cordite charges on fire. But for the presence of mind of the badly burned and dying officer in charge of the turret, Major F.J.W. Harvey RMA, who ordered the magazine doors to be shut and the magazine flooded, an explosion would have followed which would have blown *Lion* in two. Harvey died later and was awarded a posthumous Victoria Cross.

A minute later, *Von der Tann* landed three shells from a salvo of four on *Indefatigable's* upper deck. A great cloud of black smoke gushed out of her after superstructure, and she did not follow round at the next alteration of course. After about thirty seconds, *Indefatigable* began to disintegrate, her whole frame exploding, starting from forward. Sheets of flame shot up above her funnels, followed by clouds of dense dark smoke, and debris was flung hundreds of feet into the air. When the giant column of smoke had shredded away and the debris had fallen down, *Indefatigable* had disappeared. It seems she suffered the terrible magazine explosion which *Lion* had so narrowly avoided. Of her 1,019 officers and men, there were two survivors.

With *Lion* hidden in a curtain of smoke, *Derfflinger* and *Seydlitz* concentrated on *Queen Mary*, who gave as good as she got, straddling *Derfflinger* and scoring two hits on her, But at about 4.25, *Derfflinger* straddled *Queen Mary* with a salvo of four, three of which hit. At first it seemed that *Queen Mary* was not seriously hurt. Her armour had saved her. But the next salvo also straddled her, with two more hits. There was a crimson glow amidships. The ship, said an eye witness in *Tiger*, next astern, 'seemed to open out like a puffball or one of those toadstool things when one squeezes it'. After several underwater explosions, the last remains of *Queen Mary* disappeared, taking 1,266 officers and men with

was not read in *Barham*, flagship of Rear Admiral Evan-Thomas, commanding the Fifth Battle Squadron. Beatty did not wait, and by the time the signal had been made by light, and Evan-Thomas' ships had turned and worked up to full speed, they were some ten miles (16km) astern of Beatty.

The action between Beatty's and Hipper's battlecruisers began at 3.47, when both sides opened fire at a range of 15,500 yards (14km). Once again, the German gunnery was devastatingly accurate. *Lion, Princess Royal* and *Tiger* were all hit in the first three minutes, while only *Queen Mary*, the fleet's champion gunnery ship, scored two hits on *Seydlitz*.

Although Beatty had six battlecruisers to Hipper's five, *Derfflinger* was at first left unengaged. This was rectified by *Queen Mary*, but

her. When *Queen Mary* was reported sunk to Beatty, he said to Chatfield, his flag captain, 'There seems to be something wrong with our bloody ships today.'

By now Evan-Thomas' Fifth Battle Squadron had caught up and were in action, scoring hits on *Von der Tann* and *Moltke*, although the effect of their hits was greatly reduced because their armour-piercing shells broke up on impact instead of piercing the armour and exploding inside it. Nevertheless, Hipper was now in an exposed position, which his destroyers temporarily relieved with a torpedo attack, causing Evan-Thomas' ships to turn away.

A CONFUSED PICTURE

Meanwhile, far to the south, Commodore Goodenough in the light cruiser *Southampton* had sighted and reported the leading battleships of Scheer's High Seas Fleet. Soon, Beatty himself sighted them and reversed course to the north, passing Evan-Thomas' ships still steaming south. Once again, the manoeuvre was clumsily handled and by the time Evan-Thomas' rearmost ship had turned to the north, his Squadron was three miles (5km) astern of Beatty and on his port, disengaged, and most disadvantaged quarter. Further, they were now in range of the German battleships. *Barham* and *Malaya* were both hit.

As evening drew on, the sky clouded over, and visibility deteriorated markedly in mist, and smoke from funnels and gunfire. The situation was no clearer on *Iron Duke*'s flag bridge, where Jellicoe suffered from a lack of information all day. There were long yawning gaps between signals, some of which were actually wrong. Jellicoe's best informant was Goodenough and even he was occasionally in error. For much of the

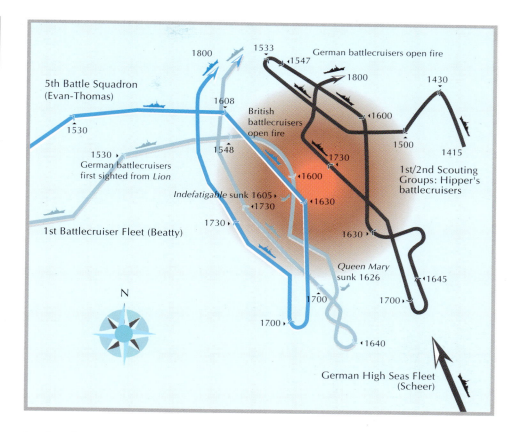

battle of Jutland, Jellicoe did not know the true strength or even the approximate position of his enemy.

The battlecruisers were in action again at about 5.40. This time the honours went to Beatty who had the better view of his enemy. *Derfflinger* was hit again and appeared down by the bow. *Seydlitz* was also hit again and set on fire. Hipper was forced to turn away, thus allowing Jellicoe's ships to stand on unreported, so that Scheer too was kept in ignorance of his principal enemy.

By now, the two battle fleets were only about 30 miles (50km) apart and closing at a relative speed of some 28 knots, a rate of one mile about every two minutes, and still Jellicoe was starved of information. After sparse and often conflicting signals from Goodenough, from the battleship

Above: First blood at Jutland. The light cruiser HMS Galatea *fired the first shot at 2.28 p.m. By 3.47 the rival battlecruisers were in action, and within 45 minutes* Indefatigable *and* Queen Mary *had been sunk.*

Below: A watercolour by Ian Marshall shows the battleship HMS Royal Oak in the thick of the action at Jutland, where she was commanded by Captain MacLachlan.

Above: 'Windy Corner' – a moment of the drama at Jutland is captured by the artist William Bishop. Jellicoe's battleships have just deployed into line ahead and are firing on Scheer's heavy units.

Marlborough away on the fleet's starboard wing, from the cruiser *Black Prince* and from *Barham*, the plotting table picture at last began to clarify.

By 6 p.m. *Lion* was in sight in the haze, *Iron Duke* signalled 'Where is enemy's battle fleet?' and repeated the signal ten minutes later. The reply, at 6.14 p.m., was 'Have sighted enemy's battle fleet bearing SSW.'

THE MOMENT OF DECISION

Jellicoe had only seconds to make up his mind. The visibility was only about five miles (8km), which meant the enemy were much closer to him than he had thought and they were on his starboard bow, when he had expected to meet them dead ahead. His 24 battleships were steaming in six columns, four ships in each column. His intention was to deploy all 24 in line ahead, stretching across in front of the enemy's van. Such a manoeuvre, known technically as crossing the enemy's 'T', would allow all his ships to fire their full broadsides, while the enemy ships would only be able to fire their forward guns.

Jellicoe had to decide whether to lead the deployment with his starboard wing, or the port. By deploying to starboard, he might be laying his ships open to torpedo attack by enemy destroyers who were sure to be ahead of the High Seas Fleet. There might already be an overlap, so that as his starboard ships advanced the enemy might already have passed ahead of them, and so crossed their T.

Jellicoe chose to deploy to port, on a south-easterly course, and made the signal to that effect at 6.15 p.m., only one minute after Beatty's signal that he had sighted the enemy battle fleet. Jellicoe

'As we turned to bring the enemy ships on our starboard beam at about 10,000 yards, the squadron opened up with all its main armament guns... We sent out a continuous ripple of flashes all along the enemy line, but, in the poor visibility, I couldn't tell where our shots were falling although I found the noise of our guns most heartening and welcome. It helped to drown the rumbling noise made by the shells passing over us and the crack of those falling short. But the enormous columns of water thrown up were only too visible and sometime uncomfortably close. We must have been constantly straddled but not once were we or Inflexible hit...'

MIDSHIPMAN FRANK LAYARD WHO SERVED ABOARD HMS *INDOMITABLE* AT THE BATTLE OF JUTLAND

himself had not sighted a single enemy ship, yet almost entirely intuitively, and in less than a minute, he had arrived at the solution which innumerable postwar exercises on the tactical floor, and extensive post-war research carried out over many years, demonstrated was the best possible.

The deployment was completed at about 6.40 p.m., when Jellicoe could see three of the enemy battle fleet – at no time during the whole battle was he able to see more than four at once – and knew that his deployment had been successful. It was as if he had drawn a figure which, by its very geometry, was imposing its pattern on the battle.

Iron Duke's shooting was fast and accurate. Of nine hits achieved by the British battleships at this stage of the battle, seven were by the fleet flagship. Meanwhile, ahead of the battle fleet, the battlecruisers had suffered another tragedy. When Hood saw Hipper's battlecruisers approaching from the south, he turned his squadron on to a parallel course and opened fire at 6.23, scoring hits on *Lützow* and *Derfflinger*. The enemy concentrated their fire upon Hood's flagship *Invincible*. At 6.33, a shell hit the fatal Q turret, pierced the roof and exploded inside. *Invincible* blew up and of her 1,032 officers and men, there were six survivors.

SCHEER'S 'BATTLE TURN'

Scheer had been no better informed that day than Jellicoe had been, and the first real indication he had of the whereabouts of his enemy's battle fleet was the actual sight of it, stretched out along the horizon, firing at his ships along its whole line. The wind shifted and carried funnel and gun smoke and fumes forward in front of Scheer so that his view, never good, became much worse. His ships were being hammered by an enemy he could barely see. He could not go on leading his ships against what seemed to be a solid wall of fire. He could not order them to turn in succession because each ship as it reached the turning point would be the focus of a storm of fire. So, at 6.33, Scheer ordered his famous *Gefechts-kehrtwendung*, or 'battle turn'. His ships all turned together through 180 degrees, and steamed back the way they had come, except that

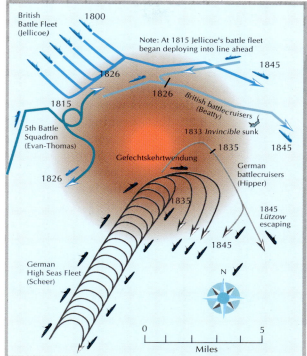

Left: *From around 6.25 p.m., Jellicoe's battleships deployed into line ahead. He had 'crossed the T' of the High Seas Fleet, briefly threatening it with destruction. Scheer skilfully extricated himself, ordering his ships to lay down a smoke screen while making a 180 degree turn – the Gefechtskehrtwendung or 'battle turn' – reversing their course. Between 7.10 and 7.40 he again encountered Jellicoe's battle line, and this time was saved by the 'death ride' of Hipper's battlecruisers.*

their order was reversed. It was well and neatly executed, and was completed by 6.45.

Several ships saw this turn away, but none reported it to Jellicoe. Ten minutes later, Scheer made another advance towards the Grand Fleet and was even more roughly received than before. Jellicoe's battleships scored 30 hits, Evan-Thomas' five, most of them on Hipper's

THE MEN OF JUTLAND

Rupert Brooke ('Now God be thanked...'), a volunteer who would die off Gallipoli, was not the only naval officer to welcome the First World War. 'In the Grand Fleet everyone was pleased it had come at last', wrote Midshipman Johnstone; 'I have had a certain amount of shooting this season which will put me in good form when the bigger game come forth to fight.' 'Johnstone', the future King George VI, was, as Sub-Lieutenant Prince Albert, to fight at Jutland as second in command of the fore turret in HMS *Collingwood*.

Perhaps the lower deck harboured less elevated sentiments, despite Fisher's reforms. Regular seamen were now better educated and better fed. Fisher, a fanatical inspector of galleys, had bakeries instituted aboard larger warships and, from 1904, decreed the free issue to ratings of knives, forks, plates and bowls. Leave was more generous, and better quarters ashore were provided, with new barracks at Portsmouth, Chatham and Devonport replacing the old accommodation hulks. The holystoned decks, gleaming brightwork and pristine paint of peace had given way to 'crabfat gray'. An

The Morning News
Saturday, June 3rd
GREAT NAVAL BATTLE
HUGE BRITISH AND GERMAN LOSSES

Above: *Jutland was front page news on 3 June 1916 – but many in Britain looked on the battle as a defeat.*

Left: *Jutland VC – Boy Cornwell (aged 16) kept his station on HMS* Chester *when mortally wounded.*

Ordinary Seaman's pay was 1s 8d (8p) per day; a Chief Petty Officer got about 4s (20p). Oilskins and seaboots had been issued on loan since 1907, but 'woolly pullies', thick socks and balaclavas were not issued free until 1916. But free food, accommodation and a non-contributory pension put the sailor on a par with the working man ashore.

Some traditions remained unchanged. Men still slept in hammocks, and many wore beards. (Seamen wore a 'full set' because Queen Victoria had said that with moustaches alone they looked too much like soldiers. The famous HMS *Hero* advertisement for Player's cigarettes, introduced in 1898, was modelled by AB T.H. Wood (d.1951), who received £2.2s.0d (£2.10p) and 'a bit of baccy for myself and the boys aboard'.) Time still taken by 'bull' might better have been employed in training, especially practice in 'Director Firing'. A Midshipman in the *Indomitable* at Jutland recalled that in the eight months before the battle the ship had only 33 days at sea, and 'we only fired our main armament four times and our secondary armament once'.

Left: *A posthumous VC was won by Commander Loftus Jones of the destroyer HMS* Shark. *Here we see a lifebelt from the sunken* Shark *and Commander Jones's watch, binoculars and medals.*

battlecruisers. Scheer now launched Hipper's battlecruisers on a suicidal run towards the enemy. They got within 700 yards (640m) of the nearest British ships, then altered to the south and then west and rejoined the main fleet. The 'death ride' mysteriously fizzled out.

Beatty's battlecruisers were in action again at about 8.20 that evening. In a short engagement, with some good shooting in poor light, *Derfflinger* and *Seydlitz* were hit once again. The action ceased at about 8.40 p.m. This was, in fact, the last time capital ships were engaged in the war.

When darkness fell at about 9 p.m., Jellicoe disposed his fleet into night cruising formation. He had no intention of fighting by night. He believed himself to be between Scheer and his base in Germany, and he confidently expected another Glorious First of June in the morning.

The confusions and missed chances continued. There were two paths through the German minefields. Jellicoe believed Scheer was heading for the southern entrance. The Admiralty decoded a signal revealing that Scheer was actually heading for the northern entrance, but did not pass this information to Jellicoe.

Throughout the night, Scheer's ships constantly nudged to the eastward, trying to find a way through or round the line of Grand Fleet ships blocking the way. Each time they sighted the Grand Fleet, they recoiled to the west, before edging over to the east again. The German capital ships were sighted, but not reported. The Grand Fleet's captains would have died for Jellicoe, but they would not send him a signal. Eventually Scheer's ships, a knot or two slower than Jellicoe's, slipped astern of their foes, passed across the rear of the Grand Fleet, and thus escaped. When dawn broke, the sea was empty of German ships.

German losses at Jutland were one pre-Dreadnought battleship, one battlecruiser, four cruisers, five destroyers and 2,551 men, against British losses of three battlecruisers, three armoured cruisers, eight destroyers and 6,097 men, The Germans at once broadcast a triumphant statement, claiming a great victory in the Skaggerak. The Admiralty's response, much slower and more equivocal, left many thinking the Royal Navy had suffered a disastrous defeat in the North Sea. The battered *Lion* was booed into harbour.

Even when more details emerged, the feeling persisted in the country that a great chance had been missed, and that it was Jellicoe who had missed it. Churchill said Jellicoe was the only man on either side who could lose the war in an afternoon. Many people wanted to know why he had not won it in an afternoon. Nevertheless, despite the controversy which continues to this day, Jutland was a great strategic victory for the

Above: The Star decided that the major sea battle of the First World War must share the front page with a cricket match! This may perhaps reflect contemporary disappointment at the failure to achieve a decisive material, as opposed to strategic, victory.

Royal Navy. As an American journalist wrote, 'The German Fleet has assaulted its jailer but is still in jail'. The High Seas Fleet never challenged the Grand Fleet again.

The High Seas Fleet did make one more abortive sortie in August 1916, when only pure chance saved it from as serious a battering as at Jutland. Thereafter, Scheer turned to the U-boats as the best way of winning the war. In October 1916 he ordered the U-boat offensive to be intensified once more.

THE U-BOAT OFFENSIVE

After the successful U-boat campaign of 1915, the Admiralty introduced new anti-submarine measures. Depth charges were developed, and hydrophones to detect sounds from a submerged submarine, By April 1916, over 1,000 merchant ships had been defensively armed with guns. Q-ships, harmless-looking vessels which were

HAMMERING THE U-BOATS

Britain was slow to counter the U-boat menace. In 1914, it is related, the armament of picket boats patrolling Scapa Flow included a sack and a hammer: any periscope sighted was to be enveloped in the bag and its lens smashed with the hammer! Cat-and-mouse tactics saw apparently unescorted and unarmed merchantmen trailed by a submerged submarine. One of this random hunt's rare successes occurred in June 1915, when *U.40* surfaced to attack the trawler *Taranaki* – to be sunk by the attendant *C.24* and the *Taranaki*'s own 1-pounder.

By late 1914, Q-ships were at sea, and in July 1915 the Q-ship *Prince Charles* sank *U.36* off the Hebrides. The most successful Q-ship commander was Commander (later Rear-Admiral) Gordon Campbell, RN, who claimed three of the Q-ships' 11 victims. On 17 February 1917, his Q.5 (*Farnborough*) was torpedoed off the Irish coast by *U.83*. A 'panic party' abandoned ship to lure the U-boat to the surface, where Campbell's gunners at their well-concealed weapons sank her – as their own ship sank beneath them. Campbell's Victoria Cross citation praised his 'consummate coolness'. Two other VCs awarded for Q-ship actions (in one of which Campbell again commanded) were unusual in that the recipients were chosen by ballot among the crews.

Such decoy tactics, however, meant that U-boats increasingly attacked with torpedoes while actually heavily armed with concealed guns, continued to be used, but with decreasing results as the enemy became aware of their secret. Patrols of the trade routes used by merchant ships and searches of areas where U-boats were suspected were increased, The majority of the destroyers, the most efficient U-boat hunters, were still required to screen the Grand Fleet, but a new Kil class of anti-submarine patrol gunboats was built.

All these measures proved ineffective. In one week of September 1916, three U-boats operated in the Channel between Beachy Head and the Eddystone Light, an area patrolled by 49 destroyers, 48 torpedo boats, seven Q-ships, and 468 armed auxiliaries – some 572 anti-submarine vessels, not counting aircraft. Shipping in the Channel was held up or diverted. Asdic, which was to play such a major part in the anti-submarine war from 1939-45, was still in the future, and the main means of submarine detection was still the human eyeball. Thus the anti-submarine vessels combed the Channel looking for signs of U-boats. But the U-boats sank 30 ships, while they themselves went unscathed.

Every defence against the U-boat peril was tried except the best of all. The Navy resolutely resisted the introduction of convoy. Even the use of the word 'convoy' in signals was taboo. Thus shipping losses continued to soar throughout 1916, 500,000 tons of British shipping being sunk in the first six months. In October, 176,000 tons were sunk, 30,000 tons more than the worst month, August, of the 1915 campaign.

Jellicoe was appointed First Sea Lord in November 1916, and put in train a vigorous anti-submarine campaign, of routeing ships independently, forming special patrol groups, increasing air patrols, with larger and longer-ranged aircraft, improving designs of hydrophones and depth-charges and introducing a system of 'safe areas'. Rear Admiral A.L. Duff came to the Admiralty from the Grand Fleet as the Director of the newly-formed Anti-Submarine Division.

It was all to no avail. On 31 January 1917, the German government announced that unrestricted submarine warfare would begin the next day. The

Above: *The battleship HMS Cornwallis was torpedoed and sunk southeast of Malta by U.32 on 9 January 1917. All but 15 of her crew were taken off safely while she remained afloat.*

Left and right: *The pre-Dreadnought HMS Britannia, sunk off Cape Trafalgar by UB.50 on 9 November 1918, and survivors from her crew photographed on HMS Coreopsis.*

Below right: *A hero of the anti-submarine campaign appears on the front page of the Daily Mirror.*

submerged, where they could neither be seen – even by RNAS airships, which included 139 purpose-built SS (Submarine Scout) 'blimps' – nor, with the primitive sound detection gear then under development, easily heard. The belated introduction of a wide-ranging convoy system from April 1917 blighted the U-boats' rich harvest. A convoy might consist of some 30 merchantmen deployed at intervals of 500 yards (460m) and in five or six columns some 800 yards (730m) apart, escorted by a

light cruiser and eight or more destroyers equipped with depth charges (cylinders containing up to 300 pounds of Amatol or TNT, detonated by a fuze activated by water pressure). In 1918, the commander of *U.68* described the peril of a lone U-boat attacking such 'a huge concourse of ships', lamented the 'poor percentage' of success, and advocated *rudeltaktik* ('wolf pack' attacks). His name was Karl Dönitz…

Opposite page: *The medals of Harold Auten include the Victoria Cross, won on 30 July 1918 when the Q-ship HMS Stockforce intercepted and sank a U-boat.*

Right: *The diorama shows a Q-ship, armed with a 4-inch gun, Hotchkiss QF, Lewis guns and a mortar, engaging a U-boat.*

U-boats sank 368,521 tons of shipping in January 1917, the last month of restricted warfare. They could be expected to double this figure at least, to nearly 750,000 tons a month. At that rate, Great Britain would lose up to 40 per cent of her remaining shipping in about six months.

In the first week of unrestricted warfare, 35 ships were lost in the Western Approaches and the Channel alone. The total figure climbed to 500,500 tons in February, to 560,000 tons in March, and to a horrifying 870,000 tons in April. One in four of the ships going to sea was not returning. For a few weeks the U-boats really were winning the war. Still, Jellicoe and what Lloyd George called the 'High Admirals' determinedly set their faces against convoy.

At last, encouraged by Lloyd George, the 'High Admirals' began reluctantly in April 1917 to introduce convoys, to Holland, France and Scandinavia, tentatively across the Atlantic in May, a full Atlantic system in September, and a world-wide system by the end of the year. Shipping losses plummeted.

NAVAL AVIATION

The Royal Navy had achieved its own air arm almost in spite of itself, and pioneered the first aircraft carriers in a series of inspired experimental lurches. *Empress*, *Engadine* and *Riviera* were converted cross-Channel ferries. *Ark Royal* was a collier, bought off the stocks at Blyth in Northumberland and completed as a seaplane

carrier. *Manxman* was a converted packet, *Nairana* an Australian mail steamer, *Vindex* an Isle of Man packet, *Pegasus* the Great Eastern steamer *Stockholm*, *Campania* a converted Cunard liner. Pre-war, the kite balloon ship *Manica* carried manure along the Manchester Ship Canal.

In March 1917, the large cruiser *Furious* had her forward 18-inch gun removed and replaced by a flying off deck, on which Squadron Commander Edwin Dunning made his historic first deck landing, off Scapa Flow, on 2 August 1917. *Argus*, the world's first true carrier, with a flush flight deck 550 feet (168m) long from stem to stern, was converted from the ex-Italian liner *Conte Rosso*; from *Argus*'s deck in October 1918, in the Firth of Forth, Commander Richard Bell Davies VC DSO, flying a Sopwith 1½ Strutter, led the first squadron to be embarked on a carrier. But by then, the Royal Naval Air Service had ceased to exist.

When the case for a 'unified air service' was debated in 1917, the Admiralty, either through ignorance, indifference, or lingering doubts about the real value of air power at sea, did not fight the Navy's corner with any force or conviction. When the Air Force Bill became law on 1 April 1918, the Royal Naval Air Service was abolished at a stroke, and all its resources – more than 100 air stations, some 55,000 officers and men, and over 2,500 aircraft – were transferred to the newly-created Royal Air Force. Squadron Commanders RN became Majors RAF, Flight Commanders became Captains, Petty Officers became Sergeants. 'Air' officers who stayed in the Navy, with dual RN-RAF ranks, suffered perennially from an occupational unease, constantly aware that their long-term career prospects were in jeopardy because they were aircrew. Having, almost by default, let control of their air arm go to the RAF, the Navy then spent the best part of the next 20 years trying to wrest it back.

Above: WRNS storekeepers at Lowestoft in 1918. 'Wrens' served in many shore posts during the First World War, notably as cooks, stewards, writers, telephonists and telegraphists, drivers and sailmakers.

Below right: The old light cruisers HMS Intrepid, *in the foreground, and HMS* Iphigenia *after their sinking as blockships in the canal at Zeebrugge on 23 April 1918. (Inset) The third blockship, HMS* Thetis.

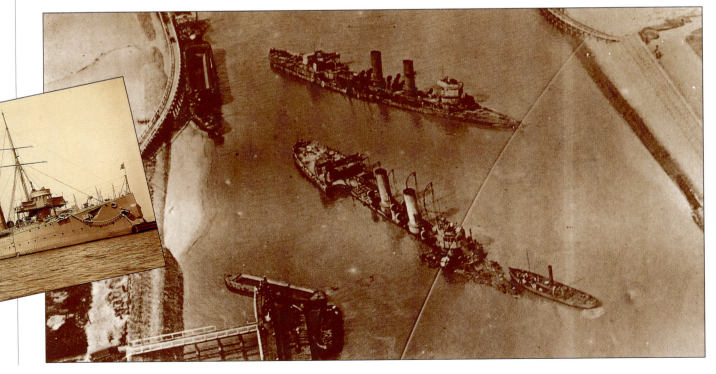

ASSAULT ON ZEEBRUGGE

As late as 1918, Bruges in Flanders was still the base for over 30 destroyers and torpedo boats, and about 30 U-boats. They reached the North Sea either through the canal exit at Zeebrugge, or, if of shallower draught, at Ostend. Plans to block Zeebrugge and Ostend had been discussed since 1914. The Flanders ports had been major objectives of Haig's great offensive in 1917. When that failed, Vice Admiral Roger Keyes, who had commanded the Dover Patrol since 1 January 1918, was authorized to make a direct attack from the sea.

The Zeebrugge canal exit was protected by the curve of a 1½ mile (2.4km) long Mole, on which the Germans had mounted gun batteries. The plan for the great raid of St George's Day, 23 April 1918, was to sink three blockships, the old light cruisers *Thetis*, *Intrepid* and *Iphigenia*, in the canal entrance, covered by a smoke screen and a diversionary infantry attack on the Mole Batteries. A section of the Mole near the shore would be blown up to prevent reinforcements arriving.

The assault force, 4th Battalion Royal Marines, and 200 bluejackets trained in close combat, were carried in the old cruiser *Vindictive*, specially prepared for the operation, supported by two ex-Mersey ferry boats, *Iris II and Daffodil*, each carrying troops. Although the canal was not completely blocked and ships could still pass, the assault on the Mole was carried out with great gallantry. That night the Royal Navy and the Royal Marines between them won eight Victoria Crosses, more than in any other single operation in their history. *Vindictive*'s people won five VCs inside one hour, putting her in the same league as Peel's *Shannon* and the *River Clyde* at Gallipoli.

There remained just one more sortie, the last: Operation ZZ. Very early on 21 November 1918, the whole Grand Fleet, of 370 ships and 90,000 men, with the 6th US Battle Fleet, a French cruiser and two French destroyers, put to sea for a rendezvous some 40 miles (64km) east of May Island in the Firth of Forth. In open water the huge line of ships split into two columns, six miles (10km) apart, each column with more than 30 battleships, battlecruisers and cruisers, with a destroyer stationed abreast each squadron flagship.

Shortly after 9 a.m. the first of 11 German battleships, five battlecruisers, eight light cruisers and 50 destroyers was sighted. Admiral von Reuter, flying his flag in *Friedrich der Grosse*, led the German ships between the two lines of British ships which had their guns loaded, although still trained fore and aft, and their ship's companies at action stations in case of last minute resistance. But there was none, and as the German ships passed by, the British turned through 180° by squadrons to escort them.

The surrender was an unexpectedly quiet, almost funereal occasion, although the fleet cheered Beatty as he passed in his flagship *Queen Elizabeth*. At 11 a.m. Beatty signalled: 'The German flag is to be hauled down at sunset today, Thursday, and will not be hoisted again without permission.' In the afternoon, lower decks were cleared and hands piped to muster aft on the quarterdeck. At 3.57 p.m., when the Royal Marine buglers sounded 'Sunset', all hands turned aft and saluted. Meanwhile the German ensigns were hauled down for the last time. Beatty sent a general signal congratulating all ships on the victory. King George V also sent a message of congratulation to his fleet.

And that, after four years, was that.

1917 The Royal Naval Division on the Western Front. Resumption of unrestricted U-boat campaign (1 February). United States enters the war (April). Admiralty reluctantly introduces convoys to combat U-boat attacks (April). First deck-landing by aircraft on Navy ship, HMS *Furious* (2 August). WRNS (Women's Royal Naval Service) formed.

1918 Dissolution of RNAS and creation of RAF (April). Blocking operation at Zeebrugge (April) and Ostend (May). Armistice Day (11 November). Surrender of German High Seas Fleet (21 November)

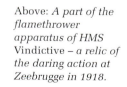

Above: *A part of the flamethrower apparatus of HMS* Vindictive – *a relic of the daring action at Zeebrugge in 1918.*

Left: *The High Seas Fleet steams into captivity. This watercolour by P.F.J. Spence shows the surrender on 21 November 1918. The German warships were interned at Scapa Flow where, in 1919, they were scuttled.*

CHAPTER EIGHT

FROM SCAPA
To
CASABLANCA

Right: *The 'Geddes Axe' threatened the Navy – but the First Battle Squadron still made an impressive sight in the English Channel in 1922.*

Previous pages: *'HMS Renown in Portsmouth Harbour in 1922', by marine artist W.L. Wyllie. Completed in 1916, the battlecruiser served throughout the Second World War.*

Below: *The fate of many of Germany's capital ships of the First World War era – scuttled at Scapa Flow in 1919.*

Below right: *A low-flying biplane is seen with the Queen Elizabeth class battleship HMS Malaya.*

It was supposed to have been the war to end all wars. For a time people believed it. The scuttling, on 21 June 1919, of 52 of the German ships interned at Scapa Flow, with another 22 beached or sunk in shallow water, was like the symbolic disappearance of the only visible enemy. Although the Navy was still in action against the Bolsheviks in the Baltic and the Black Sea, and with the Marines were similarly engaged in north Russia, there was a general feeling of war weariness and an acceptance by politicians and public that the armed forces, and especially the Navy, must be drastically reduced. In August 1919, the Navy was ordered to draft its estimates 'on the assumption that the British Empire would not be engaged in any great war during the next ten years', beginning the self-perpetuating Ten Year Rule, which lasted until 1932.

The Navy ended the Great War with 480,000 men, 58 capital ships, 103 cruisers, 12 aircraft carriers, and 456 destroyers. Savage cuts in defence expenditure were inevitable and the immediate postwar years were therefore a gloomy time for the Navy, of constant Treasury-driven cutbacks and cancellations of ships. There was resentment about the tardiness of demobilisation, with unrest and even mutiny in the Baltic ships. Ironically, under the so-called 'Geddes Axe' of 1922, some officers retired voluntarily but many others were 'selected' to retire.

There were Naval Conferences or Treaties, mainly preoccupied with disarmament, in 1921–22, 1927, 1930 and 1935. Between 1920 and 1923 there were five First Lords, seven Parliamentary Secretaries, six Civil Lords and 18 Sea Lords. The one fixture was Beatty, First Sea Lord from 1919 until 1927, but his constant presence, as a 'big ship' man, meant that the Navy continued to place its faith in battleships. Jutland influenced all postwar naval exercises, being fought and refought, on the tactical floor, over the dinner table and, most bitterly of all, in print.

Another grim bitter paper battle was waged, over the control of naval air, which lasted until the Inskip Report of 1937 returned control of shipborne aircraft to the Navy. The Air Ministry believed in the 'unity of the air': all who flew, over land or sea, should belong to a common service. The Admiralty believed that all who served in the Navy should have a 'sea-sense' and should be properly trained and led in the 'naval way', whether they served on, under, or over the sea. Both arguments had merit, but they were mutually irreconcilable.

In 1920, to the immense disapproval of the Air Ministry, the Admiralty formed a Naval Air Section, with just one officer. From this grew the future Naval Air Division. The following year, again to Air Ministry disapproval, the Admiralty formed a naval observer branch, contending that observers were naval officers first, foremost, and all the time; special air skills were certainly needed, but they could be taught by the Navy, as were gunnery and other specialisations.

The Balfour Committee of 1923 rejected the Admiralty's claim to have their own naval air service. This was upheld by the 1924 Trenchard-Keyes agreement, which did recognise the ship-borne element of the RAF as the Fleet Air Arm. All pilot training, and the control of ship-board flying, were still the responsibility of the RAF. Naval pilots still had dual Navy and RAF ranks.

Eagle, converted to an aircraft carrier from the Chilean battleship *Almirante Cochrane*, commissioned in 1923 and was followed a year later by *Hermes*, the first carrier to be designed as such from the waterline up. The battlecruiser *Furious* was reconstructed and recommissioned as a

Left: *Four Fairey Flycatchers in formation over Malta in 1930. This single-seat biplane, with a maximum speed of 133mph (214km/h) and a range of c.315 miles (507km), was the Navy's standard fighter in the 1920s and early 1930s.*

Below: *Aircraft of the Fleet Air Arm overfly the battleship HMS Iron Duke in the 1930s. The Admiralty did not gain full administrative and operational control of the Fleet Air Arm until 1937, but, even then, the RAF retained control of Coastal Command.*

carrier in 1925. Her sister ships *Courageous* and *Glorious* were also converted to aircraft carriers, commissioning in 1928 and 1930.

The RAF, themselves under constant Treasury pressure, were unlikely to give naval aircraft a high priority. Continuing uncertainty over design and tactics was compounded by the Admiralty's own indecision about what sort of aircraft the Navy required. Thus the Navy entered the Second World War without a high performance single seat fighter. The front line aircraft in 1939 was the Blackburn Skua fighter-divebomber – a contradiction in terms. The 1920s and 1930s were the biplane era. The standard naval fighter for many years was the Fairey Flycatcher, followed by the Hawker Nimrod and Osprey. The standard torpedo-bomber-reconnaissance aircraft was the Fairey IIIF, followed by the Seal and the Swordfish.

The Navy ended the Great War with 122 submarines, including the steam-driven K class, whose design was a fundamental misconception of the nature of submarines. They were intended to operate in close formation with surface ships of the fleet. As a result, they were large, over 2,000 tons submerged, and over 300 feet (91m) long, and fast (24 knots), but accident-prone, several being lost in ramming incidents, as well as individual misadventures.

Other submarine eccentricities between the wars were the M class submarine monitors, fitted with 12-inch guns, of whom *M.1* and *M.2*, (the latter converted into a submersible seaplane carrier), were both lost in accidents, and the giant submarine cruiser *X.1* armed with four 5.2-inch

Left: *The east side of Gibraltar looms in the background as a Fairey IIIF floatplane overflies a Queen Elizabeth class battleship in the 1930s. The IIIF was the Navy's standard torpedo-bomber/ reconnaissance aircraft from c.1928 to 1936.*

ceiling reduced by two or three ranks at a stroke. They could never aspire to be full admirals. There was only one engineering vice admiral (E), the engineer-in-chief. Letters of complaint from aggrieved officers were forwarded, but nothing came of them.

After a financial crisis in 1931, the National Government under Ramsay Macdonald announced drastic cuts in public sector pay. In the Navy, one shilling a day was to be cut from everyone's pay. A shilling meant little to an admiral, but to an able seaman on four shillings a day it was a cut of 25 per cent. Many sailors, who had wives and families, and rent and hire purchase commitments to pay, faced ruin.

An incompetent and insensitive Admiralty Board, who had failed utterly to present the Navy's case to the government, also bungled the announcement of the cuts. In the Atlantic Fleet, for instance, which had just arrived at Invergordon, the fleet anchorage on the east coast of Scotland, the first the sailors heard was through rumours and the newspapers, followed by bald statements on ships' noticeboards.

At that time, the so-called 'normal channels' for airing lower-deck grievances were believed to be useless. So, as the sailors had decided amongst themselves in the shore canteen the previous Sunday, early on the morning of Tuesday, 15 September, when the fleet was due to put to sea for exercises, crowds of defiant sailors mustered on the fo'c'sles of their ships and began to cheer. Echoing Spithead in 1797, the cheering swept down the line of warships, as the signal for the mutiny to begin.

It was a very polite affair, more of a sit-in than a mutiny. There was no violence. The sailors bore their officers no ill-will. Their grievance was with the Admiralty and the government. In some ships the mutiny lasted until the Friday, but it eventually ended in partial victory for the lower deck. The shilling a day was scrapped and sailors' pay cut by only ten per cent. But the mutiny sent a seismic political and financial shock around the world and forced Britain off the gold standard.

Invergordon also sent a shock through the Navy.

Above: HM Submarine M.2 in February 1930, following the removal of her 12-inch gun. It was replaced by a hangar and catapult for a small seaplane. The album was compiled by G.T. Crouch during his naval service in 1920–1931.

Below: A painting of HMS Royal Sovereign, *known to her crew as the* Tiddly Quid, *by J.H. Fry. She was lent to the Soviet Navy between 1944 and 1949, being named the* Arkhangelsk.

Below right: The battlecruiser HMS Repulse *passes through the Panama Canal c.1924.*

guns, in twin turrets. Orthodox submarine design continued with the O, P, R, and the first of the successful S, T, and U classes, with which the Navy entered the Second World War.

THE 'GREAT BETRAYAL'

The main intention of the Fisher-Selborne Scheme was that officers of all specialisations should be equally eligible to reach the highest ranks in the Navy. But in 1925 an Order in Council, in which the phrase 'executive officer' appeared for the first time, defined the branches, such as engineering, and stipulated that engineers were to ship the purple stripe between the gold again, as in the 19th century.

This 'Great Betrayal', as it was called, was bitterly resented. Many officers who had chosen engineering in good faith had their promotion

Above: *Italy's invasion of Abyssinia in 1935 caused the British Mediterranean Fleet to gather at Alexandria in readiness.*

Above: *HMS Wishart's rescue of US seamen from a burning gunboat in 1934 was rewarded by this Presidential gift.*

Below: *HMS Hunter after striking a mine during the Spanish Civil War, 1937.*

Although some captains continued to 'punish' their sailors for Invergordon, there was general acknowledgement that the great gulf which existed between the wardroom and the lower deck needed to be bridged, and some machinery introduced for airing and addressing lower deck grievances.

A DEEPING CRISIS

The aftermath of Invergordon was also the time when it was realised that the Great War was not the end, and the shape of a new war appeared on the horizon. In the autumn of 1935, the Mediterranean Fleet assembled in Alexandria in an atmosphere of deepening crisis after the Italian invasion of Abyssinia. A crisis occurred each successive autumn. A year later, the Royal Navy was involved in the Spanish Civil War, acting as peacekeeper, stationing a guardship in every Spanish port, helping refugees of both sides, and remaining impartial even after incidents such as the mining of the destroyer *Hunter* off the southern port of Almeria in May 1937.

On 4 October 1937, the destroyer *Basilisk* reported that a torpedo had been fired at her, and made a depth charge attack on an asdic echo firmly classified as a submarine. Contact was lost, but regained an hour later, and a second attack made. There was no oil, debris or other evidence. The official verdict was that if the contact was a submarine it should have been destroyed, and if there was no submarine it showed the unreliability of asdics. Therefore, 'the *Basilisk* incident did not take place'. But the incident had serious implications for the future. Very good results were being obtained with asdic at the anti-submarine school at Portland, and asdic was believed to be an almost fool-proof defence against submarines. This showed that there was a deal of difference between exercise and war.

A full scale naval rearmament programme began in 1937, with a massive expansion of the 'A' Branch for the Fleet Air Arm. Rating pilots were recruited for the first time. The first four of the new Illustrious class of 23, 000 ton carriers, with armoured flight decks, were laid down. Eight cruisers of the 9,100 ton, 6-inch gun Southampton class, eight of the 8,000 ton, 6-inch gun Fiji class, and ten of the 5,450 ton, 5.25-inch Dido class were laid down or building. Also laid down or building were some 50 destroyers of the Tribal, Javelin and Lightning classes.

An Operational Intelligence Centre, for collating and presenting intelligence and other information from all over the world, was set up in the Admiralty by Admiral Sir William James in 1937. Radar made its first appearance in the fleet: Type

Right: *A page from a photograph album showing Battle Squadrons in the 1930s – (top right; bottom left and right) in rough Atlantic weather; (centre left) illuminated for the Jubilee Celebrations in 1935; (top left; centre right) in the Mediterranean.*

1922 Washington Naval Treaty. Supply branch instituted by Order in Council.

1924 Shipborne element of RAF recognised as Fleet Air Arm as part of Trenchard-Keyes agreement on naval aviation.

1925 The 'Great Betrayal' of the Fisher-Selborne scheme.

1930 London Naval Conference.

1931 Proposed cut in Navy pay precipitates mutiny at Invergordon.

79 sets, capable of detecting aircraft at ranges of 50 miles (80km) at heights of 10,000 feet (3,050m), were installed in the battleship *Rodney* in August 1938, and in the cruiser *Sheffield* in November. In April 1939, the Women's Royal Naval Service was reformed. It had first formed in 1917 to replace men required for active service. By the time it was disbanded in October 1919, its numbers had grown to almost 7,000, carrying out not only domestic and clerical duties but acting as boats' crews and wireless telegraphists. In the war to come the Wrens performed an even wider range of duties.

THE OUTBREAK OF WAR

The Royal Navy, including Dominion Navies, entered the war on 3 September 1939 with 12 battleships, three battlecruisers, seven aircraft carriers, 64 cruisers, 184 destroyers, and 38 sloops. The German Navy had two battlecruisers, three pocket battleships, six cruisers, and 17 destroyers. Both sides were almost equal in submarines, with 58 British to 56 German.

Convoy was instituted from the outbreak of the Second World War, although there was a critical shortage of escorts. Between the wars, the mortal peril the country had faced from the U-boats in 1917 was largely overlooked. Two 35,000 ton battleships, *Nelson* and *Rodney*, were built, but the construction of convoy escorts was neglected. The numerous 1,000 ton, 27 knot Hunt class destroyers (a total of 86 were built) were approved in 1938, but the first did not commission until mid-1940. Meanwhile, the early convoy escorts included trawlers, tugs and submarines.

There was some misunderstanding in high places of the principle of convoy. Mr Churchill, who had resumed as First Lord on the outbreak of war, yearned for 'a large effective destroyer force sweeping the Western Approaches'. This was not possible. Instead, he used the Navy's few and

ELECTRONIC WARFARE: RADAR AND 'ULTRA'

In his novel *Put Out More Flags* (1942), Evelyn Waugh caricatured a 'know-all' politician who asserts in the 1930s that Britain cannot be bombed, for she has a secret weapon that will 'RDF them [enemy aircraft] out of the skies'. But Waugh's booby was then not alone in believing that RDF (Radio Direction Finding) was a potent 'death ray'. In fact, it was a basic high-frequency radar (RAdio Detection And Ranging) system developed in 1935 after long research led by Sir Robert Watson-Watt (1892–1973). Installed along the coastline in 'Chain Home' stations, it played a vital part in the Battle of Britain, naval control of the Channel and, in 1944, the D-Day invasion.

Some British warships carried Type 79 air-warning radar from the outset of the Second World War. The British origination in 1940 (and subsequent American development) of the cavity magnetron – an electronic vacuum valve for generating microwaves – resulted in more sophisticated and compact equipment. By 1942–43, Allied escort vessels in the Battle of the Atlantic were fitted with microwave (centimetric) radars. The British Type 271 sea search radar could detect a surfaced U-boat to a range of about 15 miles (24km); the Type 281 air search radar ranged to about 135 miles (215km). Also important in the anti-submarine campaign was HF/DF (High Frequency Direction Finder; called 'Huff-Duff'), which located U-boats by intercepting even their briefest radio transmissions.

Above: *Electronic equipment supplemented human surveillance in the Second World War – note the 'Huff-Duff' aerial below the lookout's post on the corvette HMS Borage which assisted in the hunt for hostile submarines.*

A further vital component in the Battle of Atlantic, as in other campaigns, was electronically-derived intelligence. All German arms had since the late 1920s communicated in supposedly unbreakable codes generated by the 'Enigma' ciphering machine. By 1940, British cryptologists at Bletchley Park, Buckinghamshire, were able to break a high proportion of Enigma-coded messages. This feat owed much to a team headed by the mathematician Alan Turing (1912–54), who developed the world's first electronic computers. The intelligence gained from the decryption of up to 1,000 messages a day was code-named 'Ultra', and was very strictly controlled (the fact that it had existed at all was not revealed until the 1970s). American cryptologists likewise broke the Japanese Navy's 'Purple' code; intelligence thus gained was code-named 'Magic'.

Above: *A surfaced U-boat spotted by a Swordfish from HMS Biter in March 1943.*

Left: *HMS Rodney was fitted with Type 79 air-warning radar in 1938.*

precious aircraft carriers as a kind of anti-submarine cavalry, to lunge about the ocean on would-be punitive expeditions to hunt and sink U-boats wherever they had been reported.

This policy was quite useless, and ultimately disastrous. *Ark Royal* was narrowly missed on 14 September 1939 by *U.39* whilst hunting U-boats off the Hebrides. Worse followed on the evening of the 17th, when *Courageous* was torpedoed by *U.29* and sunk with the loss of 519 lives whilst hunting for U-boats in the Western Approaches off Ireland. Carriers were not used on these sorties again (although other ships were).

A fleet needs a secure base. The Home Fleet had a base at Scapa Flow, but it was not secure. The flaws in the defences were known before the war but plans to remedy them had not been carried out when, on the night of 13 October, *U.47*, commanded by Kapt Lt Günther Prien, passed on the surface through Kirk Sound at the eastern end of the Flow and, early on the 14th, penetrated into the main fleet anchorage.

Prien steered north into Scapa Bay where he sighted what he thought were two battleships (actually one battleship, *Royal Oak*, and the seaplane tender *Pegasus*), and fired three torpedoes. The fourth forward tube misfired. One torpedo hit *Royal Oak* right forward. Prien then fired a torpedo from the stern tube, and finally a salvo of three from the reloaded forward tubes, all of which hit. *Royal Oak* sank, with the loss of 24 officers and 809 men. Prien retired the way he had come and returned to Kiel, after one of the most daring and spectacular *coups* in naval history.

A NEW TYPE OF MINE

From the first days of the war, it had become clear that the enemy was using a non-contact type of mine immune to normal sweeping methods. In November 1939, 27 merchant ships and the destroyers *Blanche* and *Gipsy* were sunk in home waters, the cruiser *Belfast*'s back was broken, the Port of London was effectively closed and coastwise shipping traffic brought virtually to a standstill. Mr Churchill ordered that an example of this new weapon must be recovered 'at all costs'.

On the night of 22 November 1939, a German aircraft dropped a parachute from which was suspended an object which 'looked like a sailor's kitbag' off Shoeburyness in Essex. Lt Cdrs John Ouvry and Roger Lewis, and CPO Baldwin and AB Vearncombe, all from HMS *Vernon*, the torpedo and mining school at Portsmouth, were summoned to the scene. They crossed the mudflats in darkness and pouring rain in the early hours of the 23rd to find by the light of torches what Ouvry called 'a dark, menacing looking object lying partially embedded in the sand'.

Left: *HMS* Nelson, *seen here, and her sister-ship* Rodney, *each displacing 35,000 tons and mounting nine 16-inch guns, were the first battleships designed in accordance with the Washington Naval Treaty of 1922.*

By the light of Aldis lamps held by soldiers, they found 'two unpleasant looking fittings near the fore end'. Rubbings were taken of the mine's fittings so that special non-ferrous tools could be made, the mine was photographed by flashlight and then securely lashed down.

Ouvry and Lewis returned at midday when the mine was next uncovered by the tide. By then a

Below: *The battleship HMS* Royal Oak, *seen here at the head of a battle line, was an early loss in the Second World War. On 14 October 1939 she was sunk in Scapa Bay by torpedoes from the German U-boat* U.47.

Above: *Relics of the light cruisers HMS* Achilles *and* Ajax, *which helped sink the* Graf Spee.

Below: *HMS* Achilles *in New Zealand soon after the Battle of the River Plate.*

the mine safe. It was taken to *Vernon*, where it was dismantled and its secret revealed: an electro-magnetic device which detonated the mine when the magnetic influence of a ship's steel hull passed overhead. A solution was rapidly devised, and 'degaussing coils' fitted round all metal ships' hulls to neutralize their magnetism were fitted with the utmost speed. Ouvry and Lewis were awarded DSOs, Baldwin and Vearncombe DSMs – the war's first naval awards.

The two 12,000 ton German 'pocket battleships' *Admiral Graf Spee* and *Deutschland* had sailed from Wilhelmshaven, on 21 and 24 August 1939 respectively. Designed to circumvent the 10,000-ton capital ship building limit imposed on Germany by the Treaty of Versailles, they were armed with six 11-inch and eight 5.9-inch guns and their diesel engines gave them a speed of 28 knots.

Deutschland sank only two ships before returning to Germany on 15 November. *Admiral Graf Spee*, however, commanded by Kapitan Hans Langsdorff, in an extended cruise sank nine ships of 50,000 tons as far apart as Recife in Brazil and Madagascar, refuelling periodically from the tanker *Altmark*.

THE HUNT FOR *GRAF SPEE*

Eight British and French groups were formed to search for *Graf Spee*. Force G, the 8,000 ton, six 8-inch gun heavy cruiser *Exeter* and the two 7,000 ton, eight 6-inch gun light cruisers *Ajax* and *Achilles* (largely manned by New Zealanders), was commanded by Cdre Henry Harwood, flying his broad pennant in *Ajax*, who calculated that the enemy would head for the busy shipping routes off the River Plate estuary.

Harwood was rewarded early on the morning of 13 December when smoke was sighted on the horizon to the west, and the fighting top of a pocket battleship was soon identified at a range of ten miles (16km). The enemy had already seen Harwood's ships and was closing at full speed, believing them to be a convoy. Harwood divided his squadron, *Exeter* steering west, the two light cruisers continuing to the north-east, so as to force the enemy to split his main armament fire between two targets or to concentrate upon one, leaving the other untouched.

The enemy concentrated upon *Exeter* and hit her several times, putting two of her three turrets out of action, but *Exeter* stayed in the fight, on emergency steering, with helm orders being passed from the after conning position by a line of sailors. *Ajax* and *Achilles* were also hit, *Ajax* being badly damaged, so that Harwood disengaged and retired behind a smoke screen.

Graf Spee had also been hit and suffered casualties, but her damage was only minor.

second mine had been found. It was decided that Ouvry and Baldwin would tackle the first, while Lewis took notes of what happened from a distance. He and Vearncombe would then deal with the second.

After some 40 minutes of tense concentrated work, using the greatest care but once or twice having to exert considerable force, Ouvry made

Langsdorff would almost certainly have won a notable victory had he pressed on. Instead, he turned back to the west and headed for the neutral port of Montevideo, in Uruguay, followed at a distance by Harwood's ships.

The Uruguayan government gave Langsdorff 72 hours to repair damage. Meanwhile, intelligence reports conjured up a massive but imaginary British fleet, including the carrier *Ark Royal* and the battle cruiser *Renown*, waiting outside the River Plate estuary. In fact, only *Ajax, Achilles* and (from 14 December) the cruiser *Cumberland* were still there, *Exeter* having finally been forced to go to the Falklands, with casualties of 61 dead and 23 wounded.

On the evening of 17 December, *Graf Spee* went down river with the German SS *Tacoma*. The members of *Graf Spee*'s crew who were still on board transferred to *Tacoma* and then *Graf Spee* blew herself up. Langsdorff shot himself three days later.

This first naval action of the war, 'In this sombre dark winter,' said Mr Churchill, 'came like a flash of light and colour on the scene, carrying with it an encouragement to all who are fighting – to ourselves and to our allies'.

Sixty-one Merchant Navy officers and men who had been prisoners on board *Graf Spee* were landed at Montevideo. Another 236 British Merchant Navy officers and men, and 66 Indian sailors, remained in *Altmark* which acted as *Graf Spee*'s prison ship. In February 1940 *Altmark* reached Norwegian waters, where her crew felt themselves protected by Norwegian neutrality. British intelligence learned of her presence there, and the cruiser *Arethusa* and five destroyers were dispatched, in Mr Churchill's words, to 'Find her, edge her out to sea, board her and liberate her prisoners'.

Ignoring a Norwegian gunboat, the destroyer *Cossack*, commanded by Captain Philip Vian, ran alongside *Altmark* in Joesing Fjord on the night of 16 February. Led by Lt Bradwell Turner, a boarding party from *Cossack* leaped on to *Altmark*'s deck and, after some brief fighting, the hatches were thrown open. Turner asked 'Any British down there?' There was a tremendous yell of 'Yes! We're all British!' 'Come on up then,' said Turner, in words which rang round the world, 'The Navy's here!'

1940: DENMARK AND NORWAY

The German invasion of Denmark and Norway on 9 April 1940 came as a complete surprise to the country and the Navy, although there had been signs at sea, on land and in signal traffic which, with the benefit of hindsight, should have indicated that something was afoot. But, at the time, they were discounted or disbelieved.

Above, left and below: *The end of the 'pocket battleship' Admiral Graf Spee. At Hitler's order, she was scuttled off Montevideo on 17 December 1939, in order to avoid capture or defeat by the blockading British force waiting outside the River Plate estuary.*

For *Weserübung* (Operation Weser), the naval side of the invasion, the German ships were divided into 11 Groups, Groups I to VI against Norway and the much weaker Groups VII to XI against Denmark. Group I included ten destroyers who landed 2,000 troops at the northern port of Narvik.

By chance, there was already a British operation in progress to mine the Norwegian Leads so as to force German ships, carrying iron ore south from Narvik, out of Norwegian territorial waters. Four minelaying destroyers, escorted by *Hardy* (Captain B. Warburton-Lee), *Hotspur, Havock* and *Hunter* of the 2nd Destroyer Flotilla, had sailed to lay a minefield in Vest Fjord, the approach to Narvik.

The minelaying was cancelled but Warburton-Lee, who had been joined by a fifth destroyer, *Hostile*, was ordered on the 9th to go up to Narvik to make certain no enemy troops landed there. Warburton-Lee learned from a pilot station on the way up the fjord that the enemy had already landed in some strength, but nevertheless he

1935 Mediterranean Fleet assembles in response to Italy's invasion of Abyssinia. Anglo-German Naval Treaty.

1936 Spanish Civil War begins – Navy involved in peacekeeping role.

1937 Fleet Air Arm comes under naval control. Major rearmament programme ordered. Operational Intelligence Centre established in the Admiralty

Above: *HMS* Hardy, *commanded by Captain Warburton-Lee, led five more British destroyers against a large German force at Narvik on 10 April 1940. Nine German ships were sunk for the loss of the* Hardy *and* Hunter.

Below: *Destroyers escort the battleship HMS* Warspite *(seen also in the photograph below right) into Vest Fjord, Narvik, 13 April 1940. They sank the remaining destroyers of the German force that were engaged by Warburton-Lee's flotilla on 10 April.*

intended 'attacking at dawn high water'. His ships arrived off Narvik early on the 10th and in three attacks sank six German merchantmen and a destroyer, and damaged six other destroyers, one so badly it sank next day, with torpedoes and gunfire. Whilst retreating down the fjord they also sank the German ammunition ship *Rauenfels*. However, they were cut off by three remaining German destroyers. *Hunter* was sunk. *Hardy* was disabled, and drifted ashore. Warburton-Lee, mortally wounded, was posthumously awarded the earliest-gazetted Victoria Cross of the war.

At dawn that day, 10 April, 16 Blackburn Skuas of 800 and 803 naval air squadrons, flying to the limits of their endurance from Hatston in the Orkneys, dive-bombed the German cruiser *Königsberg*, lying damaged alongside in Bergen. They scored three direct hits with 500lb bombs and several near-misses. *Königsberg* caught fire, and after a large internal explosion broke in half and sank. This was the first time a major warship had been sunk by air attack.

Warburton-Lee was avenged on 13 April when *Warspite* and nine destroyers went up Vest Fjord and sank or drove ashore the eight remaining German destroyers. *Warspite*'s Swordfish also bombed and sank *U. 64*, the first U-boat sunk by an aircraft in the war.

For the first fortnight of the Norwegian campaign neither the fleet nor the Army ashore

had any fighter cover, and both were subjected to frequent and intense enemy air attacks. It is probable that nobody at home, in the War Office or the Admiralty, really appreciated the full ferocity of the German air assault. During the fighting and in the evacuations that followed, the troops ashore and the ships at sea were constantly harassed from the air. The ships expended prodigious amounts of ammunition, but guns alone were not enough. German aircraft sank the cruiser *Curlew*, the destroyers *Gurkha* and *Afridi*, the French destroyer *Bison*, the Polish destroyer *Grom*, and the sloop *Bittern*. They also hit *Rodney*, damaged *Furious*, the cruiser *Curacoa*, the destroyer *Eclipse* and a dozen more warships, store-ships and transports. The cruiser *Suffolk* struggled back to Scapa with her quarterdeck awash, after seven hours of bombing attacks.

As the campaign went on, *Furious*, *Glorious* and *Ark Royal* tried to make up for the lack of shore-based aircraft, flying defensive sorties over the Army ashore and the ships at sea, covering the evacuations and, whenever possible, striking at enemy shipping. In May, *Furious* and *Glorious* ferried RAF fighters to Norway.

Experience in Norway showed the Navy that against determined air opposition it was not possible to maintain the Army on an overseas expedition, or even to operate ships for any length of time off an enemy coast, without proper sustained air cover.

THE LOSS OF HMS *GLORIOUS*

There was one last, cruel lesson from Norway: an aircraft carrier not operating her aircraft is one of the most helpless things afloat. On 8 June *Glorious*, escorted by the destroyers *Acasta* and *Ardent*, was detached from the fleet to make her way home independently. Earlier that day she had successfully flown on RAF Hurricanes and Gladiators from shore. None of their pilots had ever made a deck landing but they had chosen to

take the risk rather than abandon their aircraft in Norway.

At 4 p.m. that afternoon, *Glorious*'s funnel smoke was sighted by the German battlecruisers *Scharnhorst* and *Gneisenau* who were steaming north hoping to find Allied shipping leaving Narvik. *Glorious* was not flying reconnaissance or fighter patrols and so was caught utterly unaware.

Scharnhorst opened fire at 28,000 yards (26km) and, as usual, the initial German gunnery was excellent. *Glorious* was soon hit on the bridge and the flight deck. More hits brought her to a standstill. At about 5.20 p.m. *Glorious* turned over and sank.

Acasta and *Ardent* tried with great gallantry to save her, both advancing through smoke screens to attack with torpedoes. One torpedo from *Acasta* actually hit *Scharnhorst*. But both destroyers were overwhelmed and sunk by the enemy's gunfire. Only 39 men from *Glorious*, two from *Ardent* and one from *Acasta*, survived. Over 1,500 men were lost.

While these events unfolded in the north, Allied submarines were suffering a severe defeat in the Kattegat, Skaggerak and off southern Norway. The long daylight hours of the Scandinavian summer, the sudden freshwater layers and fierce tidal rips, and the constant air and surface surveillance, all made submarine patrols very hazardous. The enemy made good use of aircraft to cooperate with alert surface forces, directing them to the datum of a submarine sighting, and attacking with airborne depth-charges (a weapon Coastal Command still lacked).

These tactics, coupled with intelligent use of radio direction finders and well-placed minefields, took a steady toll. *Thistle*, *Tarpon* and *Sterlet* were lost in April 1940, *Seal* and the Polish *Orzel* in May, the Dutch *0.13* in June. But the worst months were July and August, when *Shark*, *Salmon*, *Thames*, *Narwhal* and *Spearfish* were all lost. It was the first demonstration, which was to be amply confirmed in the Atlantic, that aircraft were the natural predators of submarines, and it forced the Allies to withdraw submarines from those coastal waters.

'NINE DAYS WONDER'

Meanwhile, another drama unfolded in France: Operation 'Dynamo', an astonishing event, described by the poet laureate John Masefield as the 'Nine Days Wonder', which took place between 26 May and 3 June 1940.

At that time a defeated British Expeditionary Force was falling back on the French coastal town of Dunkirk, where the soldiers were sure that, in accordance with a centuries-old tradition, the Navy would be waiting to take them off.

Above: *A Fairey IIIF lands on HMS* Furious *in the early 1930s. Originally designed as an 18-inch-gunned battlecruiser, the* Furious *was rebuilt as a flush-decked aircraft carrier in 1921–25. In May 1940 she and HMS* Glorious *ferried RAF fighters to Norway.*

▶ **1938** Munich crisis. First radar installed in HMS *Rodney*.

1939 WRNS re-formed. HMS *Thetis* founders in Liverpool Bay. War declared (3 September). Convoy instituted. HMS *Courageous* sunk (17 September). HMS *Royal Oak* sunk in Scapa Flow by U-boat (13 October). First German magnetic mine recovered (November). Battle of River Plate (13 December).

Above: *Allied troops rescued from the Dunkirk beaches arrive at Dover. In Operation 'Dynamo', May–June 1940, some 1,300 vessels of all types evacuated 338,000 troops.*

Below: *The 41,000-ton battlecruiser HMS Hood. (Inset left) A sketch of a midship section made by Richard Beckwith in 1933. (Inset right) The* Hood *and* Valiant *under fire with Force H in the Mediterranean, July 1940.*

The Navy was not so confident. Larger ships, such as destroyers, could go alongside the Mole at Dunkirk but, since the harbour was small, many troops had to be evacuated from the beaches and there was a shortage of small boats to take them out to ships waiting off shore.

A swift inventory was made by Admiral Ramsay, Vice Admiral Dover, and his staff of ships, boats and craft in the south of England, and the call went out for volunteers to help to bring the soldiers home. A motley armada, manned by people from all walks of life, assembled almost overnight. The exact number of ships which eventually took part is not known, but it certainly approached 1,300, ranging from the cruiser *Calcutta* and destroyers to ships' lifeboats.

More than 600 were the 'Little Ships' – private yachts, motor cruisers, paddle steamers, spritsail

barges, tugs, fishing boats, a dredger, harbour defence vessels, Hayling Island ferries, Pickford's fleet of small coasters, drifters, lighters, Dutch *schuyts*, RNLI lifeboats, the London firefloat *Massey Shaw*, the Isle of Wight ferry *Gracie Fields*, *Nelson*'s captain's barge, and a 'private navy' of a pinnace and a torpedo recovery vessel from HMS *Vernon*.

The Admiralty estimated that 45,000 troops at the most would be evacuated. But with the aid of the Little Ships, the weather, which stayed miraculously calm for day after day, and Hitler, who inexplicably held back the Panzers, the final total, despite the efforts of the Luftwaffe, was 338,000, including many French troops. The majority were evacuated by destroyers (96,000) and the personnel vessels (88,000).

However, the 'miracle' of Dunkirk was not without cost. Six destroyers were lost and 23 damaged. Of the Little Ships, over a hundred were lost.

In the month of June 1940, the balance of naval power in the Mediterranean swung dramatically against the Allies. On 8 June, Italy entered the war on the side of the Axis. On the 25th, France signed an armistice with Germany. Mr Churchill was determined to show the world, and especially the United States, that Great Britain was going to continue the war alone.

The most pressing problem was the French fleet, the fourth largest in the world, with many of its major units in the Mediterranean, at Mers-el-Kebir in Algeria, and at Alexandria. French warships already in British ports were seized on 3 July. On the same day, Admiral Sir James Somerville, commanding Force H, a powerful squadron including *Hood* and *Ark Royal* formed on 28 June to fill the vacuum in the western Mediterranean caused by the French surrender, was ordered to Mers-el-Kebir to present the French admiral Gensoul with four choices: put to

sea and join the Royal Navy; sail with reduced crews to a British port where the ships would be impounded and the crews repatriated; sail with reduced crews to a French port in the West Indies; or scuttle his ships within six hours.

After some parleying, negotiations broke down. Somerville was forced, very reluctantly, to order his ships to open fire. The battleship *Bretagne* was sunk, the battlecruiser *Dunkerque* and several other ships were damaged, and 1,297 French sailors were killed. Fortunately, despite the shock the news of this caused at Alexandria, Admiral Sir Andrew Cunningham, the C-in-C Mediterranean Fleet, was able to persuade the French admiral Godfroy to immobilise his ships in the eastern Mediterranean without bloodshed.

ACTION OFF CALABRIA

The first capital ship action of the war in the Mediterranean took place off Calabria, the 'toe' of Italy, on 9 July 1940. Cunningham, known to the whole Navy as 'ABC', flying his flag in *Warspite*, with *Malaya* and *Royal Sovereign*, the carrier *Eagle*, five cruisers and 16 destroyers, had put to sea to cover two convoys from Malta to Alexandria. The Italian Admiral Campioni, flying his flag in the battleship *Giulio Cesare*, with the battleship *Conte di Cavour*, 14 cruisers and numerous destroyers, was also at sea, covering a convoy to north Africa.

On paper, ABC had the superior force, with three battleships to the Italians' two, but *Royal Sovereign* was too slow to keep up, and *Malaya* never got within range. After an unsuccessful strike by *Eagle*'s torpedo bombers, *Warspite* opened fire and obtained a direct hit on *Giulio Cesare* at the prodigious range of 26,000 yards (24km), after which Campioni broke off the action and withdrew under cover of smoke. There was some skirmishing between the destroyers, and ABC's ships came under attack by shore-based bombers. ABC pursued to the west until the evening when his ships were only 25 miles (40km) from the Calabrian coast. The enemy escaped, and ABC retired to the south, still under bombing attack.

It was a disappointingly indecisive action, but it showed the Italians' unwillingness to stand and fight, and it was the start of the clear moral and tactical ascendancy ABC was eventually to establish over his enemy.

After the arrival in the Mediterranean in late August 1940 of *Illustrious*, with her armoured flight deck and 30 aircraft, including the new two-seater fighter Fairey Fulmar, ABC enjoyed the rare luxury of having a balanced fleet in which capital ships and aircraft carriers complemented each other.

The fleet ranged freely from Rhodes in the east to Sfax in the west, its aircraft bombing airfields and harbours, laying mines in coastal waters, and strafing roads, railways and shipping in a superbly confident and successful demonstration of naval air power of which the crowning achievement was the strike at the Italian battle fleet at Taranto.

Plans for an air strike at Taranto had been discussed in the Fleet Air Arm since the mid-1930s. ABC longed to deliver a decisive blow against the Italian battleships. But they were reluctant to leave the shelter of Taranto. So, they must be hit there.

The date was fixed for Trafalgar Day, 21 October, but a hangar fire in *Illustrious* caused a postponement. *Eagle* was to have taken part, but defects in her petrol system caused by Italian bombing near-misses became worse, and she had to drop out. Five of her Swordfish, with eight pilots and eight observers, transferred to *Illustrious* for the strike.

On 10 November, RAF Glenn Maryland aircraft from Malta reported that the main Italian fleet, including at least five battleships, lay in Taranto. On the evening of the next day, Remembrance Day, *Illustrious* was detached from the fleet and escorted by four cruisers and four destroyers steamed to the flying-off point, some 170 miles (275km) south-east of Taranto.

AIR STRIKE AT TARANTO

The first strike of 12 Swordfish, led by Lt Cdr K.Williamson RN, took departure for Taranto at 8.57 p.m. Six were armed with torpedoes, four with bombs, and two had flares and bombs. Taranto was protected by balloons, nets, guard-ships and batteries of anti-aircraft guns. The torpedo-bombers were briefed to attack the battleships in the outer harbour, the Mar Grande, while the bombers attacked the cruisers and

Above: *Second World War service medals and a Lanchester sub-machine gun displayed on Jack Masters' Royal Fleet Reserve cap and jumper.*

Left: *'ABC' – Admiral of the Fleet Andrew B. Cunningham, 1st Viscount Cunningham of Hyndhope (1883–1963).*

▶ **1940** Liberation of prisoners held on *Altmark* (16 February). German invasion of Norway (9 April). *Königsberg* sunk in Bergen harbour by air attack (10 April). Battles at Narvik. Operation 'Dynamo': evacuation of BEF from Dunkirk (26 May-3 June). HMS *Glorious*, HMS *Acasta* and HMS *Ardent* sunk by *Scharnhorst* and *Gneisenau* (8 June). Italy enters the war against the Allies (8 June). Attack on French ships at Mers-el-Kebir (3 July). Cunningham's action with Italian fleet off Calabria (9 July). Calamitous shipping losses to U-boat 'wolf packs' (August to December). United States Navy transfers 50 destroyers to Royal Navy in exchange for leases of bases in West Indies (September). Abortive attack on Dakar, West Africa. Fleet Air Arm attack on Italian battleships at Taranto (11 November). Somerville's action with Italian fleet of Cape Spartivento (27 November).

A second strike of nine Swordfish, led by Lt Cdr J.W. Hale RN, began flying off at 9.23 p.m. Five had torpedoes, two had bombs, and two flares and bombs. One was left on deck after a mishap but took off later, and another had to return prematurely. But the rest could see the flames and flak of Taranto from 60 miles (100km) away and the second strike plunged through a renewed storm of fire to drop torpedoes and bomb ships and oil installations in the inner harbour.

The results went far beyond anybody's wildest expectations. The battleship *Littorio* sustained three torpedo hits which put her out of action for nearly a year. The older battleship *Caio Diulio* suffered one hit, but had to be beached to stop her foundering. A third battleship *Conte di Cavour* also had one torpedo hit and sank in shallow water; she was eventually raised, but took no further part in the war. The heavy cruiser *Trento*, destroyers and oil storage tanks in the inner harbour were damaged. Two Swordfish were lost, the crew of one being taken prisoner.

When *Illustrious* rejoined, ABC made her the marvellously laconic signal 'Manoeuvre well executed'. Taranto tilted the balance of naval power in the Mediterranean in the Allies' favour, and gave naval and air staffs all over the world food for thought. It also made the Italian Navy even more cautious. On 27 November, off Cape Spartivento, Sardinia, a powerful Italian force including two battleships retreated from a favourable tactical position on the threat of torpedo attack by *Ark Royal*'s aircraft.

Above: *A page from a photograph album that includes (top) aerial pictures of the attack on the Italian battle fleet at Taranto. Two strikes by Swordfish torpedo-bombers on the night of 11–12 November 1940 inflicted severe damage.*

destroyers in the inner harbour, the Mar Piccolo, Soon after 11 p.m., the first flares drifted down the eastern side of the harbour and the Swordfish attacked by their cold pale light, diving from 8,000 to 4,000 (2,440 to 1,220m) and finally to 30 feet (9m) above the water. The defences had had some two hours warning and were fully alert. A hail of anti-aircraft fire streamed past the cockpits as the bombers jinked and swerved at masthead height into the harbour.

TASKS AND TOOLS OF AIRCRAFT CARRIERS

In his account of the Battle of Leyte Gulf (October 1944) the US Navy's historian Admiral Morison pictures the shades of Nelson's ships of the line dipping their flags as the guns of Admiral Oldendorf's battleships fall silent, having destroyed a Japanese battleship task force. For this was the last line-of-battle action. From at least the time of the Battle of the Coral Sea (May 1942), a major naval engagement fought solely by aircraft, the aircraft carrier was the true capital ship.

By 1939, it was accepted that the principal tasks of the aircraft carrier were: (1) reconnaissance, (2) location of an enemy's battle line and strikes against

Above: *HMS Illustrious, whose Swordfish aircraft flew in the raid to attack Taranto, was the first carrier with an armoured box hangar.*

Left: *An aircraft operating from HMS Hermes in 1930. Launched in 1919, the 10,800-ton Hermes was the first aircraft carrier to be designed and built for the purpose.*

Right: *Blackburn Baffins from HMS Furious in 1936. Monoplanes like the Fulmar, Barracuda and Seafire largely replaced the FAA's biplanes in the Second World War, although the Swordfish biplane served until 1945.*

enemy carriers to achieve air superiority in the battle zone, (3) air strikes on shore targets, and (4) escorting convoys. (Many authorities then doubted that carrier aircraft alone could destroy capital ships – but the Fleet Air Arm at Taranto and the Imperial Japanese Naval Air Force at Pearl Harbor were soon to prove they could.) The Royal Navy, emphasizing tasks (1) and (4), had heavily armoured carriers with limited air wings; the US and Japanese navies, emphasizing tasks (2) and (3), opted for less protection and more aircraft. Thus, HMS *Ark Royal*, of some 22,000 tons, operated fewer than 60 aircraft, while the somewhat smaller, older USS *Yorktown* carried 80-plus. ('Habakkuk', a British project for huge 'carriers' made of ice bonded with wood fibre, proved abortive.)

The Americans and Japanese also gave more thought than the British to the development of specialized naval aircraft. In spite of its success against the *Tirpitz*, the Barracuda

At home, the Battle in France was over, but the Battle of Britain was about to begin. The Admiralty offered the Air Ministry the loan of naval pilots under training. Two courses, of about 40 pilots, volunteered and underwent operational training in Hurricanes and Spitfires. Fifty-six naval pilots took part in the Battle of Britain between August and October 1940, of whom 23 flew with RAF squadrons, and the remainder with 804 and 808 naval air squadrons. Nine Fleet Air Arm pilots were killed in the battle.

As a result of the Battle of Britain, Operation Sealion, the planned German invasion was postponed and finally cancelled, but it still left the French Atlantic ports in enemy hands. Using them as bases, the German U-boats had less distance to go to their patrol areas and could therefore spend longer on patrol. Furthermore, of the destroyers still operational after the Dunkirk evacuation, most were concentrated in the narrow seas, to guard against the threat of invasion, thus leaving the Atlantic convoys with even fewer escorts than before.

The results of this policy soon showed in the figures of sinkings. Losses (from all causes) soared: in June 1940, 140 ships of 585,496 tons; in July, 105 ships of 386,913 tons; in August, 92 ships of 397,229 tons; and in September, 100 ships of 448,621 tons. Of these, 211 ships, of well over a million tons, were sunk by U-boats, although there were only a few at sea during this period. The 289,000 tons of shipping lost to U-boats in June 1940 were sunk by only six operational boats.

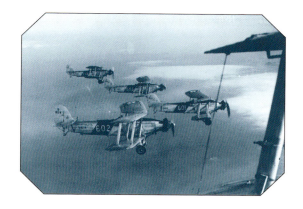

torpedo bomber made an unsatisfactory replacement for the obsolescent Swordfish; the Fairey Fulmar fighter was rugged but slow; the Sea Hurricane and Seafire (Sea Spitfire) good but in short supply. From 1943, British carriers often operated American aircraft: notably the Grumman Hellcat (Martlet) fighter and Chance Vought Corsair fighter-bomber. Thus, when the British Pacific Fleet's carriers raided Japanese oil installations in January 1945, Seafires from HMS *Indefatigable* flew Combat Air Patrol (CAP), giving air cover; Corsairs from the *Illustrious* and *Victorious* strafed enemy airfields before the strikes; and bomb-carrying Grumman Avengers and rocket-firing Fireflies made the raids.

U-BOAT ONSLAUGHT

On 15 August 1940, Hitler proclaimed a total blockade of all waters around Great Britain, and warned neutrals to keep their ships out of the war zone. The last week in August was one of the worst of the war for shipping losses – over 100,000 tons were sunk. This was what the U-boat arm called '*die glückliche Zeit*', 'the happy time', which lasted from about August 1940 until the end of the year.

It was the era of the 'aces': Gunther Prien, Otto Kretschmer, Joachim Schepke, Vaddi Schulz, Engelbert Endrass, Heinrich Bleichrodt, and Jochen Matz, all aggressive and experienced submarine captains. At first, they used orthodox submerged attacks, but informed by the German B-Dienst decrypting service and encouraged by Dönitz, head of the U-boat arm, to try methods he had pioneered himself in the First World War, the 'aces' soon began to attack convoys on the surface, at night, using their U-boats as submersible torpedo boats. Trimmed down, their small conning towers were difficult to spot, and their high surface speed made them very difficult to catch.

In September 1940, a U-boat 'wolf pack' ambushed the slow 53-ship homeward bound convoy SC2 and sank five ships of 20,943 tons. Much worse befell SC7, of about 30 ships (the number varied, with stragglers and late-joiners) in October, which lost 21 ships of 79,592 tons, with

Below: *Depth-charged by a British aircraft and captured on 27 August 1941, U.570 enters a British port. She was subsequently recommissioned as HMS* Graph

Bottom: *The battle against the U-boats: a depth charge is detonated at 50 feet.*

Above: *Seaman Cyril Stephens.*

Above: *Leading Sick Berth Attendant Howard Goldsmith.*

Top right: *With the* Warspite *and* Barham, *HMS* Valiant *took part in the battle of Cape Matapan, 28-29 March 1941. Their 15-inch guns sank the Italian heavy cruisers* Zara *and* Fiume. *She is seen here in the 1920s before she underwent a major refit.*

Below: *Italian naval prisoners at Tobruk, Libya, captured by the British on 21 January 1941. This port, vital for the logistics of the North African campaign changed hands twice more in 1941–42.*

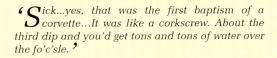

'*S*ick...yes, that was the first baptism of a corvette...It was like a corkscrew. About the third dip and you'd get tons and tons of water over the fo'c'sle.'

CYRIL STEPHENS, A SEAMAN ABOARD THE FLOWER CLASS CORVETTE HMS *ORCHIS* DURING THE BATTLE OF THE ATLANTIC

'*...I keep going on about this terrible sea, but it was; it was nearly always rough, and of course corvettes, they're like corks, they just bob about and roll around like drunken pigs.*'

HOWARD GOLDSMITH, LEADING SICK BERTH ATTENDANT ABOARD FLOWER CLASS CORVETTE HMS *SNOWFLAKE*

two more damaged. October 1940 was the happiest of the 'happy time', when U-boats sank 63 ships, of over 352,000 tons. In the week leading up to Trafalgar Day, they sank 27 British merchant ships of 137,000 tons.

This amounted to a major naval defeat, while the U-boats themselves went almost unscathed. *Gladiolus* sank *U.26* when it was attacking a convoy southwest of Ireland on 1 July 1940, but there were no more successes by convoy escorts until the end of October.

Gladiolus was the first of the numerous Flower class corvettes – there were eventually 144 of them, literally from *Abelia* to *Zinnia*. The workhorses of the battle of the Atlantic, they were 925 tons, had a complement of 85 officers and men, and were armed with a 4-inch gun, a 2pdr. pom-pom and depth charges. They had a primitive asdic set but, at first, no radar.

In September 1940, an agreement was signed with the United States to exchange 50 1918–1919 vintage four-funnelled destroyers for the leases of bases in the West Indies. Known as the Town class (all having names of towns common to both the United States and the United Kingdom), they were somewhat accident-prone, suffering from machinery defects and frequent collisions, and they took some months to enter operational service. But they filled a desperate need for convoy escorts. They also had great political significance, as tokens of possible future American participation in the war.

One convoy defence became a legend. On the afternoon of 5 November 1940, the 37-ship convoy HX84 was in mid-Atlantic, homeward bound from Halifax, when a ship was sighted to the north-east. The stranger was the 10,000 ton pocket battleship *Admiral Scheer*, who closed the convoy and opened fire with her 11-inch guns.

The convoy's sole escort was the armed merchant cruiser *Jervis Bay* (Captain E.S.F. Fegen). While the convoy scattered behind her under cover of smoke, *Jervis Bay* steered directly for the raider and opened fire with her 6-inch guns, which dated from Victoria's reign. *Jervis Bay* was soon hit repeatedly, her hull was holed in several places, and major fires started below. Three hours after sighting the raider, *Jervis Bay* sank, taking Fegen and most of her ship's company with her.

When her survivors told their experiences, the story of *Jervis Bay*'s last fight thrilled the free world. It became one of the most famous naval sagas of all time, celebrated in song, verse and on film. Fegen was awarded a posthumous Victoria Cross for his gallantry.

In the new year of 1941, no U-boats were sunk in the Atlantic until March, when the escorts gained their first real successes against the 'aces'. On 7 March, the corvettes *Camellia* and *Arbutus* sank *U.70* (Matz). A day later, the destroyer *Wolverine* sank *U.47*. Prien, the 'Bull of Scapa', and all his crew were lost. On the 17th, the destroyer *Walker* sank *U.100* with all hands including Schepke, and joined *Vanoc* in sinking *U.99* (Kretschmer). Kretschmer – the highest scoring 'ace' of them all, with 266,629 tons of shipping sunk – became a prisoner-of-war.

In the Mediterranean, 1941 began with a serious reverse for ABC's fleet. Early in January, during the passage of the Malta convoys, EXCESS

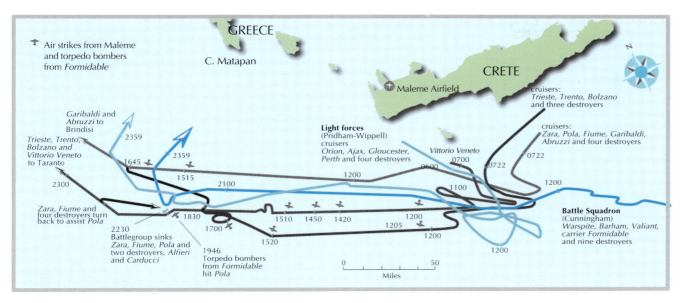

Air strikes from Maleme and torpedo bombers from *Formidable*

GREECE
C. Matapan

CRETE
Maleme Airfield

cruisers:
Trieste, Trento, Bolzano and three destroyers

Light forces (Pridham-Wippell) cruisers *Orion, Ajax, Gloucester, Perth* and four destroyers

cruisers:
Zara, Pola, Fiume, Garibaldi, Abruzzi and four destroyers

Vittorio Veneto 0700

0722

0722

Garibaldi and *Abruzzi* to Brindisi

2359

2359

Trieste, Trento, Bolzano and *Vittorio Veneto* to Taranto

1645

1515

2100

0600

0722

1200

2300

1200

1100

1200

Zara, Fiume and four destroyers turn back to assist *Pola*

1830

1510 1450 1420

1205

1200

Battle Squadron (Cunningham) *Warspite, Barham, Valiant,* carrier *Formidable* and nine destroyers

2230 Battlegroup sinks *Zara, Fiume, Pola* and two destroyers, *Alfieri* and *Carducci*

1700

1520

1200

1946 Torpedo bombers from *Formidable* hit *Pola*

1200

0   50
Miles

1941 Tenth Submarine Flotilla operations in Mediterranean. Luftwaffe attack EXCESS convoy to Malta (10 January). British reinforcements transported to Greece (March). Cunningham's victory over Italian fleet at Cape Matapan (28 March). Evacuation of the army from Greece (April). German attack on Crete (20 May). Evacuation of the army from Crete (end May). HMS *Hood* sunk by *Bismarck* (24 May). Pursuit and sinking of *Bismarck* by Home Fleet (27 May). HALBERD convoy to Malta (September). HMS *Ark Royal* and HMS *Barham* sunk (13 November and 25 November). Japan attacks Peal Harbor, Shanghai, Hong Kong, Malaya and the Philippines (7 December). HMS *Prince of Wales* and HMS *Repulse* sunk (10 December). HMS *Queen Elizabeth* and HMS *Valiant* badly damaged by Italian charioteers in Alexandria (19 December). Fall of Hong Kong (25 December).

eastbound from Gibraltar, and MW5½ westbound from Alexandria, the Luftwaffe exacted revenge for Taranto. On the 10th, Fliegerkorps X, the Luftwaffe's anti-shipping specialists, who had recently arrived in Sicily, caught *Illustrious* at sea and hit her with six 500kg bombs. But for her armoured flight deck, she must have been lost. She limped into Grand Harbour and eventually reached the United States for repairs. The destroyer *Gallant* was bombed and sunk the same day, the cruiser *Southampton* a day later.

THE BATTLE FOR GREECE

In March 1941, German troops invaded the Balkans and thus threatened Greece, which had been invaded by the Italians in October 1940. Operation 'Lustre', the transport of British reinforcements to Greece, began on the 5th. The Germans put pressure on their Italian allies to take action to interrupt the flow of British convoys which were sailing to the Piraeus every three days. At last, on 25 March, intelligence revealed that the Italian fleet was at sea in some strength.

ABC diverted two convoys from the area, ordered Vice Admiral Pridham-Wippell with the cruisers *Orion, Gloucester, Ajax* and *Perth* and four destroyers to a rendezvous some 50 miles (80km) west of Crete, and sailed himself from Alexandria on the evening of the 27th, flying his flag in *Warspite*, with *Barham* and *Valiant*, the carrier *Formidable*, which had just joined the fleet, having been delayed by magnetic mines in the Suez Canal, and nine destroyers.

At dawn on the 28th, when the fleet was about 150 miles (240km) south of the eastern tip of Crete, *Formidable* flew off a search which reported two forces of cruisers and destroyers some 100 miles (160km) to the north-west. Doubts about them were resolved at about 7.45 a.m., when *Orion's* lookouts spotted smoke to the north-west. In classical cruiser style, Pridham-Wippell's ships withdrew, to entice the enemy on to the fleet's heavy guns.

The bait was taken rather too enthusiastically. Soon Pridham-Wippell was being pursued and under fire from the battleship *Vittorio Veneto* on his port quarter and three 10,000 ton heavy cruisers on his starboard. Fortunately, a torpedo strike from *Formidable* and Swordfish from Maleme in Crete caused the enemy to turn away.

Shortly after noon, a second strike from *Formidable* scored one torpedo hit aft on *Vittorio Veneto*. But she was soon able to improve her speed and draw away. At tea time, *Formidable* launched a third strike, joined by two Swordfish from Maleme in Crete, who missed the battleship but hit the heavy cruiser *Pola*, which stopped dead in the water.

Deprived of air reconnaissance, the Italian admiral Iachino had had no reports that enemy heavy ships were anywhere near him, and so detached *Pola's* sister ships *Zara* and *Fiume* to go back and assist her.

Forewarned by radar, ABC's battleships caught their opponents completely by surprise. Searchlights illuminated *Zara* and *Fiume*, with their guns still trained fore and aft. Both were sunk by the combined fire of *Warspite, Barham* and *Valiant*. Destroyers later found and dispatched *Pola* with torpedoes. So, in this night battle of Cape Matapan, the Italians lost three heavy cruisers and, for good measure, two destroyers, *Alfieri* and *Carducci*.

Above: *Australian troops evacuated from Greece prepare to disembark from one of the 45 ships of Operation 'Demon', which in five nights, beginning 24-25 April 1941, transported some 50,000 men.*

Above centre: *The Navy lost heavily to German divebombers off Crete in May 1941. The carrier HMS Formidable, seen under attack, was badly damaged.*

Matapan was a magnificent, and much-needed, victory which made ABC as internationally famous as Nelson after the Nile. But he and his fleet were given no time to rest on their laurels. On 6 April 1941, the German army invaded Greece and, supported by over a thousand aircraft, drove rapidly south. British and Greek resistance collapsed and on the night of the 24/25th the Navy began Operation 'Demon' – the evacuation of the army.

OPERATION 'DEMON'

The evacuation, carried out by six cruisers, 19 destroyers, three corvettes, six landing craft, three fast *Glen* transports, and eight Merchant Navy transports, continued for five nights, in which some 50,000 troops – 80 per cent of those carried to Greece in Operation 'Lustre' – were taken off through minor ports or across open beaches, although much of their equipment had to be left behind. Four transports were bombed and sunk, including *Slamat*, from which 700 men were rescued by the destroyers *Diamond* and *Wryneck*. But the destroyers themselves were then bombed and sunk. From all three ships, one officer, 41 ratings and eight soldiers survived.

Early in May 1941, urged on by Mr Churchill but against the advice of ABC and his staff, the TIGER convoy of fast motor transports passed right through the Mediterranean and, largely because of a near-miraculous fog, unusual for the Mediterranean at that season, reached Alexandria safely with 43 Hurricanes and 238 tanks for the Army of the Nile. But losses from all causes left *Formidable* with only four serviceable fighters. Lack of air cover was to have a crucial effect on the forthcoming struggle in Crete.

Of the troops evacuated from Greece, some 21,000 went to Crete, to bring the garrison there up to 32,000 men. When the Germans attacked Crete on 20 May, their airborne troops suffered heavy losses, but they did seize the vital airfield at Maleme. ABC's ships prevented any German reinforcements arriving by sea, intercepting and sinking many small caiques and other craft carrying troops by night. But when daylight came, the initiative passed to the Luftwaffe, who steadily built up German strength on Crete through Maleme, and harried ABC's ships at sea.

Off Crete in May 1941, the Navy suffered its worst ordeal by air attack of the whole war. The destroyer *Juno* was sunk on 21 May. The next day, the cruisers *Gloucester* and *Fiji* and the destroyer *Greyhound* were lost, *Warspite* and the cruisers *Naiad* and *Carlisle* hit and badly damaged. On the 23rd, *Kelly*, *Kashmir* and *Kipling* of the 5th Destroyer Flotilla were returning from a bombardment of Maleme airfield when, shortly after breakfast, they were caught by a pack of Stukas. *Kashmir* was soon sunk and *Kelly* followed. *Kipling* stayed to pick up survivors and eventually reached Alexandria with 279, having survived over 80 near-misses.

On 26 May, *Formidable* launched a dawn strike against the airfield on Scarpanto, an island east of Crete, where many enemy aircraft were based. By coincidence, the same Stuka group which had attacked *Illustrious* struck back at *Formidable* who was hit twice and followed her sister ship's melancholy track, to Alexandria and through the Suez Canal to the United States.

As the losses mounted, ABC was advised by the Army C-in-C General Wavell and by his own staff that the Navy had done enough and the evacuation should be called off. ABC refused. The soldiers could not be abandoned to their fate, whatever the cost in ships and sailors might be. As he said: 'It takes three years to build a ship, it

would take three hundred to rebuild a tradition.' He signalled to his fleet 'We must not let them (the Army) down'.

As ABC had feared, the Navy paid a very heavy price to uphold their time-honoured tradition. But their reward was in the relieved faces of the soldiers and their faith that the Navy would never let them down and would be there, as expected, on the day.

HUNT FOR THE *BISMARCK*

To the men of the Mediterranean Fleet, engrossed as they were in their ordeal off Crete, news of events in the Atlantic came as though from another planet. On 18 May, the German battleship *Bismarck*, 45,000 tons and eight 15-inch guns, wearing the flag of Vice Admiral Lütjens, and the heavy cruiser *Prinz Eugen*, 12,750 tons, eight 8-inch guns, sailed from Gdynia to attack convoys in the Atlantic.

The two ships were reported passing through the Kattegat and sighted by air reconnaissance on the 21st in a fjord near Bergen where they were refuelling. They were gone by the next day. Attempting to break out into the Atlantic through the Denmark Strait between Iceland and Greenland, they were sighted and then shadowed on the 23rd by the cruisers *Suffolk* and *Norfolk*.

Meanwhile the battlecruiser *Hood*, wearing the flag of Vice Admiral L.E. Holland, the battleship *Prince of Wales* and six destroyers sailed from Scapa Flow on the 21st, followed the next day by the Home Fleet: the battleship *King George V*, wearing the flag of the C-in-C Admiral Sir John Tovey, the battlecruiser *Repulse*, the aircraft carrier *Victorious*, five cruisers and seven destroyers.

Late on 23 May, the Admiralty ordered Force H, of the battlecruiser *Renown*, wearing Admiral Somerville's flag, the carrier *Ark Royal* and the cruiser *Sheffield*, to sail north from Gibraltar. The battleship *Rodney*, with four destroyers, who were some 550 miles (900km) south-east of the enemy, were also ordered to close.

Early on the 24th, *Hood* and *Prince of Wales* (the destroyers having been detached) sighted the two German ships and opened fire at 5.53 a.m. at a range of 26,000 yards (24km). The German ships concentrated their fire on *Hood*, while the British ships were only able to use their forward turrets. *Bismarck*'s second and third salvoes hit *Hood* which blew up and sank at 6 a.m., leaving three

Above: *A battleship in pursuit: 'HMS* King George V *in the chase after the* Bismarck*', a watercolour painting by Ian Marshall.*

Below: *A painting by Paul Wright of HMS* Hood, *sunk with only three survivors during the hunt for the* Bismarck. *(Inset) The first man to sight the* Bismarck – *the lookout aboard HMS* Suffolk.

Above: 'Back Them Up!', implores a wartime propaganda poster – and reinforces its demand with a stirring depiction of a British cruiser ramming and sinking an Italian submarine in the Mediterranean.

Below: HMS Begonia leads Flower class corvettes into Gibraltar during Operation 'Halberd', a convoy that sailed to Malta in September 1941. These small, durable warships were designed as anti-submarine escorts. (Inset) HMS Nelson after a torpedo hit on her port bow sustained during Operation 'Halberd', 28 September 1941.

survivors from a complement of 95 officers and 1,324 men. *Prince of Wales*, hit by four 15-inch and three 8-inch shells, retired under cover of smoke. But she had hit *Bismarck* twice, one hit isolating 1,000 tons of fuel in forward tanks, thus reducing *Bismarck*'s endurance. This was to have an important bearing on events to come.

Tovey now realised that he could not intercept the enemy until early the next day and so detached *Victorious* to launch a torpedo strike, which was carried out at about midnight and scored one hit, which did only slight damage.

In the evening of the 24th, *Prinz Eugen* headed out into the Atlantic, while *Bismarck* steered for the French coast because of the loss of those 1,000 tons of fuel. In the early hours of 25 May the shadowing ships, who had been keeping touch in poor visibility solely through *Suffolk*'s radar, lost contact. Due to errors in plotting direction-finding bearings in the flagship, it was thought *Bismarck* had turned north, so ships and aircraft searched in that direction. Not until the evening was it known that *Bismarck* was heading for a French port. Tovey's ships were then some 150 miles (240km) astern of her.

Bismarck was lost until 10.30 on the 26th when she was at last sighted by a Catalina flying boat flown by an American pilot. Aircraft from *Ark Royal* were soon in touch and shadowed throughout the day. *Ark Royal* launched a torpedo strike of 14 Swordfish that afternoon. Unfortunately they attacked *Sheffield* who, unknown to *Ark Royal*, had been detached to find and shadow the enemy. Luckily, all the torpedoes missed or were exploded harmlessly by their magnetic pistols.

A second strike of 15 Swordfish, armed with torpedoes with contact pistols, was launched that evening and scored two hits. One was on the armoured belt and did little damage. The other

was crucial and sealed *Bismarck*'s fate, by damaging her propellers, wrecking her steering gear, and jamming her rudders. To the delight, and the astonishment, of the ships hunting her, *Bismarck*'s speed was reduced to about seven knots and, inexplicably, she was steering an erratic course around north.

At this point Captain Vian's 4th Flotilla of five destroyers arrived and between 1.20 and 7 a.m. on 27 May made several torpedo attacks, and probably scored two hits. Meanwhile, throughout the night *King George V* and *Rodney*, who had joined the previous evening, had been closing for the kill. They approached *Bismarck* from the north-west and all three ships opened fire between 8.47 and 8.49 a.m. The accuracy and volume of *Bismarck*'s fire rapidly fell away and by 10.15 she had been reduced to a flaming shambles. Finally, the cruiser *Dorsetshire* was ordered to apply the *coup de grâce* which she did with three torpedoes. Of *Bismarck*'s complement of over 2,000, 102 survivors were picked up by *Dorsetshire* and the destroyer *Maori*, three by *U.74* and two by the German weather ship *Sachsenwald*.

Prinz Eugen was due to continue her raid on Allied shipping but developed engine defects and headed for Brest, where she had arrived by 1 June.

SUBMARINES IN THE MED

In 1940, in the eastern basin of the Mediterranean, the Submarine Service sustained losses as severe as those off Norway. The Alexandria-based boats, many of them O, F and R class from the China Station, were too large, took too long to dive and were too easily seen when dived, for Mediterranean operations. Between June 1940 and the end of the year, *Odin*, *Grampus*, *Orpheus*, *Phoenix*, *Oswald*, *Triad*, *Rainbow*, *Regulus* and *Triton* were all sunk. The loss of the submarines themselves was compounded by the casualties among their crews, who were all highly trained officers and men, with years of experience in submarines.

The situation improved in 1941 with the arrival of the smaller and handier U class, based in Malta and designated in September 1941 the Tenth Flotilla. They took a steady toll of Italian warships and Axis convoys to North Africa, although ultimately suffering severe losses of their own.

Amongst several successful COs in the Flotilla, Lt Cdr Wanklyn of *Upholder* was outstanding. After a somewhat hesitant start, when his Captain S/M seriously considered relieving him of his command, 'Wanks' got his eye in and made 36 attacks in all, of which 23 were successful, and sank nearly 140,000 tons of enemy shipping, including a destroyer, two Italian U-boats and over a dozen assorted troopships, tankers, and

and placed explosive charges under *Queen Elizabeth*, *Valiant*, and the tanker *Sagona*. All three were damaged, *Queen Elizabeth* so badly that she grounded on the harbour bottom. Both battleships were later repaired, but meanwhile the Mediterranean Fleet had lost its entire battle squadron in the space of a few weeks.

store ships. He was awarded the VC, the DSO and two Bars. In April 1942, on her 25th and last patrol before going home, *Upholder* was lost with all hands.

The winter of 1941/42 was the nadir of the war for the Royal Navy, especially in the Mediterranean. On 13 November, east of Gibraltar, *Ark Royal* was torpedoed by *U.81* and foundered early the next day, with the loss of one life. On the 25th, off the Libyan coast, *Barham* was torpedoed by *U. 331*, capsized, blew up, and sank with the loss of 862 lives. On 19 December, Force K, a squadron of cruisers and destroyers operating from Malta which had had considerable success against Axis convoys to north Africa, ran into a minefield off Tripoli. The cruiser *Neptune* was sunk, with only one survivor, *Aurora* and *Penelope* were damaged, and the destroyer *Kandahar* had to be scuttled.

Early the same day, three Italian two-man sub-marine 'chariots' penetrated Alexandria harbour

DISASTER IN THE FAR EAST

But even these disasters were overshadowed by events in the Far East. The 'Kido Butai', the striking force of six Japanese aircraft carriers, had attacked Pearl Harbor, the US Pacific Fleet's main base, on Sunday 7 December 1941. It was a stunning blow, although not in the end the decisive strategic victory the Japanese had hoped and planned for, which brought the United States into the war. It was followed three days later by another disaster, inflicted on the Royal Navy. On 10 December, *Prince of Wales* and *Repulse* were both sunk in the South China Sea by Japanese aircraft of the 22nd Air Flotilla flying from bases near Saigon.

As the situation in the Far East deteriorated, Mr Churchill had pressed an unwilling Admiralty to send out a modern capital ship to act as a deterrent and a threat to the Japanese. Force Z, of *Prince of Wales*, wearing the flag of Admiral Sir Tom Phillips, *Repulse* and four destroyers, had accordingly assembled at Singapore by early in December 1941.

Simultaneously with their attack on Pearl Harbor, the Japanese also attacked Guam, Wake Island, Hong Kong, the Philippines – and Malaya, landing in northern Malaya and in Thailand on 7 and 8 December. Phillips decided that if two

Left: *The Navy took a series of heavy blows in the Mediterranean in the winter of 1941. Here, the battleship HMS* Barham *capsizes after being torpedoed by U.331 on 25 November. Her magazine exploded and 862 men died.*

Below left: *Often 'sunk' by German propaganda, HMS* Ark Royal *founders in reality after being torpedoed by U.81 on 13 November.*

Below: *The cruiser HMS* Aurora *(seen below in peacetime) was damaged when she ran into a minefield off Tripoli on 18-19 December 1941 when operating with the Malta-based Force K.*

Above: *Petty Officer Frank Clements became a PoW when HMS* Exeter *was sunk, 1 March 1942.*

Right: *Frank Clements' scanty possessions as a prisoner of the Japanese included shorts he made from calico, and a tiny measure for his sugar allowance. They are now on display in the Royal Naval Museum, Portsmouth.*

essential requirements, surprise and fighter cover, could both be fulfilled, his ships stood a good chance of destroying the invasion force. Force Z sailed from Singapore on the evening of the 8th, and steamed north.

In the event, Force Z had neither surprise nor fighter cover. It was first reported by Japanese submarines and then on 10 December found and attacked by Japanese high level and torpedo bombers. *Repulse* sank at 12.30 p.m., after sustaining multiple bomb and torpedo hits. The flagship suffered the same fate less than an hour later. 840 officers and men of Force *Z* were lost, including Admiral Phillips and Captain John Leach, of *Prince of Wales*.

This double blow was perhaps felt more deeply in the nation's core than any other the country suffered at sea. It was a severe strategic setback for the Allies, a shocking tactical defeat for the Navy, and a great personal tragedy for the officers and men of the ships involved. It was also to be the first time the Royal Navy had ever lost its supremacy in any theatre of a war at sea and failed eventually to regain it. From that day, the US Navy assumed the mantle in the Far East. When the Royal Navy

appeared again in strength it was very much as junior partners.

Hong Kong fell on Christmas Day 1941, Singapore on 15 February 1942. A mixed force of British, Australian, Dutch and American cruisers and destroyers were decisively defeated in the forlorn battles of the Java Sea in February and March. In April, the Kido Butai struck westward into the Indian Ocean, attacking Ceylon and the east coast of India, and sinking the cruisers *Cornwall* and *Dorsetshire*, the carrier *Hermes* and other warships and merchantmen.

Corregidor, the last Allied stronghold in the Philippines, surrendered on 6 May 1942. In six months, Japan had established her Greater Asia Co-Prosperity Sphere, an empire of 90,000,000 people stretching from Wake Island to Rangoon and from Manchuria to Rabaul, containing 88 per cent of the world's rubber, 54 per cent of its tin, 30 per cent of its rice, 20 per cent of its tungsten, and the rich oilfields of the East Indies. All this had been accomplished at the cost of some 15,000 men, about 400 aircraft and a couple of dozen warships, none of them larger than a destroyer.

'IT'S BEING SO CHEERFUL THAT KEEPS ME GOING'

'Roll on the *Nelson*, the *Rodney*, *Renown*; You can't have the *Hood* – the bugger's gone down!'

A sailors' song of 1942 tells us how naval ratings faced the Second World War, when the crew of a ship at sea were in combat, liable to face attack at any time. What enabled the wartime rating to do his duty was black humour, fatalism ('...if it's got your name on it'), bloodymindedness. In the words of a contemporary radio character, a lugubrious charlady, 'it's being so cheerful that keeps me going!'

The Navy expanded more than four-fold between 1939 and 1944: from 161,000 to 750,000. Physical and educational requirements were cut to a minimum – yet most 'hard bargains' served well, in spite of having plenty to grouse about. In 1939, says Captain John Wells, 'arrangements at sea for eating, sleeping and washing had hardly changed since 1919; even in new construction ships...habitability was not impressive.' For ratings in destroyers and smaller ships, 'habitability' often meant no space even to sling a hammock – sleep was snatched wrapped in a blanket (usually only one was issued; men on the Russian convoys got two) under mess-deck tables. Most food was canned or dried; meat was prepared by untrained 'butchers'. Fresh water was rationed and hygiene might mean washing in salt water.

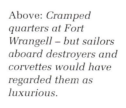

Above: *Cramped quarters at Fort Wrangell – but sailors aboard destroyers and corvettes would have regarded them as luxurious.*

Centre right: *A seaman gets a trim in HMS* Duke of York.

Right: *A popular ritual – the rum issue.*

Ratings might call a good officer a 'gentleman' – but the term now signified not the grandee of former times, but an efficient commander who both merited and was prepared to return respect. Among officers, long-standing social barriers were being broken down. In 1938–39, 45 seamen had taken advantage of the Direct Promotion to sub-lieutenant offered to specialists, but wartime saw long-serving specialist warrant officers promoted lieutenant. In 1940, First Lord Winston Churchill reversed the decision of a Dartmouth interview board that had rejected three candidates – one with a Cockney accent, the others the respective sons of a Merchant Navy engineer and a Chief Petty Officer. Yet one admires the sang-froid that preserved certain 'gentlemanly' traditions. A Fleet Air Arm pilot aboard HMS *Courageous*, patrolling the Western Approaches in

THE CHANNEL DASH

Sometimes, what appeared to be a disaster at the time turned out not to be so. The German battlecruisers *Scharnhorst* and *Gneisenau*, 'Salmon and Gluckstein' as the popular press dubbed them, had been in the French port of Brest since their successful sortie against Atlantic shipping in March 1941. They were joined by *Prinz Eugen* in June. All three were subjected to regular attacks from the air.

Early in 1942, intelligence indicated that the three ships were planning to return to Germany. Much was revealed about their intentions, but it was assumed, wrongly, that if they came up the English Channel they would do so by night. Elaborate and wide-ranging plans were laid to intercept them.

The German squadron, commanded by Vice Admiral Ciliax in *Scharnhorst*, sailed from Brest on 12 February 1942 and, escorted by a screen of small ships and massive air cover overhead, steamed up the Channel, in daylight. For the Allies, everything went wrong. The submarine watching Brest was off station. Air sighting reports were not received or were misinterpreted. Attacks by MTBs from Ramsgate, destroyers from Harwich, six Fleet Air Arm Swordfish from Manston, and by Bomber Command, all failed. Both battlecruisers were damaged by mines laid along their route (which had been revealed by Ultra) but all three ships reached Germany.

Above: *Sentimental patriotism was not much in favour – but notice that photographs of King George VI and his* consort feature alongside 'pin-ups' and cartoons in the contents of a 'typical' Second World War sailor's attaché case.

September 1939, recorded that 'officers dressed for dinner each evening'. Shortly thereafter, the *Courageous* was torpedoed and sunk: 680 men survived from a complement of 1,200.

The news of this 'Channel Dash', when heavy enemy ships had passed so close to the English coast, sent an electric tremor of indignation and outrage throughout the nation. Despite the public dismay, there were some redeeming factors. While the 'Channel Dash' may have been a tactical victory, in the event it was a strategic defeat for Germany. Those ships were much less of a threat to Allied shipping in Wilhelmshaven than they had been in Brest.

Intelligence now reported that the German battleship *Tirpitz* was getting ready for sea. If, like her sister ship *Bismarck*, she broke out into the Atlantic and then headed for a French port, there was only one dry dock on the Atlantic seaboard, the *Normandie* dock at St Nazaire on the river Loire, which could take her.

A daring Commando raid, codenamed 'Chariot', was mounted to blow up the dock gates. 'Chariot' Force, which sailed from Falmouth on 26 March 1942, consisted of the ex-US Navy destroyer *Campbeltown*, with 24 time-fused depth-charges packed in her fore peak, an MGB with the Force Commander, 16 MLs carrying Commandos, MTB 74, towed across by *Campbeltown*, with two delayed action torpedoes for use if *Campbeltown* failed, and two escorting destroyers.

The Force arrived off the Loire estuary early on 28 March. *Campbeltown*, disguised as a German destroyer and wearing a German ensign, was not challenged for some time, when she struck the Iron Cross, hoisted the White Ensign and drove foursquare into the dock gates at 1.34 a.m. – four minutes late.

Campbeltown blew up next day, while she was being inspected by German officers, and wrecked the dock gates. Of the 630 men in 'Chariot', 144 were killed and more than 200 captured, but they won five Victoria Crosses and 78 other decorations.

THE DIEPPE RAID

'Chariot' was a brilliant success. 'Jubilee', the raid on Dieppe in August 1942, was an utter failure. Ostensibly, its intention was to test the German defences of the port. Another, unspoken, motive was to provide some operational employment for the 2nd Canadian Division, who had been in the United Kingdom since 1939.

The expedition was mounted from five different ports between Southampton and Newhaven, with a force of some 5,000 Canadians, 1,000 British troops, including Commandos, and 50 US Rangers. The naval force was considerable: 237 warships and landing craft, organised in 13 groups. So too was the RAF's contribution: 74 squadrons, from nine Allied nations.

Surprise was lost when some of the 'Jubilee' ships stumbled on a German convoy in the early

▶ **1942** Continuing Tenth Submarine Flotilla operations in the Mediterranean. 'Channel Dash' by *Scharnhorst* and *Gneisenau* (12 February). Battle of Java Sea (February). Vian's victory in Gulf of Sirte (22 March). Operation 'Chariot': attack on dock at St Nazaire (28 March). Attack on Colombo by Japanese aircraft; HMS *Hermes*, HMS *Dorsetshire* and HMS *Cornwall* sunk (April). Invasion of Diego Suarez, Madagascar (May). HARPOON and VIGOROUS convoys to Malta (June). PQ 17 convoy disaster (4 July). SUBSTANCE convoy to Malta (July). PEDESTAL convoy to Malta (August). Dieppe Raid (10 August). 'Torch' landings in North Africa (8 November). PORTCULLIS convoy

Above: *Allied landing craft head for the beaches during Operation 'Jubilee', 19 August 1942. Although its planners claimed that valuable lessons were learned for later invasions, the raid on Dieppe was a costly failure.*

hours of 19 August, but the main assault landings went ahead along a ten-mile (16km) front at dawn. Some Commandos achieved their objectives, but the assaults in and near the town of Dieppe failed comprehensively. Supporting gunfire from destroyers failed to subdue the defenders who resisted vigorously with fierce fire which did terrible carnage among the attackers, especially the Canadians. Most of the tanks failed to get off the beach and into the town.

Withdrawal began at 11 a.m. and was completed by 2 p.m., when 3,367 Canadians had been killed, wounded or taken prisoner. British casualties were 275. The Navy lost the destroyer *Berkeley*, 33 landing craft, and 550 casualties. The RAF lost 106 aircraft. The Germans suffered 591 casualties and lost 48 aircraft.

After Hitler attacked Russia in June 1941, it was decided to send supplies to Russia by sea round the North Cape of Norway, the first 'Dervish' convoy sailing in August 1941. Whatever the political and moral justifications for the Arctic convoys, as naval undertakings they were always basically unsound. The merchant ships and their escorts had to make their way to and from north Russian ports along a route often restricted by ice, and always within reach of enemy air, surface-ship and U-boat bases, where Allied heavy covering forces were unable to protect them. To the dangers of the enemy and the appalling violence of the Arctic weather were added the hostility of a suspicious and ungrateful ally.

The main surface ship danger was *Tirpitz*. She never did break out into the Atlantic. Instead, in January 1942, she went up to Norway where, in her northern fjord, the mere threat of her presence affected the movements of Allied warships all over the world.

Convoy PQ 17, of 37 merchant ships, sailed for Archangel from Reykjavik in Iceland on 27 June 1942, with a close escort of three minesweepers, four trawlers, a destroyer and two auxiliary anti-aircraft ships, joined on 30 June by six more destroyers, four corvettes and two submarines. Four cruisers and two destroyers provided close cover from 1 July, and the Home Fleet was at sea as distant cover.

PQ 17 was attacked from the air from 1 to 4 July, and lost three ships on the 4th, but was otherwise

THE RED DUSTER

In 1928 the Prince of Wales became 'Master of the Merchant Navy and Fishing Fleets'. This appellation for the shipping industry, a peacetime honour, took on new meaning in 1939–40, when all ships flying the Red Ensign ('Red Duster') came under control of the Ministry of War Transport and the Admiralty. Many merchant ships and crews which had fled occupied countries, notably Norway, the Netherlands and Greece, accepted British control and became part of the Merchant Navy. Primary imports were still foodstuffs and raw materials; but now the vital exports were fighting men and arms and materiel for them and their allies – cargoes conveyed at enormous cost in ships and men. Foul weather was the least hazard: the men of the Arctic Convoys longed, during the relatively clement summer months with their 24-hour daylight, for the savage winter storms that helped shield them from attack.

Some merchant ships took combat roles, among them the CAM and MAC ships described in the text and fast passenger ships fitted as armed merchant cruisers. Luxury liners became hospital ships and troop transports (and the battleship HMS *Queen Elizabeth*, encountering the liner-turned-trooper of the same name, signalled 'SNAP'). Merchant losses in the Battle of Atlantic remained horrendous until 1943, when the mid-ocean 'Black Gap', hitherto out of range of land-based aircraft, was closed by the deployment of escort carrier groups and long-ranged B-24 Liberator bombers. It is a tribute to seamen of

Above: *A convoy steams in calm seas and clear weather – conditions that favoured attackers.*

Below: *A convoy to Malta comes under air attack in the Mediterranean, 1942.*

many nationalities serving under the Red Ensign that there was never a shortage of crews to compare with that of ships. One merchant seaman, Galley Boy R.V. Steed, aged 14 in 1943 when his ship struck a mine, is believed to be the youngest British combatant killed in the Second World War.

One measure to counter the loss in 1939–45 of some 4,700 British-flagged merchantmen was the construction of 'Liberty Ships'. The original design for these 7,126-ton cargo ships was British: some 2,700 were built in American yards, where mass-production furthered by the use of welding rather than riveting – although 'Rosie the Riveter', the archetypal female shipyard worker, became an American heroine – meant that a vessel could be completed within four weeks.

still in good heart and good order. That day, intelligence was received that German capital ships, including *Tirpitz*, had sailed and it was assumed, despite the caveats of the intelligence staff, that PQ 17 was threatened. In a period of 25 minutes on the evening of 4 July, the First Sea Lord, Admiral Pound, sent three signals in increasing priority and growing urgency, ordering the cruisers to withdraw to the westward at high speed, the convoy to disperse and proceed to Russian ports owing to the threat from surface ships, and, finally, ordering the convoy to scatter.

Without the cruisers and the destroyers, who also hauled away to the west to join the cruisers and meet the expected threat, PQ 17 fell easy prey to the aircraft of the Luftwaffe and the U-boats. The remaining minesweepers and trawlers did their best, and several mini-convoys of stragglers were formed, but PQ 17 lost another 21 ships, 13 to U-boats and eight to the Luftwaffe, between 5 and 10 July. It was a disaster which still reverberates down the years.

BATTLE OF THE BARENTS SEA

As 12 of the merchantmen sunk in PQ 17 were American, there was much criticism of the Royal Navy in the United States. Stalin, with the impudence of the landlubber, asked if the Royal Navy had any sense of glory. There is no record of any comment by him after the Battle of the Barents Sea on 31 December 1942, when 14 ships of Convoy JW 51B on their way to Kola Inlet were defended by the 17th Destroyer Flotilla, led by Captain R.St.V. Sherbrooke in *Onslow*, when they were threatened by a powerful German force of the heavy cruiser *Hipper*, wearing the flag of Vice

Admiral Kummetz, the battleship *Lützow* and six large destroyers.

Sherbrooke had a plan to deal with just such a surface attack. He led his five destroyers out on to the threatened side, while the convoy turned stern on and retired under cover of smoke laid in a long, self-sacrificing run by *Achates*.

Hipper attacked four times and was driven off each time. In the fourth attack, *Hipper* hit *Onslow* with an 8-inch shell which swept her bridge with a storm of shrapnel and badly wounded Sherbrooke in the face. *Achates* was also hit and mortally damaged but continued her run.

Kummetz also had a plan. While *Hipper* attacked from the north, *Lützow* lay in wait to the south. It worked perfectly. *Lützow* encountered the convoy at a range of only two miles (3.2km), while the escort were engaged in beating off *Hipper*. The convoy should have been annihilated by *Lützow*'s six 11-inch guns. Instead, her captain fumbled his approach, was distracted by a snow storm, waited for the weather to clear, but then made no attack and withdrew, having let slip the sort of golden chance which normally comes only once in a life time.

Hipper also withdrew, being pursued and damaged by the cruisers *Sheffield* and *Jamaica* who had come up in support of the convoy. For the loss of *Achates* and the minesweeper *Bramble*, JW 51B was unscathed. Of those 14 ships which reached Kola Inlet safely, nine were American – a fact unnoticed in the States. Sherbrooke lost an eye but won the Victoria Cross.

The battle had far-reaching consequences. A furious Hitler, who had been confidently expecting a decisive victory, ordered all the major German warships to be decommissioned. This was not actually done, but the threat, and the resignation of Raeder, to be replaced by Dönitz, further depressed the morale of the German Navy.

Right: Guardians of the Malta convoys: the cruisers HMS Euryalus, veteran of Sirte, and Hermione, which was sunk during the HARPOON-VIGOROUS convoys.

Below: In the Second Battle of Sirte, 22 March 1942, Admiral Vian's cruisers and destroyers saved Convoy MW10 from a superior Italian force.

CONVOYS TO MALTA

In the Mediterranean in 1942 the destination of all convoys was Malta, the aim – not always achieved – being to supply the island with one convoy a month. The March convoy MW10, of four ships, sailed from Alexandria on the 20th, escorted by a close escort of the cruiser *Carlisle* and six destroyers, and a covering force of four cruisers and six destroyers under Rear Admiral Vian, flying his flag in *Cleopatra*.

Brilliantly led by Vian in two engagements on 22 March which together made up the Second Battle of Sirte, Vian's cruisers and destroyers held off a vastly superior Italian force. Making judicious use of the weather gauge, as in the days of sail, with timely and skilfully laid smoke screens, advancing to open fire with guns and threaten with torpedoes, then retreating as though to lead their opponents into a trap, and advancing again, they fought off first Italian heavy cruisers and then the battleship *Littorio*.

The convoy was unscathed but it had been delayed, so that it was still at sea at daylight the next day. Two ships were sunk before reaching Malta and the remaining two were bombed in port. Only about a quarter of that convoy's cargo was safely discharged. By midsummer 1942 the situation of the people and garrison of Malta was desperate. In June, the HARPOON convoy sailed from the west and the VIGOROUS convoy from the east. Both were fiercely attacked. From the two convoys, only two HARPOON ships reached Malta, at the cost of the cruiser *Hermione*, five destroyers, two minesweepers and six merchant ships. VIGOROUS was forced to turn back.

The War Cabinet now decided that a relief convoy for Malta must be given precedence over every other naval commitment. On 10 August 1942 the PEDESTAL convoy, of 14 merchant ships including the tanker *Ohio*, steamed through the Straits of Gibraltar to begin one of the most spectacular naval actions of the war. The covering force, under Vice Admiral Sir Neville Syfret, had two battleships, *Nelson* and *Rodney*. the carriers *Victorious*, *Indomitable* and *Eagle*, with *Furious* carrying Spitfires for Malta, seven cruisers and 32 destroyers.

In its passage to Malta the convoy was attacked by aircraft, German and Italian U-boats and E-boats but not, as expected, by the Italian surface fleet. *Eagle* was torpedoed and sunk by *U. 73*. The Luftwaffe sank the destroyer *Foresight* and damaged *Indomitable* so badly her aircraft had to be transferred to *Victorious*. The Italian U-boat *Axum* fired a prodigious torpedo salvo which forced the cruiser *Nigeria* to return to Gibraltar, sank the cruiser *Cairo*, and damaged *Ohio*, which caught fire but steamed on. E-boats sank four merchantmen and disabled the cruiser *Manchester* which was scuttled (prematurely, a later court-martial decided). In all, only five merchantmen reached Malta but they included *Ohio* with her 10,000 tons of priceless petrol and kerosene. She was towed into Grand Harbour amid scenes of wild rejoicing on 15 August.

Malta had not been relieved, only reprieved. Another convoy, STONEAGE, now almost forgotten

Above: Former Signals Wren Elizabeth MacVey Cook well remembers the hazards of convoy duty in the Mediterranean .

'*First the siren or whatever they call it on the boat went…You grabbed your life jacket which had a red light clipped on to it, and you had your emergency rations which I believe were things like…I can remember the chocolate which must have been protected quite well by its waterproof cover. Don't forget there was no nylon in those days. Different sorts of fabric they had to use. A light and a whistle, I think that you had, in case you were in the dark. We expected to be in the water…When the other ships left us at Gib[raltar]: it was very scary going through the Mediterranean because you could see the periscope of the U-boats on several occasions, so there were more boat drills than ever then.*'

ELIZABETH MACVEY COOK, A SIGNALS WREN DURING THE SECOND WORLD WAR

compared with PEDESTAL, sailed in November 1942. Not until convoy PORTCULLIS arrived in December 1942 was Malta finally relieved, a relief made possible by the success of Operation 'Torch' the previous month.

OPERATION 'TORCH'

The joint Anglo-American invasion of north Africa on 8 November 1942, codenamed 'Torch', was a vast operation involving three landings, at Casablanca, Oran and Algiers. The Western Task Force, for the Casablanca landings, was wholly American, but the landings at Oran and Algiers were under the charge of the Royal Navy.

The Central Naval Task Force, for Oran, was commanded by Commodore Thomas Troubridge, flying his broad pennant in the headquarters ship *Largs*, with over 50 other warships, including two submarines to act as navigational markers off the assault beaches, 19 landing ships and 28 transports, carrying the 1st US Infantry Division and half the 1st US Armoured Division, comprising 39,000 troops.

The Eastern Naval Task Force, for Algiers, was commanded by Vice-Admiral Sir Harold Burrough, flying his flag in the headquarters ship *Bulolo*, with over 30 warships, 17 landing ships and 16 transports, to land 33,000 troops of the 34th and 9th US Infantry Divisions, the other half of the 1st US Armoured Division and the British 78th Infantry Division.

The British Task Forces and the 'follow-up' convoys were covered by an enlarged Force H under Syfret, flying his flag in *Duke of York*, with *Rodney*, *Renown*, *Victorious*, *Formidable*, and *Furious*, three cruisers, 17 destroyers and a fuelling force of four tankers.

There was some French resistance at Oran, but 'Torch' as a whole was a success. Coupled with the 8th Army offensive at El Alamein on 23 October and the breakthrough and pursuit of the Afrika Korps which began on 4 November, 'Torch' marked the turn of the tide for the Allies. As Churchill observed in a speech delivered at the Mansion House in November 1942, it was not the end, nor the beginning of the end, but it was the end of the beginning.

Above: *Cruiser HMS Coventry ablaze and sinking after strikes by divebombers off Tobruk, 14 September 1942.*

Below: *'Land the Landing Force' – a photograph taken off Oran, where the Royal Navy was in charge of the Anglo-American Operation 'Torch' landings.*
Inset: *Troops embark for the invasion of North Africa.*

CHAPTER NINE

FROM D-DAY
INTO THE
NUCLEAR AGE

Previous pages: *The
Navy in action off the
Falklands, 4 May
1982. Rex Phillips's
painting shows the
Type 21 frigate HMS
Arrow aiding the Type
42 destroyer HMS
Sheffield, ablaze after
being hit by an Exocet
missile.*

Below: *Second World
War premier Winston
Churchill with
Marshal of the RAF Sir
Charles Portal, Field
Marshal Sir Alan
Brooke and Admiral
Sir Andrew
Cunningham.*

Below right: *A Flower
class corvette that was
one of the ships that
formed the escort for
the Atlantic convoy
ONS5 in April–May
1943, a turning point
in the critical fight
against the U-boats.*

'Sink, Burn, and Destroy. Let nothing pass, Thus Admiral Cunningham, once more C-in-C in the Mediterranean, signalled to his ships to begin Operation 'Retribution', to prevent an Axis 'Dunkirk' evacuation. The land campaign in north Africa was almost over. The final breakthrough began on 6 May 1943, the first advance Allied troops entered Tunis on the 7th, and within two days a demoralised enemy was being driven up into the Cape Bon peninsula.

On 8 May, all available destroyers began a night and day patrol off Cape Bon, with coastal forces closer inshore, to foil any attempts at escape by sea. In the event, very few tried to escape in the 'Bizerta Regatta' as the destroyer captains called it.

In that same month of May 1943, there was another stupendous victory for the Allies, one which hardly seemed possible only a short time earlier. On 1 March 1943 there were nearly 70 U-boats, more than ever before, at sea in the north Atlantic. The number grew until it by the end of the month a state had been reached where the Atlantic was becoming so saturated with U-boats that it was no longer possible to route convoys so as to evade them.

In a series of savage convoy battles in March, U-boats sank 108 ships of 627,377 tons, out of a total of 120 ships of 693,000 tons sunk from all causes during the month. For a time, the Naval Staff

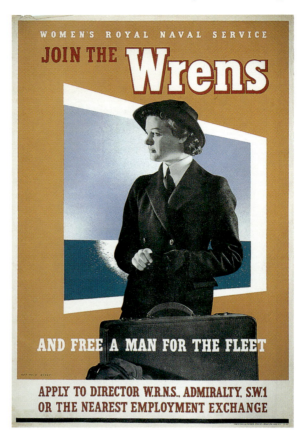

Above: *A Second World War recruiting poster for the Wrens emphasizes their trim uniform – much envied by other women's services – and vital auxiliary work which 'freed a man for the fleet'.*

began to think the unthinkable, and consider abandoning the convoy system, which was the very foundation stone of Allied naval strategy.

The most dangerous part of the ocean was the so-called 'Greenland Gap', in mid-Atlantic beyond the range of aircraft. From April 1943, when the Very Long Range Liberator aircraft arrived and the Gap was covered, the battle began to swing away from the U-boats.

The climactic battle was fought round the 43-ship convoy ONS5 which sailed from the United Kingdom outward bound for Halifax on 21 April 1943. In a ten-day battle in foul weather, the convoy was threatened by 40 U-boats. When the battle ended on 6 May, 12 merchant ships had been sunk and seven U-boats, five detected by the escorts' radar and two by collision. Five U-boats reported severe damage, and 12 more reported lesser action damage. Despite the losses, ONS5 was a resounding tactical victory for the escorts, especially in their use of radar at night.

The total number of U-boats lost from all causes in May 1943 rose to 41. U-boat Command was stunned by such catastrophic losses and on 24 May decided to halt, temporarily, the offensive against the convoys in the north Atlantic and withdraw the U-boats. In the three weeks after the battle around ONS5, 468 ships of 11 convoys passed across without loss. For the U-boats this was, in one word, defeat. The retreat of the

Atlantic U-boats in May 1943 was as smashing a strategic victory for the Allies as Stalingrad in the east and Midway in the Pacific.

Aircraft were the natural predators of the U-boats, and air cover, either by long-range shore-based aircraft or by aircraft from a carrier within the convoy, was the key to convoy safety. In the Spring of 1941, the old seaplane carrier *Pegasus* and three ex-merchant ships were converted for service as Fighter Catapult ships, used not so much against the U-boats as against their partners, the long-range Focke-Wulf Kondors. In time, some 50 merchant ships, each carrying one Hurricane, though still flying the Red Ensign, were commissioned as Catapult Armed Merchant Ships or CAM Ships.

The next development was the Merchant Armed Carrier or MAC ship, a tanker or grain carrier with a rudimentary flight deck built over her superstructure. The grainers had a lift and a small hangar and could carry up to four Swordfish. The tankers had a slightly longer flight deck but no hangar and carried three Swordfish. Both had a safety barrier and two arrester wires. They still flew the Red Ensign and still carried more than three-quarters of their normal cargo. Eventually, there were 19 MAC ships in service. Their aircraft flew about 4,000 sorties in all and made 12 attacks on U-boats. No U-boats were sunk, but no convoy with a MAC ship ever lost a ship to U-boats.

ESCORT CARRIERS

The MAC ships were necessary makeshifts. The true solution to convoy air defence was the escort carrier. These 'Woolworth Carriers', as they were called, were converted from merchantship hulls but were still genuine aircraft carriers. Most were built in America, where 20 C-3 merchant hulls were converted, ten of them becoming the RN Attacker class, of 14, 000 tons, a speed of 17 knots, carrying 16 fighters or 17 torpedo-bombers. Later, 20 more C-3 hulls were allocated, becoming the RN Ruler class.

In all, 38 C-3 hulls were turned over to the Royal Navy. Escort carriers and their aircraft sank 12 U-boats outright and their aircraft shared in a number of U-boat kills with surface ships.

Escort carriers provided fighter cover for the assault phases of a series of landings in the Mediterranean, starting with 'Torch' in November 1942, and going on to 'Husky', the invasion of Sicily, in July 1943, which was the largest amphibious operation ever undertaken until that time. Over 2,500 vessels of all types, warships and merchantmen of seven nationalities took part in the first assault, and more than 3,200 participated in the operation as a whole. 'Husky' saw the first proper use of the Combined Operations Pilotage

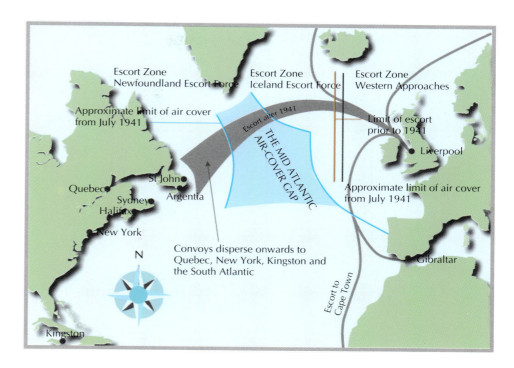

Parties (COPPs), who paddled ashore from submarines to reconnoitre possible landing beaches, and the spectacular debut of a new weapon, the Landing Craft (Rocket).

The assault forces were already on their way in September to the next amphibious operation, 'Avalanche', the landing at Salerno with the object of capturing Naples, when there were rumours of an impending Italian surrender. The first troops went ashore on 9 September, the bulk of the

Above: Convoys escorted by corvettes had to traverse the perilous mid-Atlantic air-cover gap

Below: Even a near-miss like the one viewed here aft of a cruiser might do damage, especially to smaller escorts.

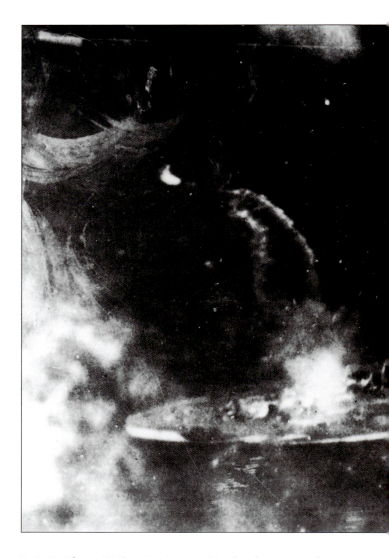

Above: *Armistice with Italy is signed aboard HMS* Nelson. *Flying black flags in token of surrender, Italian warships came under the guns of Malta on 10 September 1943.*

Right: *The German battleship* Tirpitz *is hard hit in Operation 'Tungsten', 3 April 1944. Forty-one Fairey Barracudas flew from carriers to score 15 direct hits with 500- and 1000-pound bombs.*

Italian fleet surrendered on the 10th, and next day ABC made his unforgettable signal to the Admiralty: 'Be pleased to inform Their Lordships that the Italian battle fleet now lies at anchor under the guns of the fortress of Malta'.

At first, all went well at Salerno, but the enemy counter-attacked on the night of the 11-12th. The situation rapidly became so grave that *Warspite* and *Valiant* were summoned to hold the ring with their heavy guns, which they successfully did until the danger was past. But *Warspite* was hit and badly damaged by a 3,000lb radio-controlled bomb on the 16th (the first occurrence of such an attack in warfare) and had to be towed to Malta. However, after some fierce fighting, the first advance troops entered Naples on 2 October.

THE ATTACK ON THE *TIRPITZ*

Once again, success in the Mediterranean was followed by success in the north. The menace of *Tirpitz*, lurking in her northern fastness, continued to affect Allied planning and ship dispositions. Bomber Command, the Fleet Air Arm and the Norwegian Resistance had all tried to sink her. A fresh attempt, Operation 'Source', was made in September 1943 by midget submarines, or X-craft. These were 51 feet (15.5m) long, weighed about thirty-five tons, could dive to 300 feet (90m) and make six and half knots on the surface and five dived. They were crewed by three officers and an engine-room artificer, all volunteers. They were armed with two detachable charges, each containing two tons of explosives which could be dropped on the sea-bed under the target and fired by clockwork time-fuses.

Six X-craft were built and two crews – a 'passage' crew and an operational crew – were trained for each craft. For 'Source', the targets were: *X.5, X.6* (Lt D. Cameron RNR), and *X.7* (Lt

B.C.G. Place RN), *Tirpitz*, in Kaafjord; *X.9* and *X.10, Scharnhorst*, also in Kaafjord; and *X.8, Lützow* in Langefjord. The X-craft left their depot ship *Bonaventure* in Loch Cairnbawn on 11 September and were each towed, dived, by 'orthodox' submarines to their slipping points off the Norwegian coast.

X.9 was lost with all hands on passage and *X.8* had to be scuttled because of defects. *Scharnhorst* had left her anchorage and *X.10* eventually abandoned the operation after many defects and delays. *X.5, X.6* and *X.7* began their attack on 20 September and, though *X.5* was lost, *X.6* and *X.7* both penetrated the fjords and the protective wires round *Tirpitz* and dropped their charges under or near her. They exploded at 0800 on the 22nd, damaging *Tirpitz* so badly she was unable to move from her anchorage until April 1944. Place and Cameron were both awarded the VC.

In 1944, the Fleet Air Arm launched a campaign of attacks by carrier aircraft on *Tirpitz*, beginning with Operation 'Tungsten', when she was getting ready for sea after repairs in April, continuing through the Summer with another eight operations, ending with 'Goodwood IV' in August, but could not deliver a crippling blow. A big ship needed a big weapon. After two previous raids, 32 Lancaster bombers of No. 9 and 617 (Dambuster) Squadrons administered the *coup de grâce* on 12 November with two 12,000lb 'Tallboy' bomb hits and one near-miss, after which *Tirpitz* capsized.

In September 1943, while attending the Quebec Conference, Sir Dudley Pound suffered a stroke which left his right side partly paralysed and he resigned as First Sea Lord. Pound was a 'big ship' man. He had commanded the battleship *Colossus* at Jutland and his subsequent career had followed the classical path to promotion, of a succession of appointments to flagships alternating with those in the Admiralty. He was a difficult man to serve. Someone once said of him that he was the most even-tempered of men: he was always angry. Certainly, he was apt to immerse himself unduly in detail, and to hound subordinates. But he had been First Sea Lord for four years in which he had borne the full brunt of the war, mentally and physically, and he had resisted as well as any man could the fierce pressure of Mr Churchill's personality. When he died, on Trafalgar Day 1943, victory was not yet in sight, but it was just below the horizon.

Churchill's first choice to replace Pound was Admiral Sir Bruce Fraser, the C-in-C Home Fleet. Fraser was a gunnery officer who had served with distinction in the First World War, and survived eight months imprisonment by the Bolsheviks in 1920, after which he was appointed OBE for his leadership. He was a most genial and friendly man, with the common touch to an uncommon degree.

To Churchill's surprise, Fraser did not jump at the job, but demurred, and said that, while he himself had the confidence of his Fleet, Cunningham had the confidence of the whole Navy. Andrew Browne Cunningham, ABC to the Navy, had served as a midshipman in the Boer War and had won a DSO and two Bars as a destroyer captain in the First World War. In the Mediterranean, he had fought a long and bitter battle and had won against the odds. He could be ruthless, and even cruel. He did not suffer fools gladly and he strongly objected to interference from afar. There had been several thunderous exchanges of signals between Alexandria and Whitehall. But he was also witty, humorous, eternally optimistic, justifiably self-confident, and a superb leader of men. Matapan had made him as internationally famous as Nelson after the Nile. He was the Navy's greatest fighting admiral of the war, arguably the greatest since Nelson. But he had little experience of Whitehall, and was a poor and reluctant office administrator. However, Cunningham was appointed First Sea Lord, while

Above: *A raid by RAF Lancasters with 12,000-pound bombs in November 1944 capsized the* Tirpitz.

Above: *Admiral Sir Bruce Fraser (1888–1981), later 1st Baron Fraser of North Cape.*

Left: *Churchill, a former First Lord of the Admiralty in both World Wars, was well versed in naval matters – but his 'bulldog' stance sometimes put great pressure on his senior commanders.*

Tell NOBODY –
not even HER

CARELESS TALK COSTS LIVES

Above: *Jack is warned
not to gossip on
service topics that
might interest the
enemy – even when
with his wife or best
girl. 'Careless talk
costs lives' had a
snappier American
equivalent: 'Loose lips
sink ships'!*

Below: *The End of the*
Scharnhorst *by David
Cobb. Intercepted by a
strong British force in
Arctic waters, the
German battlecruiser
fought 'to the last
shell' and went down
with almost all hands.
The Battle of North
Cape was the last big-
gun duel in British
naval history.*

Fraser went back to Scapa Flow – to finish the year of 1943 on a high note.

The Arctic convoys had been suspended early in the Spring of 1943, resuming in November with JW 54A and JW 54B, neither of which sustained any loss. The next two, JW 55A and JW 55B sailed in December. The 19-ship JW 55B, which sailed from Loch Ewe on the 20th, had an escort of 14 destroyers and three smaller ships. Also at sea to the north-east of the convoy were the 10th Cruiser Squadron, of *Belfast*, wearing the flag of Rear Admiral Bob Burnett, *Norfolk* and *Sheffield*. In the deep field to the south-west were the battleship *Duke of York*, wearing Fraser's flag, the cruiser *Jamaica*, and four destroyers.

THE BATTLE OF NORTH CAPE

Early on Christmas Day, *U.601* reported JW 55B off Bear island. *Scharnhorst*, wearing the flag of Rear Admiral Erich Bey, sailed from Altenfjord with five destroyers that evening. Next morning, the destroyers became separated from *Scharnhorst* in very bad weather and took no further part. At 8.40 a.m. *Belfast* detected *Scharnhorst* by radar, about 30 miles (50km) from JW 55B, and closed to intercept. *Sheffield* reported 'enemy in sight, range 13,000 yards' at 9.21 and a short gun action followed in which *Norfolk* scored a hit on *Scharnhorst*, who steered first to the south-east and then hauled round to the north-east.

Burnett calculated that *Scharnhorst* would make another attempt, and also steered north so that by noon his ships were well placed, some ten miles (16km) ahead of the convoy. At 12.21, it was *Sheffield* once again who signalled 'enemy in sight' and another gun action took place in which *Norfolk* was hit. *Scharnhorst* then steered south, as though to return to base, while *Belfast* followed close astern, reporting the enemy's position, course and speed every fifteen minutes.

Meanwhile, Fraser's ships were closing from the south-west. *Duke of York* detected *Scharnhorst* by radar at 4.17 p.m., range 22 miles (35km), illuminated the target and opened fire at 4.40 at a range of 12,000 yards (11km). For the third time that day, *Scharnhorst* was caught by surprise, with her turrets still trained fore and aft. Under fire from *Duke of York*, *Jamaica* and *Belfast*, and hounded by destroyers, *Scharnhorst* fled to the east and for a time it seemed she might escape. But after one of *Duke of York*'s hits, her speed slackened, and the destroyers closed in. At 5.24, Bey signalled 'Am surrounded by heavy units'.

At about 6.20, *Scharnhorst*'s guns fell silent and her speed dropped to about five knots. Bey signalled to Hitler 'We shall fight to the last shell'. By 7.45 *Scharnhorst* had been reduced to a blazing shambles. All that could be seen of her was a dull glow in a dense smoke cloud. She eventually sank, having suffered at least 13 heavy shell hits from *Duke of York* and many more from the other ships. Of 55 torpedoes fired at her, probably 11 hit. Only 36 survivors were picked up, from her complement of over 2,000. This Battle of North Cape, which Fraser eventually chose for the title of his peerage, was the last slogging match between dinosaurs, with aircraft playing no part.

D-DAY

It had to happen in 1944. The Allies had to invade occupied north-west Europe. 'Overlord' was the overall code name for the invasion. The assault phase, the Normandy landings and the associated operations, were codenamed 'Neptune'.

The Baie de la Seine, between Le Havre and the Cherbourg peninsula, was chosen for the assault. It was within range of Allied fighters. The shore defences could be neutralized. There were firm, sheltered beaches over which the troops could be landed and then supported at a rate equal to that of the enemy for at least 90 days. Until a major French port (Cherbourg, it was hoped) was captured, all supplies were to be landed via two artificial harbours, codenamed 'Mulberries', with breakwaters formed by old ships towed across and sunk on site, while fuel was to be pumped across the Channel by a specially designed and laid Pipe Line Under The Ocean (PLUTO).

The limiting factor was the number of landing craft available. The landing at Anzio in January 1944 had taken the enemy by surprise. The road to Rome lay open. But the chance was not seized, the enemy counter-attacked, and the army ashore had to be supplied by sea for four months. Every ship at Anzio reduced or delayed those for 'Neptune'. The landing in the French Riviera, planned to coincide with 'Neptune', and 'Neptune' itself, were delayed.

The date of 'Neptune' had to be carefully chosen. To neutralize the shore defences, the air and naval forces needed daylight, so the assault had to be made at dawn, and an hour after low water so that beach obstacles would be exposed. The airborne troops needed a full moon. These factors narrowed the choice of possible dates to 5, 6 and 7 June. 5 June was chosen, but the weather, which had been calm and fine for much of May, worsened early in June. 'Neptune' was postponed one day to 6 June – D-Day. H-Hour was 0630.

'Neptune' was the most massive and complicated undertaking in all naval history, carried out by the largest and most varied fleet that ever put to sea. Even the mere statistics are staggering. Including Allied merchant navies, 195,700 naval personnel, and 6,833 ships, including 1,212 warships (six battleships, 23 cruisers, and 104 destroyers), 4,026 landing craft, 731 auxiliaries and 864 merchant ships, took part. On D-Day itself, 75,215 British and Canadian and 57,500 American troops were landed over five beaches, codenamed from west to east Utah, Omaha (both

Above: *The khaki tunic was worn by RN Commando A. Laing for the D-Day landings in Normandy, 6 June 1944. The Enfield revolver and British steel helmet are issue items relating to the same occasion.*

Left: *Landing craft off the Normandy beaches are sheltered by a specially prefabricated 'Mulberry' harbour.*

Left: *A fraction of the Operation 'Neptune' armada, in which 6,833 Allied merchantmen and warships took part.*

▶ **1944** 'Shingle' landings at Anzio (22 January). Fleet Air Arm attacks on *Tirpitz* (April). Eastern Fleet air strike against Sabang (19 April). D-Day landings in Normandy (6 June). 'Dragoon' landings in southern France (15 August). Formation of British Pacific Fleet (November). Bombardment of and assault on Walcheren Island (1 November). *Tirpitz* sunk by bombers (12 November).

Above: *The first white ensign ashore on D-Day. The plaque says it was 'hoisted at 0800 (H+30) on D-Day June 6th 1944, Sword Area, Queen Red Beach, Lion-sur-Mer, at the outset of the campaign in Normandy'.*

Below: *One of the Normandy landing beaches on D-Day. A logistical feat unparalleled in history would see 850,279 men, 148,803 vehicles and 570,505 tons of supplies landed between 6-30 June.*

American), Gold, Juno and Sword (British and Canadian). There were some 4,300 British and Canadian, and about 6,000 US, casualties.

'Neptune' officially ceased on 30 June, by which date 850,279 men, 148,803 vehicles and 570,505 tons of supplies had been landed, for the loss of 59 ships sunk and 110 damaged. From D-Day to the capture of Le Havre in September, warships had carried out 750 bombardments, swept 600 mines and fought 28 surface actions. In those three months 352,570 men, 1,410,600 tons of stores and 152,000 vehicles had been successfully landed in Normandy.

EASTERN ENCOUNTERS

While 80 per cent of the ships in 'Neptune' had been British or Commonwealth, the Royal Navy had had not much more than a token presence in the Far East. For years there had been disagreement over where a British fleet should

operate in the Far East. The Admiralty wanted British ships to join the US Navy in the main offensive against Japan in the central Pacific. Mr Churchill and the Foreign Office argued that the centre of gravity of the British counter-attack should be in the Indian Ocean, with the ultimate object of recovering Singapore. Remote islands in the Pacific might be of great strategic importance in the general drive towards Japan, but they meant nothing to people in Japanese-occupied Burma, Malaya, Hong Kong and the Dutch East Indies. In other words, the Japanese must not only be defeated, they must be seen to be defeated.

The situation was not resolved until the Quebec Conference of September 1944, when Mr Churchill offered President Roosevelt the British Fleet to operate in the Pacific. The President accepted, to the dismay of Admiral King, the head of the US Navy, who wanted no British ships in the Pacific. Admiral Sir Bruce Fraser hoisted his flag as C-in-C British Pacific Fleet in November 1944, with his headquarters ashore in Sydney. The fleet was commanded at sea by Vice Admiral Sir Bernard Rawlings, flying his flag in the battleship *King George V*.

The carrier squadron, of four fleet carriers commanded by Rear Admiral Sir Philip Vian, carried out air strikes against oil refineries in Sumatra on their way to Australia in January 1945. But when the British Pacific Fleet sailed from Sydney in February 1945, the future was still shrouded in political uncertainty. Fraser and Nimitz, the US C-in-C Pacific, wanted the fleet to operate in the Pacific under Admiral Spruance. King wanted the fleet to serve under General MacArthur and Admiral Kinkaid in the South-west Pacific.

At last, late in March, the signal arrived, ordering the British Pacific Fleet, designated Task Force 57, to take part in Operation 'Iceberg', the invasion of Okinawa, which began on 1 April

Left: *The British Pacific Fleet's carrier strikes on Japanese oil installations began in January 1945. This picture shows burning oil tanks on Sumatra.*

Far left: *Corsairs on the flight deck of HMS* Victorious *during a raid on Sigli, Sumatra, 17 March 1945.*

1945 Fleet Air Arm strikes against oil refineries at Palembang (January). Campaign in Burmese Arakan (Spring). East Indies Fleet bombards Sabang, Padang and Nicobars (January to April). British Pacific Fleet takes part in invasion of Okinawa (March to May). VE Day (8 May). 26th Destroyer Flotilla sink *Haguro* (16 May). Fleet Air Arm strike against Truk (15 June). British Pacific Fleet takes part in final operations off Japan (July and August). Atomic bombs exploded over Hiroshima (6 August) and Nagasaki (9 August). VJ Day (15 August). Japanese surrender signed on board USS *Missouri* (2 September). First landing by a jet aircraft on a carrier, HMS *Ocean* (3 December).

1945. For 'Iceberg', the fleet was stationed semi-independently, on the left of the US 5th Fleet's battle line, off the islands of the Sakishima Gunto, south-west of Okinawa. Its task was to prevent the Japanese staging replacement aircraft through the Sakishima islands, which ran like a chain of stepping stones between Formosa and Okinawa, by neutralising the airfields on the two main islands of Miyako and Ishigaki.

It was a necessary but an unglamorous task, in which the fleet stood no chance of glory and every chance of being attacked. Furthermore, it had to be undertaken with the support of a few slow tankers. The Fleet Train, of tankers, store ships and assorted supply ships, which assembled in 1945, was the most motley collection of vessels in the Navy's history. But against the odds, it managed to support the Fleet by a sustained exercise of improvisation.

When the British Pacific Fleet returned to Sydney in June it had been at sea for 62 days, broken by eight days at Leyte, the longest period since Nelson's day, in which the news of Hitler's death, victory in Europe and VE-Day 8 May had

been to the men of the fleet like news from another planet. All five carriers which had taken part in 'Iceberg' had been hit at least once by kamikaze suicide bombers but were saved from crippling damage by their armoured flight decks.

The fleet sailed from Sydney on 28 June, after three weeks' rest and refit, and joined the US 3rd Fleet, under Admiral Halsey, some 300 miles (480km) east of Japan on 16 July, taking station on the right of the line. Though designated Task Force 37, the fleet was only as big as one of the three American Task Groups but, size for size, pulled its full weight in the air strikes and bombardments of the Japanese mainland in July and August 1945. However, when the 3rd Fleet began the annihilation of the last remnants of the Japanese fleet, Task Force 37 was disappointed to be allotted only subsidiary targets. The US Navy did not want to share the full and final revenge for Pearl Harbor.

There was one final disappointment. VJ-Day was declared on 15 August. When Admiral Fraser, flying his flag in *Duke of York*, signed the Japanese surrender document on behalf of the United

Left: *Grumman Avengers from a British carrier fly over the battleship* King George V, *26 March 1945, on the way to make the first of many strikes on Japanese island airfields between Formosa and Okinawa.*

Right: *Remains of a kamikaze suicide bomber – Japan's weapon of despair in 1944–45 – are cleared from the flight deck of HMS* Formidable.

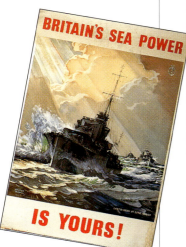

Above: An i*mage of sea power – destroyers in line ahead, painted by the Liverpool artist Walter Thomas, are the subject of a morale-building wartime poster.*

Below: *Jubilation in London's Trafalgar Square as crowds cheer VE (Victory in Europe) Day, 8 May 1945.*

Kingdom on board USS *Missouri* in Tokyo Bay on 2 September, the bulk of the British Pacific Fleet had already had to withdraw, for lack of fuel.

British ships had returned to Hong Kong on 27 August, and to Penang on the 28th. The surrender of Singapore and Johore was signed on 4 September, and Operation 'Zipper', the invasion of Malaya, took place as planned on 9th.

On VE-Day, 8 May 1945, the British Commonwealth Navies had 9,460 ships of all types in commission, refitting or in reserve, including 14 battleships, 52 aircraft carriers, 62 cruisers, 257 destroyers, 131 submarines, 235 frigates, 257 corvettes, 1,265 major and 3,777 minor landing craft. By the end of the war, the Fleet Air Arm had 70 strike and fighter squadrons. The Navy had grown from a prewar strength of 129,000 men to a wartime peak in mid-1944 of 863,500, including 72,000 Wrens.

But in the six years of the Second World War, the British Commonwealth Navies lost 431 major

warships, including warships manned by Allied navies and Allied ships operating under British control. Among these were four battleships, five aircraft carriers, 33 cruisers, 154 destroyers, 90 submarines, and 38 corvettes. The British, Dominion and Allied navies also lost 1,035 auxiliary and minor warships, and 1,326 landing ships and craft.

In the same period, the Royal Navy, the Royal Naval Reserve and the Royal Naval Volunteer Reserve together suffered casualties of 73,642 officers and men (50,758 killed, 820 missing, 14,663 wounded and 7,401 prisoners of war). The WRNS had 102 killed and 22 wounded. The British Merchant Navy lost 30,248 men through enemy action, and these were but a fraction of the total number of merchant seamen of all nationalities lost from all causes.

THE POSTWAR NAVY

The end of the war brought the inevitable running down and clearing up. By the end of 1946, 840 warships had been struck from the Navy List, and orders for 700 new ships had been cancelled. In the same period, a start was made on the gigantic task of sweeping the enormous number of mines, laid by both sides.

The first act in the Cold War took place on 15 May 1946, when British destroyers steaming through the Corfu Channel, an international waterway, were fired on by Albanian shore batteries. To uphold the legal right of free passage, subsequently confirmed by a decision of the International Court of Justice, in October the destroyers *Saumarez* and *Volage* were sent down the Channel. Both struck mines, and 43 men were killed. *Volage*'s bows were blown off, and *Saumarez* was so badly damaged she had to be scrapped.

Hardly had the last British troops and ships left Palestine when the British Mandate ended in May 1948 than an insurgency broke out in Malaya where communists attempted to seize control. In a campaign which was to continue for some years, naval aircraft from Sembawang flew sorties against communist guerrillas, and surface ships such as the frigate *Amethyst* patrolled the coast to prevent guerrilla sea traffic.

In 1949, when there was civil war in China between the Communists and the Nationalists under Chiang Kai-Shek, the Navy stationed ships ready to evacuate British nationals from danger areas. In April, *Amethyst* was on her way up the Yangtse River to relieve the destroyer *Consort* in Nanking when she was fired on by communist guns on the river bank. Several of her people, including her captain, were killed, and the ship ran aground. In July, under a new CO, Lt Cdr Kerans, she was refloated and in an exploit which thrilled the world escaped down river to rejoin the fleet.

After the war, all existing and building submarines were fitted with the Schnorkel, a Dutch device used by German U-boats in the latter stages of the war. It consisted of a hollow metal mast, formed by an inlet tube fitted at its head with a float-controlled stop valve, and a shorter open-ended exhaust tube. This mast enabled a submarine to run its main diesel engines for propulsion and/or charging the main batteries whilst submerged at periscope depth. The earlier

'snort' masts were retracted by a hydraulic ram, so that they lay in crutches on the submarine's casing. In later designs, the 'snort' mast was raised and lowered like a periscope.

Trials were held of another system of submarine propulsion, fuelled by High Test Peroxide (HTP), a German invention giving very high underwater speeds which, happily for the Allies, had not been fully developed in time for operational wartime service. An HTP-powered U-boat, *U.1407*, was towed across the North Sea after the war, refitted

Above: Admiral Sir Bruce Fraser signs for the UK at the Japanese surrender aboard USS Missouri, 2 September 1945.

Left: No longer a potent threat to democracy, the captured German submarine U.776 is seen on the Thames River near the Houses of Parliament, Westminster, 25 May 1945, when she went on public display.

1946 First nuclear air-burst explosion over unmanned fleet at Bikini atoll (July). Mining of HMS *Saumarez* and *Volage* in the Corfu Channel off Albania (22 October).

1947 Operations off Palestine. First helicopter squadron in RN.

1948 (and later) Counter-terrorist operations off Malaya.

Above: *A failed experiment. HMS* Excalibur *(with her sister ship* Explorer*) was built in the 1950s to try out High Test Peroxide (HTP) propulsion. Submariners called them 'Excruciator' and 'Exploder'!*

Above: *P.O. Marine Engineer Ken Flemming remembers the efficiency of the gas turbine.*

Below: *Joiner James Anderson saw synthetic materials increasingly supplant wood from the 1960s.*

by Vickers and commissioned as HMS *Meteorite*. The trials were successful enough for two British experimental HTP-powered boats, *Explorer* and *Excalibur*, to be built in the 1950s. HTP was a very volatile, not to say dangerous, substance, and work on an HTP-fuelled torpedo, 'Fancy', was discontinued after the accident which caused the loss of the submarine *Sidon* at Portland in 1955. *Explorer* and *Excalibur* proved to be technological dead ends, being made obsolete by nuclear power.

Successful trials began in gunboat *MGB 2007* in 1947 on a new type of propulsion, the gas turbine. Gas turbines were fitted in the single shaft Tribal class Type 81 frigates in the 1960s, which had combined steam and gas turbine (COSAG) machinery. The first Royal Navy ships to be propelled entirely by gas turbine (COGOG) machinery, of one Rolls-Royce Olympus and one Rolls-Royce Tyne on each of two shafts, were the Amazon Type 21 frigates of the 1970s. Eventually, gas turbines replaced steam turbines as the principal propulsion system in the Royal Navy.

The Cold War prompted the West, for mutual defence against Soviet hostility, to draw up a North Atlantic Treaty, signed in Washington on 4 April 1949, and form a North Atlantic Treaty Organisation (NATO), with Belgium, Canada, Denmark, France, Iceland, Italy, Luxembourg, the Netherlands, Norway, Portugal, the United Kingdom and the United States as members. The

> '...the gas turbine was probably the fundamental change in the machinery side, because it meant that you could leave harbour within half an hour...you could be [away] to whatever emergency, or just out of harbour, straight away...flashed up and gone.'
>
> KEN FLEMMING, P.O. MARINE ENGINEER
>
> '...the phasing out of wood started really about the middle 1960s...you would get a new modern type of ship coming out and it was all plastics and Perspex and vinyls and things like that.'
>
> JAMES ANDERSON, JOINER, ARTISAN BRANCH, 1ST CLASS

Royal Navy contributed ships to NATO forces such as the Standing Naval Force Atlantic (STANAVFORLANT), Standing Naval Force Channel (STANAVFORCHAN), and later the Naval On-Call Force, Mediterranean (NAVOCFORMED).

THE KOREAN WAR

In the event, the Navy's first major commitment after the establishment of NATO was well outside the NATO area. On 25 June 1950, six divisions of the North Korean People's Army, with artillery and Soviet tanks, crossed the 38th Parallel and advanced into South Korea. The United Nations' response was swift. British and American warships of Task Force 77, representing the United Nations, were off the Korean coast by 2 July. The first naval action of the Korean war took place that day, when the cruiser *Jamaica* and the sloop *Black Swan* engaged six North Korean E-boats and sank five of them.

The Royal Navy's main carrier strength in 1945 was in the six large fleet carriers, *Illustrious, Victorious, Formidable, Indomitable, Indefatigable* and *Implacable*. They had all seen hectic wartime service but were hardly used operationally after the war, being employed mostly as trials and training ships until *Victorious* finally emerged after much modernization in the 1960s. Thus, the Navy's air war in Korea was fought by the light fleet carriers.

WRENS: THE WOMENS ROYAL NAVAL SERVICE

In November 1917, Dame Katherine Furse (1875–1952) became first Director (equivalent to Rear Admiral) of the Women's Royal Naval Service (WRNS), established to fill shore posts and release men for sea duty. The first ratings, single women over 18 recruited through employment exchanges, mustered at the Crystal Palace Depot in January 1918. After basic instruction in drill and naval customs, their many specialties would include cooks, stewards, writers, telephonists and telegraphists, dispatch riders, drivers and maintenance technicians, storekeepers and sailmakers. One of the first Wren officers – recruited through advertisements in *The Times*, and from the outset distinguished by their tricorn hats – was Vera Laughton, who as Dame Vera Laughton Mathews (1888–1959) was to be Director from 1939–46.

More than 6,000 Wrens served in the First World War, but the service was stood down in 1919. In 1939, when the WRNS re-formed, a call for 1,500 volunteers produced 15,000 – and by 1945 there were some 74,000 Wrens. As well as their 1918–19 duties, Wrens operated port motorboat services (ferries, water ambulances and mail boats), undertook ordnance and gunnery maintenance and

Air strikes, the first of many thousands flown in the next three years, were launched at dawn on 3 July from USS *Valley Forge* and the light fleet carrier *Triumph* in the Yellow Sea. The cruiser *Ceylon* and the ferry carrier *Unicorn* each embarked a battalion of British troops in Hong Kong and took them up to Pusan in August. *Triumph*, *Kenya* and *Jamaica* took part in the successful amphibious assault landing by US Marines at Inchon in September.

In October, *Triumph* was relieved by her sister ship *Theseus* who made eight patrols 'up the coast' in the Yellow Sea with rest and maintenance periods in Japan between each one. *Theseus'* Sea Fury fighters and Firefly fighter-bombers flew on a variety of tasks: maintaining a Combat Air Patrol (CAP) overhead; armed reconnaissance; strikes against pre-briefed targets; close support for the troops ashore, the sorties being controlled by the Joint Operational Centre at Seoul; photo-reconnaissance; interdiction strikes against roads and railways; and bombardment spotting.

Truce talks began in the Summer of 1951 which lasted, with breaks, for two years and resulted only in an armistice (which is still in force today). Meanwhile, the situation on land had stabilised around the 38th Parallel. At sea, the watch on both coasts was kept by Task Force 95, with ships of the Royal, Canadian, Australian, New Zealand, Netherlands, Siamese, South Korean and United States Navies.

Theseus was relieved by her sister ship *Glory* which began the first of her three tours of duty off the Korean coast in May 1951, operating with USS *Bataan*. *Glory* normally worked a nine-day

operational cycle, flying for four days, replenishing for one day, returning for a second four-day period and then handing over to *Bataan*, returning to Sasebo or Kure in Japan for maintenance, and then sailing for another nine-day cycle. Her Sea Fury XIs and Firefly Vs operated a 14-hour flying day, of some 50 to 60 sorties. On her last patrol, she raised the light fleet carrier record for daily sorties to 84.

Glory's relief was HMAS *Sydney*, the first Dominion carrier ever to go into action. In October 1951, she put the record up to 89 sorties in a day, but *Glory* returned in January 1952 to raise it to 104. Another light fleet carrier, *Ocean*, arrived in May 1952. She and *Glory* operated off the west coast, and with US Navy carriers, until the armistice in July 1953, and for a time afterwards.

Ocean put the daily light fleet record up to 123 and was the only British carrier to experience serious enemy air opposition off the west coast. In

Above: *Cruiser HMS Ceylon carried troops to Korea in 1950.*

Below: *This detail of the Coronation Review of the Fleet in 1953 was painted by Rowland Langmaid.*

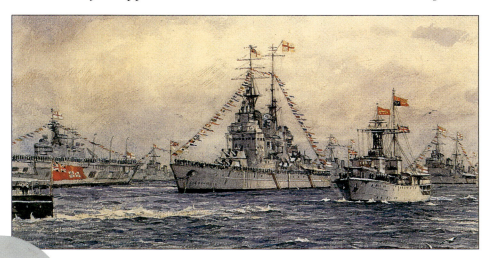

repair – and proved especially skilled in photo-reconnaissance interpretation and coding. As plotters and communications personnel, many women played vital roles in the Normandy invasion, which WRNS Chief Officer Dorothy Faith Parker, as Assistant Staff Officer for Escorts, watched from a destroyer's bridge.

Surviving a postwar threat of abolition, the WRNS acquired a permanent training establishment, the "stone frigate" HMS *Dauntless*, in 1953, and by the 1970s recruiting was so buoyant (as it always had been) that 80 per cent of more than 6,000 applicants per year for a nine-year engagement were refused. The increasing empowerment of women in society was reflected in the admission of WRNS cadets to RNC Dartmouth in 1976; the inclusion of Wrens in the Naval Discipline Act in 1977; and the beginning of mixed-sex training at HMS *Raleigh* in 1980. On 6 February 1990, WRNS Second Officer Chella Franklin (b.1963), joined the Type 23 frigate HMS *Norfolk* as Weapons Engineering Officer; however, the employment of women in sea-going and combatant posts remains somewhat controversial.

Above: *Shown on the mess dress tunic of a Director, WRNS, are the wartime medals of First Officer Helen Minto, along with specialists' insignia and a copy of the WRNS Testament 1918.*

Left: *Wrens parade at the shore station HMS Daedalus, Lee-on-Solent. In 1994, around the time that this photograph was taken, the WRNS was fully integrated into the Royal Navy.*

Left: *Wrens did not enter combat in the Second World War, but made a significant contribution to the manufacture of armaments. Here, at HMS Vernon, they assemble the firing apparatus of magnetic and acoustic mines.*

Right: HMS Bulwark, commissioned in 1960 as the Navy's first 'Commando' carrier, operates her helicopters.

August 1952, four Sea Furies were attacked by eight MiGs. Lt 'Hoagy' Carmichael, the Sea Fury flight leader, became the first, and only, Fleet Air Arm pilot of a piston-engined aircraft to shoot down a jet.

The Royal Navy and Royal Marine casualties in the Korean war – killed, died of wounds or in captivity, missing, wounded, or prisoner-of-war – were 182. Twenty-two Fleet Air Arm pilots were killed in action and another 13 in accidents; these were light, considering that the ten squadrons involved flew nearly 23,000 operational sorties.

HELICOPTERS AND JETS

Below: Smartness fosters self-respect, so correct dress – this example is from the 1950s – is a Royal Navy requirement. The poster was originally issued by the Publications Section of HMS Excellent in April 1957.

Since the earliest days of naval aviation, an aircraft carrier always had at least one 'planeguard' destroyer following close astern while she was operating her aircraft, ready to pick up aircrew after an accident. On *Theseus*' final patrol off Korea early in 1951, the destroyer was replaced by a helicopter. It had been found that a helicopter could recover ditched aircrew from the sea in a fifth of the time taken by even the most alert and

well-trained destroyer – as well as releasing that destroyer and her crew for other duties.

In Korea, helicopters demonstrated the full range of their versatility. They not only rescued ditched or crashed aircrew, but evacuated wounded to hospital, acted as aerial staff cars, carried mail or blood plasma to units in the line and ships at sea, spotted for bombarding ships, buoyed a crashed MiG in a river estuary and then guided recovery vessels to the spot.

The Royal Navy had become interested in helicopters during the Second World War and the first Sikorsky R-4Bs arrived from America in January 1945. The Naval Helicopter Training Squadron, 705, formed in May 1947 to fly the Hoverfly I, as the R-4B was named. But it was a primitive and under-powered design. The Royal Navy's first 'real' helicopter was the Sikorsky S.51, built by Westland under licence as the Dragonfly.

The Royal Navy's first operational helicopter squadron, 848, equipped with the Sikorsky S.55, the Whirlwind, was formed in October 1952 specifically for operations in Malaya, where they arrived in January 1953 and dramatically transformed the tactical situation on the ground. One Whirlwind could take a 'stick' of five fully-equipped soldiers and fly them in 12 minutes to a position in the jungle which would have taken them 12 hours to reach on foot.

The first controlled landing by a true jet aircraft was made on 3 December 1945, off the Isle of Wight, when Lt Cdr 'Winkle' Brown landed a Vampire I on *Ocean*'s flight deck. Two days of trials, with 15 take-offs and landings, convinced

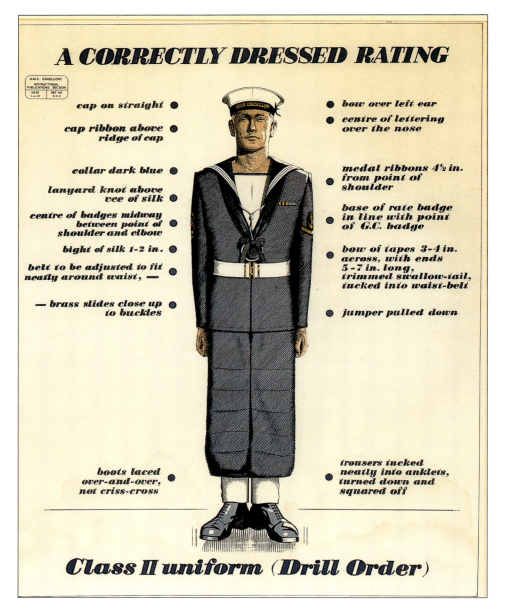

A CORRECTLY DRESSED RATING

H.M.S. EXCELLENT
INSTRUCTIONAL
PUBLICATIONS SECTION
DATE | REF No
3-4-57 | S.O.4

- cap on straight
- cap ribbon above ridge of cap
- collar dark blue
- lanyard knot above vee of silk
- centre of badges midway between point of shoulder and elbow
- bight of silk 1-2 in.
- belt to be adjusted to fit neatly around waist, —
- — brass slides close up to buckles

- bow over left ear
- centre of lettering over the nose
- medal ribbons 4½ in. from point of shoulder
- base of rate badge in line with point of G.C. badge
- bow of tapes 3-4 in. across, with ends 5-7 in. long, trimmed swallow-tail, tucked into waist-belt
- jumper pulled down

- boots laced over-and-over, not criss-cross
- trousers tucked neatly into anklets, turned down and squared off

Class II uniform (Drill Order)

the high-ranking spectators embarked that jet flying from carriers was feasible. The Royal Navy's first operational jet was the 590mph (950kph) Supermarine Attacker, which began carrier trials in 1947. 800 Squadron was equipped with Attacker F.ls in August 1951. The Attacker and the Sea Fury were both replaced in 1953 by the 560mph (900kph) Hawker Sea Hawk jet fighter. For anti-submarine warfare, the Fairey Gannet entered front-line service in 1955. The Royal Navy's strike aircraft of the 1950s was the 380mph (611kph) Westland Wyvern.

Higher landing speeds and heavier aircraft (a wartime Supermarine Seafire was 7,000lb or 3,175kg, a fully-loaded Westland Wyvern in 1953 was 24,000lb, 10,900kg) made obsolescent – and dangerous – the traditional flight deck layout, with arrester wires, crash barriers, and the forward half used as deck park for other aircraft.

The solution, devised by Cdr D.R.F. Cambell and Mr L. Boddington, of R.A.E. Famborough, was staggeringly simple: slew the direction of the approach and landing a little to port, so that an aircraft which missed the wires could simply put on the power, take off and go round again. The first experiments were made by painting new lines on the flight deck of *Triumph*. Further trials required an extension of the flight deck out to port and realignment of the arrester wires. After trials, the angled deck was adopted for all carriers, first

with a 5½ degree 'interim' deck, then by a full 10½ degree angled deck.

The mirror landing aid, whereby the pilot himself could monitor his own approach, originally devised by Cdr H.C.N. Goodhart, consisted basically of a number of white lights shining into the curved inner surface of a concave mirror. The pilot flew so as to keep this apparently horizontal line of white lights aligned with green datum lights fixed on the sides of the mirror. The pilot could see by the lights whether he was too high, too low, or correct. The 'mirror' was adjustable, to give different flight approach paths for different aircraft and gyro-stabilized, to compensate for the ship's motion.

The 'mirror' was introduced into service in 1954, the same year as the third important British flight-deck innovation of the 1950s, the steam catapult. Fully loaded modern aircraft could not take off without a catapult, but the hydraulic and compressed air catapults were reaching their design limits. Cdr C.C. Mitchell RNVR had the idea of using steam from the ship's main boilers to operate the catapults. As finally developed by Brown Brothers of Edinburgh, and first fitted in *Perseus* in 1951, the steam catapult gave power and to spare to launch any naval aircraft of the foreseeable future. *Ark Royal*, commissioned in 1955, was the first British carrier to have the operational steam catapult.

Above: *The Navy's first operational jet, the Supermarine Attacker, is seen at the rear of this line-up on HMS* Eagle, *January 1952. The other aircraft (front to back) are Hawker Sea Fury, Blackburn Firebrand, Fairey Firefly, and De Havilland Sea Hornet.*

Left: *Note the* Eagle's *angled flight deck – an important innovation in carrier design.*

▶ **1949** WRNS becomes permanent and integral part of the Naval Service. North Atlantic Treaty signed (4 April) and NATO set up. HMS *Amethyst* escapes down the Yangtse river to rejoin the fleet.

1950 Beginning of the Korean War (25 June); invasion of Inchon; air strikes launched by carrier-borne aircraft.

1951 Korean War continues. Ships deploy to the Persian Gulf after Mossadeq's nationalisation of oil fields.

Right: *A selection of Naval insignia in various colours and materials.*

Far right: *Cap badges (clockwise from left) of RN officer; Admiralty Board civilian; Chaplain; Petty Officer (PO); FCPO; CPO.*

Above: *Admiral Sir Frank Twiss KCB, KCVO, DSC, Second Sea Lord and Chief of Naval Personnel, 1967-1970.*

Right: *Oil tanks ablaze during the Anglo-French assault on the Suez Canal in November 1956. (Inset) Commandos fly in from HMS* Ocean *and* Theseus – *the first helicopter-borne assault landing in history.*

1952 RNR and RNVR adopt straight stripes with 'R' in the curl. First Allied Supreme Commander of NATO appointed. First experiments with the angled flight deck on aircraft carrier.

1953 Exercise Mariner, first time troops lifted into action by naval helicopter, in Malaya.

1954 Introduction of mirror deck-landing sight and steam catapult on aircraft carriers.

'*...the whole business of looking at life in a ship began to take on a much more civilised view...the regulation of life became much less rigid.*
....it was not really considered good enough to have forms of feeding where the stuff was dolloped out from a ladle and you sat down in your mess deck and ate it. [The sailors] wanted choice, they wanted menus.'

ADMIRAL SIR FRANK TWISS KCB, KCVO, DSC,
SECOND SEA LORD AND CHIEF OF NAVAL PERSONNEL
1967–1970

With developments in technology went changes in personnel. The age of officer cadet entry, 13 since the start of the century, was raised in 1948 to 16, and when this proved unpopular especially with headmasters, the age was eventually stabilised at 18. In 1949, the WRNS became a permanent and integral part of the Naval Service. In 1952, the RNR and RNVR adopted straight stripes with 'R' in the curl. A review of officers' career structure and training resulted in Admiralty Fleet Order 1/56, whereby the General List was instituted. Distinguishing cloth on sleeves was abolished. Technical and supply officers could command shore establishments and hold Admiralty appointments previously reserved for executive officers. Executive officers were either promoted on the 'Post' List, who could expect sea command, or on the 'General' List, who could not. These 'Wet' and 'Dry' Lists, as they inevitably became known, were so profoundly unpopular and divisive that they were eventually abolished. Suitability for sea command was thereafter decided by a committee which scrutinised each officer's record.

THE SUEZ CRISIS

On 26 July 1956, President Nasser of Egypt nationalised the Suez Canal Company. Had Britain and France, who owned the Canal, at once taken military action in a spirit of righteous retribution, world opinion would probably have been on their side. But, despite the strategic importance of the Mediterranean and the Suez Canal, sufficient forces were not immediately available. In the event, the British had 45,000 men, 12,000 vehicles, 300 aircraft and 100 warships at Suez, the French 34,000 men, 9,000 vehicles, 200 aircraft and 30 warships. But this force took months to assemble.

Operation 'Musketeer', the seizure of the Suez Canal, had three stages: air attacks by RAF aircraft from Cyprus and Malta, and by carrier air groups off shore, to neutralize the Egyptian Air Force; an airborne landing by the British 16th Independent Parachute Brigade and the French 10th Airborne Division; and a sea-borne assault by the 3rd Commando Brigade, supported by a tank regiment of 48 Centurions.

Air strikes from *Eagle, Bulwark* and *Albion*, and the French *Arromanches* and *Lafayette*, began on

1 November and had effectively eliminated the Egyptian Air Force by noon the next day. Targets that afternoon and on 3 November were vehicles, camps, barracks, bridges and railways. On the 1st, in the Gulf of Suez, the cruiser HMS *Newfoundland* challenged and then sank the Egyptian frigate *Domiat*.

The airborne assault took place on 5 November, all objectives being secured. On the 6th, the whole of 45 Commando, some 425 men and 23 tons of stores, were flown ashore from *Ocean* and *Theseus* in 90 minutes, in the first helicopter-borne assault landing in history. The forces ashore were well established and preparing for their drive down the Canal when a ceasefire came into effect at 11 p.m. on 6 November. Political uproar soon drowned out the noise of battle. Whatever the politicians who had themselves been responsible for the debacle might say later, 'Musketeer' was reckoned a success by those who carried it out, The opinion of the men in the fleet, had they ever been consulted, was that whether or not it was wrong to begin the Suez operation, it was certainly wrong to end it prematurely.

Suez was a pivotal event in the postwar history of the Navy. No longer was it possible to claim that the Royal Navy was able to operate as a major force worldwide on its own. Thenceforth the Navy would have to co-operate with other navies. In 1957, Duncan Sandys published his Defence White Paper. National Service was to end. Much greater reliance would be put on nuclear weapons. As for the Navy, 'the role of naval forces in total war is uncertain'.

Above: *Trouble in northern waters, as the the Icelandic Fisheries Patrol Vessel Baldur (right) confronts a British trawler during the third 'Cod War', 23 February 1976.*

A slow retreat, already underway, accelerated. In the years ahead, bases and dockyards all over the world were closed or turned over to private hands. Much greater emphasis came to be laid on the Navy's role in NATO, especially in the eastern Atlantic, leading first to the reduction and finally to the withdrawal of all permanent naval forces east of Suez.

But, as always in naval history, it was wise to expect the unexpected, whether in or out of the NATO area. In 1958 Iceland declared a 12-mile (20km) fishing limit round her shores, and the first of three so-called 'Cod Wars' (the second and third were in 1973 and 1975–76) began. Icelandic gunboats attempted to obstruct or even board British trawlers and were prevented by Royal Navy frigates, manoeuvring in close encounters which stopped just short of the use of firearms. Eventually, Britain had to concede at least a partial diplomatic defeat.

A CHANGING ROLE

It was a seeming paradox that while there was increasing political pressure to restrict the Navy's sphere of action to the NATO area, ships were being launched and aircraft designed which would retain the Navy's worldwide capability. In 1960, *Devonshire* was launched, the first County class guided missile destroyer, armed with four 4.5-inch guns, Seaslug and Seacat missiles. On Trafalgar Day, HM the Queen launched *Dreadnought*, the Royal Navy's first nuclear submarine.

In the same year, *Bulwark* commissioned as the first 'Commando' carrier (*Albion* followed two years later). Her catapults and arrester wires had been removed, gantries for assault craft built on her sides, and her messdecks and magazines

1956 President Nasser nationalises the Suez Canal (26 July). Operation 'Musketeer', the seizure of the Suez Canal – the first helicopter-borne amphibious assault (6 November).

1957 Defence White Paper places much greater reliance on nuclear deterrence. Reserve fleet scrapped.

1958 First 'Cod War' with Iceland.

1959 HM Dockyard, Malta, privatised (March). East Indies Station closed (September). Hong Kong dockyard closed (November).

1960 HMS *Bulwark* commissioned as first Commando carrier. End of National Service. HMS *Devonshire*, first Guided Missile Destroyer, launched (10 June). HMS *Dreadnought*, first RN nuclear-powered submarine, launched (21 October).

1961 Kuwait deployment to deter Iraq.

Above: *The RN's first nuclear submarine, HMS* Dreadnought, *surfaces during exercises.*

Above right: *Flown in by Wessex helicopters, men from the guided-missile destroyer HMS Kent take part in jungle operations during the Malaysian 'confrontation', 1964.*

Right: *Bearing the names of its winners, the 'Beira Bucket' was a trophy for intership sports among the crews of ships enforcing the UN oil embargo on Rhodesia, 1966–75.*

Below: *Planned as a carrier for the Navy's earlier jet fighters, HMS Bulwark was, as seen here, converted to a 'Commando' carrier in time for the Kuwait landings in July 1961.*

converted to carry a Royal Marine Commando of some 600 officers and men, with their arms, stores and vehicles, and a squadron of Fleet Air Arm helicopters. *Bulwark* was soon in action, landing her Commando in July 1961, in support of Kuwait, threatened by Iraq. The Marines were ashore until the crisis abated in September.

In December 1962, an armed revolt by the 'North Borneo Liberation Army' who were opposed to the newly-formed Federation of Malaya, broke out in Brunei and in nearby Sarawak and North Borneo. *Albion*, the cruiser *Tiger*, along with destroyers, frigates, minesweepers and tank landing craft brought up troops and provided valuable fire power. Supported by helicopters from sea, the Commandos had the situation under control in a week.

In September 1963, a new independent State of Malaysia was formed from the Federation, the State of Singapore, British North Borneo (renamed Sabah) and Sarawak, which was violently opposed by President Sukarno of

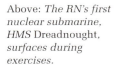

Indonesia, who refused to recognise the State of Malaysia and threatened a 'terrible confrontation'. Indonesian guerilla attacks and infiltration began along the 970-mile (1,560km) border between Malaysian Sarawak and Indonesian Borneo. Troops were supported and transported by Fleet Air Arm Westland Whirlwind and Wessex helicopters flying from *Albion* and *Bulwark* and from a small airfield ashore, named HMS *Hornbill* after the national bird, and from an advanced base 150 miles (240km) inland and only 30 miles (50km) from the Indonesian border. Confrontation ended in 1966 with the ousting of Sukarno and the signing of an agreement. It had been a full scale war, involving a total of 100 warships over a period of nearly three years, but it was played down in the media by both sides and the contribution of the surface ships, cutting off Indonesian incursions, the helicopters, and fixed-wing aircraft from *Victorious*, operating for prolonged periods in Borneo and along the coasts of Malaya was, and still remains, largely unsung.

In 1964, there were mutinies in the armies of the newly independent countries of Uganda and Kenya, and in Tanzania (formerly Tanganyika) where President Nyerere asked for British help. *Centaur* embarked 500 men of 45 Commando and their equipment at Aden and landed them by helicopter on 24 January at Dar-es-Salaam to restore order, which they did in a week. In May, after an armed insurrection by tribesmen in the Redfan mountains north of Aden, four Wessex helicopters from *Centaur* lifted nearly 550 men and their equipment into the Radfan area in one day. In 1966, *Eagle* and *Ark Royal* in turn, followed through the years by a succession of frigates, maintained the 'Beira Patrol' in the

Mozambique Channel, to enforce the United Nations oil embargo on Rhodesia.

While the large but ageing fixed-wing carriers ranged the world, their future was being thrown into doubt. Carriers were the most flexible and speediest means of providing air power world-wide. But they were expensive. The Navy had plans for new 50,000 ton carriers. The first, designated CVA01, was already on the drawing board. But such a large ship was an easy political target. The RAF argued with great skill that their aircraft, flying from island bases around the world, could do everything that Navy aircraft from carriers could do, and do it more cheaply.

The facts and the figures used to support this argument were both wrong. But, after a Defence Review, one of many, CVA01 was cancelled in February 1966. It was also pronounced that Britain would never again embark on major naval operations without allies, and an opposed amphibious landing was not envisaged and could be ruled out for the foreseeable future. The existing carriers would continue in service until the 1970s. After that, the Fleet Air Arm would become not much more than a helicopter-equipped anti-submarine force, operating solely in the NATO area.

NEW CARRIERS, NEW SUBMARINES

In the general atmosphere of gloom, the seeds of a new birth had already been sown. In February 1963, the first touch-and go landing was made on board *Ark Royal* by the experimental Vertical Take Off (VTO) aircraft P1127. This was the start of a new era, eventually leading to the delivery to the Navy in 1979 of the British Aerospace V/STOL (Vertical/Short Take Off and Landing) Sea Harrier,

which made its first deck landing, on *Hermes*, in 1978 (the year Ark *Royal* paid off for the last time).

In the aftermath of the CVA01 debacle, the concept emerged of a 'through-deck' cruiser (the words 'aircraft carrier' were not used, to avoid alarming the Treasury and the RAF). After many compromises and delays of several years, the first of the class, *Invincible*, was laid down in 1973, launched in 1977 and commissioned in 1980 as a 16,000 ton aircraft carrier, the largest ship built for the Navy since the Second World War, equipped as a command ship, and capable of operating helicopters and STOVL (Short Take Off, Vertical Landing) aircraft in a NATO role: the helicopters for anti-submarine warfare, the STOVL aircraft for operations against Soviet shadowers and warships. *Illustrious* and *Ark Royal* followed at two-year intervals. All three were eventually fitted with the full 12 degree 'ski-jump' for operating Sea Harriers.

The NATO commitment had a further dividend for the Navy. The nuclear submarine was acknow-

Above: *The aircraft carrier HMS* Invincible *is seen in the early 1980s with one of her British Aerospace V/STOL FRS.1 Sea Harriers, in this case from 800 Sqn. For the Falklands campaign aircraft were repainted in low-visibility grey.*

▶ **1962** Borneo Rebellion (lasts until 1966). US agrees to provide UK with Polaris ballistic missiles.

1963 HMS *Dreadnought* commissioned. First experimental touch-and-go landing by VTO aircraft P1127 on board HMS *Ark Royal* (February).

1964 Board of Admiralty becomes the Admiralty Board of the new Defence Council. Helicopter-borne landing by Royal Marines from HMS *Centaur* to put down rebellion in Tanganyika. Indonesian Confrontation.

Left: *This view of the Invincible's sister-ship HMS* Illustrious *clearly shows the 'ski-jump' ramp at her bow. This gives Sea Harriers added lift, enabling take-off with less fuel expenditure or greater weapons payload.*

Above: *The nuclear-powered ballistic missile submarine (SSBN) HMS* Renown, *built by Cammell Laird at Birkenhead, is launched on 25 February 1967. The four Resolution-class boats were the Royal Navy's first SSBNs.*

At a meeting at Nassau in the Bahamas between Harold Macmillan and President Kennedy in November 1962, it was agreed that Britain should be supplied with the American submarine-based Polaris intercontinental ballistic missile. A Polaris programme began early in 1963 which produced the first British nuclear-powered ballistic missile submarine (SSBN), the 8,000 ton *Resolution*, on time and on budget – an unprecedented, and unrepeated, feat in British naval history. It was decided at the outset that *Resolution*, launched in September 1966 and commissioned in October 1967, would fire her first missile off Cape Canaveral at 1115 Eastern Standard Time on 15 February 1968, and it duly took place (actually fifteen milliseconds late).

Resolution was followed by *Repulse, Renown,* and *Revenge,* their names showing their status as the Navy's new capital ships They were armed with 16 Polaris 35,000lb (15,875kg), 2,880-mile (4.635km) range A3 missiles, and six torpedo tubes. Navigation was by a system of gyro compasses known as SINS (Submarine Inertial Navigation System) which could consistently give a submerged submarine's position to within a few yards.

SSBNs had two complete crews, Port and Starboard, of 145 officers and men. While one crew was at sea, the other had leave, or went on courses, and prepared to support the boat on its return. The Polaris SSBNs maintained their deterrent patrols until *Repulse,* the last one, decommissioned in 1995, handing over to Trident.

ledged to be the best anti-submarine weapon against the Soviet nuclear submarine fleet. *Dreadnought* was followed by two Valiant and three Churchill class 4,000 ton nuclear fleet submarines in the late 1960s and early 1970s, six 4,500 ton Swiftsure class in the 1970s, and seven 5,000 ton Trafalgar class in the 1980s. Four 2,400 ton diesel-electric Upholder class were built but were soon taken out of service and placed on the disposal list for sale after one of the frequent defence cut-backs of the 1990s.

FIREPOWER FOR PEACE: THE NUCLEAR NAVY

Since its establishment in August 1968, the activities of two very different groups have centred on HMS *Neptune* at Faslane on the Clyde. One comprises the officers and men of the Royal Navy who man and maintain Britain's nuclear submarine force, based there; the other consists of members of organizations which denounce nuclear weapons as a threat to world peace. There are arguments for both sides; practically, however, we may note that there has been no global conflict since 1945 – and that the 'nuclear fleets in being' of the great powers have had some bearing on this fact.

The D5 Trident missile is described later in this chapter. On 18 November 1998, the Royal Navy entered an era of advanced tactical (and possibly strategic) weaponry, when the Swiftsure-class SSN HMS *Splendid* accomplished Britain's first live-firing of the US Tomahawk cruise missile. Shorter ranging than Trident, some 1,000 miles (1,600km) as opposed to 6,500 miles

(10,500km), and carrying a single 200KT nuclear or 1,000 pound conventional warhead against Trident's multiple ordnance, Tomahawk is distinguished by its accuracy.

Britain has purchased 65 Tomahawk Block III Sea-Launched Cruise Missiles (SLCM), designated when conventionally armed as Tomahawk Land Attack Missiles (TLAM). Tomahawk, 20.9 feet (6.37m) long and with a body diameter of 1.7 feet (0.52m), can be launched from the 21 inch (533mm) torpedo tubes used for the Tigerfish or Spearfish torpedoes of Britain's five Swiftsure and seven Trafalgar class SSBNs. Tomahawk is sub-surface launched, sheds its booster rocket and deploys its stubby wings (8.6 feet [2.62m] span) after surfacing, and flies at a cruising speed of 550mph (885km/h) and an altitude over land of only 100 feet (30m) on a turbofan engine. A triple guidance system – global positioning via fixed satellites; Terrain Comparison and Matching Guidance (TERCOM), using ground-mapping radar; and a video camera system that identifies pre-programmed ground features – is claimed to give it near pin-point accuracy. On 24 March 1999 HMS *Splendid* was called into action as part of NATO's response to the crisis in Yugoslavia and she fired Tomahawk missiles at a military target in Kosovo.

Left: *A Swiftsure class submarine. The first RN firing of Tomahawk was from such a warship.*

Above and below: *A Tomahawk cruise missile breaks the surface and detonates in the target zone during the Royal Navy's first live-firing of this advanced weapon system, 18 November 1998.*

NEW FRIGATES

The NATO requirement for anti-submarine warfare naturally laid particular emphasis on the provision of frigates. Postwar, the Navy began by converting wartime destroyers into frigates. The first frigates to be designed after the war were the Type 14 Blackwood class of the 1950s: 1,500 tons, three 40mm guns, four torpedo tubes and two Limbo three-barrelled ahead-throwing mortars. One of this class, *Exmouth*, was the first naval vessel to be converted to gas turbine power. Also in the 1950s were the 2,500-ton Type 12 Whitby class, and the 2,500-ton diesel-engined Type 41 Leopard class anti-aircraft frigates, designed to operate in pairs with the 2,300-ton Type 61 anti-aircraft direction Salisburys, the 41s providing fire power, the 61s radar direction. Some famous names were revived in the Type 81 general purpose Tribal class frigates.

In the early 1960s, the Modified Type 12 Rothesay class were fitted with a flight deck for a helicopter. They were followed by their logical development, the numerous and very successful 2,800-ton Leanders: two 4.5-inch guns, Seacat missiles, Limbo mortars, and a Wasp helicopter. The later broad-beamed Leanders had more modern Lynx helicopters.

The 1970s saw the advent of the 3,250-ton Amazon class, the first privately designed (Vosper-Thornycroft and Yarrow Shipbuilders)

frigates to be constructed for the Royal Navy and the first to be propelled completely by gas turbines: one Rolls-Royce Olympus and one Rolls-Royce Tyne to each of two shafts. They were armed with Exocet and Seacat missiles, a 4.5-inch gun, anti-submarine Mark 46 torpedoes, and had either a Wasp or a Lynx helicopter.

By the early 1980s, frigates had grown to the size of prewar light cruisers. The Type 22 Broadsword class dual purpose surface/anti-aircraft and anti-submarine frigates were 4,400 tons, armed with Exocet and Seawolf missiles and anti-submarine torpedoes, and had two Lynx helicopters. However, they were the first frigates since the Blackwoods to have no main gun armament.

Destroyers also grew to the size of prewar cruisers. The unique Type 82 *Bristol*, the only one built of a projected class of four designed to escort the cancelled CVA 01, was 7,000 tons. Commissioned in 1973, she was the last major British warship to be built which was not capable

Above: *Type 81 Tribal class warships, like HMS* Ashanti *seen here, were designated GP (general purpose) frigates. The first Tribal commissioned in 1962; the class was finally withdrawn in 1983–85.*

Below left: *Type 22 frigates of the Broadsword class – the name ship is seen here – were specifically armed for anti-submarine duties.*

Below: *The 7,000-ton Type 82 destroyer HMS* Bristol, *commissioned in 1973, was the only one of her kind.*

Above: *The Type 42 destroyer HMS Coventry. Twelve of this large class remain in service in 1999. Armed with 4.5-inch guns and Sea Dart missiles, four were committed to air defence duties in the Falklands.*

1966 Beira Patrol instituted. Aircraft carrier CVA01 cancelled. HMS *Resolution*, RN's first Polaris-armed SSBN, launched (15 September).

1968 NATO Standing Naval Force Atlantic (STANAVFORLANT) formed. HMS *Resolution* fires the first British Polaris missile submerged off Cape Canaveral (15 February). UK Defence Policy focuses on NATO commitments.

1970 Last issue of rum.

1972 First glass-reinforced plastic (GRP) warship, the minelayer HMS *Wilton*, launched.

1973 Second 'Cod War' with Iceland.

1975 Operations Branch formed. Suez Canal reopens after eight years' closure. British naval presence at Singapore ends after a century and a half.

1975–76 Third 'Cod War' with Iceland.

of operating her own helicopter, but she had three new weapon systems: the Sea Dart surface-to-air missile, the Ikara anti-submarine missile, which was a small delta-winged rocket-propelled launch vehicle carrying a Mark 44 or 46 homing torpedo, and the 4.5-inch automatic gun.

The 6,200 ton *Devonshire* was followed by seven more of the County class in the 1960s, and by the numerous Type 42 destroyers in the 1970s and 1980s, which grew from the 4,100 tons of the first Batch I ships to the 4,800 of the Batch III. All had Sea Dart missiles, 4.5-inch guns, and Lynx helicopters.

WAR IN THE SOUTH ATLANTIC

It was the greatest irony of the Royal Navy's postwar history that much of its NATO-orientated force – aircraft carriers, aircraft and helicopters, destroyers and frigates, missiles and guns, nuclear submarines, minesweepers, and the tankers and store ships of the Royal Fleet Auxiliary which contributed to NATO's logistic effort – were all deployed in the largest naval confrontation since the Second World War in a part of the world which could hardly have been further from the NATO area.

The announcement in 1981 that the Antarctic patrol ship *Endurance*, the only permanent British naval presence south of the Equator, was to be withdrawn convinced the governing *junta* of Argentina that the United Kingdom government was no longer interested in the sovereignty of the Falkland Islands.

On 1 April 1982, Argentine ships and commandos began to carry out Operation Rosario, the invasion of the Falklands, whose garrison of 85 Royal Marines surrendered by order of the Governor on 2 April. Argentine forces landed at Grytviken, South Georgia on 3rd.

In a mood of indignant outrage at home, the nucleus of a Task Force, the carriers *Hermes* and

Invincible, each with squadrons of Sea Harriers and Sea King helicopters, sailed from Portsmouth on 5 April to begin Operation 'Corporate', the recovery of the Falklands.

On their way south to Ascension Island, whose value as an intermediate base the Argentines appeared to have overlooked, the carriers were joined by destroyers and frigates who had been exercising off Gibraltar. In all, 44 warships took part in 'Corporate', including the amphibious assault ships *Fearless* and *Intrepid*, two County class guided missile destroyers, four Type 42s, and *Bristol*. The frigates included two Type 12s, seven of the eight Amazon class Type 21s, four Leanders, and two Type 22s. Aircraft from 15 Fleet Air Arm squadrons, some of them formed specially for the Falklands, were engaged, flying from the carriers, the surface ships or from shore.

There were also two offshore patrol vessels, three survey vessels employed as 'ambulance ships' with prominent Red Crosses, five trawlers from Hull, fitted out as minesweepers and wearing the White Ensign, three Valiant class and two Swiftsure class nuclear fleet submarines, and the diesel-electric patrol submarine *Onyx*. Last but not least was *Endurance* herself.

Twenty-two Royal Fleet Auxiliary ships took part: fleet oilers of the O and Tide classes, modified commercial tankers chartered by the RFA as support oilers, fleet replenishment ships such as the Fort class, and *Stromness*, which was converted into an assault platform, the Helicopter Support Ship *Engadine*, and six Landing Ships (Logistic), such as *Sir Galahad*.

The P&O cruise liner *Canberra* (nicknamed 'The Great White Whale') sailed from Southamp-

ton on 9 April with 40 and 42 Royal Marine Commandos and 3 Para embarked, having had two helicopter landing platforms and replenishment at sea and communications kits fitted, to turn her into a 'Landing Platform Luxury (Large)' in a matter of days.

Canberra was one of 45 Ships Taken Up From Trade (STUFT) which varied in size from the 67,000-ton liner *Queen Elizabeth II* (also converted into a LPL(L)) to 600-ton salvage tugs.

The Carrier Battle Group and its escort, the amphibious force, the expeditionary force (40, 42 and 45 RM Commandos, 2 and 3 Para, the Scots and Welsh Guards, the Gurkhas, the Blues and Royals), the RFAs and the STUFT were all assembled, fitted out and dispatched in the space of a few weeks, after an extraordinary display of national determination and improvisation.

The first operation was Paraquat, the recapture of South Georgia. The County class destroyer *Antrim*, the Type 22 frigate *Brilliant* and Type 12 frigate *Plymouth, Endurance* and RFA *Tidespring* arrived off the island on 21 April and a reconnaissance party of SAS were landed by Wessex helicopters on Fortuna Glacier. But the SAS radioed next day that their position on the Glacier was untenable. The whole party, and survivors of two crashed Wessex Vs, were rescued in a superb feat of flying by the pilot of *Antrim*'s Wessex 'Humphrey', Lt Cdr Ian Stanley.

On 25 April, 'Humphrey' detected and attacked the Argentinian submarine *Santa Fe* with depth charges. Badly damaged, *Santa Fe* made for Grytviken where it was attacked by helicopters from *Brilliant, Plymouth* and *Endurance*. After a short bombardment, troops were landed by helicopter, and the Argentinian garrison surrendered. The formal documents were signed on board *Plymouth* on 26 April.

As the Task Force neared the Falklands, there was intense diplomatic shuttling to and fro, and the declarations, first of a Maritime and then of a Total Exclusion Zone (TEZ) of 200-mile radius around the Falklands. But despite the RAF Vulcan and Sea Harrier bombing of Port Stanley on 1 May

Above: *The carrier HMS* Invincible *was on the point of being sold to Australia early in 1982 – but then the Falklands conflict erupted.*

Left: HMS Hermes *leaves Portsmouth for the Falklands, 5 April 1982. (Inset) The amphibious assault ship (LPD) HMS* Intrepid.

1977 First through-deck cruiser HMS *Invincible* launched (3 May). Royal Navy leaves Malta after 169 years. Silver Jubilee Review of the Fleet, Spithead.

1978 First deck landing by a Sea Harrier, on HMS *Hermes*. HMS *Ark Royal*, last fixed-wing aircraft carrier, paid off.

1980 Outbreak of Gulf War (Iran-Iraq); Armilla patrol instituted.

1982 Argentine forces land on the Falkland Islands (1 April) and South Georgia (3 April). Task Force sails from Portsmouth to begin Operation 'Corporate', the recovery of the Falkland Islands (5 April). South Georgia retaken (26 April). HMS *Conqueror* sinks the *General Belgrano* (2 May). Landings at San Carlos Bay (21 May). Surrender of Argentine Forces at Port Stanley (14 June).

Above: *HMS* Sheffield *on fire after an air-launched Exocet strike, 4 May 1982.*

1983 Gibraltar dockyard closed.

1986 HMS *Upholder*, first non-nuclear submarine launched since 1963 (2 December). First Trident-armed submarine, HMS *Vanguard*, ordered.

1990 Kuwait invaded by Iraq. Wrens go to sea in combatant ships.

and the air attacks on the County class destroyer *Glamorgan* and the Type 21 frigate *Arrow* the same day, there was still a general feeling that this Falklands affair would not come to anything really serious.

HOSTILITIES INTENSIFY

All such doubts were resolved on the evening of 2 May, when the nuclear submarine *Conqueror* torpedoed and sank the Argentinian cruiser *General Belgrano* south of the Falklands. There was, and still is, controversy over her course,

away from the Task Force, and her position, outside the TEZ, but her mere presence at sea was a threat, and her loss had a powerful deterrent effect on the Argentinian Navy.

The Carrier Battle Group had no airborne early warning, a lack which had a fatal result on the afternoon of 4 May when the Type 42 destroyer *Sheffield* was hit starboard side amidships by an air-launched Exocet missile. The missile did not explode but its fuel started major fires. The frigates *Arrow* and *Yarmouth* went alongside to render firefighting assistance and later take off survivors. *Sheffield* was abandoned, with the loss of 21 lives, and capsized and sank on 10 May.

On 21 May the ships assembled east of the Falklands for the forthcoming landings in San Carlos Bay. In the Carrier Battle Group were *Hermes*, Rear Admiral Woodward's flagship, *Invincible*, *Glamorgan*, *Arrow* and *Alacrity*, the Type 42 destroyers *Glasgow* and *Coventry*, the oilers *Olmeda*, *Tidepool*, and *Pearleaf*, the storeships *Resource* and *Regent*, the personnel transport *Elk*, *Fort Toronto*, and *Atlantic Conveyor*. In the Amphibious Group were *Fearless*, wearing the broad pennant of Commodore Clapp, Commodore Amphibious Warfare, *Intrepid*, *Antrim*, *Brilliant* and *Broadsword*, the Type 21 *Ardent*, *Plymouth* and *Yarmouth*, *Stromness*, *Sir Galahad*, *Sir Percival*, *Sir Tristram* and *Sir Lancelot*, *Europic Ferry*, *Canberra* and *Norland*, and *Fort Austin*.

D-Day was 21 May, H-Hour was 0740. 40 Commando and 2 Para were ashore by 0905. Argentine air attacks began early in the afternoon,

THE ROYAL FLEET AUXILIARY

Logistics is not the most glamorous branch of warfare – but since it embraces all operations necessary to maintain the effectiveness of a fighting force, it is most vital. The logistical aspect of sea warfare assumed prime importance in the Pacific during the Second World War, when the US Navy, often operating far from its bases, established a huge 'Fleet Train' of oilers, supply ships, repair vessels and other auxiliaries. The British Pacific Fleet, formed late in 1944, at first relied largely on US support services, but by August 1945 had its own 'floating bases' – some 95 ships of the Royal Fleet Auxiliary (RFA).

The RFA, whose ships, although owned and administered by the state, are manned by merchant seamen and fly the Blue Ensign, has become increasingly important in the later 20th century, when Britain's decline as a world power has seen the dismantling of her once global network of naval bases. Indeed, the withdrawal in November 1967, without significant loss, from one such base, Aden, under threat of hostile action, was only successfully accomplished because eight RFAs were deployed with the task force to lift off stores and personnel while keeping the rearguard ashore supplied with materiel.

In 1982, the Falklands War brought the vital role of the RFA increased public recognition – at a high

Above: *The Tiger-class helicopter cruiser HMS* Blake *refuels at sea from an RFA oiler. The* Blake *led a Task Group on a round-the-world voyage in 1974–75.*

Right: *A little sister of the 36,000-ton Auxiliary Oiler Replenishment ships acquired in the 1990s, RFA* Green Rover *is a small fleet tanker of the Rover class. These ships were delivered in 1969–70.*

price, when on 8 June Argentine Skyhawk bombers hit the RFA *Sir Tristram* and sank *Sir Galahad* in Bluff Cove. (Since some sources fail to make the distinction, it should be pointed out that of the 75 auxiliaries that accompanied the 51 warships of the Task Force, 21 were RFAs and the rest, including the liner *Canberra* and the ill-fated *Atlantic Conveyor*, were STUFT; that is, Ships Taken Up From Trade.)

Further experience in the Gulf War (1991) and currently in the Gulf and the Adriatic, has shown the Admiralty's wisdom in the 1960s in opposing swingeing reductions in RFA strength. Its most recent additions include two 32,300-ton multi-role Fleet Replenishment Ships of the Fort Victoria class, which each carry five ASW helicopters and can, in emergency, operate Sea Harriers.

Antrim was hit aft by a 1,000lb bomb which failed to explode but did considerable damage. *Argonaut* was hit by two 1,000lb bombs, neither of which exploded but both caused extensive damage. *Ardent* was attacked three times, hit by six bombs, and was finally abandoned, sinking next day. At the end of the day, of the seven escorts, only *Plymouth* and *Yarmouth* were undamaged, and only one of the damaged escorts, *Broadsword*, was still fully operational. However, by going for the escorts instead of the troopships the Argentine Air Force had made a grave mistake, allowing the majority of the troops to get safely ashore.

On 23 May, the Type 21 frigate *Antelope* escorted *Stromness* and *Norland* to San Carlos Water, and was hit twice by 1,000lb bombs which failed to explode. She blew up during bomb disposal and was abandoned. She sank the next day, 24th, when *Sir Galahad* was hit once and *Sir Lancelot* twice by 1,000lb bombs, which all failed to explode.

On 25 May, National Day of Argentina, *Coventry* and *Broadsword*, who had formed a 42/22 'Combo' 'Missile Trap' the day before, shot down two Skyhawks before *Coventry* was hit by three 1,000lb bombs, of which at least two and probably three exploded. *Coventry* rolled over on her beam ends within 15 minutes and capsized. *Broadsword* was hit by a bomb which ricocheted off the sea, passed through the side and the flight deck, wrecking the Lynx helicopter, and fell into the sea without exploding.

On the same day, *Atlantic Conveyor*, some 70 miles (115km) north-east of Port Stanley and on her way into San Carlos, was hit port side aft by an air-launched Exocet, caught fire and had to be abandoned. Although the Harriers and some of the helicopters she had carried had already been flown off, three Chinook and six Wessex V helicopters and a huge amount of stores were lost, making *Atlantic Conveyor* the most serious loss suffered by the Task Force.

VICTORY IN THE FALKLANDS

On 27 May, 2 Para began their attack on Goose Green, and the first ground troops broke out of the bridgehead, to start the long 'yomp' to Port Stanley. Meanwhile, the Navy continued to wage what was a curiously old-fashioned war, with many of the tactics the Navy had used for centuries: decoy and deception, blockade and bombardment, covert operations and convoy.

The Carrier Battle Group experienced its final air raid when it was attacked on the afternoon of 30 May by two Super Etendards, one equipped with an Exocet, and four Skyhawks, two of which were shot down. The Argentinians continued to claim an Exocet hit on *Invincible*. On 8 June, the long-serving and long-suffering *Plymouth* was hit by two bombs, neither of which exploded, but a Mk 11 depth charge on the flight deck was detonated by a cannon shell, causing fires and considerable damage.

At about the same time, *Sir Galahad* and *Sir Tristram* were attacked by five Skyhawks in Fitzroy Cove. *Sir Galahad* was hit by two and possibly three 500lb bombs, not all of which exploded, but the ship caught fire and had to be abandoned, with great loss of life, especially among the Welsh Guardsmen still on board. *Sir Tristram*, hit by two bombs which did not explode, and a near-miss which did, also caught fire and was abandoned, but was later recovered.

Four days later, on the 12th, *Glamorgan* was hit port side aft by a shore-launched Exocet, which caused severe damage, fires, and casualties. But this was a Parthian shot. White flags were seen flying over Port Stanley on 14 June. Argentinian

1984 Chatham dockyard closed.

1991 Naval units take part in Operation 'Desert Storm' to liberate Kuwait from Iraq.

1992 HMS *Vanguard* launched (4 March).

1993 Naval units operate in Adriatic in support of forces ashore during crisis in Bosnia.

1994 WRNS dissolved as a separate service and absorbed into RN.

1995 HMS *Victorious*, second Trident submarine, enters service. HMS *Repulse*, last Polaris submarine, paid off.

1997 Navy leaves Hong Kong.

1998 Royal Yacht *Britannia* paid off.

Above left: *A life belt from HMS* Antrim *and an anti-flash helmet to protect from burns. The destroyer was hit by a 'dud' bomb in the Falklands.*

Left and below: *The destruction of HMS* Coventry, *25 May 1982. After shooting down two Argentine A-4B Skyhawks with Sea Dart missiles, the destroyer was struck by three 1,000lb bombs and capsized.*

THE PENGUIN NEWS

30th JUNE 1982

VICTORY

FREEDOM

AND A

FUTURE

Above: Mementos of the Falklands War. (Left to right) A set of commemorative stamps issued on the first anniversary of the liberation, 14 June 1983; the obverse and reverse of the South Atlantic Campaign Medal; the badge of HMS Hermes; the 30 June 1982 issue of the 'Penguin News', the Falkland Islands news magazine, which celebrated the defeat of the Argentinian forces.

forces in East Falkland surrendered at midnight.

Naval casualties in the Falklands were: *Coventry*, 18; *Fearless*, two; *Glamorgan*, 14; *Sheffield*, 19; *Hermes*, three, *Invincible*, three; *Ardent*, 22; *Argonaut*, two; *Antelope* one; *Atlantic Conveyor*, three Royal Navy and five Merchant Navy. The RFA suffered five casualties, in *Fort Grange* and *Atlantic Conveyor*, and three in *Sir Galahad*. Eight Chinese ratings were lost, serving in *Coventry* and *Sheffield*, and two in *Atlantic Conveyor*, *Sir Galahad* and *Sir Tristram*. The Royal Marines lost 27.

The resounding success of the Falklands campaign enabled the Navy to claw back some of the assets, especially the carrier and amphibious capabilities, which it had been due to lose under the 1981 Defence Review. The Falklands also strengthened the position of those who argued that the Navy should remain capable of taking action outside the NATO area. However, Treasury-driven defence reviews continued almost biennially through the 1980s.

In 1989, the Soviet Empire and the Warsaw Pact crumbled, like the Berlin Wall itself, with astonishing speed. The Cold War had effectively been won, in a manner which immediately questioned the need for NATO, which had been specifically formed to fight the Cold War.

One obvious question was: is there any longer any need for an independent British nuclear

deterrent? It was planned to replace Polaris with Trident. It might have been politically and financially tempting to discard Trident. But the same argument, that Polaris was the most cost-effective deterrent, also applied to Trident. The first of a projected class of four 16,000-ton Trident-armed SSBNs, *Vanguard* and *Victorious*, had been laid down in 1986 and 1987, before the Cold War ended, and it was decided to retain Trident. Each SSBN was armed with 16 Lockheed D5 Trident missiles, with a range of 6,500 miles (10,500km). *Vanguard* commissioned in 1993, *Victorious* in 1995, and *Vigilant* in 1996. *Vengeance* is due to follow in 1999.

THE GULF WAR

The Royal Navy's first major commitment of the 1990s was, once again, outside the NATO area. When Iraq invaded Kuwait on 2 August 1990, the Type 42 destroyer *York*, the Type 22 frigate *Battleaxe* and the Leander frigate *Jupiter* were already in the Gulf on the Armilla Patrol, which the Royal Navy had maintained since the Iraq-Iran war broke out in 1980.

As the months passed, international resolve hardened against Iraq, and more ships were sent out, including the Type 42s *Gloucester* and *Cardiff*, and the Type 22 *Brazen*. The Type 22 *London* was fitted with the communications equipment required to act as the flagship of the Senior Naval Officer Middle East (SNOME), commanding the British Task Group 321.1.

A Multi-national Maritime Interdiction Force (MIF) was formed to enforce United Nations sanctions against Iraq. Iraqi ships were boarded, often jointly with Coalition partners, by RN and RM parties in boats and helicopters. By December 1990, 2,000 vessels had been challenged, 25 boarded and one diverted.

As tension in the region mounted, the Task Group was ready in all respects by 14 January 1991, and hostilities began with Operation Desert Storm on 17 January, with the Type 42 destroyers up-threat in the northern Gulf. In all, five Type 42s, four Type 22s, *Jupiter*, eight Brecon class Mine Counter-Measure Vessels, *Hecla* and *Herald*, and six Fleet Air Arm squadrons took part in operations in the Gulf and in the subsequent clearing and harbour opening. The RFA played a vital part, with 11 ships, including oilers and store ships, *Argus* (ex-*Contender Bezant*, from the Falklands) fitted out as a Primary Casualty Receiving Ship, and the Repair Ship *Diligence* (ex-*Stena Inspector*, from the Falklands).

In Desert Storm, Wrens served on board the warships taking part, having first gone to sea in combatant ships in 1990. The WRNS was dissolved as a separate service and absorbed into the Royal Navy in 1994.

Right: Women have served afloat on equal terms with men since 1990. In February 1999, the Royal Navy's total personnel of 43,747 included 3,279 women (including the Royal Marines, Queen Alexandra's Royal Naval Nursing Service and Careers Service). At that time the Lieutenant seen here received annual basic pay of £24,400-£28,345. On entry, a Midshipman received £10,165 per year, a 17-year-old rating £6,768.

Left: *One of the four Vanguard class ballistic missile submarines laid down in 1986–93. The 16,000-ton boat carries 16 D5 Trident missiles.*

(Inset) *Wayland Austin was a Flight Controller on HMS* Gloucester *in the Gulf War, 1991.*

Below: *The Navy is ready for the new millennium. Here, members of a warship's Abovewater Warfare (AW) Team operate sensors and weapons that protect the ship from air and surface threats.*

It was the final irony of 20th century naval history that the first shots fired by NATO in anger were after the end of the Cold War, in Bosnia, where the Royal Navy following an old tradition, sent ships including the aircraft carriers *Invincible* and *Illustrious* to the Adriatic in support of forces ashore. But another old tradition, going back to the reign of Charles II, the first Royal yacht-master, came to an end in 1998 when the Royal Yacht *Britannia* was finally decommissioned.

For the 21st century, it will be, in the words of the Preamble to Charles II's Articles of War, 'upon the Navy under the Providence of God that the safety, honour, and welfare of this realm do chiefly depend'. But anyone who ventured to predict how that will be fulfilled in the next century should mark Sir Walter Raleigh's words in the Preface to his *Historie of the World* when he was asked why he did not write the history of his own times, 'having been permitted to draw water as neare the Well-head as another: "To this I answere, that who-so-ever is writing a modern Historie, shall follow truth too neare the heeles, it may happily strike out his teeth".'

INDEX

Ship names are in *italics*. Page numbers in *italic type* indicate an illustration. Subheadings are in chronological order.

Picture Credits

Unless otherwise credited below, all the photographs and illustrations reproduced in this book were supplied by, and are the copyright of, **the Royal Naval Museum**.

Quotation Boxes
Several of the extracts quoted in the personal recollection boxes distributed throughout the book are taken from the manuscript and oral history collections of **the Royal Naval Museum**. Their RNM references are as follows:
Page 35: RNM Manuscript Collection 1981/454
Page 51: RNM Manuscript Collection 1973/323
Page 66: RNM Manuscript Collection 1996/2
Page 73: RNM Manuscript Collection 1998/2
Page 85: RNM Manuscript Collection 1992/442(2)
Page 91: RNM Manuscript Collection 1997/65
Page 95: RNM Manuscript Collection 1995/88
Page 110: RNM Manuscript Collection 1994/414(1)
Page 134: RNM Oral History Collection (3/1996)
Page 169: RNM Oral History Collection (426/91)
Page 180: RNM Oral History Collection (3/1993 Stephens) and (43/1993 Goldsmith)
Page 190: RNM Oral History Collection (168/1992)
Page 204: RNM Oral History Collection (5/1993 Flemming) and (218/92 Anderson)
Page 208: RNM Oral History Collection (407/91)
Page 219: RNM Oral History Collection (274/91)

The quotations on pages 152 and 158 are reprinted from *The True Glory – The Royal Navy: 1914–1939* by Max Arthur (© Max Arthur 1996) and are reproduced by permission of Hodder & Stoughton Limited.